His Majesty King George VI.

GAUNTLET
TO
OVERLORD

The Story of the
CANADIAN ARMY

by
ROSS MUNRO

HURTIG
Publishers
EDMONTON

Published by Hurtig Publishers
by special arrangement with
the Macmillan Company of Canada Limited, Toronto

Copyright, Canada, 1945 by the
Macmillan Company of Canada Limited

International Standard Book No. 0-88830-061-1

First Hurtig edition published 1972

PRINTED IN JAPAN

To
My Wife
STEVIE

It has been a matter of great satisfaction and pride to have had Canadians with me both in the Eighth Army during Sicily and Italy and also during the Invasion of North-west Europe. They have proved themselves to be magnificent fighters, truly magnificent. Their job along the Channel coast and clearing the Scheldt Estuary was a great military achievement for which they deserve the fullest credit. It was a job that could have been done only by first-rate troops. Second-rate troops would have failed.

1 Feb., 1945
TAC. HQ. 21 Army Gp.

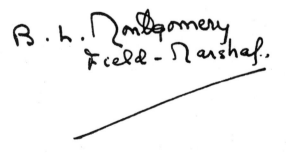

INTRODUCTION TO THE NEW EDITION

LOOKING back on those years, it was all rather quaint and old-fashioned, long before the peaceniks and the beatniks.

It was a war that our soldiers, sailors and airmen *believed* in—that people at home supported to the full. The issue was black and white, with no grey areas. Hitler's Nazi regime was a tyranny that had to be destroyed or we would be engulfed by it. This dedication to the allied cause was not flaunted and seldom articulated by the troops but this Canadian volunteer army that swelled from one division to five was bound together and fought together out of a conviction that it was a war that had to be waged and had to be won. And far from home, in battles through northwest Europe and in the Mediterranean, our men achieved more in five years of conflict than anything else to establish Canada as an independent nation and a significant middle power.

Many political and economic events have altered things since then, but this country never stood taller in the world than she did when it was all over on May 8, 1945. Alongside the giants of the west in battle after battle, the Canadian units on land, sea and air won the respect of all for the contribution that this then small nation of twelve million people made to the final victory.

As a war correspondent for the Canadian Press, I followed the Canadian soldiers through their training and their campaigns—from England to Spitzbergen; to that bloody, anguished day at Dieppe; to Sicily and Italy; to Normandy and across northwest Europe into Germany; from the wintry mountains of Tunisia to the Elbe. Five times I landed from the sea with our assault troops, was at Wageningen in Holland when the German forces on the Canadian front surrendered and at Rheims when the German high command capitulated unconditionally to the Allies.

Through the mist of years, I retain vivid recall of the great events that transpired and of the men who directed them. The most memorable twenty-four hours of all was D-day in Normandy when the British, Canadian and American forces stormed ashore from the most massive armada of ships ever assembled.

If Shakespeare had been with us in the landing craft in the smoke and turmoil of that assault he might have quoted from *Henry V*:

And gentlemen of England, now abed
Shall think themselves accurs'd they were not here,
And hold their manhoods cheap whiles any speaks
That fought with us upon St. Crispin's day.

Attacking between the British on the left and the Americans on the right, the Third Canadian Infantry Division and the Second Armoured Brigade worked their way in a choppy sea through the underwater obstacles at dawn to land on the sweeping beaches at Courseulles, Bernieres and St. Aubin. As the allied air forces and the navy hammered the coastal defences inland the Canadians stormed the fortifications on the beaches, cut through the masses of barbed wire in the sand dunes behind and burst out in heavy fighting into the wheat fields and woods beyond.

Throughout the day, the Third Division advanced inland making the deepest penetration of any allied formation. Before dawn, the Canadian parachute battalion had landed with the British airborne division north of Caen and east of the Orne river to protect the left flank of the invasion forces.

The British Third Division established itself between Caen and the sea and to the west two American infantry divisions and two airborne landed on a broad front.

The allied beachhead was won on that warm and sunny June 6, 1944, and from it were to be waged the titanic battles ahead.

Nearly two years before, on August 19, 1942, there had been Dieppe. It is the most searing memory of the entire war. The Second Canadian Infantry Division was cut to pieces on that eight-hour raid across the channel from England.

It was the Canadians' first engagement of the war and their most disastrous. I was with the Royal Regiment from Toronto and it was decimated in the gulch at Puits to the east of Dieppe as it landed, late, in broad daylight under the blazing German guns. Fifty-eight of us from a regiment, out of more than 600, got back to New Haven that night in shattered landing craft.

On the main beach at Dieppe, three regiments and the tanks got ashore and some troops fought their way into the town. But most of them were pinned down on the beach and finally the survivors had to surrender in the early afternoon.

To the west at Pourville, two other battalions successfully landed, thrust several miles inland, but with the failure on the other two beaches, they had to withdraw and escape to the sea as best they could. Many were captured but a Victoria Cross was won by an officer on the bridge at Pourville.

Dieppe was the most hotly debated action of the

war. Many contended it should' never have taken place; that it was but a suicide sacrifice of one of the top Canadian divisions; that the planning was atrociously faulty; that the Germans knew we were coming and were waiting.

Nobody has been able to determine for sure whether the enemy was alerted ahead of time. I'm inclined to think they were not. The planning had many deficiencies. Far, far from enough bombardment support was provided by the navy and airforce. No troops could possibly have captured Dieppe that day with the meagre support provided them from sea and air.

But it did prove to the British High Command, who were all powerful in those days, that an assault from the sea should never take place on a fortified port. It is incredible that this lesson had to be learned at Dieppe. But the War Office and Combined Operations Headquarters in Whitehall had to be shown with heavy casualty lists that it couldn't be done.

After Dieppe, every landing was done across wide-open beaches, without a port within dozens of miles. The raid by the Canadians in an inverse way paid off in every subsequent sea assault. And none of them missed. This was small comfort to the casualties and the prisoners but the men of Dieppe have always had a special place in the hearts of Canadians.

But now to return to the start. In 1939, Canada was poorly prepared for any kind of conflict. Her regular army had been starved for years and was but a skeleton of dedicated officers and men who had stayed with it. Prime Minister Mackenzie King detested war and was immensely suspicious of the British. But strong men in his cabinet persuaded him that support for Britain was support for Canada and it was the only choice when war broke out.

So the First Division was recruited in the fall of 1939 and arrived in Britain just before Christmas. The seemingly endless training for battle began. The threat of the German invasion hung heavy over the land. The Battle of Britain raged in the skies over the Canadian camps in the southern counties.

The First Canadian Corps was formed. Then the Second as the Third and Fourth Divisions arrived. Finally, the First Canadian Army came into being under General A. G. L. McNaughton, who had brought the First Division overseas and who was the father of the overseas forces. The Fifth Division was then in the U.K.

But by Christmas 1943 McNaughton was out. Officially, he retired because of ill health. In reality, he was fired. First, the British knocked him down. Personal enmity of long standing between him and the British Commander of the Imperial General Staff, Sir Alan Brooke, was one factor. The poor showing on a major invasion manoeuvre called Spartan was another. But the major consideration was the long battle between the general and Defence Minister Ralston over the splitting of the army, in which Mackenzie King sided with Ralston.

The army was split, with the First Corps operating in Italy after the highly successful campaign of the First Division in the conquest of Sicily. The Second Corps was held in England for the invasion of Normandy but by then General H. D. G. Crerar had taken over and during the Normandy operations and beyond British, Polish and other formations were under his command.

The Italian campaign was a gruelling one for the Canadian corps and it didn't receive the attention of the more dramatic invasion of Normandy and the drive into Germany. But the First and Fifth Divisions were as fine troops as Canada ever fielded. When they joined up with the rest of the First Canadian Army in Holland in the last phases of the war, they proved it once again.

Of our generals, Andy McNaughton stands the highest in my estimation and I had every opportunity for three years to see him at close quarters. Canadian troops would have followed him anywhere. The end was a sad day for the army and for the general. But he was no politician and politics finally brought him down.

We had few poor divisional commanders. Most of them were highly competent soldiers and fine leaders. Our best corps commander was an icy cold General Guy Simonds who knew what he wanted, knew his tactics and his strategy, and could get along well with the high command from Eisenhower to Montgomery down.

So this is a book about the Canadian soldiers in the Second World War, a reprint from the volume published right after the war. It's a story largely of first-hand observation of what happened when there was little divisiveness in Canada and the total nation worked towards one goal.

ROSS MUNRO

Edmonton, Alberta
February 1972

CONTENTS

CHAPTER   PAGE

I—INTRODUCTION -   -   -   -   -   -   1

II—THE STORM GATHERS -   -   -   -   -   9

Through the winter of 1943-44 and into the spring the Allied
Expeditionary Force mustered in Britain, training and prepar-
ing for the Normandy landings. As the opening of the Second
Front approached, tension in Britain reached fever pitch.

III—THE LIGHTNING STRIKES   -   -   -   -   45

On June 6, 1944, British, American and Canadian assault troops
landed from the air and the sea on the Normandy coast. A
beach-head was won and the titanic battle in the west roared on.

IV—STRUGGLE ON THE BEACH-HEAD   -   -   97

The Allied forces beat off German counter-attacks and held the
beach-head. The Canadians near Caen fought many savage
actions as the stage was set for the big offensive to break from
the beach-head.

V—THE BATTLE FOR CAEN   -   -   -   -   137

Canadian and British troops broke through the defences screening Caen. The Canadians took Carpiquet and with the British
stormed into Caen. One of the great victories in Normandy
was won.

VI—THE PUSH TO FALAISE   -   -   -   -   163

Driving down the Caen-Falaise highway, the First Canadian
Army shattered the German northern pivot in Normandy.
Falaise was captured and under pressure from the Allied
armies the German Seventh Army began to disintegrate.

VII—TRIUMPH AT TRUN—ON TO THE SEINE -   182

The Trun gap was closed tightly and the German Seventh
Army was wiped out, with the Canadians taking a major share
in administering this defeat to the enemy. From Trun the
Canadians sped east to the Seine with the British and the
Americans.

VIII—RETURN TO DIEPPE   -   -   -   -   198

The 2nd Canadian Division went back to Dieppe, which it
raided at heavy cost two years before. The enemy evacuated
the port and the Canadians returned without losing a man or
firing a shot.

CHAPTER   PAGE

IX—CHANNEL PORT BLITZ - - - - - 210

Attacking eastward, the Canadian Army thrust through to
Belgium and the Channel Ports were invested. Le Havre was
captured by the British in the Canadian Army. Calais,
Boulogne, Cap Gris Nez and Ostend fell to the Canadians.

X—THE *Polders* BATTLE—INTO GERMANY 223

The Canadians, aided in the last phases by British troops,
cleared the Schelde Estuary of the enemy to open the port of
Antwerp to Allied shipping. Terrific battles raged for a
month. Canadians then crossed Reich frontier.

XI—ENGLAND AND THE LONG WAIT - - 260

In the training camps of England the Canadians prepared for
the battles they fought in the Mediterranean and in Western
Europe. Enduring tedium and boredom with stoic patience,
they learned how to campaign.

XII—ARCTIC FORAY - - - - - - 279

In August and September, 1941, a Canadian force carried out
a raid on the Arctic island of Spitsbergen. It was a bloodless
operation, made in the infancy of combined operations.

XIII—DIEPPE—KEY TO INVASION - - 293

The 2nd Division raided Dieppe on August 19, 1942. For eight
terrible hours, the troops fought on the beaches. It was a
reconnaissance in force, made with heavy losses, but one which
paid off in every combined operation which followed.

XIV—DETOUR VIA NORTH AFRICA - - - 347

When British and American forces were driving the Axis from
North Africa, groups of Canadians served with the British
First Army in Tunisia, gaining valuable battle experience from
Kasserine to Tunis.

XV—SICILY'S THIRTY-EIGHT DAYS - - - 359

On July 10, 1943, British, Canadian and American troops went
ashore in Sicily to gain the first foot-hold from the sea on
enemy soil. Battling through the mountains, they drove the
enemy from the island.

XVI—FROM REGGIO TO THE PO - - - - 435

Canadian and British troops of the Eighth Army landed on the
toe of Italy on September 3, 1943. They advanced through
Calabria as the Fifth Army landed at Salerno Bay. In the
long struggle up the length of Italy, the Canadians took part
in most of the major operations.

ILLUSTRATIONS

HIS MAJESTY KING GEORGE VI - - - - *Frontispiece*

Facing page

(TOP): How the Allies built two "portable" harbours capable of handling vast armies of men and millions of tons of cargo. Ships were sunk off the Normandy coast to form breakwaters behind which concrete pontoon jetties, prefabricated in England and towed across the Channel, were strung together. Ships of the Royal Canadian Navy protected them as they were slowly pulled by tugs.

(LOWER): The troops come ashore on these at Arromanches - - - - - - - - - - 50

(TOP): A group of Canadians wounded as invasion forces from Britain made their way ashore on the French coast, wait on the beach to be transferred to a Casualty Clearing Station.

(LOWER): A Nazi machine-gun nest knocked out of action as Canadian invasion forces quickly silenced shore installations - - - - - - - - 82

(TOP): When the flag was unfurled over the ground where the Canadians had been fighting, Dominion Day was celebrated in France, and Canadian pipers led a parade.

(LOWER): During the hard-fought February offensive of the First Canadian Army, Field-Marshal Sir Bernard Montgomery joined Canada's General H. G. D. Crerar and Lieut.-General Guy Simonds, as they moved forward to confer with senior officers - - 114

(TOP): He's away! This remarkable picture, snapped at 500th of a second, caught a Canadian paratrooper going "over the side" of his aircraft.

(LOWER): F. O. Robinson of Montreal, shot down, hid in the woods and joined Canadian paratroopers, who were the first to land in France. (Photo by Sgt. Dave Reynolds of Toronto, who jumped with the paratroopers and made his way back with pictures) - - 146

Facing page

(TOP): Moving ahead under the protection of a tank, these Canadians advance through the streets of Falaise, looking for snipers hidden after other Germans had fled.

(LOWER): Amphibious Canadians at Nijmegen, Holland. In the Schelde Estuary, during the *polder* warfare, the Canadians perfected an original technique in the field. This won special notice from the British War Office, which requested the preparation of special reference records - - - - - - - 178

(TOP): Canadian infantry flushing Germans from the mass of rubble which was once a thriving French city. Panzer troops fought stubbornly here.

(LOWER): Western Canadians hitch-hiking to victory, on tanks that sank deep in mud as the spearhead of the Allied attack in the West pushed into Germany in the spring of 1945. It was a typical scene in the advance - - - - - - - - - - - 210

(TOP): Canada in Germany. Past battered buildings but along well-preserved roads, traffic moves up the lines with the Canadians, in the Big Push. "Monty" held the first Allied investiture of Canadians on German soil.

(LOWER): A dream comes true! The sign tells the story, as Corporal Urban Mayo of London, Ontario, who has fought many a weary mile, reaches his primary objective - - - - - - - - - - - 242

(TOP): Canadians take over a German town. They are here seen in Cleve, a Rhineland village captured in the advance.

(LOWER): Lieut.-General A. G. L. McNaughton greets officers of a Canadian Machine-Gun Reinforcement Unit. An especially favoured army mascot is lying at the General's feet. There were many such dogs with the Canadians - - - - - - - - - 274

(TOP): At Dieppe, the plan called for an unopposed surprise landing at dawn, to gain the headland overlooking the harbour, knocking out the guns there and eventually circling back to re-embark in early

Facing page

afternoon. (These pictures are from captured German films.)

(LOWER): The main attack was to go in on the main beach. It was good for landings but loose shale and pebbles prevented tanks from getting a grip, and some foundered - - - - - - - - - 306

(TOP): The beach at Dieppe after the raid. The Royal Canadian Engineers were to blast the length of the main beach to enable tanks to get up on the Esplanade, visible here in the background. (From a captured German photograph as is the lower picture.)

(LOWER): Wounded and captured Canadians in front of a building in the town proper. "They fought on and on, until they had nothing left with which to fight." 338

I

INTRODUCTION

THROUGH a boiling sea in the sullen hour after dawn, flotillas of landing craft splashed towards the beaches of Normandy. Assault troops crouched in the craft, tensed for the first shock of battle.

A gigantic fleet of fighting ships, troop-carrying vessels and supply boats lay off the coast and as the assault forces sailed to the beaches a thousand guns thundered out a drumming barrage from the sea. Bombers and fighters droned through the smoke and mist to their targets.

This was D-Day—June 6, 1944. This was Invasion Day. This was the day for which the Allied world had waited with grim suspense, gnawing fears, unbounded hopes and patient confidence. It was a day earmarked for history.

A few hours before dawn, a British and two American airborne divisions had dropped from the night skies to the Norman fields to open the attack. Now two British infantry divisions, three American and one Canadian were going in to land from the sea.

Along the Bay of the Seine, between the Orne River and the base of the Cherbourg Peninsula, thousands of men poured ashore in a bedlam of supporting gunfire. They flooded over the beaches, punched into the sand dunes, stormed the concrete casemates from which the German guns were spitting out their hate.

They attacked ugly machine-gun posts, enemy batteries, trench systems and fortified houses. They cut through masses of barbed wire, made paths through the mine fields and their tanks churned forward in the sand, firing as they went, firing at houses, casemates, the enemy in the trenches and the dunes.

The quiet fields of Normandy were torn by the tumult of this battle, as the Allied Expeditionary Force hurled itself against the German coastal defences.

Through that first warm June day, with planes flying continuous patrols overhead, the fighting raged, and a foothold was gained on the French coast.

The 3rd Infantry Division and the 2nd Armoured Brigade, with the 1st Canadian Parachute Battalion in the British Airborne Division, were the Canadian Army contributions to that grim assault landing in the greatest combined operation ever undertaken. Ships of the Royal Canadian Navy were in the invasion fleet and bombers and fighters of the Royal Canadian Air Force flew in the vast air armadas.

The Canadian ground forces served in the second British Army for the first phase of the campaign and later they rejoined the First Canadian Army when that formation took the field at Caen.

This was the most fateful D-Day of the war, yet the Canadians had known other D-Days—the dawn landings at Dieppe, in Sicily and Italy.

In the Mediterranean and on the western front, Canada has taken a proportionate place among the Allied nations in a world engulfed by war. A fighting force of five divisions and two independent armoured brigades, formed into two corps under an Army Headquarters, was gradually created. The year 1944 saw every unit in action—the 1st Corps in Italy and the 2nd Corps, with the Army formation, on the western front.

*   *   *   *

The war was only four months old when the 1st Division arrived in Scotland just before Christmas in 1939. It was the first contingent of Canadians to come to this new conflict and the other formations followed it overseas. But the road to battle was slow and tedious. The Canadians missed action by narrow margins during the Norwegian and French campaigns of 1940. After Dunkerque, they were, for a perilous period, the only force in Britain equipped and ready to meet a threatened German invasion. But the Germans did not invade.

Month after month, the Canadians trained in southern England and built up their fighting strength as new divisions arrived from the Dominion. The training was a bitter test of patience but crack formations were created under the leadership of General McNaughton. They kept at the task of preparing for battle and they waited their moment.

There was the expedition to Spitsbergen—a bloodless operation, successfully carried out—and then the moment came at Dieppe. The raid was a tragic foray against the fortress coast of German Europe and yet, in the balance of the war, the world could later see its significance in the final victory.

The endless training went on in England. Manoeuvres, exercises, schemes. They were hard to endure. But the Canadians were prepared for the campaigns ahead of them like no other troops of this war.

Groups of officers and non-commissioned officers were sent to Tunisia to gain battle experience with the First British Army and in the spring of 1943 the 1st Division and the 1st Armoured Brigade prepared to join the Eighth Army for the Sicilian invasion.

*   *   *   *

The Canadians landed in Sicily and through July and into August they fought in suffocating dust and heat through that rugged country. A brief rest, a refit, and they crossed Messina Straits to land on the toe of Italy in early September. The Division and the Armoured Brigade fought through Italy, and at Ortona, on the Adriatic coast, at the tag end of the year these troops waged one of the bitterest battles of the campaign and won it.

The 5th Armoured Division and 1st Corps H.Q. were sent to Italy to form a Canadian Corps in the Eighth Army and it fought on the road to Rome and on the Adriatic coast again in the craggy mountains and endless hills that led to the Lombardy Plains.

In England, the rest of the Canadian Army—the 2nd Corps of three divisions and an independent armoured brigade, with Corps and Army troops and Corps and Army Headquarters—finished its preparations for D-Day in western Europe. General Crerar, after commanding the Corps in Italy, had succeeded General McNaughton as Army Commander after the latter had been forced to leave his command at Christmas, 1943. In June, the Allied Expeditionary Force struck in the west.

The 3rd Division and the 2nd Armoured Brigade won a fierce fight on the beaches when they landed at Courseulles, Bernières and St.-Aubin and for weeks bore a heavy burden of the responsibility for maintaining the beach-head perimeter west and northwest of Caen.

Many German counter-attacks were thrown back by the Canadians . . . Bretteville . . . Putot-en-Bessin . . . Villons-les-Buissons . . . Authie . . . those were towns which figured in the early struggle.

These Canadians were in the forefront of the attacks which saw the Second Army burst from the beach-head. Carpiquet was captured . . . there were bitter fights at Buron . . . Gruchy . . . Authie again . . . at Cussy and the ancient Abbey of Ardennes . . . then on to capture Caen with the 3rd British Division. The 2nd Division went into the line after the weary 3rd, having fought without rest for fifty-six consecutive days, was given a few days' respite. The 2nd Canadian Corps took the field and when the 4th Division went into the line south of Caen the First Canadian Army, under General Crerar, became operational with the 1st British Corps and the Canadian Corps under command.

The climax of the Normandy campaign came in the early days of August when huge attacks were made which led to the destruction of the Seventh German Army.

Down the Caen-Falaise highway roared the three Canadian divisions and the 1st Polish Armoured Division, with British divisions under General Crerar operating to the north and the east. The Caen-Falaise hinge was shattered in two thundering attacks, in which thousand-bomber raids were made in close support of the ground forces.

May-sur-Orne . . . St.-André-sur-Orne . . . Roquancourt . . . Tilly-la-Campagne . . . Verrieres . . . some of the towns the Canadians fought for in those desperate brown fields and slopes south of Caen. And further south towards Falaise . . . Quesnay Woods . . . Hill 195 . . . the Laison Valley . . . Falaise itself.

Falaise was captured by the 2nd Division, and the 4th and the Poles raced on to Trun, followed by the 3rd. At Trun and at St.-Lambert-sur-Dives the Trun gap was closed, cutting off the last escape route of the Seventh German Army.

This army was slaughtered in the gap by the converging British, Canadian and American forces and General Crerar's formations struck east through the hills, the green woods and the rolling farmland to the Seine, in hot pursuit of the fleeing rabble.

Over the Seine . . . the 3rd Division took Rouen . . . the 2nd went back to Dieppe in triumph . . . the 3rd, 4th and the Poles rolled east to cross the Somme at Abbeville and storm through the Pas de Calais in the great pursuit.

The Canadian Army drove on into Belgium . . . through Ypres and the old battle-fields to Ghent and Antwerp where it linked with Second Army forces. Le Havre was besieged and captured by the 1st British Corps . . . Boulogne, Calais and Cap Gris Nez fell to the indomitable 3rd Division.

The pace was hot and heavy . . . hundreds of V-1 sites were overrun by the Canadians racing along the "rocket coast". The coastal guns at Calais and Cap Gris Nez were silenced.

The task of clearing the Schelde estuary to enable the huge port of Antwerp to be used as a gigantic supply base was given the Canadian Army.

The 3rd Division opened the operation with an attack over the Leopold Canal and in bitter fighting finally cleared the south side of the estuary by destroying the German force in the Schelde pocket. The 2nd Division advanced north from Antwerp and struck along South Beveland Island in an operation co-ordinated with the work being done by the 3rd. Four seaborne landings were made in this complicated Schelde operation and in the final phase the 52nd Lowland Division shared in the fighting. In one month the Schelde was cleared of Germans and within a few weeks the first Allied convoys sailed into Antwerp.

While the Schelde battle raged, the 4th Division, with British, Polish and American divisions under General Crerar, drove the Germans from southwestern Holland with the assistance of Second British Army forces, striking west from the Nijmegen salient.

A broad phase of the war in the west was over and in the re-grouping which followed the Canadian Army took over the Nijmegen salient. Troops of the 3rd Division were the first Canadians to cross the German border.

The battle for Germany itself lay ahead.

For the Canadian Army it began February 8 when British and Canadian troops in the Army attacked southeast of Nijmegen to clear the west bank of the Lower Rhine. The Reichswald Forest and the northern end of the Siegfried Line were overrun. The Canadians broke through the Hochwald Line to the south and in one month's heavy fighting the Germans were driven back over the river. A springboard for the Rhine crossing had been provided.

On the night of March 23-24 the Rhine was forced by British and American troops. The Canadians passed into the bridgehead and struck north along the east bank . . . Emmerich was captured . . . the Canadians crossed the Dutch border to liberate northern Holland . . . part of the Army swept back into Germany along the northern flank of the Allied drive into the Reich. These were the last days for Hitler's Germany.

In this final phase of the European war the 1st Canadian Corps was transferred from Italy and rejoined the First Canadian Army. Canada's whole overseas force was then together again. The 1st and 5th Divisions went into their first Western Front action in Holland, driving the Germans out of an area from Arnhem to the Zuider Zee . . . the 1st Corps besieged fortress Holland and the 2nd Corps closed in on Emden and Wilhelmshaven . . .

On May 5 the fighting ended for the Canadians in Europe when German forces surrendered unconditionally along the fronts of the First Canadian Army and the Second British Army. At Rheims, two days later, the German representatives signed the unconditional surrender of all Germany and the war was over. This was officially announced May 8, which became Victory Day in Europe.

*   *   *   *

This is a book about the Canadian soldiers . . . from Spitsbergen to Dieppe, from Sicily and Italy to Normandy and Germany.

I was fortunate in being able, as a war correspondent of The Canadian Press, to follow them in their campaigns. Here I have tried to relate in a narrative of events the story of their achievements, their ordeals, their sacrifices and their boundless courage along the tortured paths to our victory.

To The Canadian Press for an assignment which took me to the battle-fronts with my countrymen and to officers and men in every Canadian division and formation who have helped me gather the news during these years of war, I owe a debt of gratitude.

I thank Gillis Purcell, Assistant General Manager of The CP, for constant encouragement in writing this book, and Charles Bruce, CP London Superintendent, for helping it along in so many ways.

II

THE STORM GATHERS

IN THE fall of 1943, with Sicily conquered and the Italian campaign successfully launched, British and American leaders made their final decision that the Second Front would be opened in late May or early June the following year—and that the target would be the flat beach areas along the Bay of the Seine, between Le Havre and Cherbourg. Prime Minister Churchill and President Roosevelt travelled to Teheran with their military advisers and in that Persian city the die was cast. In the meeting with Marshal Stalin the plan, the target and the time were discussed and the whole issue of the Second Front was settled.

But the story of invasion planning goes back to the days after Dunkerque. The battered British Expeditionary Force had scarcely come back to England before high-ranking men in the War Office and in the British and Canadian forces in England began to ponder the problems of getting an army back on the continent. General McNaughton of the Canadians was one of them. He kept his eye on the continent even through those months in the summer, fall and winter of 1940-41 when a German invasion of Britain was regarded as more than a possibility. The menace of German invasion passed and the British High Command turned its planning to the offensive.

The Commandos had been formed; they carried out small but significant raids on enemy-held coasts. In August, 1941, a Canadian force went to Spitsbergen, stayed there ten days, denied the valuable coal mines to the Germans who controlled the Arctic island from Norway, and came back to Britain. In the sweeping panorama of the war it was not consequential—but it was important because it was offensive. The wheels were slowly and ponderously turning in England. Britain had recovered from the shock of Dunkerque and the French collapse and now her leaders, her people and her new Army, then taking shape, were thinking of attack. This switch from the defensive to the offensive was reflected most clearly in the training of the troops. In Surrey and Sussex the Canadians went on invasion manoeuvres instead of practising the anti-invasion role that had been theirs. In the fall of 1941, General McNaughton gave an interview to a group of Canadian editors in England on tour. Sitting in his office at Headley Court near Leatherhead, where his Corps Headquarters was located, he spoke a sentence that endured: "The Canadian Corps is a dagger pointed at the heart of Berlin." And a few months later during a visit to Washington he held a press interview in the Canadian Legation there and told the newspapermen: "We will give it to the Hun —right in the belly." He was thinking continually of the great offensive to come—the return to the continent, and there were others like him in high places who were planning ahead for this huge task.

The invasion was only a dream then, with comparatively meagre forces available in Britain at that time. The new British Army was far from ready for such an enterprise and the science of combined operations on a large scale had not been explored. Much had to be done. Many more troops, *matériel* and ships were needed. Then in December, 1941, the United States came into the war. The picture altered sharply.

The Americans had that extra man-power. They had great war industry potentiality. Link the two with the magnificent contributions of Britain and the Empire and you had the stuff for invasion.

American staffs came to London in the spring of 1942, with invasion on their minds. But D-Day was a long way off. The British command had the Dieppe raid on the books; the American and British chiefs were planning the landings in North Africa.

Other campaigns had to be fought before the Allied forces crossed the Channel to stay on French soil.

The Dieppe raid was staged on August 19, 1942. It proved many things which had to be proved in battle, and, apart from the vitally important lessons in combined operations which were learned in those terrible eight hours at Dieppe, it convinced the Allied Command that an invasion assault on a heavily defended port was not feasible.

The attack must be made across open beaches, beaches, say, like those in the Bay of the Seine, the commanders reasoned. These beaches are distant from big ports, yet they are between Le Havre and Cherbourg and comparatively near the Breton ports of Brest, St.-Malo and Lorient. The Germans were defending the ports; they were not defending the beach areas in between with the same strength. But to invade over open beaches involved a staggering supply problem. The invasion armies might have to be supplied over the beaches for weeks, even months. Yet this seemed the only way to launch the attack without colossal casualties in the initial assault. This problem of supplying over beaches had to be worked out, they said. So in London and in Washington officers went to work planning a supply system to keep an army in the field without port facilities. This was back in the

fall and winter of 1942-43. Even then the tentative
plan was to land on the Normandy coast between
Le Havre and Cherbourg; but it was not until the
fall of 1943 that the plan firmed up.

After Dieppe, the American and British forces
under General Eisenhower landed in North Africa.
The Mediterranean had priority over western European operations for one whole year. The First Army
fought bitterly in the ragged mountains and valleys of
Tunisia and the Second American Corps joined in the
struggle there, which went on into 1943.

The Eighth Army fought from El Alamein through
the western desert for the last time. At Casablanca,
Churchill and Roosevelt and their military staffs
reviewed the war they were waging and reached the
conclusion that the campaign in the Mediterranean
should be pressed. North Africa would be cleared of
the enemy and attacks on Sicily and Italy would
follow. The invasion of northwest Europe was not to
be attempted until the Mediterranean campaign was
well advanced. At Casablanca there were champions
of a Second Front in 1943; but this view was overruled by the decision to seize every opportunity in the
Mediterranean.

British and Canadian troops in Britain, earmarked
for invasion roles, and the Americans who were flooding into the United Kingdom, were given another
year to train and prepare.

The Tunisian campaign was brought to a sweeping
conclusion and the fall of Bizerte and Tunis in May
marked the end of the Axis in Africa. The Eighth
Army and the new American Seventh Army looked to
Sicily. On July 10, a huge fleet landed the two armies
on Sicilian beaches. By mid-August the island was in
Allied hands and the 1st Canadian Division, which

had gone direct from England into the assault as part of the Eighth Army, shared in this Allied victory.

The Eighth Army went on to Italy and on September 3 the 1st Canadian and 5th British Divisions crossed Messina Straits and landed on the continental mainland. They poured through mountainous Calabria, meeting little opposition, and the Fifth Army, composed of British and American troops, struck at Salerno Bay.

A tremendous and critical battle took place at Salerno and the landing succeeded in face of heavy German resistance. The advance up the length of Italy began and the "hot rake of war" was dragged across the country.

From the accumulated knowledge of the Dieppe raid and the four major combined-operations landings in North Africa, Sicily, the toe of Italy and Salerno, the secrets of successful seaborne attack had been determined.

While this Mediterranean campaign marched from one success to another, the British and American planning staffs in London kept working on the vast and detailed plan for invasion of northwest Europe. Every bit of information from the other landings helped them as they built up the plan. By the fall of 1943, great progress had been made. It was agreed that the target would be the Normandy coast between Le Havre and Cherbourg. The date would be late May or early June.

*   *   * · *

Special training for the assault was started even before the invasion of Italy. The 3rd Canadian Infantry Division was detached from the First Canadian Army in the late summer and went into the 1st

British Corps, which was the assault corps of the British force. Designated now as an assault division, it began a long period of training. The troops first went to Scotland for intensive combined-operations training and carried out many practice landings on the rugged Scottish coast under fire support from the sea. This was the special feature of their training and it was this Division that carried out all the experiments and improved this bombardment method. It proved a great success in the real show.

At first ordinary twenty-five-pounder field guns were loaded on tank-landing craft and after a good deal of adaptation it was found that they could lay down accurate fire on the beaches, shooting from the craft as they went in to shore behind the assault infantry. Even when the sea was rough, the gunners were able to maintain a good rate of fire. In the initial experiments, a battery of guns supported a company of infantry and this was gradually increased until several regiments of guns were firing with an infantry brigade as it landed. For several weeks the Division was on one manoeuvre after another in Scotland. Then it moved south to a concentration area on the Channel coast between Bournemouth and Southampton.

I got back to England from Italy in early October to find the Division already training with the special Royal Navy force which was to carry it to France. On this divisional level the opening of the Second Front seemed to be very close, for the troops were ready even then for the job and many in the camps thought they might be going at any time. In Italy, I had heard rumours among Eighth Army officers and in the 1st Division area that the invasion might go in before the winter to seize a beach-head and hold it during the bad weather until big operations could start in the spring.

A similar story was going around Algiers when I got there on my flying trip to Britain on the incredible wartime air route that took you from the Italian battle-front through Sicily, Tunis, Algiers, Casablanca, Marrakesh and then to Scotland in one last long hop.

But an enormous lot of work had still to be done until everything was ready. In the fall of 1943 the plans for the Normandy assault were far advanced but a tremendous volume of detail had still to be handled, meaning months more work. Other divisions had to train with naval forces just as the 3rd Canadian was doing. Troops had to be brought from the Mediterranean to be part of the expeditionary force. There had to be certain changes in command. Supreme Headquarters had still to be set up. General Eisenhower was in Algiers, and General Montgomery was with his Eighth Army. But the invasion was taking sure and certain shape in the war councils and in the planning staffs in London, Washington, and Algiers and in the training camps of Britain.

On the surface there was little to indicate that all this preparation was going on. And some people in London and in New York still expressed doubts that there ever would be a Second Front.

With the 3rd Division on a landing manoeuvre called "Pirate" in mid-October, I saw the proof that the invasion preparations were going ahead well and I was convinced then that the operation was going to take place. This highly secret exercise drew most of the senior officers in Britain to Bournemouth to see the Canadians land on Studland Bay, just east of the city. The feature was a demonstration of the new fire support plan.

It was the newest thing in combined operations and was considered to be the answer to an opposed landing on a fortified beach. The 3rd Division had developed this fire plan in the months of its training. Now it was being displayed for the High Command.

The talk in the messes the night before the demonstration landing was all Second Front, fire support and artillery plans. I talked with a lot of senior officers that night in the Royal Bath Hotel and it was obvious that the Second Front was no myth. It was definitely going to take place, but not before spring at the earliest. I don't think there were half-a-dozen of these high-ranking officers who knew the where and when of the big plan but they all took it for granted the job was coming off and concentrated on their own specific tasks in the undertaking.

They watched the landing from a headland by Studland Bay. It was done in broad daylight, a significant hint of what was to happen later, and we saw the fleet of several hundred landing craft and ships carrying the Division come out of Southampton and sail towards the beaches in perfect formation. The destroyers came up and opened fire.

They pumped shells on to the flat beach; then the Canadian field artillery on the landing craft drummed forth with its barrage from the sea. At first, most of the shells fell short but the range was corrected and the beach was showered with bursting high explosives. The rocket craft sailed in towards the shore and did their stuff, hitting the target dead on. Small craft swept the beach with fire from close in and infantry in assault landing craft landed under this curtain of fire, as fighter planes cannoned and machine-gunned dummy pillboxes. Assault engineers landed in armoured vehicles to blow paths through concrete walls and other obstacles. Tanks landed right with the infantry and shot up the pillboxes and "enemy" strongpoints. It was a minute, but accurate demonstration of the D-Day plan. Many features had to be tidied up and improved, but the great secret was this new conception of devastating fire support from the sea. Everything was to be done to give the infantry more than a fighting chance once they got ashore. Dieppe had clearly shown the need for this.

*   *   *   *

The pace quickened toward the year's end. General Eisenhower was appointed Supreme Commander of the Allied Expeditionary Force and SHAEF—Supreme Headquarters, Allied Expeditionary Force—was set up in London. At first there were only a few hundred officers in the Headquarters, most of them from the planning staffs which had done all the preparatory work. Then SHAEF really expanded until it became the biggest Allied headquarters of all time.

General Eisenhower came to London and General Montgomery, who had been appointed Commander of the British ground forces for the invasion, left his Eighth Army and joined him. Montgomery was to be more than British Commander. He was to direct all the British, American and Canadian ground forces in the first stages of the continental operation. His headquarters was 21st Army Group.

During the fall, it had appeared that General Sir Bernard Paget, who had been Commander-in-Chief, Home Forces, had commanded Southeastern Command in England and before that directed the ill-starred Norwegian campaign in the spring of 1940, would lead the British invasion armies. He was Commander of 21st Army Group when it was first formed in the fall and under him as Commander of the Second British Army—the invasion army—was General Anderson, who had led the First Army in Tunisia. But Montgomery was given 21st Army Group and when he got to London changes occurred.

General Anderson went to Britain's Eastern Command and General M. C. Dempsey was brought from Italy to command the Second Army. Dempsey had commanded a Corps under General Montgomery in the Mediterranean and in the summer and fall of 1940 he had been Brigadier, General Staff, to General McNaughton in the 7th Corps, a composite Canadian-British formation which at that time was Britain's principal anti-invasion force.

In the Second Army there were four British corps and the 1st Corps, to which the 3rd Division was attached, had the most important British task in the assault. It was to gain the eastern end of the beach-head from the mouth of the Orne River, north of Caen, to Courseulles, twelve miles to the west. The 3rd Canadian Division was bolstered with the 2nd Canadian Armoured Brigade of three Canadian tank regiments, and also had an additional artillery regiment and engineers. Other divisions in this Corps were the 6th Airborne, including a Canadian parachute battalion, and the 3rd British Division. These were the assault divisions of the Corps; the 51st Highland Division was to follow up in reserve.

Another corps also was to be on the assault, but on a smaller scale than the 1st Corps, sending in the famous 50th Division to beaches around Arromanches, west of Courseulles. The 7th Armoured Division was also to land after the 50th had won its section of the beach-head.

One of the most intriguing secrets of the invasion preparations was the return to England for the Second Front of three crack British divisions which had seen

long service in the Mediterranean. The 50th was one
of these. It had been with the Eighth from El Alamein
and had been in the vanguard of its hardest battles
right into Tunisia. Others were the 51st Highland,
which had also fought from El Alamein and like the
50th had been through Sicily as well, and the 7th
Armoured—the "desert rat" division—a legendary
formation of the western desert. In addition to
these full divisions, several experienced independent
brigades of armour and infantry came back to Britain.
Not a word was let out about this switch-over from
the southern theatre. Thousands of people knew of
the home-coming of these forces but you seldom heard
it mentioned even in casual conversation. The troops
went to their homes on leave. They were all over
London, wearing the battle flashes of their own
divisions and formations and wearing their Africa Star
ribbons, yet nobody talked unduly about them. It
was one of the best-kept secrets of the war. Several
experienced American divisions, too, were brought
from the Mediterranean to Britain and the Anglo-
American mystery force for Europe gathered its
strength.

Naval forces were mustered in home waters. Warships crowded into the big British naval bases and
assault ships and landing craft sailed home from the
Mediterranean. From the United States and Canada
and from the factories of Britain came thousands of
newly-built landing craft and escort ships of a dozen
types all ticketed for the attack.

The air forces were ready for the assault and bombed
with increasing intensity from the winter through the
spring to D-Day. American airmen flooded into
Britain and joined with the old hands of the United
States Army Air Corps, with the Royal Air Force and

Royal Canadian Air Force in the long programme of air attack, the destructive prelude to the landing.

*   *   *   *

In December the commanders of assault formations went to London for planning conferences. On maps bearing bogus names but which were actual maps of the Normandy coast target, they fought their battles on paper. These men who were to lead the troops in the real actions did not officially know the target or the time then, and the secret still rested with a handful of British and American statesmen and military leaders.

Another planning conference started in London in January; on January 25, the assault leaders were told where the landing was to be and the approximate date. Like the other divisional commanders, Major-General R. F. L. Keller of the 3rd Canadian Division was there with a few senior members of his headquarters staff. The conferences lasted through February and it was not until some weeks later that brigade commanders and their staffs knew the Second Front secret.

The broad plan drawn up by the invasion planning staffs over the previous year and more was not greatly altered by General Eisenhower and General Montgomery when they assumed their new command at the start of 1944. The most significant change was the inclusion of an additional division—the 50th.

General Montgomery insisted that the British invasion force must have this extra formation and so it was brought back home with the 51st, the 7th and the independent brigades, and given a spearhead role. The addition of the 50th involved a great deal of extra staff work, because the complicated loading tables for shipping had to be altered to fit in 15,000 more fighting men. Supply calculations had to be adjusted.

But the job was done and inclusion of the 50th proved later to have been a decision of great wisdom.

All this went on behind the scenes in Whitehall and in the planning rooms at SHAEF. Never had any operation been so wrapped in mystery.

I was working in London, with occasional visits to the Canadian camps in southern England, through the winter and the spring, and the tension of approaching events compounded with every passing week. We knew that invasion was in the making; that it was a dead certainty to come off; that several large armies were going through the final stages of training; that the plan was ready and that the colossal machinery to put it into action was grinding into gear.

We could not write much about invasion preparations in those days. We were told not to speculate on time and place. Training could be described only in the broadest terms. One censorship restriction followed another. The High Command was taking no chances. Yet correspondents, sensing the greatest news story in centuries, flocked to London. They came from the Mediterranean; they came from the southwest Pacific; scores of freshman war reporters joined the old hands at this job and Fleet Street and the Strand were the base for literally a battalion of reporters waiting for the invasion. Meantime they were practically unemployed.

I tried to cover other assignments. They put me on the Whitehall beat and I went the rounds, writing about post-war plans, pay-as-you-go income tax, Churchill, Eden, Cabinet rumours, London pocket blitzes, Tito and Balkan politics and the Russian thrust into Rumania. I wrote about German generals and what the German coastal defences might be like. That was about as close as you would get to writing

about the Second Front possibilities. It was not because
we knew any deep secrets. We did not know the time
or the place, and as a matter of fact the stretch of
Normandy beach where we did land was the spot least
considered in private speculation that went on in
offices and flats.

In the Canadian camps, I could see the preparations
going ahead at top speed. Masses of new equipment
went to Canadian formations in the early spring and
the various headquarters began to move around the
south with their fighting units. It was practice,
practice, practice.

At First Canadian Army Headquarters in southern
England there was unusual activity. An operational
planning staff was there with General Crerar and the
staff was working out the Canadian Army's specific
job. While the 3rd Canadian Division was in the 1st
British Corps for the early phase, the First Canadian
Army H. Q. and the Canadian formations in England
which were all under its command were to go to
France in the follow-up phase after the assault. The
Canadian Army was to take its place alongside the
Second British Army and the American armies on the
continent and some British formations were to come
under General Crerar's command to give the army
full stature. Like the Second Army, the Canadian
Army was part of 21st Army Group and was
closely linked with General Montgomery's headquarters during the planning period.

I saw the 2nd Canadian Division training on the
South Downs behind Brighton and watched the 4th
Armoured Division working in its area south of East
Grinstead. They knew they were on the last lap. The
final proof for the troops was in the equipment they
were getting. Nothing was denied them. The gates

were wide open and guns and vehicles and arms flowed right to them.

They knew they had a follow-up role to the assault and viewed the 3rd Division with awe. They called them the "death or glory boys" and there was a rumour that the Division estimated that its probable losses on the beaches would be 50 per cent. A lot of people believed this wild rumour. Once, at 2nd Division, I mentioned to a staff officer that I expected to go with the 3rd and he looked at me as if it was the last time he would see me.

In the south, the big base camps mushroomed around the ports and British, American and Canadian troops raced through their final training. The 3rd Division kept up its intensive combined-operations work and every few weeks went to sea with its naval force to make more landings along the south coast. The fire plan was gradually improved and after three or four more practices the Canadians and the Navy had it down pat. That coastline was one of the most bombarded strips of land in the world. New assault equipment was given the 3rd Division, including self-propelled guns. These were the American "priests", 105mm. guns mounted on tank chassis, and they could run right off a landing craft and go into action immediately on the beaches. For the artillery bombardment from the sea, they were easy to handle on the landing craft.

February passed, March passed, and General Montgomery toured practically every division in Britain— British, Canadian and American. He talked to his troops, told them little but primed them for the task and the ordeal ahead as only he can do.

The Canadian correspondents saw him one evening at Euston station aboard his special train in which he had travelled up and down England seeing his forces. He was affable and talked freely—talked freely about anything but the invasion. We came away knowing less than ever about what the future held.

In London the tension grew. We knew we were going with the Canadian assault formation and the waiting was a nerve-racking experience. Week after week, we haunted the public relations office at Canadian Military Headquarters on Trafalgar Square, hopefully expecting that Colonel Bill Abel or Lieutenant-Colonel Eric Gibbs would tell us to get our kit and report for this assignment.

We tried to do other work around London but it was difficult to keep one's mind on anything else. Occasionally we would go on sorties to American or British formations to see Allied commanders inspect troops but this only increased the tension. It is a wonder some of us did not wind up in the Canadian Army's neurological hospital.

London was jam-packed with officers and men. SHAEF personnel were all over the city. Thousands and thousands of soldiers, airmen and sailors crowded into the capital for last leaves. You had to reserve a hotel room weeks in advance and were lucky to get it even then. Hostels were filled with troops and restaurants and movies were flooded with customers. To get a beer in most London pubs was like elbowing your way to a bargain counter.

But London was not in any carnival mood. It was expectant, hopeful, serious.

At the beginning of April, leaves were cancelled for most of the services. Even the luckiest serviceman could get only twenty-four hours away from his unit. London emptied of men in uniform, except for those stationed there, working in the big headquarters. The barber and the pub-keeper, musing over this situation, said: "London is very quiet. It can't be far off now. I suppose you'll be going soon?"

You answered a vague "maybe" and your mind was jumbled with excitement, uncertainty, confidence and doubt. We became very cautious about discussing the invasion or anything to do with the army. We just waited and waited. We packed our kit carefully, repacked it and sorted it all out again. I thought I had the perfect field kit for an amphibious assault, with everything in it from can-opener to an extra typewriter ribbon. A week after landing in France, German shells destroyed the lot and left me with just the clothes I was wearing when I plunged into a slit-trench.

In mid-April I went down to see the 3rd Division again and it was ready almost to the last detail. A few hundred more vehicles had to be waterproofed, some special equipment for the assault had yet to arrive, but generally the formation was all set for D-Day. For several days I lived at Headquarters on the south coast and then we went to sea on the big dress rehearsal.

It took several days for the guns, tanks and troops to be loaded and we sailed into the Channel to land on a south coast beach. Ashore were members of the Supreme Headquarters staff watching the landing and the bombardment of the coast. This was the last practice for the fire-support plan. Everything was being used in this divisional manoeuvre, including two cruisers.

I left Headquarters Ship with some of the staff officers in a landing craft and we lay off shore about half a mile as the divisional artillery pounded out its barrage and the rocket craft, destroyers and cruisers added their weight to the bombardment. The infantry and tanks landed and the beach organization followed behind them. The whole practice went off with a precision that you seldom get on these manoeuvres and although there was some quibbling as to whether the bombardment was laid right on the target it seemed to satisfy the top men who witnessed it.

We sailed back to port again and the troops unloaded, to return once more to their camps in the concentration areas. I went to London with an enormous amount of background information on the invasion in my mind and a tip from a general that there was time for only one more manoeuvre. That meant the real show was only a matter of weeks away.

As D-Day came closer, the Allied Command fought their own brand of nerve-war as hard as they could. The Germans were jumpy about the concentration of shipping in south coast ports, and for that matter in ports all around the United Kingdom, and their aircraft also could spot the great troop concentrations in the south.

By deception, rumour and false alarms, the enemy was made more confused than ever and the supreme secret of the date of D-Day was fogged up so well that the people of Britain were just as muddled about it as the Germans.

The 3rd Division was given orders to go on one more manoeuvre. No correspondents were permitted to accompany the troops, yet I was ordered to report to the public relations headquarters of 21st Army Group in South Kensington with a score of other reporters. At the first of May all the correspondents with the various armies had been accredited to SHAEF and "alerted" to stand by for orders to move. This seemed like the big move, so we checked quietly out of our hotel rooms and flats, packed our kit for the Channel crossing and went out to South Kensington at the appointed hour. A British brigadier, who was chief of PR for the Army Group, was there. He blandly informed us that this was all part of the war of nerves and that we were to be used in the broad deception plan.

"Our intelligence is concerned about the problem of getting a large number of correspondents out of London when the real show starts, without giving information to the enemy," he said. "The disappearance of you people under these circumstances could indicate to an alert enemy that D-Day was near. So we have decided to take you away from London, twenty or so at a time, for about a week, to accustom Fleet Street and your friends in London to seeing you go and also to confuse any enemy agents who might be around. Please tell your offices you are on an assignment, but do not give any further details."

Off we went to Euston station and laden down with our kit walked along the crowded platform. We all wore our correspondents badges, and an officer with us edged up to me as we stood by the train for Scotland and whispered like a conspirator: "I wonder if your departure will be reported to Berlin tonight. We certainly hope there is an agent in this crowd."

We felt like immensely important personages, not that we were being used in the deception plan, but because we had first-class sleepers on this night train to Scotland. For the last two years I had seldom enjoyed the luxury of a first-class sleeper on any train in Britain. You had to be a full colonel or above to rate sufficient priority, but here we were, each with his own compartment. I felt as if I were wearing red tabs.

Our hideout was on the coast southwest of Glasgow and we arrived there in the morning. It was a British combined-operations training centre and now that the rush of training for the invasion was over this spacious camp was empty so we moved into the officers' quarters there. It was a pleasant week. We had good food; we attended combined-operations lectures and demonstrations put on for our benefit by the staff, and we walked the long sandy beaches. It brought back a lot of memories for me, for it was in this same area that the 1st Canadian Division had concentrated and done its practice landings before sailing for Sicily a year before. And the Scottish weather was just as foul in the spring of 1944 as it was in 1943. One rain squall followed another and a chill wind blew down the coast. But the week gave one a chance to get adjusted properly to the attack ahead. Most of us were in a pretty bad frame of mind from this seemingly endless waiting through the winter into spring; now we settled down and got things into the right perspective.

The evening we left to return to London, the colonel commanding the camp dined with us in the mess and after dinner he proposed a toast, "happy landings", and wished us luck. Back in London we went over our precious kit again, for the time was getting short.

In the south, the 3rd Division had carried out its final exercise and British and American formations which were to share in the assault had finished their rehearsals.

The last great convoys had arrived from the United States and Canada with invasion materials, stores, personnel and ammunition. The south of England was overflowing with the greatest armed force assembled by Britain, the United States and Canada. The south for miles and miles was packed with troop concentrations, ammunition dumps, tank harbours and vehicle and gun parks. The whole thing was on a colossal scale.

The bombing of Germany and occupied France, of communications, factories, bridges, concentration points and defences was reaching its climax. The German radio, in a wildly unsettled state, sought to draw information from Allied sources by broadcasting invasion stories. But on this invasion eve London and Washington kept mum. The Supreme Command continued to play its war-of-nerves cards skilfully.

General Montgomery held a press conference at his headquarters in west London and spoke to two hundred of us in the incisive, clipped manner which is characteristic. He laid down some definite rules for us, talked glowingly of his troops, mentioned his own activities, told us the principles on which he fights a battle. He emphasized the Allied aspects of the expedition. He told us that he expected Rommel to react immediately and fight it out on the beaches. This is not what happened, but General Montgomery was equal to the new situation of a slow German reaction. Nothing fazed him. We thought when we went to his headquarters that we might be briefed on part of the plan. But he told us nothing about the plan. That was to come later.

In a few days we were summoned *en masse* to General Eisenhower's headquarters. In the big conference room, hung with the flags of the United Nations, the Supreme Commander, genial and buoyant as ever, chinned in his Kansan way about his attitude to the press and told us there would be no political censorship of copy coming back from France. There were many reporters in the audience who had worked out of Algiers when the General was head man there, and they remembered the political censorship which followed the assassination of Admiral Darlan.

We waited for the General to say something about
the invasion, but he chatted on about the press and
wound up on his pet topic—Allied co-operation. He
waved to us and smiling his big, wide smile strode out
of the room. We had been told nothing, but his
appearance of utter and complete confidence had an
influence on everyone there. General Bedell Smith,
Eisenhower's chief of staff and the man with the
sharpest, shrewdest mind behind the Supreme Commander, then gave us some details. He was as emphatic
as a machine-gun. The last big conference of the
corps commanders was taking place that day, he said.
Several large convoys of ammunition ships still had to
be unloaded. Without saying it in words, he told us
D-Day was almost here.

We were put on three hours' notice. I locked myself
up in a room in the Park Lane Hotel and worked on
the Sicilian and Italian chapters of this book. It was
a good antidote for invasion nerves to write about
other invasions, already history. On Tuesday, May
30, at nine A.M., the telephone in my room jangled.
I knew what is was before I picked up the receiver.
A PR officer at C.M.H.Q. said: "Please report with all
your field kit to 17 Pall Mall at four-thirty this
afternoon."

This was the final call. I tried to be cool and
collected, but found myself dithering around like a
cub reporter on his first big assignment. Louis Hunter
came up to the room. Lou was the veteran in the
Canadian Press Bureau in London. He had come
overseas in August, 1940, had been through the blitz
from start to finish, had been with the Canadians in
Sicily and Italy and now he was assigned to the
R.C.A.F. to cover the start of the invasion. He had
received his marching orders too. He was reporting

back to his air station that afternoon. I checked out of the Park Lane, said one of those strange goodbyes to Lou, and rushed up to Fursecroft apartments in Marylebone where my field kit was.

For nearly four years of war, practically all the CP London staff had lived at one time or another in a six-room flat in that apartment block. It had been a bachelor home for the London staff and it had always been a place of great hospitality to me when I came in for week-ends in London from the Canadian camps in those training years before the Canadians went out from Britain to fight. It was always a place where you found a welcome when you came back to London from some assignment outside England. One of the members of Fursecroft Bureau, as we called it, was there when I arrived, sorting out his kit. Bill Stewart was going with the 3rd Division too. We were the CP team on the assault.

We got our stuff together—two packs and a typewriter each—the bare essentials to keep us going for a week or so on the continent. We had been warned to take every precaution to prevent our departure from our hotels or flats from being too obvious—and just as we were about to leave, the charwoman came in for the daily cleaning job and brought a friend with her. As the two women chattered in a back room, we dodged down the hall like ten-second men, lugging our kit. Out of the door we went, down the stairs, through the lobby and into a waiting cab.

Number 17 Pall Mall was across from the Royal Automobile Club and it was the headquarters of the Canadian Army Film and Photo Unit. Today it was our invasion rendezvous and here the small group of "assault correspondents" with the 3rd Division gathered. It amused us to be tagged with this name. You can't assault much with a typewriter and a notebook. There were Matt Halton and Marcel Ouimet of the Canadian Broadcasting Corporation, Ralph Allen of the Toronto *Globe and Mail*, Lionel Shapiro of the North American Newspaper Alliance and *Maclean's Magazine*, Charlie Lynch, a Canadian writing for Reuters, Bill Clark of British United Press, Joe Willicombe of International News Service, Stewart and myself.

Captain Placide Labelle, who was with Montreal *La Presse* before joining the army, was in charge of our PR unit on the assault. Nobody had much to say. We got into jeeps and the little convoy whisked west through London and down the broad highways leading to Portsmouth and Southampton. It was a beautiful afternoon. Children were playing by the hundreds in the parks. England was fresh, green and luxuriant and you noticed with a start that there were practically no men in uniform on the streets. They were getting ready in the army camps, airfields and naval bases all over this crowded United Kingdom.

I felt elated as we whizzed southwest from London; it was a great relief to be moving. At last we were on our way. But looking at England now I found it had a stronger grip on me than I thought. Leaving it was almost like leaving home. England had been good to the Canadian Army.

The roads were nearly empty. The heavy movement to the ports was over. The men and *matériel* for the Second Front were loading on the ships now on a time-table schedule. In this area through which we passed you could not drive a mile in the preceding few months without being bogged in traffic as huge convoys moved to the ports. It was all over.

Our first destination was an estate in the south, and

there in a large country home we joined the British and American writers attached to other divisions in the Second Army. We had a meeting with the PR chiefs there and were given our allocations in the assault. All the Canadians knew approximately what their positions were going to be, but there was one British correspondent who to his consternation found he had been assigned to the airborne troops. He had never made a jump in his life! Another correspondent, a well-groomed, monocled French writer, was told he was going with the "ducks". He had never heard of the amphibious trucks that bear that name and leaning over in his chair, taking the monocle carefully from his eyes, he asked the PR colonel: "But, sir, what is a duck?"

Allocations were adjusted, "duck" was explained and the Canadian group went off to its own "camp". They called it a camp but the place sticks in my mind as one of the loveliest spots I have seen. It was a fine old timbered house down a winding lane, with early summer flowers blooming profusely on either side. It made you at ease just to cast your eyes over this picture of peace and composure.

This was the starting-point for a new adventure— one that was inevitably going to make you witness of the greatest military event of the war, yet one of death and destruction and sorrow and pain. This country home, set in spacious acres, scarred with barbed wire which contained us for some unknown reason of security, had been the home of a retired admiral. He must have lived splendidly. From the drawing-room, you walked into a garden where there were flowers, humming-birds, flagstones and a lily pond. And beyond was a brick wall with ivy clinging to it and a Chinese moongate with weeping willows drooping beyond.

We stayed there overnight and were given our detailed instructions for our positions in the assault by Lieutenant-Colonel Dick Malone, in charge of the Canadian PR field organization with the expeditionary force.

I did not sleep much that night. Like a lot of others, I was thinking back over the years the Canadians had spent in England. Now they were going to leave for the struggle on the continent. The years in England had not been wasted. The troops had trained hard under circumstances of tedium and boredom. They put up with routine, with repetition and waiting. The soldiers had done magnificently here in England and the commanders who guided them through this difficult period of inactivity deserve the highest praise. I thought particularly of General McNaughton, who had given everything he had to this Canadian force overseas and who was not here for the fulfilment of his plans and his dreams. This was going to be his kind of war. A war of guns and machines operated by brave men. A war of science, too.

I thought of the assault troops of the 3rd Division. I knew hundreds of them. They were friends and they were going into the most perilous operation in history. Anything could happen but they were willing to go. My mind drifted off to personal things and I fell asleep.

In the morning we went south again to Southampton. For the last ten miles leading to the port, we passed through the marshalling areas where a large portion of the Second Army was concentrated and being fed through to the ships. The Canadians called it the "sausage machine".

There was an immense amount of work involved in merely getting the expeditionary force aboard ships, without considering the battle at all. For months and months this work had been going on, with staff officers sweating over loading tables to ensure that the right bodies and the right vehicles and weapons were on the right ships in the right places to sail from the right ports at the right time.

We passed through the marshalling area and went down to Southampton docks where a naval craft took a party of us down Southampton Water towards Cowes where we were to report to the 3rd Division H.Q.

Every port in the United Kingdom had invasion shipping in it at that time, but Southampton was probably more crowded than any other. Ships were moored along wharves for miles and in the inlets and in Southampton Water itself there were hundreds upon hundreds of white-and-grey landing craft, assault ships, troopers, gun-boats, destroyers and the *mélange* of surface craft that go into making a combined operation. Smoke screens covered a good portion of the fleet to protect it from any venturesome German aircraft. But the *Luftwaffe* made no real raids against this great concentration of shipping. In the Thames Estuary there was another great concentration; it was the same in Bristol and Cardiff, in Plymouth where many of the Americans loaded, in Glasgow, Liverpool and Hull.

We splashed down Southampton Water into the Solent and our craft dropped me off at the ship which served as headquarters for the 3rd Division and the 1st Corps, as well as for the naval force carrying the Division. She looked anything but a H.Q. Ship. She looked more like a banana boat which was doing some rum-running on the side. But she was a valuable vessel and a floating wireless set. She had been a H.Q. Ship for the 1st Division on the Sicily invasion, and her officers and crew were great friends of the Canadians. In the wardroom, the first naval officer I met was Lieutenant Des Lenthall. Des was R.N.V.R. He was typical of R.N.V.R. men who are in the navy for the duration only. I met him first at Dieppe. He brought me back from France that time in his landing craft. In the winter of 1942-43, I went with No. 1 Commando on a raid up towards Bizerte and in the big lighthouse at Cap Serrat, down the coast from the Tunisian port where the Commandos holed up for a day, I bumped into Des again. He was operating a flotilla of landing craft along the North African coast. Now he was in charge of the landing craft flotilla on the H.Q. Ship. We figured it was a good omen meeting again on this job.

The Headquarters staffs had not arrived aboard yet and they told me I was a little early. So the next morning, June 1, I went ashore at Cowes and joined up with Halton, Lynch, Labelle and Major Roy Oliver, a British public relations officer. The other correspondents had gone through the "sausage machine" routine with the troops they were accompanying or else went direct to their ships.

Third Division H.Q. was in an apartment building and here the staff was taking it easy until they went aboard the ship. All the work was done; what a grind it had been! For the past six months General Keller and his staff had slaved at this task of preparing the Division for the assault; it meant working day and night here in Cowes, over on the mainland and at the big planning conferences in London where everything was finally tied together. Now the staff relaxed before battle. They told us we had a few days to wait with them and we were "sealed" on the Isle of Wight. We were to be briefed in detail later.

All five of us took rooms at the Fountain Inn, one
of the few hotels in Cowes still open for business. That
evening, we gathered in one of the rooms and Roy
Oliver told us the secret which had been out of our
reach for all these months. He spread out maps of a
section of the French coast. For a minute I could not
identify just where it was. Then he unrolled another
map showing the Cherbourg Peninsula and Le Havre.

"This is the plot," he said in a low voice—the walls
of these old English inns are thin. "We are landing in
the general area here between Cherbourg and Le
Havre. The Americans are on the right—the Western
Task Force. We are on the left—the Eastern Task
Force. The 1st British Corps is going in here to take
Caen and the road to the west. Another corps is going
to land and go for Bayeux."

He told us in general terms how the various British
and American divisions were to be deployed, gave us
some details on the naval and air bombardment. It
was about all we could digest at the time. My own
immediate reaction was an overwhelming relief at
knowing at last where we were going. I had thought
that possibly we were going to attempt a frontal attack
on the Pas de Calais and I knew it would be a terrible
and bloody battle with the chance of success possibly
slim. I had thought some of us might be going back to
Dieppe and that idea did not appeal to me. Here we
were to land on broad beaches, extending for miles
without a break. There were no cliffs from which
German guns could cover the beaches completely.
There were plenty of beach obstacles, including masses
of underwater ones, but there was a plan to overcome
them.

Looking over the broad picture, though, it did not
measure up to what we had expected for the Second

Front. We were going to bite off a piece of north-western France—a small piece, very small. That was all it seemed to be. The number of divisions on the assault was not really large. I think we felt a little disappointed that the plan for the first attack was not on a more grandiose scale.

However, there it was. D-Day was Monday, June 5, and H-Hour was 7:30 A.M.

But we only had a snippet of the full story that evening. As we fully realized later when we were briefed in complete detail, this was a scheme on a grand scale in every sense of the word. And we realized it too when we learned the full story of the planning and when we saw the superb plan unfold in France in the months to follow.

The troops were crowding aboard the ships now and by Saturday, June 3, everything was ready for the expedition to sail. I went to the H.Q. Ship again and the others went to their ships. Around us was the bulk of the fleet carrying the Eastern Task Force. It overflowed from Southampton Water into the Solent and down the Spithead past Portsmouth to the open sea. The sky was cloudy and a gusty wind kicked up whitecaps. This was not good weather.

Saturday evening all the Canadian correspondents were called ashore for briefing by Lieutenant-Colonel Don Mingay of Windsor, Ont., the General Staff Officer Grade I of the Division and General Keller's right-hand man.

He sat at a bare desk in a bare room with a few maps before him and told us first of the steps leading to this day. For nearly a year the 3rd Division had been training in combined operations and carrying out experiments in assaulting a defended coast. Last fall the divisional staff had begun work on the detailed planning and they had been hard at it ever since. Now the plan was ready for execution.

He made one particularly significant comment when he said: "I assure you, this invasion could not have been put on one day earlier."

There had been many reports and rumours that the invasion had been planned to take place months earlier and that it had been postponed again and again. We were all puzzled about these reports but it was clear that the Allied Command had carried out its intentions without deviation.

The Colonel then went into details. On his maps he showed us the assault plan. The 6th Airborne Division would land during the early morning of D-Day east of the Orne River and northeast of Caen, seize the important bridges over the river and the Caen canal and hold the little bridgehead on the Allies' left flank.

For months this airborne division had been training on Salisbury Plain; the 1st Canadian Parachute Battalion was in one of its parachute brigades. To the right of the airborne troops, the 3rd British Division was to land west of the mouth of the Orne. Alongside the 3rd British, the 3rd Canadian was to go in at St.-Aubin, Bernières and Courseulles and the 50th Division was to land on the extreme right flank of the Second British Army on the beaches near Arromanches. The Americans had other beaches to the west near the base of the Cherbourg peninsula.

Tanks supported the infantry on each beach and with the Canadians was the 2nd Canadian Armoured Brigade commanded by doughty Brigadier Bob Wyman of Edmonton, who led the 1st Canadian Armoured Brigade through Sicily and also through Italy to Ortona.

In addition to the four assault divisions, there were several Commandos going in with the first wave of infantry and tanks to carry out specialized tasks.

The plan for the assault was this: the fleet would arrive off the Normandy beaches about six A.M. on D-Day. The bombardment preceding the landing would begin. Destroyers would shell beach targets, the artillery regiments on the landing craft would lay down their barrages on the beaches while rocket craft were to blast the beach strip with their high explosives. Numerous types of gun-boats and support craft would go in close to the beach to sweep the sands and dunes with fire and masses of heavy and medium bombers would attack a series of targets from Le Havre to Cherbourg. Fighter bombers and rocket-firing Typhoons were assigned to attacks. Fighter cover would be provided throughout daylight hours.

The assault itself would be carried out by infantry, engineers and tank crews with their support troops, and the first big problem to cope with was a profusion of under-water obstacles the enemy had placed right along this flat stretch of beach. At low tide the tops of these obstacles were visible and some were high and dry at that time. First, there was what was called Element C, which looked like a big iron gate. Each was about fifteen feet long and twelve feet high with powerful legs bracing it firmly against pressure from the seaward side. These were set in the water three or four hundred yards from the high-tide mark on the beach. At low tide a foot or two of these obstacles was visible. The Germans evidently had intended to have a complete fence of these gates right along the beach but had not finished the work. They were fairly well spread out with gaps of fifty or sixty yards between them in places.

Between Element C and the shore, there were hundreds of hedgehogs—four-foot-high triangles of steel or wood, each with a German mine or an old French shell, primed to explode on contact, tied to the top of it. At high tide all these hedgehogs were under water and any craft that scraped over them was certain to be holed.

When the plan for attack was first drawn up, the Germans had not many of these under-water obstacles along the Normandy coast, but during the late spring they speeded up work and by June the beaches were bristling with them.

On the beach itself, just ahead of the sand dunes, was a mass of barbed wire and in the dunes were the coastal fortifications, lines of concrete and steel pill-boxes, big-gun casemates, elaborate trench systems, underground chambers, hidden machine-gun posts, gun batteries sunk in the earth and well camouflaged from air observation. Houses near the beach were fortified and guns on slopes behind the beaches were sighted on the sandy beach and the approaches to the dunes.

This was the immediate beach defence along the West Wall sector which the Canadians were to storm. Stretching back inland were numerous other positions and defence lines hinged on towns, villages and cities. The German Todt organization had worked on these defences and the army itself had elaborated on them in their long occupation of the area.

There also existed a natural obstacle for the Canadian and British troops, for screening the approaches to the beaches was a line of reefs, four to five hundred yards from shore. At low tide some of their rocks jutted out of the water and at high tide they could be a menace to ships moving to the beaches.

In selecting the time for the landing, the planning staffs had to give minute consideration to tides. It was mathematically determined that from June 5 to about June 10 the tides were such that a landing could be made at the desired time. The plan was to land on a rising tide and the assault had to be timed so that the assault craft could clear the rocks and work their way through the Element C and hedgehogs to the beach. But the timing had to be such, too, that the tide did not rise to its full height to cover the hedgehogs completely before the assault engineers got to the beach with special armoured bulldozers and demolitions to clear lanes for follow-up craft through these angle-iron obstacles. If these lanes were not cleared before the tide rose to its full height then the build-up would be delayed until the next tide.

It would be broad daylight at H-Hour, but daylight was necessary for the big bombardment plan, as good observation was essential. Colonel Mingay told us that they feared the long-range coastal guns at Le Havre would be able to shell the anchorage of the Eastern Task Force and that there also were big guns on the coast at Houlgate, seven miles east of the Orne, which could hit the ships. However, heavy bombers were striking at these gun positions and if the bombing did not stop any shelling they would be engaged by battleships and cruisers.

The Germans had coastal defence troops manning all the positions on the immediate beach strip on the sector to be assaulted and although they were not élite troops they had been in Normandy for several years, knew their areas thoroughly and were backed up by large reserves of crack troops being held in the west to strike at the main Allied success.

Elaborate mine fields had been laid back of the

beaches and the exits from the beaches through the mine fields were covered by artillery and usually by machine-guns as well, the Colonel said. He did not minimize the German strength. He, like the others on the staff, was under no illusion about the hard fight ahead. And neither were the troops. They had been given the story in as exact detail as we had.

While the Bay of the Seine was one of the points where the enemy possibly least expected an Allied landing, the defences were strong and a great deal of labour and thought had gone into them. A few days before the attack, Rommel himself toured the area around Bernières and Courseulles, we learned later from the French people there. He showed particular interest in the additional underwater obstacles being erected, but the work was going too slowly. It was increasingly difficult to get material to the west. The railways were bombed day and night. The bridges over the Seine were gone. The roads were beaten up by Allied fighter planes.

We asked Colonel Mingay about Canadian casualties anticipated on the assault. He said the estimate was 1,800 killed, wounded and missing. They turned out to be much less.

The 3rd Division was practically a pocket-edition corps. Under General Keller's command were the tank formation, extra gunners and engineers and a large British beach group—responsible for maintaining the beaches once they were taken. Over the beaches would come the build-up troops and the supplies and ammunition for the inland advance.

The beach group would even defend the beaches if the Germans broke through and several good British infantry regiments, with long training in England, were among the troops in the group. On the first night ashore these battalions were used to plug a gap on the front at a critical moment.

It was nearly dark when the Colonel finished the briefing. He was a member of the Essex Scottish, one of the Dieppe regiments. I had a strange foreboding as I walked down the dark stairs, for all this took me back two years. Here in this very building, we had been briefed for the Dieppe raid on a sultry summer night. A few rooms down the hall from where Lieutenant-Colonel Mingay had told us the plan for the invasion, another young lieutenant-colonel, Church Mann of Toronto, had detailed the plan for Dieppe.

We went to the jetty and a launch delivered us back to our ships. The sea was rougher than ever and our craft tossed wildly in the white-tipped waves.

III

THE LIGHTNING STRIKES

ON BOARD the H. Q. Ship on Sunday, June 4, there was a Sabbath quiet. Staff officers of the 1st Corps and the 3rd Canadian Division were aboard now and they had little to do but await the start of the battle they were to direct. The plan was fixed and nothing could alter it.

But the weather could dictate whether the attack could be made or not and the wind was still whipping down the Solent from the white-capped Channel. Even in the lee of the land the sea was rough and the small craft clustered around us tossed sickeningly. Finally the signal was flashed to the invasion fleet: "Twenty-four hours postponement."

It was dismal news but those buoyant Canadian officers did not let it dismay them. "If we can't do it tomorrow, we'll do it the next day or the day after that," said Major Bill Seamark of Galt, Ont., who was on the divisional staff. "We have four or five days leeway now—that is, the tides will still be okay for that period—and if the weather is completely impossible there will be a postponement for a few weeks until the tides are right again. But the attack is going in."

We went up on deck every few hours to look at the sea. The wind did not abate. The rumours started. A gale was sweeping in from the Atlantic . . . ships were being swamped in the Channel . . . a Spitfire pilot reported the sea quite calm near the French coast, so the grapevine reports ran . . . the Germans knew now we were going to Normandy . . . no, the attack would be a complete surprise . . . the navy was going to land the expeditionary force come hell or high water. I believed the last story.

The navy was ready for anything and even this devilish, freakish Channel weather would not upset its carefully-laid, long-matured plan for the greatest amphibious operation in history.

We had waited for such a length of time for D-Day that this additional day did not mean a thing. It merely gave those of us on board a chance to get some sleep, eat a few more good meals and gather more detail about the operation. It was the troops on the hundreds and hundreds of landing ships who would suffer if there was another postponement. They were in cramped quarters and on the landing craft tanks (LCTs) in particular had very little shelter and limited cooking facilities.

All the men had been completely briefed. Now they worked over their maps and their air photographs, fixing every little detail firmly in their minds. Great care had been taken that every soldier knew his sector fully and completely, knew the enemy positions, the roads, where the beach exits might be made, and the lie of the land back of the beaches. On no other combined operation had the ordinary soldier been briefed so thoroughly.

Through Sunday and Monday morning the colossal fleet idled. Destroyers and motor gun-boats came and went through our anchorage. They were prowling the Channel with other fighting ships, keeping it clear for the force to sail for France. At noon on Monday, word came that the operation was on. Tomorrow morning, Tuesday, June 6, 1944, British, American and Canadian troops would storm the Normandy coast. The weather was not good, but the Supreme Commander and his staff had decided to go ahead. On the navy rested the tremendous responsibility of getting the expedition to France despite the heavy sea.

I made my own last-minute preparations, spread my maps in the wardroom, and with the help of Lieutenant-Colonel Ernest Coté of Edmonton and Major Bill Fess of Toronto, went over the specific Canadian plan.

On the right, the western brigade was to go in at Courseulles, a little fishing town at the mouth of the Seulles River. The Royal Winnipeg Rifles were to assault the beach and the sand dunes which extend for half a mile between the town and the sea west of the inlet at the river's mouth. A company of the Canadian Scottish from Victoria was also to go in with this first wave on the right flank of the Winnipegs. To the east of the inlet, where a line of buildings runs down from the town to the sea, the Regina Rifles were to land. Each battalion had assault engineers with it, and tanks of the 1st Hussars from London, Ont., were to land with the infantry and give them immediate fire support with their guns. The rest of the Canadian Scottish battalion were to land shortly after the first assault.

In the centre of the Canadian sector, which was about four and a half miles wide, the Queen's Own Rifles of Toronto were to land at Bernières, a small resort town set back from the beach a few hundred yards. On their left, the assignment of the North Shore New Brunswick Regiment was to storm the beaches near St.-Aubin, another resort town. The Fort Garry Horse, an armoured regiment from Winnipeg, was to land with each of these battalions. Assault engineers also were with these units. The reserve battalion for the left-flank brigade was the Regiment de la Chaudière.

The reserve brigade comprised the Stormont, Dundas and Glengarry Highlanders, the North Nova Scotia Highlanders and the Highland Light Infantry from Galt, Ont., supported by tanks of the Sherbrooke Fusiliers from Sherbrooke, Que. This Highland brigade was to be committed by General Keller as soon as the situation on the beach crystallized and the best beach possible was cleared of the enemy.

The Cameron Highlanders of Ottawa, a support battalion with Vickers machine-guns and heavy mortars, were spread through the assault units. Troops of the 17th Duke of York's Royal Canadian Hussars from Montreal also were with the Division. This was the divisional reconnaissance regiment and although the whole unit was not on the assault and did not go into the line until several weeks later, a group of officers and men went in with the assault troops to do reconnaissance and special liaison work for Divisional H. Q.

All told, there were troops from fourteen Canadian regiments involved in the assault, in addition to six artillery regiments. The 12th, 13th and 14th Field Regiments, R.C.A., equipped with the American "priests", the self-propelled 105mm. gun, were the regular divisional field artillery, and the 19th Field Regiment with twenty-five-pounders was added.

The 3rd Anti-Tank Regiment and the 4th Light Anti-Aircraft Regiment, as well as assault units from the Army Service Corps, Signals, Medicals and Ordnance, were in the force. It was a closely-knit force packing a punch far heavier than a normal division.

The Canadians' task was common to that of the two other seaborne divisions in the Second Army. General Montgomery had given the specific, simple order to assault the beaches, break through the immediate coastal defences and then exploit inland without stopping to clean up enemy pockets that could be by-passed. That would be done later. The fundamental principle of the D-Day assault was to attack and to exploit, to gain a beach-head rapidly into which the follow-up formations could pass.

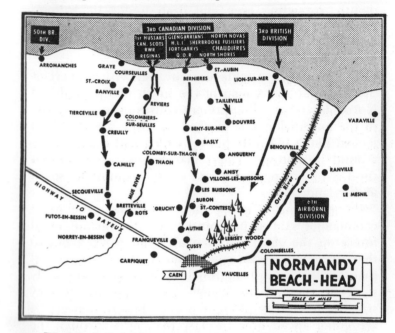

The 3rd British was to capture Caen the first day. The Canadians were to thrust inland to the Caen-Bayeux highway and hold the slopes astride the road. The high ground northwest of Caen and along the highway was the objective of the Canadian reserve brigade, while the western brigade was to go south to Bretteville and Putot-en-Bessin on the highway. The 50th Division was to take Bayeux and consolidate in that area, linking up with the Canadians on the left.

*   *   *   *

All afternoon, ships had been clearing from the Solent and the Spithead, moving south into the turbulent Channel. We lifted anchor at six P.M. and swung past Cowes and out the Spithead as the main portion of the fleet put to sea. I had a quick last look at Portsmouth, sprawling grey and drab under its balloon barrage, and went into the operations room to get the details of the naval and air operations from a commander and a group captain.

The big, square table was covered with a chart of the Channel and a map of the south of England and Normandy coast. The present course of every convoy in the expedition was marked in white and England looked like a big milk bucket which had sprung leaks around its bottom. Chart markings showed convoys coming out of ports big and small, around the south of England.

"The sailing is going on a schedule," the naval commander said as he pointed out the various naval forces on the chart. "It has all been worked out so that there will be no congestion in the Channel and that the right assault combinations will arrive at exactly the right time off the French coast, even though they start from several different ports. The minesweepers are going ahead now to clear the paths through the mine fields and the assault convoys will pass through during the night."

He was just as casual as that. Already the slower convoys were well out into the Channel, with some leading ships forty miles south of us. Others were sailing from Portsmouth and Plymouth. The gigantic fleet was moving to its rendezvous points in the Channel. Destroyer flotillas were screening the convoys and hundreds of escort vessels worked up and down the lanes through which the fleet passed to France. Capital

(TOP): *How the Allies built two "portable" harbours capable of handli armies of men and millions of tons of cargo. Ships were sunk off the N coast to form breakwaters behind which concrete pontoon jetties, prefe in England and towed across the Channel, were strung together. Shi Royal Canadian Navy protected them as they were slowly pulled*
(LOWER): *The troops come ashore on these at Arromanches.*

ships were in the Channel and with them cruisers, monitors and gun-boats. The Royal Navy, with destroyers, landing ships and fighting ships of the Royal Canadian Navy, were taking the British-Canadian force to Normandy. Ships of the American Navy, aided by some of the Royal Navy, were doing the job with the American forces.

The assault was only part of the navy's task in the Second Front. It had to get the troops there first and then see that the expeditionary force was maintained by a steady stream of convoys from Britain, carrying more troops, equipment, ammunition and supplies. The force was to be supplied over the beaches for an indefinite period and the navy had its own scheme for creating a synthetic port off the Normandy beaches.

The Commander finished his naval briefing and then the group captain crouched over the chart and told us how the Allies' greatest air effort to date would be carried out. The strongest German coastal positions from Le Havre to Cherbourg were to be bombed heavily. Fortresses and Liberators of the American air force and night heavies of Bomber Command were to give their full support to the job. Medium bombers and fighter bombers were to be out in great force before and after the seaborne and airborne attack and the air cover by the fighters was to be complete.

My mind bewildered with facts and figures of this perfectly co-ordinated, three-service combined operation, I went up to the top deck as we sailed around the east of the Isle of Wight. England disappeared in evening mist and from horizon to horizon ships were massing under the dull, cloudy sky. The wind blew right down the Channel from the west and the sea made even our solid ship roll slightly.

What a spectacle that armada made sailing steadily

south to France! On our right were lines of LCTs, carrying our self-propelled artillery regiments, infantry and tanks. The lines extended for two or three miles, with the craft low in the water and all flying the white ensign of the Royal Navy. On the other side of us were more LCTs and beyond them were scores and scores of landing ships of every type and size. Some had been at Dieppe and were going back to France, taking Canadians into battle again. Others had been on the North African landings, at Sicily, Reggio, Salerno and Anzio. They were the veterans of combined operations. Other ships were new. They came right from the yards in the United States, Britain and Canada.

Troopers, cargo boats, supply boats, and hundreds of small craft were there. Through this shipping, fanned out over the Channel, were the protecting escort ships of the navy. Behind us was the Canadian destroyer *Algonquin*, in light blue camouflage, which curiously was the same colour as the battle patches of the 3rd Division. A flotilla of small landing craft, carrying commandos, lurched through the sea beside the *Algonquin*, taking each wave with a graceful bob of her bow while the little craft nearly foundered.

Other destroyers weaved through the fleet; corvettes and frigates kept a vigil for submarine attacks. Overhead were patrols of Spitfires, winging out from England in relays until dark.

On board you would never have known at first glance that this was one of the greatest nights in history. The officers gathered in the wardroom as usual for a drink before dinner. They sat down to a good meal. There was some talk of the operation, but not a great deal. A naval officer at our table recalled his yachting days around Cowes away back in peacetime. This seeming indifference is common before big actions, and it always covers an undercurrent of electric emotion, but this time I had thought that possibly the sheer magnitude and drama of these hours would stir the participants to a point where they should display some excitement. It was just the same as before. It might have been another manoeuvre. Looking around the wardroom as the officers smoked their pipes and cigarettes after dinner, I thought how similar it was to those training days when we had made landings on the English coast.

But in the cabins and in the mess decks the officers and the men of this force were writing letters later that evening. They were their last letters home before going into battle.

We got our packs ready for the landing and I had the old problem of waterproofing my typewriter. They issued us with twenty-four-hour rations, which were in a neat new package being used here for the first time. In it was concentrated vitamin food which had the advantage, unusual in the army, of being tasty as well as compact.

We were now far out in the Channel and as darkness closed in, blotting out the fleet, we tried to get some sleep. Some of the men aboard slept soundly for hours, but a lot of us tossed fitfully, as we thought ahead to the hours of the dawn when the guns would roar.

About one A.M.—it was D-Day now—I got up and went to the wardroom and set up my one-man news desk on a mess table. Beside me the ship's doctor had prepared his dressing station to handle a possible overflow of wounded from the sick bay.

Out on deck the wind howled through the wireless masts which spouted profusely from the upper deck. The sky was black as the inside of a gun barrel and spray and rain lashed the deck. It was a terrible night for the crossing. The sea seemed worse than ever and the ship creaked and groaned as she ploughed her way through it.

The *Algonquin* just astern of us was a blob in the night and you could barely pick out the silhouettes of other ships near us in this curtain of darkness, spray and rain drawn tightly over the rolling sea. The night seemed ominously quiet, apart from the elements. I had expected that German surface craft would make suicide attempts to intercept some portions of the invasion fleet but they never showed up on our sector. At four A.M. flares were dropped by German aircraft flying to the west of us. Apparently they had spotted the American convoy. There was no ack-ack fire from the ships. The flares snuffed out and darkness closed in again.

Occasionally there was a great flash over the French coast as Royal Air Force heavy bombers struck at gun positions in Le Havre area. A number of those big guns had a range of twenty miles. Some star shells arched into the sky.

Up on the bridge naval officers told me they had heard our troop-carrying planes and tug planes returning from Normandy after dropping the airborne troops.

We were now going down the channels swept through the mine fields and the French coast was only fifteen miles away. At five A.M. action stations was sounded as we sailed into the danger zones and everyone went to his post. The operations room filled up with staff officers. Army, Navy and Air Force officers took their places around the big chart where the battle would be plotted minute by minute and where the commanders were to make their decisions from information coming in from the beaches over the wireless networks.

It was becoming light and in the first glimmer of the dawn we saw the ships still massed around. The navy had brought the armada to French coastal waters through the inky darkness and the mine fields without serious mishap. Over to the east, explosions rumbled as the bombing continued and the heavy naval guns fired several salvos that grumbled up the Channel.

The wind had gone down considerably and a haze misted the sea. D-Day morning was raw and sullen. We moved slowly towards the coast as the assault craft and ships jockeyed on their start line for the run-in and the bombardment ships of the navy, with the rocket craft and the craft carrying the regiments of artillery, got into position for the shoot.

Just before six, we saw the French coast, lying low and dark against a slate-grey sky.

*   *   *   *

We got closer, and as the light improved and the mist cleared we made out landmarks—the strips of white beach and the brown dunes, slender church spires at Courseulles, Bernières and St.-Aubin, the water towers behind the towns. Back of the dunes were the rich green and brown fields on gentle slopes where some of the finest crops in France are grown. Woods dotted the fields and ribbons of roads led back from the coast toward Caen and Bayeux, over the slightly rolling countryside. This was the new Canadian battlefield, but at that moment it looked like a travel poster.

Not a single gun fired from the shore. The entire fleet was now in full view of the German coastal garrisons, with the first line of landing ships and support craft only a mile or so from shore. Others were massed for miles and miles out to sea. The Bay of the Seine was choked with Allied shipping. Four thousand ships and landing craft were participating in this operation and most of them seemed to be here off the Normandy shore at this tense time between the dawn and H-Hour.

The vast panorama of fighting ships and ships carrying fighting men must have dumbfounded the enemy. Even for us, it was a staggering sight. I stayed on deck and waited, my nerves tingling, for the opening crash of our guns.

With careful, ponderous deliberation, our ships took up their assault stations. They did it as if they were in a huge convoy forming up in Halifax harbour or in Southampton Water back over the Channel. The immunity of the fleet, the lack of gun-fire from the coast was something I had never expected.

The larger ships anchored several miles off shore and the landing craft assault (LCAs) were lowered, each with its load of thirty assault troops. The flotillas formed up in the leaping waves and soon there were hundreds of these small, armour-plated craft bobbing about prepared to go in to the beaches. We had thought the sea might be calmer in the lee of the land, but it was nearly as rough as the open Channel.

The minutes crept by. At 6:30 A.M. wireless silence was broken and messages flashed through the fleet. Lines of assault craft, lashing through the sea, passed by our ship. You could see the infantrymen and sappers crouched in their craft, gripping their weapons, their battle-dress soaked already by the spray. These were the heroic, first-wave troops, going now to the battle on the beaches. Flanking the assault craft were LCTs carrying Canadians in Sherman tanks, and with them were support craft with their guns pointing to shore. Assault engineers, in special armoured vehicles, were in other first-wave craft.

The bombardment ships were in position. Destroyers were in a straight line parallel with the beaches; the craft carrying the army artillery were massed to the right and left of them; the long, black rocket craft, their decks covered with rocket racks that looked like clusters of pipe organs, were manoeuvring about slowly. Our ship, the *Hilary*, was in the centre of this concentration and behind us were the big ships—cruisers and monitors. Battleships were in the Channel that morning as well. Our planes droned over us.

The bombardment started; the tension broke. The battle had begun. The destroyers' guns flamed and roared. They got the range and salvo after salvo slammed down on the beach positions.

Cruisers and monitors opened up from far out to sea, throwing great shells on inland strongpoints. The cruiser *Diadem* concentrated on an enemy gun position at Beny-sur-Mer behind Courseulles, and blew it to pieces. The monitor *Roberts,* which had supported the Canadians on the Sicily landing, went into action in support of these other Canadians. The blast of the heavy guns swept over the sea and our ears rang with the thunderous crash and explosions of the bombardment. But this was just the start. Medium and heavy bombers raced through the clouds and dropped their bombs on the enemy. The army's seaborne artillery began to shoot. A few batteries fired. The range was corrected by artillery officers in the leading landing craft. A few more batteries hammered away and with a heavy boom all the regiments began a devastating barrage. They did not let up. Hundreds of gunners, working their guns on the swaying decks, loaded, fired, loaded again and fired again. The guns were like automatics, and even in the heavy sea the artillerymen maintained a fierce and steady rate of fire. The barrage sounded like the rhythmic beating of a gigantic drum as it boomed along the coast.

The beach was torn by this concentrated shell-fire from the artillery and naval guns and the shore-line was clouded with dust and smoke from bursting shells. Through my binoculars I watched the assault boats moving steadily nearer to shore. Some of the beach defences spurted flame. German guns were firing on the boats. The craft were getting close to the line of under-water obstacles.

On our flanks, similar attacks were going in under the same type of bombardments and the coast-line, as far as the eye could reach on either side, was being blasted like no other section of shore had been before. It was the turn of the rocket craft now. Eight of them were near us and they turned their bows to shore to sight their rockets. With an awful "swoosh" they fired their salvos. Sheets of flame burst from the long decks of these craft as the rockets went off, and you waited for the bursts ashore. There they were, hitting the beaches and the slopes behind them, hundreds of dancing lights in the murky smoke. The sea itself seemed to shake with the explosions. Our ship shuddered.

The assault craft surged into the beaches, riding the swell over and around the underwater obstacles. Some craft hit hedgerows, though, and the mines attached to them exploded, blowing gaping holes in the boats and causing heavy casualties. From big concrete gun-casemates which had not been knocked out by the bombardment, the enemy shot at the craft with artillery and machine-guns. German fire laced the beach, and just before eight A.M. leading companies of the western brigade touched down on the Courseulles beaches. The Winnipegs were on the right, the Reginas on the left of the inlet as planned. Tanks of the 1st Hussars were with them.

This cryptic message was flashed back to *Hilary*: "Under fire on all beaches."

On the left, at Bernières and St.-Aubin, the Queen's Own and the North Shores were on their beaches, too, after perilous passages through the obstacles and over the reefs screening the shore. Tanks of the Fort Garry Horse ploughed ashore with them. Every unit had to cross from one hundred to two hundred yards of open beach, littered with hedgehogs still not covered by the rising tide.

Many of the beach defenders had been made casualties or were stunned by the bombardment but others in deep shelters and under concrete came up fighting, as the shelling lifted inland when the Canadians landed.

The Germans responded rapidly, shelling the beaches, mortaring them and spraying them with machine-gun bullets. The Canadians ran down the ramps of their assault craft into the face of this fire. Men dropped crossing that open beach but the main force got over it and struggled through the snarled mass of barbed wire at the base of the sand dunes. Gaps were cut and the infantry stormed into the German defence positions. Tanks worked along the beach helping the infantry by shelling casemates and pillboxes and machine-gunning the trenches. Naval craft which had closed in to the shore lent their fire support to the attack on the beach strip defences, while out to sea the big guns of the fleet pounded away at inland positions which were firing on the beaches.

Bloody fighting raged all along the beaches. On the right the Winnipegs had to battle their way past five major concrete casemates and fifteen machine-gun positions set in the dunes, commanding a long sweep of the beach. From dune to dune, along the German trench systems and through the tunnels, these Manitoba troops fought every yard of the way. They broke into the big casemates, ferreted out the gun crews with machine-guns, grenades, bayonets and knives. The Canadians ran into cross-fire. They were shelled and mortared mercilessly even in the German positions, but kept slugging away at the enemy. The 1st Hussars' tanks churned through the dunes in close support and after a struggle which was as bitter and savage as any on the British-Canadian sector, the Winnipegs broke through into the open country behind the beach. The company of Canadian Scottish shared this heavy fighting with the Winnipegs.

On the east side of the inlet, the Reginas had another fierce and deadly fight at close quarters. They had four or five big casemates to deal with as well as a line of fortified houses which clustered around the Courseulles railway station by the inlet. Here again there was wire to get through, then the dunes to assault. Machine-gunners and snipers were well dug in and hard to get at. One by one the casemates were captured, the pillboxes destroyed, the trenches cleared of living Germans.

With the sea behind them and the Norman fields ahead, they broke through the first line of defences and took on the next string of pillboxes and line of trenches. They went for the fortified houses, blew their way through them and worked into the town of Courseulles, fighting up the streets leading from the inlet to the market square. By now the Germans were in confusion, but they stood to fight in small groups at every corner. Off the market square was the German headquarters for this coastal sector. It was in a big château with an orchard behind it, in which were located sturdy air raid shelters with steel and concrete roofs and walls. The officers had fled when the fighting Reginas broke into the building. They found a few snipers; wiped them out; cleaned up obvious opposition in the town and passed through to the farmland south of Courseulles.

The rest of the Canadian Scottish landed on the Winnipegs' beach and moved through the captured dunes, past the German dead sprawling in every trench and by every casemate and pillbox. Canadian dead were there too, men who had trained for a year for this assault and died fifty yards and two minutes inside France. But they had won this smashing victory on the beaches, the men who died and the men who lived to fight on into France.

Canadian wounded were being collected in the shelter of the captured casemates, and men of the Royal Canadian Army Medical Corps, who had come in on the first wave assault with the combat troops, were caring for them under fire with the tenderness that only man can show to man in war.

It took about two hours of terrible, ugly, brutal fighting for the beach defence system to be shattered and for the infantry and tanks to exploit rapidly inland as General Montgomery had ordered. They did not think of their flanks. They kept going south, fighting their way through town after town.

While the battle was raging at Courseulles, there was stern and savage fighting too along the rest of the Canadians' beach-front at Bernières and St.-Aubin. The Queen's Own and the North Shores also met heavy machine-gun fire sweeping the beaches from great casemates and lines of pillboxes. Guns shelled their beaches as well and the mortars crumped around them as they raced over the sand and attacked the enemy positions.

At Bernières, the Queen's Own had a sticky time right in front of the town, where the largest casemate was located.

The German defenders there had not suffered heavily from the bombardment and they blasted the riflemen as they came over the sand. But the Toronto troops somehow reached the sea-wall which extends along the back of the beach at Bernières, got over it, and worked their way through the dunes towards the casemate. Meanwhile, some of their troops, including Bren-gunners, got into the buildings near the casemate and gave covering fire to their comrades, who battled their way into the concrete fort and wiped out the garrison. The Queen's Own then captured one line of trenches after another and made forays through the dunes to the west of the town, where they knocked out a string of pillboxes that was holding them up. Into the shattered town of Bernières they went and there they coped with snipers and machine-gunners in houses and in the little shops by the fine Gothic church.

The North Shores landed by the western outskirts of St.-Aubin and they too had a battle to get through the system of concrete and trench defences. The Germans were strong in the centre of St.-Aubin and a company of New Brunswick troops was sent into the town, with British Commandos, to deal with the opposition there while the rest of the battalion went inland fast.

Tanks of the Fort Garry Horse were with these two battalions and the reserve battalion, the Regiment de la-Chaudière, landed to pass through the Queen's Own and strike over the fields as fast as they could go.

The self-propelled artillery rolled ashore from the landing craft and these regiments went into action right on the beaches, firing on targets passed back to them by forward observation officers with the leading infantry.

Immediate fire support for the infantry ashore was fundamental to the assault plan. The tanks provided the first support that was very vital and then these 105mm. "priests" followed up to give the infantry the help they needed.

On the beaches, the Royal Canadian Engineers, many of whom landed with the assault troops, blew exits through concrete walls and prepared roads for the vehicles and tanks to get clear of the beaches. They also had to clear gaps in the mine fields and there were plenty of mines laid just behind the beach defences. Every road through a mine field was covered by German artillery and machine-guns and there were delays until these were silenced.

Armoured bulldozers crunched around the beach areas, making paths through rubble, levelling sand, filling in gaping craters, pushing down buildings. Other sappers were at work removing the hedgehogs to enable the larger ships to beach. Much of the time they were under fire, for the enemy artillery on the slopes behind Bernières and Courseulles were not leaving the captured beaches alone.

The momentum of the attack was wonderfully maintained during the morning, and from the coast the infantry and tanks made good advances, while the beach organization got itself established to handle supplies, ammunition and the follow-up forces that would come in with each tide.

On the *Hilary,* from which General Keller controlled the battle in the early phase, running reports came in over the wireless from the formations ashore.

At 10:30 A.M. the General was able to send a message to General Crerar in England: "Beach-head gained. Well on our way to our intermediate objectives."

There was no question then of the success of the initial assault. It was going better than anyone had expected. I met the General on the deck which was serving as the Headquarters' observation post and he gave me the text of his brief message to the Army Commander. "It is hard fighting but our troops are doing great," he said. "I'm committing the reserve brigade now and it is landing at Bernières where the best beach exits have been made."

The *Hilary* closed in to the shore between Courseulles and Bernières and we had a grand-stand view of the battle-field, which sloped gradually to the sea. Battered landing craft pulled alongside us, and the first wounded were brought aboard. Bleeding, gasping, badly hit, they were carried to the sick bay ˙and the emergency dressing station in the wardroom where the ship's doctor worked over them.

Some had been terribly wounded by shell-fire as the boats went in to the beach, and they died in a few minutes. Others with lighter wounds were patched up and later transferred to ships going back to England.

There was smoke all along the coast, lingering from the bombardment and from the engineers' demolitions ashore. Part of Courseulles was burning and a white smoke screen had been laid along the fields southwest of the town. St.-Aubin rocked with half a dozen explosions and debris flew high in the air, followed by billows of black smoke. They were still fighting for the town and this fight went on all day until the North

Shores' company and the commandos got the situation fairly well under control by evening.

Destroyers and gun-boats moved along the coast only a few hundred yards from the beach, shooting at any German positions they could reach. Some destroyers already had run out of their store of ammunition and were turning back to England to restock.

It was one of those destroyers which carried back a story of mine which by chance and by luck got out ahead of any other correspondent's with the ground forces. In it I had told of the Canadians' success in gaining the beach-head in two hours and a half fighting and had quoted General Keller's message to General Crerar.

All night and morning I had been writing my head off in the wardroom, attempting to describe this incredible invasion scene. At my disposal, I had minute-by-minute information which was flooding in over the wireless from shore. I knew exactly how the fight was going and could see a good deal from the deck of our ship. But we were not permitted to use naval wireless to England and there was no other available link. We had to trust to sending our copy by any available dispatch boat or ship that was going in the direction of England. It was a haphazard system at best. I sent back several long stories on a dispatch boat which were delayed in reaching London, but the one sent by the destroyer clicked.

The commander who had given me the naval briefing the evening before would have made a good communications chief for a news service for it was he who tipped me off about the destroyers returning to England for ammunition.

"It's a sure bet for you," he said, showing almost as much interest in this communications problem as mine. "You see that destroyer lying off the port bow? Well, she is going back to England for ammunition but is also going to pick up Montgomery and bring him to France by tomorrow morning. She won't be sidetracked on the way by other orders."

The commander even sent one of his lieutenants to the destroyer with my copy. Somehow it got from Portsmouth to London; somehow it got through the wild confusion of the SHAEF copy room at the Ministry of Information into the hands of the London bureau of The Canadian Press. Once it was there, it was practically in the papers at home. That is how it happened.

The reactions of the German air force to this landing had been a doubtful point in the minds of many of our commanders. It was difficult to forecast whether the *Luftwaffe* could come up and fight or not. I had been told by a senior air force officer that the enemy had 2,500 aircraft available for combat in the west, but he would not commit himself on any prognostication.

On this D-Day morning we watched the cloudy skies expectantly for the German planes. They never came in strength. Our own air cover was magnificent to see, and Spitfires and Lightnings patrolled over the fleet in steady relays from England. We knew the raiders would be over every night striking at the beach-head, but our overwhelming air superiority in daytime kept the beach-head area clear of German planes in those critical few hours after H-Hour. And after that there were only scattered daylight raids. The *Luftwaffe* had decided against a knock-down, drag-out battle in the west.

The uncertainty and tension of the first phase of the attack was over by eleven A.M. and with the beach in our hands it was imperative now to win the objectives inland. Divisional Headquarters was going ashore, and first went the tactical H.Q. which was composed of General Keller and a handful of staff officers. I went with the Tac H.Q., and we set off from the *Hilary* in a landing craft, plunging through the heavy swell towards Bernières. Tank-landing craft, and landing craft infantry were beached there, unloading more troops, guns and tanks, and the wreckage of first-wave assault craft which had been smashed up going in was strewn along the shore. The beach was crowded with vehicles and tanks, grinding laboriously through the sand to the beach exit-roads leading into Bernières. The engineers were working all over the beach, trying to clear it rapidly. Smoke was still pouring up from St.-Aubin and there was gun-fire on the slopes behind Bernières and over by Courseulles. Our landing craft passed by several disabled craft, damaged by underwater obstacles they had hit. On the crest of a swell, we ran up on the beach, skimming past a line of hedge-hogs, with menacing mines still attached to them, and Tac H.Q. splashed ashore as the craft grounded.

The shelling had stopped on the beach and we walked into Bernières with the reserve brigade infantry which had just come off craft. The French civilians, who had fled to the fields for shelter during the bombardment, were returning to their shell-raked village now. Old men and women, young girls and children, stood on the sidewalks of the littered main street, clapped their hands, waved the troops on their way and tossed roses in their path.

This first spontaneous reaction of these Norman people was an almost unbelievable thing to see. Our shells and rockets had blown down their homes; they had lost everything they owned; their town was a shambles, with even the fine church on the square scarred by battle; they had been terrified by the bombardment and some of the people of Bernières had been killed. But there they stood in little groups on this dusty street amid the havoc of their village and smiled and laughed and cheered our men along the road that wound up the slope through the wheat fields to battle.

A girl handed me a crimson rose and there were tears of despair and joy in her eyes as she said: "There is my home, over there. It is gone. It is ruined by the bombardment, but the Allies are here! The Canadians are in our village now, and the Boche has gone."

She smiled, and seemed to forget about her personal tragedy as she picked another armful of flowers and tossed them to the tank crews as the Shermans thundered by.

Everyone I spoke to in Bernieres seemed genuinely glad to see the Allied troops in France. They used ugly words to describe the Germans who had been living here in their midst for four years. I was cynical at first at this welcome, and thought that possibly it was partly feigned, but as time passed and we got to know the Norman people better we realized how sincere was that spontaneous reception on D-Day morning.

But I was more concerned with the war just then than I was with any implications of the civilian welcome, and the war was just down the road from the village. The Queen's Own Rifles and the Fort Garrys had run into a battery of 88mm. guns in the fields between Bernières and Tailleville, two miles south. They were fighting now to destroy these guns which were causing a pile-up in Bernières of the reserve brigade. This brigade was all ashore and there was a first-class traffic jam in the village. The road leading south from Bernières was covered by German guns and every tank or vehicle which went past the orchard into the open on the southern outskirts, came under accurate fire.

Four of our self-propelled guns were knocked out in a few minutes near the orchard as they tried to take on these enemy guns. Two of our tanks swung around to the left through the waist-high wheat and hit mines.

The Germans fired on everything that came out of Bernières, and the village itself was not a healthy spot with trucks, tanks and troops jammed in the narrow streets. I could never figure out why the Germans did not shell and mortar it with everything they had. A few shells came over, but this fire was nothing to speak of. The enemy evidently was so confused that no co-ordinated fire plan seemed to have been worked out, but it looked alarming enough to force me to dig a slit-trench by a ruined house! Holed up in this trench at the cost of a couple of big blisters, I hammered out more copy.

The German guns were finally knocked out, and the Canadians flooded down the narrow Tailleville road. The North Nova Scotia Highlanders, riding on the tanks of the Sherbrooke Fusiliers, went through Bernières to a thrilling thrust inland which carried them to within a mile of Carpiquet airdrome just west of Caen. There they were to fight one of the most savage actions of those early days. A lot of those fine troops that I had watched go up the line at noon in the dust, died in battle the next day near the villages of Authie and Buron.

The Glengarrians went up the line too with the H.L.I., and on the beach the British beach group organization, under the 3rd Division command, got itself established and began to handle ammunition and supplies which were already being brought ashore. Scores of barrage balloons tugged in the sky over the beach-head, and over them the Spitfires passed back and forth. The weather cleared a good deal in the afternoon and there were patches of blue sky in the white clouds. A warming sun shone.

A few shells whizzed over Bernières and a couple of rounds fell in an orchard where a battery of our self-propelled guns was located. There was a crackling sound overhead and a Spitfire chased a German fighter from cloud to cloud, its guns sputtering. That was the only German plane I saw on D-Day! These distractions did not help get my story done, but I finished it and walked down the lane to the half-wrecked hotel on the main street where Captain Jack Wilson of Halifax, one of the public relations officers, had set up his headquarters to handle our copy and get it away to England by any available means. The only bet, at first, was landing craft returning to the other side and Jack made trip after trip to the beach and waded out to the craft to hand the skipper the canvas press bags.

Many of the stories about the Canadians got through by this means. Some good stories were lost but we could do nothing more than write all we could and then hope and pray the ship would not be sunk, that the skipper would not put the copy in his tunic pocket and forget about it, that the press pickets at the English ports would be on the docks all right—that somehow the stories would get through to the papers and to the people at home!

In Bernières I bumped into Major Steve Lett of Toronto, who was second-in-command of the Queen's Own. Last time I had seen him was on a hilarious evening in the regiment's mess at Bournemouth about

three months before D-Day, but Steve was grimly serious now. "Some of the companies had a rough time
on the beaches," he told me. "That goddam casemate
there in front of the town just hammered the beach
with stuff. But some of our men got into the house
over there and pegged the casemate with everything
they had, while others worked through the dunes and
got into it. Bloody going. We've collected our casualties by the casemate now and they'll be going back to
England soon."

Several hundred German prisoners were sitting and
standing in a long line on the beach by the casemate
and our wounded were lying in the German trenches
and on the trampled grass by the big concrete fort.
There must have been a hundred and fifty wounded
men there — Queen's Own, sappers and gunners.
Germans too. They lay on stretchers and on the
ground wrapped in blankets, their faces ashen grey.
Doctors and medical orderlies were with them and the
ships to take them to England were nearly ready now
to receive them.

Around the casemate lay German dead, blankets
over them. There were some Canadians too who had
been killed on the assault on this position. I went
down into the tunnels and the concrete chambers that
were part of the fort and marvelled at the job done
here by the Toronto battalion. Smashed German
heavy machine-guns were there; several smashed artillery pieces too. It had taken fiercely determined troops
to capture this commanding fort. Linked in the enemy
defence system with the casemate were pillboxes and
deep trenches and tunnels screening Bernières, and
each had been captured by the old, reliable expedient
of troops closing right with the Germans and beating
them man to man.

You felt an intense pride in your countrymen to
see what they had achieved here on the Norman coast,
but your exhilaration was tempered by the sight of
wounded friends who talked to you with pain in their
faltering words.

The Divisional Headquarters was first set up in a
grove of trees in Bernières and then it moved to an
orchard south of the town, once the road had been
cleared of the German guns. At 2.30 P.M. the General
held a conference and new orders were issued for the
advance which was going forward well. On the right,
the western brigade had overcome immense difficulties
getting clear of the beach and now the Winnipegs had
captured Banville, two miles southwest of Courseulles
on the road to Bayeux; the Canadian Scottish had
cleared St.-Croix, a mile west of Banville on flat
ground, where the first airstrips in France were laid
and from which fighter planes were operating by the
end of the week; the Reginas held Reviers, two miles
south of Courseulles. This was on the main lateral
road on the Canadian front, running east through
Tailleville to Douvres and the Orne River.

The crossings of the River Mue were also held by
the Reginas at Reviers. The 1st Hussars' tanks were
all ashore, supporting these infantry advances.

On the left the North Shores, with some Fort Garry
tanks, were in Tailleville and were attacking numerous enemy strongpoints in that area. The Queen's
Own and the Chaudières were over the Tailleville
lateral road with the rest of the Garrys. General Keller
had ordered this brigade to take Beny-sur-Mer, a mile
and a half southwest of Tailleville. The infantry and
tanks moved over the fields, went through the heavy
wood on the north side of the village and by 3.30 P.M.
the town was captured, although there were still
snipers infesting the woods and some of the houses.

The reserve brigade was rolling now, and it was ordered to pass through the other brigade at Beny and go on to the divisional objective on this left flank— the high ground northwest of Caen.

The Chaudières took out a troublesome 88mm. battery about a mile east of Beny, and a German radar station—one of the strongest positions on the inland defence line—was by-passed. For twelve days this radar station held out, completely surrounded and supplied from the air at night. It was finally stormed and captured by British commandos and assault engineers.

By six P.M. the Westerners on the right had made more advances, capturing Tierceville, two miles southwest of Banville, and Colombiers-sur-Seulles between Tierceville and Reviers, with the Reginas working south into the Mue River valley where there was a strong force of enemy.

Before nightfall, the western brigade had reached the Camilly area, west of the Mue valley and about eight miles inland, after taking the big town of Creully and the villages of St. Gabriel, Pierrepont, Lantheur and Cainet.

East of the Mue, the progress was also good. On the road to Caen, towns of Basly, Anguerny, Anisy and Colomby-sur-Thaon were captured. The "Jock Column" of the North Novas and the Sherbrooke Fusiliers reached Villons-les-Buissons, four miles northwest of Caen, measuring an advance of eight or nine miles from the beaches, and the other Canadian regiments in this sector were spread out along the road leading back to Beny and Tailleville.

In all these villages there was fighting before they were taken, and the Germans had fiercely resisted every one of these rapid thrusts which the Canadians had made from the shore-line. On every slope the

Germans had guns sited along roads and at exits from
mine fields, and infantry stood to fight in long-
prepared trench systems and in strong positions, all of
which had deep underground chambers.

The Canadians maintained the momentum of their
exploitation all of the first day. They did not think
of stopping to consolidate any gains until nightfall,
when they did take precautions against counter-attacks.
They just kept going on and on, capturing a town,
going through it rapidly without clearing it completely, advancing to the next slope, driving the enemy
from the wheat fields and descending on the next
village in their path. They moved through fairly open
country with no dominating hills. But there were
scattered bits of woods where the enemy was concealed
and all had to be fought for. The slopes gave the
German gunners good observation for direct shots
at the attacking infantry and tanks. This countryside over which the battle swept on that first day
greatly resembled the farmland of Ontario and
those country districts of Quebec along the St. Law-
rence. The Canadians felt at home on this kind of
ground.

The fighting had been fierce from H-Hour to nightfall but the casualties were far less than anticipated.
As Colonel Mingay told us in the briefing, he anticipated 1,800 on the landing. They were assessed at
Headquarters at 800 for the whole first day, including
killed, wounded and missing. Six hundred German
prisoners were taken.

*   *   *   *

Between the Canadians and the Orne, troops of the
3rd British Division landed with the intention of
storming down the roads to Caen and capturing the
city, which had been heavily bombed.

They failed to reach their goal but they made a determined effort to break through to the city. They came so close to getting there that there was a premature announcement in London that there was fighting in the streets of Caen. There was no fighting in Caen in those early days. The nearest the British got to the city was to reach Lebisey Woods, two miles north of it. German tanks, infantry and guns blocked their advance there and for more than a month the enemy firmly held the perimeter defences of Caen.

The 3rd British did not have the same difficult assault role as the Canadians and landed only one infantry brigade in the initial attack. The brigade went ashore at Lion-sur-Mer, two miles west of the mouth of the Orne. Although it met machine-gun and mortar fire it cleared its beach within an hour and advanced inland.

The Division's two other infantry brigades and an independent armoured brigade under command followed up this first landing during the morning and as leading troops got close to Caen, enemy resistance stiffened.

The Germans maintained a wedge between the Canadian and British forces which proved troublesome and endangered the narrow beach-head for the first day and night.

The British concentrated on attempting to break through to Caen, however, during the first day, and infantry and tanks fought stubbornly over the slopes and through the woods. They got to Lebisey, from which you can see Caen in the valley of the Orne and at that point twenty enemy tanks, supported by a strong force of infantry, attacked the leading troops. Heavy, confused fighting went on for hours, but the spearhead thrust to Caen was blunted. The British were forced to consolidate on the ground they had won, and give up the plan to capture Caen immediately.

Crack German S.S. troops flooded into Caen to bolster the defences and man the prepared enemy positions which covered approaches to the city from the north and west, where the main British and Canadian pressure was in evidence.

Later when Caen was finally captured, French civilians said that the entire German force in the Caen area nearly folded up on D-Day. With a little more pressure, the city would have fallen, for until the arrival of the S.S. troops the regular German soldiers were preparing to leave the city and fall back to the hills south and east of it.

On the right flank of the Canadians, the British 50th Division landed at Arromanches and had better fortune in its advance on Bayeux. It got ashore without a great deal of trouble and skilfully moved south to capture Bayeux against only slight opposition, the following day. It was the first city of France to fall to the Allied Expeditionary Force.

*   *   *   *

The First American Army, the spearhead of the American forces, made its assault at the same time as the Second British Army, landing on two beaches at the base of the Cherbourg peninsula, west of the British. The immediate intention of the Americans was to gain a beach-head, cut the peninsula and capture Cherbourg. In twenty days, by June 26, this was achieved.

For the assault, three infantry divisions and two airborne divisions were used. The 1st and 29th Infantry Divisions were landed on a beach near St.-Laurent-sur-

Mer, nine miles east of the Carentan estuary at the base of the peninsula, and west of the estuary the 4th Infantry Division went ashore. The airborne divisions were dropped behind the 4th Division's beach, with the 101st going down in the area of Ste.-Mère Église, on the Carentan-Cherbourg highway, and the 82nd landing southwest of there.

As on the Second Army sector, the attack began with the landing of parachute troops shortly after midnight. This phase of the operation was carried out smoothly and of 800 aircraft used to fly in the parachute elements of the two divisions, only twenty were lost. The night of D-Day, 510 more aircraft brought in gliders carrying the rest of the men and only eight of these were shot down.

The airborne troops made good landings and although there was inevitable confusion, they carried out their tasks and finally both divisions linked up with the 4th Division to create a broad arc of a beachhead north of Carentan.

The forces landing from the sea were handicapped from the start by bad weather. The Channel was terribly rough even in the lee of the Cherbourg peninsula, and through tumultuous seas, the Americans went into the heavily-defended beaches at about 6.30 A.M.

The hardest fight took place at St.-Laurent, where the invasion forces ran right into the German 352nd Division while it was carrying out anti-invasion manoeuvres on the coast.

As the landing craft thrashed through the surf to the sandy beaches, they came under accurate artillery and machine-gun fire and losses were severe in men as well as in equipment. The men of the 1st Division and the 29th fought their way ashore, however, and all day long the battle raged on the strip of beach.

American Ranger units fought on these beaches too. By D-Day night, only narrow gains had been made, but troops were into St.-Laurent and one of the coast roads had been cut. Reinforcements were landed despite the fierce fight right on the beaches. One of the big difficulties was getting the support weapons ashore in the boiling sea.

Despite their losses, the 1st Division, which had been in action in the Mediterranean, and the 29th Division, which like the 3rd Canadian was new to battle and had trained for months on end in England for this assault, overcame the German resistance and slowly shoved inland.

On the other beach west of the Carentan estuary, the 4th Division had a comparatively easy time and won a sizeable beach-head on the first day to link up with the airborne forces.

Fierce naval and air bombardments supported the landings on both beaches and practically the same artillery plan as was used on the Second Army sector was also employed on the American front.

By June 7—D-plus-one—the Americans who had landed at St.-Laurent had linked up with the British 50th Division west of Bayeux, and by June 10 the difficult job of linking up the two American beach-heads through Carentan was completed.

Using masses of artillery that poured ashore once the bridgeheads were won, the Americans slammed north towards Cherbourg. On June 26 the port was captured by the joint efforts of the 4th Division and the 79th and 9th Infantry, which had come in following the assault.

I remained around Bernières all D-Day, for our jeeps had not landed and Divisional Headquarters in the orchard was the only source of accurate news. The

Canadians were sweeping over the fields and through the towns and yet I shared the forebodings of many others about the hours ahead. German counter-attacks were bound to come and if they were made today or tonight or even tomorrow in great strength, the Division would be in a tight spot.

It was a race against time, for the Canadians must gain the slopes on the Bayeux-Caen road and the area northwest of Caen to meet the enemy counter blows with any real advantage.

All through that hectic, frantic first day, with our nerves taut as piano wire even there in the village on the fringe of the battle, we gathered our news and wrote it and got it away to England by the landing craft that plied the Channel in their hundreds.

I had not slept much for a couple of days and I was dopey with weariness. This is always the threat on these landings for us correspondents. You get so tired you cannot write what you see and learn. I munched a benzedrine tablet every four hours and it cleared the cobwebs from my mind for a while. It was an old expedient for landings.

In the early evening our little group decided to find a bivouac for the night and Ralph Allen and I trudged through Bernières and its outskirts, lugging our type-writers and our packs and one spade which a French-man had given me as his contribution to our welfare. Ralph and I had shared another D-Day together and we went through the same routine at Bernières as we did at Reggio the September before when the Can-adians crossed Messina Straits into Italy. We plodded down the battered main street, past the post office where some soldier had draped a large Canadian flag, the first to be put up in France, past the church and down the road that curled out into the fields. We searched around the orchards and the woods on the outskirts of the town for a good spot for the night but German *Minen* signs all over the place, indicating mine fields, made us very cautious. Later on we learned that many of them were "phoney" and had been put up for the benefit of Rommel, who inspected the area a few days before. For a couple of hours we walked about, and at eight P.M., saw several hundred Fortresses drone overhead in formation and bomb the Caen area and targets beyond. An angry, dirty, black curtain of flak rose from Caen and Carpiquet, and it seemed close enough to be over the next ridge. The Forts were riding high and several were hit, streaking down to earth with a long white plume of vapour trail and smoke marking their fall.

Eventually Ralph and I, with Lieutenant Frank Dubervill of Ottawa and Sergeant Grant, the two Army Film Unit photographers who went in with the infantry at Bernières and got pictures that were world beats, wound up at Divisional H. Q. in the orchard just south of the town. There were enough trenches in that orchard for a battalion. Every couple of feet there was a hole big enough for a man. The Germans had been there before us and the Canadians, already wise to the tricks of the trade, had dug even more trenches and looked as if they had been campaigning here for weeks.

The H.Q. was really under the guns that night, for there was fighting only a few miles away in the Tailleville area where enemy strongpoints continued to resist. Occasionally a salvo of mortar bombs crumped in the neighbouring fields, and our guns were in action around us.

Just before dark, information came down from 1st Corps H.Q., which was now ashore in the Courseulles area, that we could expect German parachute landings within the narrow beach-head during the night and that precautions should be taken. Relays of guards were mounted throughout the night, with staff officers and everyone bearing arms in the H.Q., sharing in the watch for the enemy from the sky.

It was the jumpiest night I can remember and I lay in my slit-trench, with only a gas cape for warmth, miserable with the cold and wondering why I was in this hole in Normandy waiting for some German to come out of the air and land in our orchard. I had no arms. I was useless to the defence of H.Q. and if the enemy pounced on us there would be no story written by us, for the chances were remarkably good that I wouldn't be alive to write it and neither would Ralph.

Wild, unsettling thoughts raced through my mind and then I tried to be rational about it and put it down to inevitable D-Day nerves. After all, the beach-head had been won and was now being consolidated. It had been a great victory. But could the Canadians hold it? They were uneasy, uncertain hours and the most critical ones of the landing, for if the Germans had counter-attacked then, if they had been prepared and ready for the invasion at this point, if they had struck at us with a division of armour, with airborne troops, with infantry and guns, they might have broken through to the sea. The Canadians would have fought like demons, but their formations on that first night were loosely scattered. They had exploited, as the plan had called for them to do, and they had performed a magnificent feat, but they were not prepared for any savage thrust from Caen and the south. The German reaction to the landing was ponderously slow, though. The night passed without any counter-attack. The paratroops did not land right in the beach-head, although one group came down four miles south of us and were dealt with by forward Canadian elements who wirelessed back to H.Q.: "We are now playing with German paratroops".

The bombers did come over, however, and the night was a mad confusion of streaking tracer, roaring flak, guns and diving planes. They went for the ships, for the beach zone and for orchards and woods where troops might be. We clung to the damp earth of our slit-trenches and held our breath as each plane whined past and as each bomb fell.

I have never got to that point in fatalistic thinking that I can say to myself as some men can: "If it's going to get you, it's going to get you." The more I saw of bombing, shelling and mortar fire as the war went on, the more nervous I was of it. I never got used to it and never would. Every time I experienced enemy fire, I compared it to something before and it always seemed worse. This nervousness was cumulative, for I suppose I was figuring out the odds and when I compounded a lot of sporadic incidents they added up to quite a sum over four campaigns and two raids!

By the odds alone, my luck would not hold indefinitely and I got more cautious than I ever was. Yet to put things in proper perspective, I only had to think of the infantry and I felt like kicking myself.

No dawn was as welcome as that one on D-plus-one, even though it was grey and drab, and rain threatened. We hauled ourselves out of the fox-holes and walked down into Bernières again. Today the Canadians were going on to their objectives, the Westerners moving down to the Caen-Bayeux highway and the Highland brigade, led by the column of North Novas and Sherbrooke tanks, was advancing towards Carpiquet to gain the high ground if it possibly could.

(TOP): *A group of Canadians wounded as invasion forces from Britain made their way ashore on the French coast, wait on the beach to be transferred to Casualty Clearing Station.*

(LOWER): *A Nazi machine-gun nest knocked out of action as Canadian invasion forces quickly silenced shore installations.*

Canadian in Bernières itself had had a rocky night, with bombs whistling down on the beaches and the flak guns clattering for hours on end. There also was a "flap" on about snipers. Rumours spread rapidly that hidden enemy, in houses and trees, were shooting up small groups of troops. Some claimed that French civilians were doing it; others claimed they were Germans in uniform or in civilian clothes who had been left behind as the Canadians rushed inland. I never could find irrefutable evidence that any snipers I heard about were French civilians, although one case of a French woman sniper was later confirmed. However, there certainly were German snipers in places like Bernières and Courseulles, and although the threat was exaggerated to extravagant proportions by rumour and alarms, you had to keep a wary eye open for them all that first week.

For instance, two days after the landing, the Canadians had to go through Bernières from house to house and thoroughly clean it up, for their men were being hit by snipers in the streets and on the beach. They got them as they worked at unloading stores and ammunition from the landing craft that came and went in a steady stream of shipping. A couple of snipers were located in the church steeple which had to be partially blown down to get the Germans out.

It was miraculous that a lot of Canadians in and around Bernières that first night were not shot, for although the town was occupied, probably thirty or forty Germans were lurking in the houses and in the woods. We walked around in complete ignorance of any such threat, assuming that with the front line now a few miles away, all was clear behind it. But it was not that kind of war!

Some of our jeeps showed up and I drove down the

coast road to Bernières and on to Graye-sur-Mer, where I had heard Bill Stewart might be. Bill had gone in with the western brigade on the Courseulles beaches and I had a terrible feeling that he might have been hit on the landing, for we had heard how tough it had been and that casualties had been heavy. But in a little Franch house in the little village of Graye, Bill was safe and sound. He had landed just west of the inlet, had dug himself a slit-trench and written his first story there on the edge of the dunes while fighting was still going on not far away and wounded were coming back every few minutes. With Matt Halton and Placide Labelle, he had followed the infantry into Graye-sur-Mer and an old French couple had offered them the hospitality of their home. The first night in France this trio slept between white sheets, in comfortable beds, and it was the only decent sleep they had for the next two weeks or more.

The PR unit had collected from the two beaches by now, and we set up our press H.Q. in the former German headquarters in Courseulles, the place the Reginas had captured. Labelle and Roy Oliver were looking around about noon on D-Day for a spot and drove into the courtyard. They went into the house and to their utter astonishment found a group of Germans! Some of them were armed but they held up their hands and surrendered to the two officers. Oliver went to get some troops to take them to the prisoner-of-war cage, and Labelle, with a spade in his hand, for he had left his gun in the jeep in the courtyard, kept guard.

Several German dead were lying on the second floor of the château, and after the prisoners were taken away and the dead were buried in the orchard outside the door, we moved in.

The château had been smashed up in the Reginas' attack and by the bombardment, but it must have been a superb headquarters. There was a long room on the ground floor which had been a German staff conference room. At one end of the white-washed walls there was a six-foot red-and-black German flag, complete with swastika, painted on the wall. Across the wall at the other end, was the standard Nazi emblem of eagle with wings spread.

In the big room was a sand table and the terrain represented was the coastal area at Courseulles and Bernières which the Canadians had successfully attacked. This sand table had been used by the Germans here in their anti-invasion training. Every gun position and trench system was represented on the model, every slope and road was there. It was a fine replica of the shore-line and the beach defences. On the area representing the sea, there were toy landing craft nosing in towards the beach—British landing craft. From a switchboard you could flash lights from points on the model to represent gun-fire. Any youngster would have had the time of his life playing with this model and it struck me as ironical that we set up our invasion news room right alongside this table where German officers only two nights before were probably devising new tactics to meet landing attempts.

There was so much to write about the Canadian advance inland that we scarcely knew where to start.

At 7.30 A.M. on this day after the assault the western brigade west of the Mue went south from the Camilly area and against comparatively slight opposition seized ground on the Caen-Bayeux highway, with the Winnipegs at Putot-en-Bessin, south of the highway, the Reginas in Bretteville d'Orgueilleuse right on the highway with forward troops in Norrey-en-Bessin to the south, and the Canadian Scottish in Secqueville-en-Bessin, north of the highway.

This was their final objective and they reached it by daring exploitation from the beaches, taking all kinds of chances of being cut off and surrounded. Later, General Montgomery himself especially praised the work of this western brigade and its tough, forthright brigadier, Harry Foster of Picton, Ont. He had led the Canadians on the Kiska operations in the Aleutians.

The brigade dug in quickly on these objectives and the counter-attacks it expected developed in the evening. For days and nights the attacks kept up, with German infantry and tanks hammering at the Canadian positions. But the Westerners hung on through it all and hit back hard at the enemy. The official Divisional report says: "Every one of these strong probes by enemy infantry and armour were well and truly smashed."

While the western brigade seized its objectives astride the highway, the North Novas rode south from Villons-les-Buissons on the tanks of the Sherbrooke Fusiliers towards their objectives on the high ground around Authie and towards Carpiquet airfield.

The hamlet of Les Buissons, a few hundred yards south of Villons-les-Buissons, was cleared without difficulty and by one P.M. the vanguard was in possession of Authie and had pressed on to within a mile of Carpiquet.

Then the Canadian force was counter-attacked by German tanks and infantry. It was the first major enemy blow on the Second Army front and was struck by the forces which Rommel had mustered hurriedly in the Caen area.

The North Novas and the Sherbrookes, far out

ahead of the rest of the Division, closed with the enemy and for several hours the bloodiest battle of those early days in Normandy raged.

German Panther tanks swept along the slopes and the roads from Caen and Carpiquet, and infantry followed them up, as Germans in defence positions in the little towns around Authie hammered the Canadians with artillery, mortars and machine-guns.

Two companies of the North Novas were cut off in this fierce struggle and fought to the end with Germans all around them. Deeds of gallantry were legion as the Canadian infantry and tank crews battled the enemy along the slopes and through the battered streets and houses of Authie, which was the focal point of the action.

Commanding the North Novas was Lieutenant-Colonel Charles Petch of Montreal, and commanding the Sherbrookes was Lieutenant-Colonel Mel Gordon of Ottawa. These youthful C.O.s displayed magnificent leadership in the mad confusion of the battle, which was the first of many that their regiments fought together in the grim struggles on the Caen front.

About four P.M., the battle eased up and the German forces withdrew towards Caen, leaving about forty smouldering tanks littered over the fields.

Several hundred German infantry had been killed or wounded, but the cost to the Canadians was heavy. The Sherbrookes lost about twenty-five or thirty tanks and the North Novas had made a great sacrifice too, with about half the battalion casualties.

The Canadians were ordered to fall back on the Glengarrians around Les Buissons, where the Ontario troops had dug in along a wooded slope by the tiny village.

They came back into Les Buissons from the hell of

the Authie battle but there was little respite. The
Germans attacked again at ten P.M. moving up the
slope through the sweeping fields of wheat. The Canadians threw them back and the position was stabil-
ized.

The H.L.I. moved up to Villons-les-Buissons to back-
stop the Glengarrians, North Novas and Sherbrookes,
and some tanks of the Fort Garry Horse also came up.

In the thrust towards Carpiquet, the North Novas
and the Sherbrookes had gone right into the main
German defence line on the Caen perimeter. These
defences had been prepared a long time before and
were the German bulwark behind the beach defences.
Hinged on villages like Authie, Buron and St.-Contest,
there were elaborate trench systems, gun positions and
underground chambers. Manned by crack German
troops, these defences were a tremendous obstacle.

It was little wonder that the Canadian "Jock
Column" did not get to Carpiquet on that day after
the landing. It was simply too tough a job.

The objectives on the left flank of the Canadians
here had not been attained, but a magnificent and
courageous effort had been made, and even if they had
got south right to Carpiquet the position probably
would have been untenable, for the 3rd British Division had been stopped at Lebisey Woods, and could go
no further.

The other Canadian regiments operated most of this
second day in France in the Douvre area trying to
clean up the radar station, and although several positions around it were captured, the main underground
fortress remained in enemy hands. The North Shores
and tanks of the Fort Garry Horse fought in the
Douvres and Tailleville area most of the day rounding
up groups of enemy, and the Queen's Own and the

Chaudières were attacked by a German column retir-
ing from Douvres after a successful commando attack
from the coast to Douvres. The Canadians engaged the
Germans, broke them and took sixty prisoners.

The area behind the fluid front was still far from
consolidated, and when you drove around the beach-
head you never knew where the next shot was coming
from. Those were hectic times for everyone in the
beach-head. With practically no sleep, the troops kept
going for days on their nerve. Many sections of the
beaches were shelled by German heavy artillery; supply
and transport concentrations in the divisional administration area were shelled and occasionally German
planes whisked over the area scattering bombs, although our air cover was very laudable.

But for all the fighting that went on further inland,
the great story of the invasion was the assault itself.
In the afternoon of the second day in Normandy, after
we had written what we could about the new advance
and what we could learn from the confusion of the
battle at Authie, I went down to the beach at Courseulles and went through the German defence system.

Those were sombre hours I spent walking through
the dunes, the trenches and the casemates where the
Canadians had wrought this incredible victory. The
German dead were littered over the dunes, by the gun
positions. By them, lay Canadians in blood-stained
battle-dress, in the sand and in the grass, on the wire
and by the concrete forts. I saw friends I had known,
men who had joined the army in the first months of
the war, who had trained hard, had endured the
tedium of endless manoeuvres and now had died in
their first action here on the Norman beach. They had
lived a few minutes of this victory which they made.
That was all. On their shoulder flashes you read "The

Royal Winnipeg Rifles", in white letters on rifle green, and "Regina Rifle Regiment", in green on a red background.

To see these defences that they had stormed and captured awed you, made you proud of the Canadians and left you astounded. Time and time again as I walked along I kept asking myself in my mind: "How did these men ever do it: how did they break through?"

This was the Atlantic Wall. It was not one solid line of gigantic concrete forts as popular fancy might have thought it would be. It was a series of formidable casemates, the largest about thirty or forty feet square, with walls four and five feet thick—all reinforced concrete. Between these casemates were lines of concrete pillboxes, dug deep into the ground with just the top above the earth. Trench systems and tunnels also linked each strongpoint and there was not a yard of the beach that the cross-fire from machine-guns and rifles could not cover. There were three or four lines of pillboxes at more vulnerable spots and for five or six hundred yards inland this belt of bristling positions extended from the shore.

Weeks later I read a report from someone who had been on some beach after the assault. It described the defences as the "biggest bluff in the world". That person did not go to Courseulles; he did not carefully examine the intricate system of inter-locked defences there; he did not see the casemates with their guns and their concrete and the pillboxes and the tunnels and underground chambers where the Germans could find refuge from the bombardment. He did not see the dead lying there stiff and grotesque and bloody. No, at Courseulles and at Bernières and at St.-Aubin, the German defence system was no bluff.

Courseulles was one of the strongest sections on the British-Canadian sector and where there were not concrete, forts and guns, there were guns, mine fields and fortified houses. Behind this line were the mortar positions and the artillery batteries sited on the beaches, and the strongpoints ringed with barbed wire and dug far down into the earth, like the radar station near Tierville and Douvres, which was the finest of them all.

Take a half a mile of the Courseulles defences on either side of the inlet and this is what I found that day after the battle, as the burial parties moved over the dunes. On both sides of the inlet were two large casemates. I went into the one on the east side which the Reginas had taken with the help of several tanks from the 1st Hussars. It was thirty-five feet across and the concrete walls were four feet thick. There was a heavy artillery piece in the casemate and empty shell cases were piled deep on the floor. Six members of the gun crew sprawled there dead. They had fired until they had been killed. Their gun covered the beach right down to Bernières and also the approaches. Two of those German gunners wore the Russian front ribbon on their tunics. There was a machine-gun in the casemate too, a heavy machine-gun, and it looked as if it had been run over by a truck.

Outside the casemate was a concrete-walled trench which ran to the water's edge of the inlet and there were three machine-gun posts, well protected by concrete. Each one had been defended, and half-empty ammunition boxes, belts of bullets and the broken guns were still there. Behind the casemate was an anti-tank gun, also in concrete and on a swivel so it could fire in any direction. There were several underground chambers in this one position and the Germans had been improving them with more concrete **and steel.**

Some Canadian tankmen from the 1st Hussars were there. They were crews of tanks which had fought on the beach, whose tanks had been knocked out and now they waited for replacements to go into battle again. One of these knocked-out Sherman tanks was on the beach thirty feet from the muzzle of the big gun in the casemate. The corporal said: "That tank there waddled right up to this fort thing here when the assault troops came in. It waddled right up close like where it is now and it pumped 75mm. shells into the fort. It put some right into the opening where the Jerry cannon was sticking out. It got away twenty-eight rounds before it was holed."

"How about your own tank, corporal?" I asked him.

"We came in alongside him," he replied. "The fire was very heavy. Guns were popping off everywhere and the machine-gun bullets pelted our hull. We broke through the wire into the dunes a hundred yards or so over there past this fort and we got among those fortified houses there."

These were the line of fortified houses which were clustered around the Courseulles railway station near the inlet and north of the town proper. They had been hit hard by the bombardment but in their shelters some Germans had still fought there.

"We figured we'd help the Reginas on this strong-point here so we wheeled around and spotted this anti-tank gun behind the casemate. The Jerries were manning it, but we crashed through a brick wall and surprised them so much that before they could get at us we had put some 75mm. shells into them and blown them up."

The gun shield had two neat 75mm. holes through it.

I walked through the dunes down in the direction

of Bernières over the Reginas beach. It was a ghastly sight with its dead and its ruin. The pillboxes were chipped and blasted by grenades and shell-fire. Some of the casemates had received direct hits from heavy artillery but they had withstood them. It had been the Reginas themselves who had battled their way into them with grenades, Sten guns, Bren guns and the bare, gleaming bayonet before they were captured.

I looked at these defence positions and tried to picture the hell that broke loose in that terrible fight, but it was impossible to envision. "How did those troops ever get through?" I asked myself again and again and found no answer.

I crossed over the inlet and went along the Winnipegs' beach. Like the Reginas' beach, each pillbox, gun-post and trench showed evidence of the battle which had raged. Each one had been fought for. Each one took its toll. Each one held its own dead. Patches of grass had been trampled down in the struggle of men fighting in close combat and there were patches of dark red blood on the ground. German potato-masher grenades were scattered in the trenches and shell holes pitted the beach strip. Your boots kicked jagged chunks of shrapnel. On the beach were more derelict Sherman tanks, and close to the big casemate on the west side of the inlet, was a tank in about the same position as the one before the fort on the east bank. It had shelled the casemate at practically muzzle-blast range and its crew had died there.

The underground chambers and the tunnels were still giving up Germans even at that time, and as we got fifteen feet from one tunnel entrance eight Germans suddenly sprang out with their hands high in the air saying "Don't shoot, don't shoot," to a commando who was standing by the entrance with a Tommy-gun.

The ninth German lay wounded inside the tunnel entrance, and he died there before one of our doctors could reach him.

The wind was blowing hard and the rain fell on this grey beach scene. I drove silently back to the old German headquarters, stirred as I never had been, by the raw, inhuman, savage sights of war which that tour of the beach had given me.

"How did they do it?" The question hammered on my mind and the only answer was the indomitable, determined spirit of those magnificent troops.

It was their first fight, and they went into the face of those guns; they clambered and battled over and through the casemates and the trenches; they fought on and on, ferociously, savagely, grimly in the wild tumult that raged that D-Day morning until they had broken through.

The splendid, shining heroism of the Canadian assault troops themselves was the immediate reason for the success of the coastal attack at Courseulles, Bernières and St.-Aubin. And there were several other reasons, reasons which go back to the days at Dieppe where other heroic Canadians stormed a different type of fortified beach on an eight-hour raid, from which only a tragic few returned, but which was the prelude to nearly two years' successful combined operations in the Mediterranean and which had its climax in this Normandy triumph.

The holocaust of shells and high explosives which the pre-landing bombardment spread along these beaches was a major contributory reason for the success. Dieppe proved conclusively that such a bombardment was absolutely essential. A half-dozen destroyers and medium bombers and fighter bombers were not enough, not nearly enough.

It required naval might, with cruisers and battle-ships. It required massed artillery firing those hellish drum barrages from the sea. It required destroyers and gun-boats and monitors and rocket ships, all blast-ing the coastal positions. It required heavy and medium bombers, carpeting the area with bombs. It required all this to give the assault infantry, engineers and tank crews a fighting chance. On D-Day it was all used.

And when the infantry and engineers were ashore, they had immediate close fire support from tanks that were landed in an ingenious fashion which is still a war secret as this is being written. Other assault weapons were used which still remain secret.

The amazing technical development which was made during preparations for the invasion was another big reason. The 3rd Canadian Division carried out experi-mental work in coastal assault for months on end, inventing, adapting, adjusting plans until a system had been devised which seemed workable. And it was.

The training of the assault divisions was a factor. The Canadians trained longer than any of the others, but all the assault force was the most highly skilled which had ever undertaken a combined operation.

The troops were provided with the finest equipment any force of its kind ever had. The staff work on the operation was painstaking, accurate and professionally done.

The navy was a fundamental factor in the success and the masterly manner in which they landed the expedition in the rough sea was an achievement that will rank in naval annals with the finest exploits of the service.

But from Dieppe had come the lessons which had been the basis for the planning. As General Crerar said in his order to the Canadians as they sailed for France:

"Plans, preparations, methods and technique which will be employed are based on knowledge and experience, bought and paid for by the 2nd Canadian Division at Dieppe. The contribution of that hazardous operation cannot be over-estimated. It will prove to have been an essential prelude to our forthcoming and final success."

Later, after the 2nd Division had returned to Dieppe and occupied the port without losing a man or firing a shot, the Army Commander added that without the experience of the Dieppe raid, the basis of the planning and execution of the Allied landings on the Normandy coast would have been lacking.

IV

STRUGGLE ON THE BEACH-HEAD

THE initial assault by the Allied invasion forces had achieved, by the afternoon of D-plus-one, practically everything the High Command had hoped at that uncertain phase of operations. Caen had not been captured, but a satisfactory beach-head, narrow as it was, had been gained by the Second Army from the Orne River, which flows through Caen to the Bay of the Seine, west to Bayeux. The assault troops of the First American Army had established their beach-head on the right flank of the British and Canadians.

The next stage of the operation on the Second Army front, was to build up strong forces in the beach-head for exploitation inland. Many more divisions were following up the assault formations; ammunition, transport and supplies were ready to be poured into this strip of liberated Normandy.

The job of the British and Canadian troops who had won this beach-head between Caen and Bayeux was now to hold it firm while the build-up was accomplished. They dug in to meet inevitable German counter-attacks and the beach-head struggle began.

Through June and into the early days of July, this fierce struggle went on with little let-up. It was costly, bitter warfare in confined areas. Day after day the fighting raged along the beach-head perimeter, with the heaviest actions in the Caen area. It was a struggle that required immense endurance, stamina and courage and the Second Army showed it had all these qualities. It held its beach-head, which later became the pivot point for the spectacular advances which broke the German armies in the west and freed all France.

The German reaction to the landing was ponderously slow on our front, and there is no question that the assault on this section of Normandy took the enemy by surprise. It required twenty-four hours before the German mobile reserves were rushed in strength to the Caen area to put in strong counter-attacks, and in this time the Second Army assault forces were in a position to cope with them.

But for days it was touch and go, with the Germans threatening day and night to break into the beach-head. If they had been able to penetrate that outer defence of infantry, tanks and guns and sent their armoured columns roaring down to the beaches, the invasion might well have been turned into a gigantic disaster that first week.

The story of how the British and Canadian troops prevented the break-through is a jig-saw of a dozen scrambled actions. The stand of the western Canada brigade in the Bretteville area is one of the highlights, for it was in this district that German tanks and infantry made probably their most desperate attempts to penetrate the Second Army line.

The Royal Winnipeg Rifles, commanded by Lieutenant-Colonel J. M. Meldram of Victoria who had led them on the beach assault, were in the Canadians' forward position at Putot-en-Bessin, south of the Caen-Bayeux highway. Putot is merely a cluster of houses on flat farmland, dotted with clumps of trees, and the German forces, moving up from Carpiquet and Caen, struck particularly hard at this area.

The attack began with artillery and mortar fire slamming down around the Winnipegs' slit-trenches, and machine-gun fire was added to pin down the battalion. Enemy tanks and infantry followed up this bombardment and drove right into the Canadian positions. Three company positions were overrun and wild man-against-man combats raged over the fields, with the Winnipegs refusing to give up Putot even when the Germans were milling around among them. Heavy casualties were suffered by the battalion, including three company commanders, but somehow the remnants of the regiment hung on to some of the vital positions until nightfall when the Canadian Scottish, commanded by Lieutenant-Colonel F. N. Cabeldu of Victoria, came up with some tanks of the 1st Hussars to relieve them.

The stand at Putot was one of the most heroic actions the Winnipegs fought in France. The Scottish also had heavy fighting in and around Putot and this regiment too showed its stern fighting qualities as it drove back German attacks which, if they had been successful, might have been the beginning of the end for the Second Army beach-head.

The town of Bretteville on the Caen-Bayeux highway was held by the Regina Rifles, commanded by Lieutenant-Colonel F. M. Matheson of Prince Albert, Sask., and the Germans tried for more than a week to capture the place. Enemy tanks fought their way into the town several times but the Reginas destroyed them in the streets. At one time, Panther tanks shelled and machine-gunned Battalion Headquarters in a building near the church in the centre of the town.

At another time, with enemy tanks reported on every point of the battalion front, a German tank broke into the town and its commander demanded the surrender of Bretteville by shouting in English to Reginas crouched in the rubble heaps. The reply of the

Westerners was to knock out the tank and kill the crew. During these close-range actions against tanks, the Reginas proved to their own satisfaction the value of the new Piat mortar. "Piat" stands for "projector infantry anti-tank". They had been doubtful about its merits, but in Bretteville they knocked out half a dozen German tanks with this weapon and the regiment became the foremost champion of the Piat in the 3rd Division.

When the tanks failed, the Germans sent waves of infantry against the Reginas, who mowed them down from their positions among the buildings and from slit-trenches dotting the outskirts of the town. In one attack, these western troops allowed a company of German infantry to come within forty yards of them and then, opening up with every weapon they had, practically wiped out the company. At least one hundred and fifty Germans were killed or wounded in a few minutes of furious firing.

This slaughter made the Germans pull back, and no further attempts were made to close with the Reginas in the town. However, enemy guns and mortars hit at Bretteville continually, and it, like Putot, was one of the hottest spots on the front that first week.

Many times these two positions looked quite untenable, but the western troops hung on grimly, suffering casualties every hour. Brigade Headquarters was in the thick of the marathon battle and few such headquarters on the Normandy front went through such days of tumult. With Brigadier Foster were staunch officers like Major Peter Bennett of Toronto, the brigade major, Major Lou Rounding of Victoria, Captain Bob Knechtel of Saskatoon, the staff captain, and Captain Warren Stewart of Winnipeg.

The 1st Hussars, commanded by Lieutenant-Colonel

R. J. Colwell of Toronto and Halifax, fought many
fierce tank actions in the Bretteville-Putot sector in
support of the three western infantry battalions, and a
company of Vickers machine-gunners of the Cameron
Highlanders of Ottawa also saw a great deal of fighting
here. This company was commanded by Major John
Rowley of Ottawa, who when the fiercest actions were
over, immediately donned his Cameron kilt and wore
it around the front. His brother, Major Roger Rowley
of Ottawa, was second-in-command of the Camerons,
which were led by Lieutenant-Colonel Percy Klaehn
of Saskatoon. Later Roger Rowley commanded the
Glengarrians.

Fighting in the Hussars' squadron led by Major
D'Arcy Marks of Toronto, Lieutenant Gordie Henry
of Montreal created a sensation in the Division one
afternoon at Bretteville, when he and his tank crew
knocked out five German tanks with five shots. This
was an individual record which stood through the
French campaign.

The climax of the terrible Bretteville struggle came
on the Sunday following the landing. The Germans
had tried in vain to break the line and had suffered
severely but they still had one big punch left. On
Sunday, June 11, enemy tanks and infantry were seen
massing in the orchards and fields two miles south of
Bretteville. General Keller took quick action and
ordered the 1st Hussars, with infantry of the Queen's
Own Rifles, to attack before the enemy got his forces
rolling.

The Hussars thundered forward with the Queen's
Own, and in the orchards south of the Caen-Bayeux
railway line the battle was joined. The attack caught
the Germans unawares but they soon steadied up and
as confused and tumultuous an action as the Brette-

ville area saw took place. When tank formations were broken up by gun-fire, the Canadian crews fought as infantry. The violence of that struggle, with Canadians and Germans fighting hand-to-hand with grenades, bayonets, pistols and knives has had few equals. Losses were heavy on both sides but the sacrifice of those Canadian tank crews and infantry broke up the threatened German attack. General Keller assured the regiments that their magnificent effort, costly as it was, killed a German counter-attack which would have endangered the entire Canadian front.

Bretteville in those stormy days was practically cut off, and it was a perilous job to get ammunition and rations up to the brigade along the straight, flat road leading from the beach zone. Even dispatch riders went forward to brigade and battalions in armoured scout cars when they could, for they were too easy prey for snipers on their motor bikes.

Accurate information about what was going on in all this fighting was extremely scanty. Reports that whole battalions were wiped out would be contradicted an hour later with word that an attack had been repulsed and casualties were not as serious as at first thought.

Even at Divisional H.Q. it was difficult to piece the story together into any kind of a balanced picture, for the fighting was as confusing as any prolonged battle could be. Divisional H.Q. itself was in the gun lines. There were few places immune to shell-fire in the beach-head and the sniping menace was prevalent everywhere that first uncertain week. On D-plus-one, Divisional H.Q., which was my main point of contact in the early stages, moved to Beny-sur-Mer, three miles south of Courseulles. It came under shell-fire several times, which is not orthodox battle procedure, and

it also was plagued by snipers to such an extent that
the divisional staff organized sniper-hunting parties
through the woods at Beny and bagged a good many
prisoners.

One of the major problems in the Canadian sector,
apart entirely from the Germans attacking at Bretteville and on the left flank at Les Buissons, was the
wooded Mue River valley which ran right through the
divisonal area towards Courseulles and split the western brigade on the right from the other forces on the
left.

It had not been cleaned up in the initial push on
D-Day and D-plus-one, because it would have delayed
exploitation. Now the valley was very troublesome,
for it was full of Germans. They weren't particularly
good troops, being the left-overs of the coastal garrisons, but they were a nuisance, sniping Canadian lines
of communications to the forward units and shelling
everything they could with a couple of batteries of
88mm. guns they had in the valley.

This business of having the Germans in one's midst
added to the difficulties the Division had to overcome,
so after several small parties had probed into the valley and found it contained a considerable force of
enemy,. General Keller ordered the Regiment de la
Chaudière, with some British commandos and tanks of
the Fort Garry Horse, to clear the valley. The French-
speaking troops and the others did it with great *élan*,
hunting the Germans through the woods and caves
that honey-combed the valley.

The "Chauds", as they came to be known, had done
well right from the landing. One of the best jobs they
did in the first two days was to ambush a German
armoured car column on the Caen road just north of
Villons-les-Buissons. They caught the convoy on a

slope and the Germans did not know what hit them. The Quebec soldiers tore into them with every weapon they had and destroyed the entire convoy. Major Hugues Lapointe of Quebec City, the son of the late Ernest Lapointe, former Minister of Justice and one of Canada's great Liberal statesmen, took a prominent part in this action with his company.

While the struggle went on at Bretteville and while the Mue valley was mopped up, there was another fierce and important action taking place on the Division's left flank at Les Buissons where the Highland brigade, with tanks of the Sherbrooke Fusiliers, were beating off other German counter-attacks.

Les Buissons commanded the main highway leading from Caen to Courseulles and if the Canadian position there had been overrun the German armoured forces could have shot right through to the beaches. There was practically nothing behind the Highland brigade, except some miscellaneous beach troops, and some 1st Corps units. Youthful, buoyant Brigadier Ben Cunningham of Kingston, Ont., was determined that not a single German would get through his brigade. The hard fight on D-plus-one at Authie had reduced the ranks of the North Nova Scotia Highlanders and the Sherbrookes, but the brigade was still strong and it held firm as a rock at Les Buissons, which the troops soon dubbed "Hell's Corner", not very originally but very accurately.

The Stormont, Dundas and Glengarry Highlanders led by their imperturbable commanding officer, Lieutenant-Colonel G. H. Christiansen, a Kingston, Ont., high school teacher before the war, had their first big action here, fighting with the North Novas and the Sherbrookes, as well as some Fort Garry tanks. The Germans threw in the first attack on the night of

D-plus-one, six hours after the Authie fight, and they received a sound trouncing.

The following day they came back and for three or four days after, brief but heavy actions flared up. Each time the Highland units held every yard of their own ground, and even prolonged and concentrated artillery fire interspersed with German multiple mortars did not budge them from their slit-trenches.

Even when they were on the defensive, the Highland units did not lose their aggressiveness and kept sending out numerous patrols to nearby enemy-held towns like Buron and Gruchy, which were strongly held by the enemy, being anchor points for the Caen defence system. It took a full-scale attack a month later to capture these places and open the way to Caen and it was the Highland brigade which did it then.

The western brigade and the Highland brigade with their tank regiments bore the brunt of these defensive actions along the beach-head line but the third infantry brigade of the Division, commanded by Brigadier Kenneth Blackader of Montreal, also had an important share in the tasks the Division accomplished during the first fierce weeks.

Its regiments mopped up half a dozen pockets of resistance behind the front and the Chaudières' job in the Mue River valley is typical. The Queen's Own had the one particularly heavy fight south of Bretteville and the North Shore Regiment from New Brunswick was in the line steadily.

Behind the infantry and armoured regiments were the Royal Canadian Artillery regiments. Several of the self-propelled regiments had gone into action right on the beaches and they were the greatest support the forward troops had in the perimeter fighting. Time and time again German attacks were blasted by concentrations brought down by these regiments. German positions were hit hard by shell-fire and the Canadian gunners did themselves proud in the beach-head struggle as they did right through the French campaign and beyond.

The 3rd Anti-Tank Regiment was in action many times and the 4th Light Anti-Aircraft Regiment had more shoots than its gunners ever dreamed it would. After a few weeks it claimed to have brought down more than thirty enemy planes, most of them in the dusk and dawn hours when the German aircraft usually made their most threatening raids.

The services of the Division carried out their jobs remarkably well in the face of many complications and difficulties. The Royal Canadian Corps of Signals kept the communications going; the Royal Canadian Army Service Corps kept the ammunition, rations and gasoline moving to the front; the Ordnance Corps kept the Division in vehicles and repaired plenty, too, in its beach-head workshops; the Royal Canadian Army Medical Corps cared for the casualties.

The 3rd Division and the 2nd Armoured Brigade were served well by its services and without their efficiency the battle would not have gone so well.

After a week of vicious fighting, the big German counter-attacks petered out. They had failed in their attempts to crack the Canadian line and other attacks on the British line also had been blunted.

The troops had some opportunity now to get a breather in their positions but there was still a great deal of artillery fire and life was far from quiet on the front.

According to the plan, the Second Army was to hold what it already had gained, without attempting any advances of any considerable degree until the build-up was satisfactory. Then the British and Canadian troops would strike out with a vengeance.

*   *   *   *

To live in the centre of this beach-head maelstrom was an incredible experience. While the battles raged along the perimeter, events crowded on one another inside the beach-head too and each hour brought some new excitement. There were no dull moments for any of us during that doubtful early period when anything might have happened and the fate of this West Front operation hung in the balance.

The area we possessed was small and the fighting was very close to everyone. The war was concentrated and personal and one's most vivid memories are of personal experiences in those sleepless, haggard days and nights when we lived on the excitement of the moment and the steaming stew and hardtack that our stalwart cook produced at all hours in our press camp.

We had that weird first night at Divisional Head-quarters outside Bernières and then Press H.Q. moved to Courseulles to the German H.Q. building. Information was skimpy and the fighting was so fluid the divisional staff was having trouble getting accurate word from the front, which was only a few miles ahead of it.

Still, there was an avalanche of stories to write. The assault itself was an epic that required a week to tell properly. We had to tell it in a few hours' labour on our typewriters. The story of the German beach defences was another and again it had to be skimmed over, for the battle had gone on to Bretteville and Les Buissons and we had to try our best to keep abreast of it.

We worked madly in Courseulles, with frequent

trips in speeding jeeps up the traffic-jammed roads to Divisional H.Q. in the sniper belt at Beny where steady, unruffled Lieutenant-Colonel Mingay or Major Phil Strickland of Saskatoon and Galt, Ont., the G2, would sort out the situation for us as calmly as they would read a balance sheet at a directors' meeting.

Back to Courseulles we would hustle to send more copy to England by landing craft or by pigeon, but these perverse birds all seemed to fly towards the German lines. We had brought about twenty with us but I never heard of one getting back to its English loft. After a day or so, we had a small wireless set which cleared brief stories to England direct from former German coastal H.Q.

An hour or two in Courseulles and we'd be off again to Division or any other points farther forward which you could reach in a jeep without getting thoroughly shot up. Rumours of snipers and ambushes spread like wildfire all over the Division. Some of them were true but many were utter rot. They were contagious, though, and they did not help a bit to steady the men in the beach-head.

A good deal of fire was coming from the Mue River valley, however, and from the valley the enemy there could cover many of the roads leading to Bretteville and Les Buissons. In addition to the valley, the radar station near Douvres was holding out and small-arms fire and occasionally some shell-fire came from there.

The nervous tension in the beach-head was terrific and on the second night I decided to try and be comfortable for one night at least. So I went off to Graye-sur-Mer with Bill Stewart and Captain Jack Golding of Saint John, N.B., to sleep in that French home which had the beds with sheets. The old people who owned it had asked any of us back who wanted to accept their hospitality.

After the excitement of two days in France, I tumbled into bed but it was scarcely dark before German night bombers were over the town, hitting at the beaches nearby and the roads through Graye. The planes growled and snarled through the night, as tracers streaked from hundreds of ack-ack guns which roared into action. We were getting rather used to the inferno when a stick of bombs fell across the town near our house and shook the ancient building to its foundations. I thought it had been more comfortable in the slit-trench at Bernières the night before, cold and miserable as that was. There was nothing we could do but sit and take it here in Graye. It would be madness to go out and wander around in the dark, looking for a less vulnerable spot, for every soldier in the area had a trigger finger, with these sniper rumours going around, and he would probably shoot first and challenge afterwards.

The bombing kept up for hours and the few lulls were punctuated by the sharp clatter of small-arms fire in the street outside. I never found out whether there were any enemy in the town, although the soldiers we saw in the morning swore there were batches of them, but there certainly was enough rifle and machine-gun firing to do honour to a battalion in close action. An unarmed correspondent has the most helpless feeling in the world when bullets are popping about, and I have never felt more helpless and useless than that night in Graye when I was not at all certain that the street fighting was not going to overflow into our rooms.

Until the crack of dawn, the German planes zoomed over the beaches and over the town and in the dawn light I saw four fighter bombers on the last sortie, scattering bombs over the edge of Graye, chased by clouds of flak bursting on their tails.

Bleary-eyed from that nightmare night, we stumbled down to the street and the best sight of the day greeted us—hundreds of German prisoners marching in single file down to the beaches. They had been captured in the Mue valley and in strongpoints which had been destroyed. It helped make up for the beating we took during the night.

We hustled back to Courseulles and started the daylight routine again, rushing anywhere we could in the beach-head to get news of the fighting that was flaring up now all along the divisional front with increasing fury.

Down in Bretteville the western regiments were in their furious fights and at Les Buissons the Highland brigade was battling with everything it had. In the Mue River valley the Chaudières, the commandos and the tanks were rooting Germans out of caves and clearing them from the woods and the undergrowth. Our artillery was firing steadily hour after hour, taking on a score of urgent targets as the forward observation officers with the front-line units passed back targets over field wireless sets.

Allied fighters, still flying from southern England, patrolled the beach-head skies in threes and fours and only the odd enemy fighter bomber showed up.

I talked to tank crews of the Sherbrookes, who had come back from the hellish fight at Authie to refit, and I talked to their running mates, the North Novas. What struck me most was the attitude of these troops who had been through one of the heaviest actions of the initial phase of the campaign. They didn't grouse. They figured they were very lucky to get out alive, but the important thing was that they wanted to go back— to go back firing every weapon they had. Troops like that are unbeatable, as the remarkable 3rd Division and 2nd Armoured Brigade proved so conclusively. The Division and the Armoured Brigade had the feel of battle now. The troops had gone in superbly trained, but it was their first action. They had things to learn. They learned with amazing rapidity. They were veterans in a week. Probably no new Allied division or brigade in the Allied Expeditionary Force became battle-worthy so quickly.

At Press H.Q. scarcely a day or night passed without some uproar of some kind. Our former German building was a fine spot for our purposes but the night bombers seemed to show a preference for sighting their aim on it, standing as it did on the highest point in Courseulles. So we soon determined that the best spot after dark was in the elaborate air-raid shelters the Germans had fitted out in the orchard. They had been used by the German staff and had panelled walls with concrete and steel roofs. The Nazi officers had slept there all the time, so we moved in.

German uniforms, weapons, grenades and ammunition littered the shelters and the orchard—the shambles of a very rapid departure when the Regina Rifles had stormed into this place on D-Day morning. I had resolved I'd get away from the beach during the nights after any landing, for we'd been plastered both in Sicily and Italy after the assaults there, but here I was again, right in Courseulles, in the centre of the Second Army beach.

The bombs rocked us about on the first night in those shelters but it was mostly from the earth tremors set up when they landed about half a mile away. None was very close. Still, it was an uneasy, sleepless night, lying there in our clothes listening to the planes, the flak and the whistles of the bombs.

We were all getting nearly as ragged as the fighting

troops, with practically no sleep since several days
before D-Day, and the climax to our dizzy existence
came on Friday night, June 9. We were finishing off
our stories in the evening—the stories of the counter-
attacks being repulsed on our front—when we heard
the crack of rifle fire outside our château. There was
one burst of firing and then another. Lionel Shapiro
looked across the table doubtfully, his ears cocked for
some more shots. They came. They were very close.
A couple of Royal Marines raced across the courtyard
outside the windows, with rifles, followed by a British
officer with his pistol drawn.

We left our typewriters and took cover behind the
wall as a fusillade of bullets whined across the courtyard. The PR officers, our drivers and cook grabbed
their weapons to join in the fray with the Marines.
It was all more comical than alarming but after four
days in the beach-head we were getting windy about
any disturbance. Our armed bands hunted the snipers,
but they could not tell where the firing was coming
from. Ralph Allen swore it was from the cemetery
behind the orchard. Somebody else said it was from
the barn across the courtyard. Then the Marines
decided it was coming from the church steeple a
hundred yards away.

Bren guns fired at the slits in the steeple and someone shouted that they saw a white flag fluttering from
the top slit. I was watching it from a window at the
top of the château and did not see a thing. Anyway,
an officer went into the church and began to climb into
the steeple. Some misguided person, by this time, had
got in touch with a Bofors gun crew and a tank crew,
and they both fired shells into the steeple, knocking
the side off it.

The officer climbing up the steeple came down

unhurt but covered with dust and debris, cursing the gunners. We never found the snipers but the firing stopped abruptly.

I tell the story to give an idea of the type of wild situations that arose in the beach-head.

It was dark by now and down we went to the shelters. Hardly had we got settled for the night when the bombers came over and this time they did not miss the château. Their aim was accurate and a shower of anti-personnel bombs crashed into the courtyard among our jeeps. It was a disaster for us, for most of our vehicles were hit, and the next day we were immobile while we sought new tires, radiators and jeeps.

No one was wounded, however, and the shelters had proved their worth, although we thought the whole works was going to collapse on us when the bombs landed.

We felt, though, that we were too far from the front back at Courseulles and so on Sunday we moved up to another château near Beny. The Divisional H.Q. which had been there eluded us, however, by going in the meantime to Camilly, on the west side of the Mue valley, which still contained some enemy.

The château seemed satisfactory for our Press H.Q. and we settled down again. But it was a snare and a delusion. On Monday a British armoured brigade— an independent brigade in the Second Army—moved into the park surrounding the château. This was one of the most famous brigades in the British forces. It had fought through the desert wars, through Tunisia, Sicily and into Italy and now led by its great brigadier, decorated with the D.S.O. and two bars, was making more history in the Normandy campaign.

We felt very comfortable at Beny with the armoured

brigade around us. Then trouble came in big quantities. Monday night the bombers hit our area heavily with anti-personnel bombs and the old château, which had been a German regimental headquarters, rocked like the other buildings we had been in. We were standing around in the hall watching the fireworks and ducking when it was appropriate when the intelligence officer of the brigade shouted "Parachutists!" It looked as if German airborne troops were being dropped around the park.

Again the PR unit grabbed its weapons and Captain Golding and the others organized the defence of the château. As usual the correspondents had no choice but to stand around helplessly as spectators to a potential fight.

Nothing happened. We were just as glad, but it was an anti-climax. Nobody attacked the château and the air raids stopped. We went to bed, although Goldie and his detachment of drivers and cooks stayed on guard all night.

I had had a fever that night which I attributed to a recurrence of malaria I contracted in Italy and not the "flap". I had the professional word of the brigade medical officer that it was malaria, so I went to bed doped up with a lot of pills and fortified with some cognac Shap had brought from Bayeux.

I woke up about ten A.M. on Tuesday still with the fever and there was some artillery firing a few fields away. I thought it was our guns and dozed off for two more hours. At noon there was a crump which was definitely not our guns. I got out of bed fast, for my ear knew that sound. It was German 88s. Hardly had I got my battle-dress on over my pyjamas when a shell landed in the park. I went down the stairs like a gazelle and when I got to the hall, where half a dozen

(TOP): *When the flag was unfurled over the ground where the Canadians had been fighting, Dominion Day was celebrated in France, and Canadian pipers led a parade.*

(LOWER): *During the hard-fought February offensive of the First Canadian Army, Field-Marshal Sir Bernard Montgomery joined Canada's General H. G. D. Crerar and Lieut.-General Guy Simonds, as they moved forward to confer with senior officers.*

other Canadian correspondents were standing, a shell hit the centre of the château over our heads and plaster and masonry flew in all directions.

Another shell hit a gasoline dump we had outside the kitchen, and the building caught fire. We headed for slit-trenches in the park and the British brigadier with his D.S.O. and two bars and I landed in the same one. He was known as the man with the charmed life. He had been through endless battles and had never been hit. I felt I was in the best possible company. But even brave men crouch in slit-trenches, and he crouched on top of this correspondent who hit the bottom first, as shell after shell crashed into the château and the park.

The building was smoking and blazing by now and Golding, aided by Captains Jack Wilson and Bill Cornforth, had gone back to try and save some of our kit. Halton and Allen worked with them and got some of their stuff out of the second-storey window but mine, along with most of Shapiro's and Stewart's in our room at the end of the corridor, was a total loss.

After firing twenty shells, the German guns stopped. The armoured brigade headquarters made an unceremonious departure and so did our PR unit.

We headed back to Courseulles to get re-organized and we spent the next two nights in the Lion d'Or Hotel in Bayeux, which the British correspondents had practically taken over.

All these minor incidents had not helped us in our job of covering the army so we settled next in a farm at St.-Gabriel, near Second Army H.Q. at Creully, half-way between the beach and the front. The air raids went on night after night, however, until the breakout from the beach-head was made.

I felt very, very weary as we went into our second

week in France, for it had been a difficult job to keep up with the fighting in the midst of our own series of adventures. However, the first phase of the campaign was over and a more settled and stable atmosphere was evident around the Second Army area.

General Dempsey and his headquarters were at Creully now and we had two conferences a day there with Lieutenant-Colonel "Spud" Murphy, chief of the Intelligence branch. These conferences kept us completely up to date on what was happening along the whole army front, while as usual at our own division, we were given abundant assistance from General Keller and his helpful staff. Our field press censors were established with the British PR unit in the Norman castle in the centre of Creully, and there were some wireless sets there too which sent our stories to London. There also was an air courier service we could use.

Although there were exasperations from time to time over censorship and communications, these were by far the finest facilities with which war correspondents had ever been provided.

*   *   *   *

General Montgomery also established his tactical headquarters of 21st Army Group near Creully and we saw him several times there in the first few weeks.

The great plan was unfolding as he wanted it to. The Americans were fighting their way up the Cherbourg peninsula towards the port of Cherbourg, while the British and Canadians attracted the great bulk of the German forces in the Caen sector. Once Cherbourg fell, the American forces would be turned loose for the wide sweep to Brittany and then eastward through France. The main German force must be forced to remain on the Caen-Bayeux sector, however, until the Americans should have time to swing.

This was the broad scheme, and it worked out practically as it was drawn up on paper. The surprising feature of this French campaign was the way in which the Germans reacted as we wanted them to react. They played into the Allied hands and in addition made several incomprehensible blunders that sealed their fate in Normandy and in France, even ahead of the Allied schedule for annihilation of the German forces.

General Montgomery would never talk about the future at our conferences, but he would appraise what had taken place and each time he found little to criticize. The fighting was hard and bitter, sometimes our casualties were terribly high, especially around Caen, but the plan was working, it was working with ruthless, devastating, relentless precision.

Von Rundstedt and Rommel strove desperately to find a weak spot, but failed completely. The German Seventh Army in Normandy simply could not cope with the vast array of Allied forces, backed up by tremendous quantities of guns, transport and supplies. The invasion might have been broken in the first forty-eight hours if the Germans had been able to counter-attack with half a dozen divisions from their reserve of crack *S.S.* and *Panzer* forces.

Then they had their only chance of inflicting a decisive defeat. But they could not do it. Their reserves, held forty and fifty miles inland or around the Paris area, could not be deployed in time. The German army was not mobile enough. It still used a great deal of horse-drawn transport. Allied air attacks had hammered enemy communications in France for months and now in these first critical days and weeks they went all-out to beat up roads, railway lines and enemy troop concentrations.

The German High Command also lacked decisive-
ness in its handling of its forces in Normandy. After
the failure to counter-attack in great strength and
drive right through to the beaches, German armour
and infantry were thrown in piece-meal. The counter-
attacks which the Canadians had to meet were the first
of these. While they meant bloody battles for the
Canadians, the German forces employed were only a
small portion of what was available in the reserve.
The 21st *Panzer* Division, the 12th *S.S.* Hitler Youth
Division, and several other armoured and infantry
formations were identified on our front in the early
phases but they were employed in what the British
always called "penny packets".

The build-up in the Second Army beach-head was
going along well while the Germans frittered away
their forces trying to break through the outer
perimeter. But on June 18 the weather turned foul.

General Crerar arrived from England that day with
tactical H.Q. for First Canadian Army, brought to
France by the Royal Canadian Navy in the destroyer
Algonquin. I saw him come ashore on the beach at
Courseulles which the Winnipegs had taken on D-Day.
A gale was blowing up then. The beach organization
was finding it more and more difficult to land vehicles
and supplies in the heavy seas.

The gale swept the Channel for nearly a week and
in that time perilously little was landed. If the
weather had turned like this in that first week after
D-Day it would have been a disaster for the Allied
Expeditionary Force, but now, although it was a
serious handicap and delayed the build-up, it was not
a fatal stroke of ill luck.

Before the storm came, thousands of fresh troops
had been landed and masses of ammunition and stores

were got ashore. Still more was needed and a full-scale attack, the first to be launched from the Second Army beach-head, was put off until the storm blew out. The Second Army impatiently waited on the whim of the weather; on June 23 the sea abated enough for the beach organizations and the navy, by a super-human effort, to get ashore thousands of tons of war material and make up in good part for the delay.

On Saturday night, June 24, Lieutenant-Colonel Murphy called the Second Army correspondents to Headquarters at Creully and briefed us on the imminent attack which was to be made from the beach-head.

This was the start of the Battle for Caen.

*   *   *   *

The amazing engineering and naval achievement of the invasion landing was the creation of the artificial harbour off the beaches at Arromanches, north of Bayeux. The June gales smashed up part of this harbour, but it survived the gale and through it, after the storm, flooded the supplies which allowed the British, American and Canadian troops to launch the offensive which carried them through France.

Through this pre-fabricated port, the first of its kind in history and one of the most astounding developments in any war, the Allied armies were supplied for weeks and months until the captured ports took the supply convoys. The ordinary beaches were used in addition to the harbour, but the artificial port was the real key to the supply problem during the summer months. It was such a tremendous success that it was even being used in the late fall when Cherbourg, St.-Malo, Le Havre, Boulogne and Ostend were all operating.

The artificial harbour was one of the greatest surprises to the Germans. As I mentioned previously, the enemy made their plans on the premise that the Allies would have to capture a port rapidly. But the invasion forces were sent to Normandy under a plan which called for them to be supplied over the beaches for an indefinite period. Under that phrase "over the beaches" was included this fabulous construction which was floated across the hundred miles of channel in sections, and fitted together like a jig-saw puzzle, off the beaches of Arromanches.

At best it was a big gamble, but it worked better than the most optimistic had hoped. Invasion secrets were all well kept, and the secret of the pre-fabricated port—as important as the time of D-Day and H-Hour to the enemy—was scrupulously guarded. Even in our briefing we were not told many details about this ace in the Allied hand. I remember, before D-Day, seeing huge concrete blocks, like small apartment blocks, floating in the Solent and in the Spithead, but nobody on any ship I was on knew what they were for. "Something to do with the landing, I suppose," was the vague answer I always got. I concluded that they likely were some kind of super fort which was heavily gunned and would be beached on D-Day to give fire support to the assault troops. It sounded Wellsian, but in those days before the landing nothing was too fantastic to believe in the midst of the preparations for the greatest sea and air attack of all time.

In reality the concrete blocks were caissons for the Arromanches harbour. The biggest weighed 7,000 tons and 150 of them had been constructed during the winter at scores of places in the United Kingdom.

But they were only part of the harbour installations floated to Normandy on D-Day and the days and

weeks following. The method of providing the necessary sheltered water was to sink a line of block ships
off shore as a breakwater and then to extend this line
with the caissons sunk in pre-arranged positions, so
as totally to enclose the anchorage. Inside this breakwater, ships could unload into barges, despite freaks
of Channel weather.

All told, it took more than a million tons of
material to prepare this port. Fifty-eight merchant
ships—a good-sized fleet in themselves—were first
taken to the beaches in the wake of the invasion troops
and they were blown up and sunk two miles from
shore. The caissons then were floated into position
and sunk, and a huge concrete wall took form like a
street of mansions rising out of the sea.

Piers were built out from shore at which ships
could unload inside the shelter of the anchorage and
the Royal Engineers assembled miles of bridging and
pier material, frequently under air attack and sometimes under shell-fire, as they built these long roadways into the anchorage.

*   *   *   *

In the interval of the storm, when overcast skies also
restricted daytime air force operations but seldom
seemed to keep the German planes away from our
beaches at night, the 3rd Canadian Division hung on
to its positions on the Caen perimeter. Day and night,
there was fierce shelling and mortaring and the troops
got little rest, although there were no serious German
attacks. Canadian infantry patrols went out each
night into the enemy lines at Buron, Gruchy and
towards Carpiquet, and proved that the enemy was
in strength in these areas.

On the right of the 3rd Canadian Division, a British

corps was working south from Bayeux, with the 7th Armoured Division carrying out several well-executed armoured thrusts, backed by the 50th Division.

On the Canadians' left, the 3rd British Division, in very confined space, endured endless shelling from the Germans around Caen. A cluster of tall factory chimneys at Colombelles, over the Orne from Caen, gave the enemy almost complete observation of the divisional area and although every attempt was made to knock down the chimneys, they were never destroyed.

Even 1st Corps H.Q., which was at Douvres in the 3rd British area, came under shell-fire several times, much to the amusement—yes, amusement—of the grand group of solid British officers who served in that fine headquarters.

But by far the most perilous area on Second Army front was in the bridgehead won by the 6th Airborne Division east of the Orne and northeast of Caen.

The 51st Highland Division had been sent over the river to join the airborne troops and it shared the ordeal with them for weeks. It is the story of the sky men that I want to relate, however, particularly the epic deeds of the 1st Canadian Parachute Battalion in the Division.

I knew the Canadian Parachute Battalion had landed on D-Day morning and I knew a number of officers and men in the unit, having visited them on Salisbury Plain when they were training for this operation. But I had no word about how they had made out until about D-plus-five when some of the British correspondents who had dropped with the airborne forces, and whom I rate the gamest reporters on our front, came back to Courseulles to file some stories over our wireless.

Leonard Mosley, who was writing for the Kemsley newspapers in Britain, said: "You ought to go over and see those Canadian boys. They have done a simply terrific job. Your friend 'Brad' is expecting you."

"Brad" was the commanding officer. He was Lieutenant-Colonel Bradbrooke from Saskatoon, and back in 1941 when he was a captain with the Saskatoon Light Infantry machine-gun battalion we had gone to Spitsbergen together. He was commanding machine-gunner there, but later he joined this Canadian parachute battalion and became its colonel.

In England before the invasion, I had told "Brad" I was going with the infantry but would get to his outfit as quickly as I could.

The 3rd Division was "priority one" for those first few weeks, but then I tried to get to the Canadian airborne soldiers. I asked one morning at 1st Corps if I could get over the Orne to them and an intelligence officer said: "You can get to them if you are bullet-proof. I'd bet ten to one you won't make it even then if you try."

He wasn't being pessimistic about the Canadians' position, but the route to their positions was a couple of miles of hell. The Airborne Division had landed between midnight and dawn on D-Day morning on the east banks of the Orne River between Caen and the Bay of the Seine and also at the vital bridges at Benouville, five miles northeast of Caen. Its troops had seized the bridges intact and had held their bridgehead on the left flank of the Second Army sector. Every German attempt to deprive them of their positions was beaten off and few fights of airborne troops equal the heroism of the 6th Airborne Division.

Divisional H.Q. was set up at Ranville, a few hundred yards beyond the east end of the Benouville bridge and even Headquarters was shelled and mortared incessantly. The airborne troops were holding a perimeter about three miles in depth around Ranville and one German attack followed another. It was very close country here and the battle developed into guerilla warfare with man hunting man through the woods and along the narrow lanes. Snipers infested the trees. The fighting was chaotic and in the rest of the beach-head they talked in words of awe of the troops "over the Orne".

It took three attempts for me to get to the Canadian parachutists, for the Benouville bridge was shelled with methodical persistence by the Germans who could direct the fire from the Colombelles chimney lookouts. Strangely enough, the shell-fire never wrecked the bridge. Actually it was two bridges in line, one crossing the Caen canal and the other the Orne, a distance of about five hundred yards in all, with a narrow island between the two waterways.

The first time we got to within two miles of Benouville at the western edge of the bridge, when a concentration of shell-fire blasted the town and the bridge area. It kept up and we gave up the idea of reaching the Canadians that day. I returned to Creully to the jibes of my colleagues.

The next time I got into Benouville, racing down the last mile of straight road with its line of burlap and canvas screens along the south side to block the vision of the German spotters at the Colombelles chimneys. They seemed to lean right over the road although they were four miles away!

It was just after the Beny-sur-Mer shelling and my nerves were not very steady. As we entered Benouville, a truck ahead of our jeep pulled down a signal wire stretched across the road and the wire ripped a line of tile off a roof over our head. It sounded for all the world like a mortar bomb exploding beside us. Then a couple of shells landed near the bridge, and without more ado I postponed the trip.

But the third one was to be final, and Shap and I set off. We had travelled together most of the way through Sicily and teaming up in France again we had found our luck had held. This time it was right on the beam. We went into Benouville and stopped to speak to a military policeman by the first bridge. "Sure, go right ahead," he said with a grin. "You'll be all right over the first bridge, but when you hit the second, start to pray."

That was the attitude of the British Tommies in this area. However, over the first bridge we went, and then we sailed over the second and not a shot was fired. The Canadians were in the woods along the banks of the Orne, north of the road, so we turned left along a trail, going through the gun lines of the airborne division. The airborne troops had their small howitzers dug in along the river banks. This was practically all the artillery they had had through these rough weeks, apart from support they received from 3rd British Division guns and 1st Corps artillery from the west bank of the Orne.

We poked along through the woods and the fields until we found the Canadian battalion, half-way between Ranville and the mouth of the Orne. They were supposed to be out of the line resting for a few days, but their camp was within easy mortar range of the Germans crowding the bridgehead. We found them dug in as they would be at the actual front. It was some place for a rest, but for them it was a paradise of quiet and comfort after Le Mesnil.

I met Lieutenant-Colonel Bradbrooke again and some of his officers—Major Jeff Nicklin of Winnipeg, a famed football player with the Blue Bombers, Captain John Hanson of Montreal and Captain Peter Griffin of Toronto.

The Colonel told me the story of the battalion, as heroic a one as I heard during the French campaign, and he particularly told me about the long fight at Le Mesnil. This was the story I wrote at that time:

For eleven wild days and nights the 1st Canadian Parachute Battalion in the British 6th Airborne Division fought German infantry and snipers on this incredible battle-ground east of the Orne and northeast of Caen.

It was savage, chaotic fighting in closely-wooded country which the Canadians call "squirt gun territory". After dropping by parachute before dawn on D-Day, this unit took up positions right on the outside perimeter of the beach-head gained by the airborne division east of the river, and there the Canadians stood and battled the enemy. They were shelled and mortared mercilessly and German infantry stormed at them but they did not yield a yard. For eleven days they held the vital cross-roads and the little hamlet of Le Mesnil on the main Cabourg-Caen highway, and two and a half miles east of the bridges which cross the Caen canal and the River Orne at Benouville.

This is one of the hottest spots in the entire Allied beach-head, and in these green woods of Le Mesnil and in the ditches along the hedgerows, these Canadians showed unbreakable spirit.

They could not be beaten. Even when they were cut off and had to be supplied by air, they never wavered and they stuck on the cross-roads, grimly determined men from every province of the Dominion, wearing their maroon berets and loose camouflaged battle-smocks. They fought like men inspired.

The battalion had gone to its airdrome in England on the evening of June 5 and got into Douglas transports about 11.30 at night, taking off for France. In a high wind, squadron after squadron of troop-laden planes winged south past the invasion fleet pounding through the heavy seas in the Channel below. As they crossed the Normandy coast at the mouth of the Orne, heavy flak burst around the planes and inside, the parachutists were knocked about as the aircraft weaved in over selected dropping zones. It was one A.M. on June 6 when the first Canadian company dropped in the Varaville area, three miles southwest of Cabourg.

Here the Canadians had their first fight. A German headquarters was located in Varaville and it was the assignment of this company to wipe out the headquarters. They did it with machine-gun and grenades, cleaning out the town as well.

Captain Hanson, who was with the Royal Montreal Regiment before joining the parachutists, was with this company and he said: "We dropped in a swamp east of Varaville and it took us a while to get the mix-up straightened out. However, some of our boys teamed up and we linked with some British paratroops who were in the wrong place. Gradually we worked through the bogs to the highway leading to Varaville."

There were only about fifty parachutists in this group, but at dawn they went into Varaville and first attacked and captured the big château which was the officers' mess for the German H.Q. They were fired on heavily by a German anti-tank gun and machine-guns.

The company commander was killed by this fire,

coming from a huge pillbox at the cross-roads in the
town. There were twelve machine-guns in this strongpoint and while the airborne sappers blew the bridge
at Varaville, the parachutists surrounded the pillbox.
There was a fierce exchange of fire and finally they
picked off the German captain in command. Shortly
afterwards the pillbox surrendered and forty-two
Germans came out with their hands up. The Canadians were then relieved by British commandos who
came up on bicycles after landing from the sea, and
Hanson and his men went down the road to Le Mesnil
for the struggle there.

Hours before the parachutists got into Varaville,
Major Nicklin had created a one-man sensation there
by dropping alone and by mistake right in the centre
of the German-garrisoned town! His parachute caught
on the roof of a house and the husky major dangled
down the side of the wall as the Germans, thrown into
utter confusion by the airborne landings in the area,
scurried about the town. Several of them spotted him
and fired at him but he cut himself loose and took
cover. He looked around for other paratroops, but not
a single one was in the town yet. He was trapped alone
in Varaville. He worked his way from building to
building with platoons of excited Germans stalking
him. It took him an hour to get clear of the buildings
and get into the fields where he linked up with other
Canadians and made his way to the rendezvous at
Le Mesnil.

While the major part of the battalion came down
in the Varaville area after the first company, Captain
Griffin and a small band of parachutists carried out an
almost suicidal task deep in German territory. Their
job was to land near Robehomme, nine miles east of
the Orne and the farthest eastern point of any of the

invasion forces. They were to blow up a bridge over
the Dives River there, hold high ground for several
days and then withdraw to the main Canadian defence
position at Le Mesnil.

Despite the fact that Griffin and his troops were
badly scattered when they landed, they carried out this
job, and then they got back to share in the stand at
Le Mesnil.

"Although we were scattered about in that boggy
country, little groups gathered together and finally
we were up to strength of one hundred and sixty men,"
said Captain Griffin, who with Captain Hanson was
later awarded the Military Cross. "Our sappers blew
the bridge okay and then we got back on high ground
west of Robehomme. On the afternoon of the second
day the Germans came at us and tried to get across
the river which blocked their path. We got a Vickers
gun on them and there was one of our platoons by the
blown bridge. Every time the Germans tried to make
the river crossing, we let them have it plenty. They
never set foot on our side, and then stopped trying.
Meantime we carried out fighting patrols around us
and raided westward into the German positions
between us and Le Mesnil where we knew our other
men were holding out."

This Canadian outpost was ordered back finally to
Le Mesnil.

As for the main part of the battalion, the high wind
and the heavy flak prevented them coming down with
planned precision on the dropping zone near Varaville. Instead, they came down all over the place, in
woods, on roads, in towns and in the muddy bogs
dotted with ponds. Companies were scattered and it
took hours for groups to collect and for order to be
brought out of this inevitable confusion in the dark-

ness. Lieutenant-Colonel Bradbrooke himself came down in a bog, all alone, and plunged into three and a half feet of water. Then he met his intelligence officer and they hustled to a rendezvous point near Varaville, from where they went four miles down the highway in a southwesterly direction to Le Mesnil. This was the point the Canadians had been told to hold at all costs, and there they dug their slit-trenches and got strong positions ready in a brick factory.

In Le Mesnil the Canadians were sniped at from the buildings when they established themselves about six A.M. and the Colonel posted a six-pounder anti-tank gun, which had come in by air, on the cross-roads. Only a dozen rounds of ammunition were available for the gun, but with eight shells the gunners drove the snipers out of the buildings and the situation was well in hand.

During the first day, more and more men from the scattered Canadian unit drifted into Le Mesnil and for three and four days afterwards, they kept coming in. By D-Day evening there were two hundred parachutists in Le Mesnil ready for the enemy. The Germans came at them the next day and were beaten off by machine-guns and rifles. On the second day, the Canadians received artillery support and before long the unit's mortars and Vickers machine-guns reached them there. The Germans put in a bang-up attack on this second day. The Colonel described it as being "a dilly". The Canadians hurled it back too, and killed dozens of Germans in the woods and on the roads.

"The country around Le Mesnil is very close, with its ditches and hedges, and it was just a perfect position for determined men like ours," the Colonel said. "We were just one little pocket out on the end of nowhere but after three days of this rough going we had three hundred men which was quite a good force. We held there for eleven days and the Germans threw in many attacks. But we also took the offensive and sent out strong patrols to the little towns outside the perimeter, giving the Jerries a bloody nose a couple of times. The Germans were methodical as the devil in their attacks but with our mortars and Vickers we waited for them regularly and knocked Hell out of their infantry.

"Between two and three hundred dead Huns piled up in the fields in front of us, and for days we could not even get out to bury them because of incessant sniping from those monkeys hiding in the trees. They were so methodical they even came down the same ditches several nights running and we machine-gunned them every time. We found them following our patrols into our positions too and caught them that way a couple of times good and proper."

The Canadians' position was under shattering German artillery fire between attacks but the unit's entire invasion task was carried out, as was the whole task of the 6th Airborne Division in this highly successful air-landing operation.

The Canadians proved their toughness, and their hard training paid off for them, for there were only three cases of battle exhaustion during the fight. Some wounded men went back into the line after getting patched up and one casualty was evacuated right to the beach but went absent without leave and rejoined the battalion at Le Mesnil despite his wounds.

Following a few days' rest after the eleven-day battle, the battalion again went into the perimeter line at Le Mesnil, but nothing again could be as tough as those first eleven days.

*   *   *   *

We had one capsule action right in the centre of the Second Army beach-head which was a sparkling little scrap and like a movie to watch. It was the fight for the German radar station between Douvres and Beny-sur-Mer, where two hundred Germans were holding out in a strong underground position about a mile square, all ringed in with barbed wire and mine fields.

The radar station was of no particular value to the enemy, for it was completely surrounded, but with the blind stubbornness that Germans can show, the garrison would not give in. The Germans had resisted there since D-Day. The Canadian assault troops had attacked it on the morning and afternoon of D-Day but found it too formidable and by-passed it. A few days later Highlanders of the 51st Division attacked it but they could not crack the position.

Finally, a Royal Marine Commando unit, which had been begging 1st Corps for the chance to clean it up, was given the job and on June 17, twelve days after the invasion, stormed the radar station with the support of assault engineers.

And this was one battle we really had a chance to watch. Normandy had proved to be the worst theatre in this war to see actions first-hand, for there were no high hills or mountains on which we could perch and get a panoramic view of the fighting as we did so often in Tunisia, Sicily and Italy.

In Normandy we were lucky if we could see even part of the action without being directly embroiled in the actual fighting, for the battleground inevitably was a series of rolling hills where there was no observation to speak of.

But for the radar station fight that warm Saturday afternoon we had ringside seats. The three-dollar ones

were in the big church steeple at Douvres from where
you could look right down on the German position
less than a mile away. Most of the 1st Corps staff
seemed to be crowded into this steeple along with
about a dozen war correspondents, and Charlie Lynch
of Reuters really gave it a press-box touch by taking
his typewriter into the steeple with him and writing
a blow-by-blow description of the actions as if he were
covering a football game.

The fight opened with artillery blasting the German
position over open sights. The shells screeched over
the fields and soon the few shattered buildings among
the underground chambers were smoking, blazing.

The assault engineers in their assortment of
armoured vehicles moved in on the enemy. Their
tanks with heavy chain flails on their bows went
through the wire and the flails beat paths through the
mine fields, with mines exploding every few feet.

Tank guns roared and a few German guns fired
back to add to the inferno, which was noisy enough
for a divisional attack.

Several breaches were made through the wire and
the mine fields and the commandos went to work.
Firing from the hip, they raced into the German
stronghold, fierce, ruthless fighting men with their
faces smeared dark with smudge and wearing their
green commando berets. These men disdained steel
helmets.

Moving among the burning buildings they broke
into the underground forts and within an hour it was
all over. We left the church and trailed the commandos into the position just as the first prisoners
were coming down the road. They had not put up
much of a fight this time, although their resistance had
been stern in the other attacks made on the place.

They had given up, the first of so many thousands of Germans who were to throw in the towel to the Second Army men, in the long advance across France.

Dirty and dishevelled, they trudged down the road past the grinning, triumphant commandos and the assault engineers. After many days of bitter fighting in the beach-head, this Saturday afternoon clean-up job, done with practically no casualties, was a real fillip to the spirits of our troops.

*   *   *   *

The spirit of the beach-head forces never flagged, all through those fantastic first weeks of the campaign. I have seldom seen troops so confident, so assured, so certain that their victory was inevitable.

One of the finest expressions of the confidence everyone felt was the visit of the King to the beach-head. The campaign was not two weeks old before His Majesty came to Normandy. He visited several formations, and at General Montgomery's tactical H.Q. at Creully he held the most unusual investiture of this war. On the lawn of a château where the Army Group Commander had his caravan, the King made General Keller a Commander of the British Empire and also decorated a number of British officers and men for gallantry.

The ceremony was utterly simple, without red carpets and bands. The King, wearing his naval uniform, stood there in the open, while special Spitfire patrols droned overhead, and honoured these men.

For General Keller, the award of the C.B.E. was a tribute to his work in preparing his 3rd Division for the assault and in carrying out invasion experiments in the long months of training. The General had done well and his handling of the Division right through to Caen brought much well-deserved praise.

*   *   *   *

General Keller had a fine staff with him at Headquarters and the success of the Division in training and in battle was due in good measure to the work they did and the skilful way they directed the combat troops and the services in the campaign.

The senior officers were all anonymous during the fighting but they can be named now and these are some of the officers who worked with General Keller: Brigadier P. A. S. Todd of Ottawa was the chief artillery officer directing the strong artillery support of the Division; Colonel M. C. Watson of Toronto was head of the Division's medical services; Lieutenant-Colonel G. O. Gamble of Ottawa and Toronto was chief of the signals, and Lieutenant-Colonel R. J. Cassidy of Ottawa led the divisional engineers. The very competent "A and Q", handling the Division's supply and administrative problems, was Lieutenant-Colonel Ernest Coté of Edmonton. Lieutenant-Colonel Dew was the ordnance chief.

I have mentioned Lieutenant-Colonel Mingay, and among others who served on the Division staff through the heavy fighting were Major Strickland, Major Seamark, Major Fess—whom I've also mentioned before—Captain Glenholme Black of Montreal, Captain Ross McMaster of Montreal, Major Pat Haszard of Trail, B.C., and Calgary, Major John Craig of Toronto, Captain Bill Lovering of Montreal, Captain Dudley Dawson of Toronto, Captain Danny Osborne of Winnipeg, Major Hugh Kennedy of Windsor, Ont., who won the Military Cross on the Dieppe raid, Captain Earl Olmsted of Ottawa, Lieutenant Gordon Bradshaw of Toronto, Lieutenant Charles Askwith of Montreal and Captain Charles Turton of Montreal.

V

THE BATTLE FOR CAEN

By THE END of the third week in Normandy, the Second Army was ready to take the offensive and begin operations to exploit inland and break the Germans' hold on the pivot point at Caen.

The beach-head was an amazing place, for in the history of British arms there had never been so many men or so much *matériel* packed into such a confined space. Four army corps were in the narrow beach-head—three British, plus the Canadian corps—and another British corps was moving in rapidly. In addition there were masses of army and army group troops, beach organization troops, along with the various air components. Airfields had been rapidly built within the beach-head and fighters were flying off them shortly after the landing, although some of the airfields were under shell-fire for some weeks.

At Second Army H.Q. they talked of getting more "elbow room". They most certainly needed it. Originally it had been planned to use the areas in and around Caen during the build-up but this area was still in enemy hands and the problem of finding space for all the forces was a ticklish one.

Practically every field in the beach-head had some unit in it. The roads were jammed with convoys of trucks, tanks and half-tracks as men and material kept flooding off the ships. They piled up like water at a dam.

The British corps, which had been given the task of breaking out of the beach-head southwest of Caen in the first of a series of operations which led to the capture of the city, massed behind the Canadians who

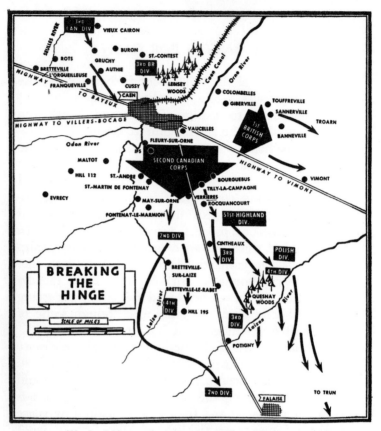

were still holding the Bretteville area. Every day
more and more guns moved up for the great barrage
which was to precede the infantry and tank attack to
be carried out by the 11th Armoured Division and
the 15th Scottish Division. They were to pass through
the Canadians in the Bretteville district and strike
south to the Odon, cross it and swing to the Orne. This
should eventually place them south of Caen. The
Guards Armoured Division was to follow up the other
two divisions.

The attack went in on June 26, after a diversionary thrust by the 49th Division on the right flank. The 49th, which had fought in the ill-starred Norwegian campaign in the spring of 1940 and had served for a long and dreary period in Iceland, battled its way forward through the Fontenay district, southeast of Bayeux and ten miles due west of Caen.

The next morning at 7.30 on the dot, the Second Army barrage for the corps attack began. More than 650 guns let go with one terrific blast and for more than two hours this mass of artillery raked a path for the infantry and tanks.

The infantry plodded through the fields of red poppies in the crisp, damp morning air, and a mile south of Bretteville the battle was joined on the farm fields and in the orchards of that war-torn district.

The guns grumbled and rumbled. We had never heard anything like this since D-Day morning when the coast was bombarded by many of these same guns now pounding away here in this barrage.

The artillery work of the British Army and particularly these devastating barrages had been one of its greatest strengths since El Alamein. General Montgomery was never the general to use the same tactics twice in a row, but he had a pattern for his artillery preparation to any attack, and the only variation it had was to become larger and more intense.

This barrage supporting the British corps was the first of many that were fired in the Caen-Falaise operations and they were a tremendous factor in the victories won. It was the same in Sicily and Italy. Every major attack was preceded by a thundering artillery shoot by field and medium guns. The Germans could never match such barrages; they never attempted to, in my experience. The Germans would shell fiercely, but it was nothing compared to the fire from twenty or thirty regiments that we put on enemy positions time and time again.

The enemy was skilled, though, in the defensive use of his artillery. The long-barrelled 88mm. gun was a potent menace to any attack, for with its great range it could lie back and carry out direct shoots against attacking forces. These 88s were the thing that could stop our tanks quickly. The Germans also had a good number of self-propelled 88mm. guns, which looked a great deal like Panther tanks and which often were mistaken for them. The Panthers themselves mounted 88mm. guns and with this arsenal, limited as it was in France and in the Mediterranean, the Germans were dangerous opponents once our forces came within range for direct shoots.

The enemy in Normandy also showed all his old skill with the regular mortar and machine-gun, and the multiple-barrelled *Nebelwerfer* mortar, which troops called "Moaning Minnie", made its appearance early in the French campaign.

The first objective for the British corps was the village of Cheux, three miles south of Bretteville, and in twenty-four hours the tough British Tommies captured the village. The attack created a salient right into the German positions and the British came under fire from three directions. Grimly, they battled south, crossed the Caen-Villers-Bocage highway and reached the Odon, seven miles southwest of Caen. The Germans mounted counter-attacks. Some of them were broken up by our artillery fire; but some slammed right into the salient and the fighting was long and bloody.

The 15th Scottish and the 11th Armoured, as well as the Guards Armoured, which shortly joined in the battle, were fighting their first actions, and it was a grim ordeal as they maintained the salient and struggled forward. Around the clock the guns roared and flamed.

The weather turned bad and deluges of rain beat down on the battle-field. But the battle raged on. The British tanks crossed the Odon and struck out into the open rolling country between the Odon and the Orne. This was supposed to be what was called "good tank country". But it proved to be just what the German gunners with their 88mm. artillery wanted. The fighting was hot and heavy south of the Odon around Maltot, Hill 112 and Evrecy.

The enemy had more than 150 tanks massed around the salient and they threw them into battle in groups of twenty or thirty. The gallant British soldiers kept slugging away at these strong enemy forces and the ferocious fighting continued all week.

The long-range objective on the Orne was not reached but the first break from the beach-head had been made. Thin, gaunt, intense General Dempsey held a press conference at his headquarters after the Odon was crossed and he told us: "I am completely confident in the situation here now. We have got to fight the Hun and kill him and defeat him in battle. This is as good a place to kill him as any."

The day before Dempsey spoke to us, I felt that Lieutenant-Colonel Murphy had been somewhat enthusiastic when he had said, as the Second Army spokesman, that the Germans on the Odon River line and beyond were in "complete confusion". When you went down to see the enemy in this confusion you found that there was a very real and grim battle going on and that if the enemy was in such turmoil he was doing a pretty fair job of fighting too.

The salient held and, although the advance was limited to seven or eight miles, the operation had been successful in that it brought the enemy to battle in good strength and his forces had been whittled down materially.

Now other Second Army operations were to be launched.

*　　　*　　　*　　　*

North and northwest of Caen, the British and Canadian troops had been nibbling away at the German defence perimeter screening the city. They were not supposed to do any more than that at this time. It involved strong patrols day and night, some local actions and a considerable amount of shelling and mortaring by our batteries, which invariably brought salvos of German shells and mortar bombs in return.

Various plans were being considered to crack the Caen defences and each day the intention changed. Information from patrols would alter situations drastically and the 3rd Canadian Division, as well as the 3rd British, had to be restrained in their desire to strike at the defence perimeter before the time was ripe.

The 3rd Canadian H.Q. was at Thaon in the Mue valley three miles behind the front at Les Buissons, and each day that I called, there seemed to be some new scheme afoot. However, after the fighting in the Odon salient decreased and the British had firmed up their gains there, it was decided to send the Canadians against Carpiquet village and the airfield, west of Caen.

This was believed to be one of the most heavily defended districts in the entire area. The airdrome had not been used since D-Day, but the enemy were strongly entrenched in the village and around the airdrome, with a number of concrete fortifications adding to the defence line.

Thirty to forty tanks kept moving around the area and a number of gun and mortar positions were on high ground behind the airdrome. Carpiquet also was protected from the north by the German positions in the towns of Authie, Gruchy and Buron which dominated the hollow where Carpiquet and the airdrome were located. All approaches to this defended locality were over open wheat fields.

Canadian patrols had scouted the area for two weeks and found out considerable information about enemy positions, but Carpiquet was still a great deal of a mystery. In the first few weeks of the campaign Carpiquet was jammed with German ack-ack guns and a curtain of flak used to rise, black and ugly in the sky, when our planes would fly over. The flak guns had evidently been taken away now.

The Regina Rifles, with the Winnipeg Rifles and the Canadian Scottish, had moved into position in the Mue River valley east of Bretteville, holding towns like Villeneuve and Rots, and they did a good deal of the patrolling to bring in information on which the Carpiquet attack was based.

Lieutenant Lorenzo Bergeron, a French-speaking officer from Montreal and a member of the Regina Rifles, did several patrols right into Carpiquet which were phenomenal. He became a legend on the front for his skilful and daring patrolling, and later led the first Canadian patrol over the muddy Orne at Caen.

His specialty was night work, and one night he crept through the wheat fields to the fringe of Carpiquet airdrome. A full moon was shining but he crept right across the wide airdrome into the end of Carpiquet village, noting every enemy position as he went along. He was challenged by German sentries but ghosted back again to his own lines. He did the same job another night but was delayed around the village until after daylight, when he began to return. Nobody fired at him. He got up and walked to the railway tracks which skirt the village and standing there waved his handkerchief to draw fire so he might know of some more enemy positions. The Germans would not fire. He walked back along the tracks to his own lines in disgust!

By July 3, the reconnaissances had been completed and the attack was to be made the following morning at five A.M. Brigadier Blackader's brigade was given the job of capturing the village and the Royal Winnipeg Rifles, temporarily attached to this brigade, were to take the hangars on the south side of the airfield. Tanks of the Fort Garry Horse commanded by Lieutenant-Colonel R. E. A. Morton of Calgary and Winnipeg, were to support the infantry. Troops of the British 43rd Division were to operate on the Canadian right flank, south of the airdrome to reduce the fire from positions there.

In the chilly dawn the attack began with another thunderous artillery barrage and the five Canadian units moved towards Carpiquet behind the screen of bursting high explosives. They advanced from the village of Marselet, only a mile and a half west of Carpiquet, over an area which had no cover at all.

Rocket-firing typhoons drove on the German positions, sailing out of the dull skies like black meteors and firing their rockets from about two thousand feet up. A plume of white smoke marked the path of the projectiles. From a slope behind Rots, I watched the attack go in, but it was like most of the other attacks in this area—you could see very little. Our hill gave some observation but soon the battle-field was wreathed in smoke from the shelling.

The Regiment de la Chaudière, commanded by Lieutenant-Colonel J. E. G. P. Mathieu, advanced with the North Shores to lead the attack on the village. Lieutenant-Colonel D. B. Buell of Vancouver and Montreal was leading the North Shores. The Queen's Own Rifles, under buoyant, rugged Lieutenant-Colonel "Jock" Sprague of Toronto, followed them closely.

Visibility was limited at times to ten feet as the infantry went through the smoke over the open wheat fields and up the gradual slope that leads to Carpiquet. Some German machine-guns opened up on them and then you would hear the hard clatter of our Bren guns. Mortars and shells crashed down among the three battalions but on they went with Fort Garry tanks firing as they rolled beside them.

Vickers machine-gunners of the Cameron Highlanders of Ottawa pelted the German positions with bullets, firing over the heads of the advancing infantry.

The Chauds and the North Shores reached the hangars on the northwest side of the airfield and from there fought their way into the village. Street fighting went on among the shattered houses of Carpiquet, where there wasn't a place left standing. By eight A.M. the village had been captured and the Canadians were clearing the last of the defenders out of strong concrete forts at the west end of the village. Major Doug Cunnington of Calgary, former personal assistant to General McNaughton when he was Army Commander, was commanding a company of Royal Canadian Engineers with the infantry, and his men located one fort which still contained twenty Germans.

They refused at first to come out, and the sappers went to work. They first poured gasoline down the ventilators and set fire to it, trying to smoke out the enemy. They still did not come. So they put big explosive charges against the roof of the fort and literally blew the twenty Germans out of the place. They tumbled out wildly when the explosions went off and fell into the waiting arms of the Queen's Own.

The three battalions, with their tanks, sappers and some Cameron Highlanders, dug in to hold the village against the bombardment and counter-attacks that were certain to follow.

The Winnipegs, however, had not fared so well. They were shelled and mortared in the Marselet woods even before they began the attack, and all the way over the open ground towards the hangars on the south side of the airfield they came under savage fire. Somehow they kept going. Their orders were to capture the hangars and they would make a desperate attempt to do it, despite their already heavy casualties.

The regiment did reach the first cluster of hangars, but the enemy fire became worse and worse. Much of it seemed to come from a ridge behind the hangars which it had been hoped might be dominated by troops of the 43rd Division on the right flank. They had not been able to get as far as they had wanted and the guns and mortars on the slope had not been silenced.

The Winnipegs also were under fire from about twenty dug-in tanks among the administration buildings at the eastern end of the airfield. Still they fought on, with some Garry tanks with them. They fought on a good part of the day. It would have been madness to leave them there longer. They were withdrawn into the Marselet woods again and the airfield once more was in German hands.

(TOP): *He's away! This remark-able picture, snapped at 500th of a second, caught a Canadian paratrooper going "over the side" of his aircraft.*

(LOWER): *F. O. Robinson of Mont-real, shot down, hid in the woods and joined Canadian paratroopers, who were the first to land in France. (Photo by Sgt. Dave Reynolds of Toronto, who jumped with the para-troopers and made his way back with pictures.)*

The Germans then hit Carpiquet with everything they had in the area. For hours on end they shelled it with guns of all calibres; they threw hundreds and hundreds of mortar bombs into the rubble piles; they machine-gunned the village and they sniped everyone that moved.

The Canadians went deep to ground but the bombardment was almost more than human nerves could stand. During the first night the Germans hurled four counter-attacks against the village and each one was repelled. The enemy struck with tanks and with infantry who followed up the armour shouting their heads off in the night. The Canadians beat off the tanks with anti-tank guns and Piat mortars and mowed down the infantry. Some enemy tanks got right into the village where they were destroyed. About ten tanks were knocked out that night.

All the next day the village was pounded again by guns and mortars.

The Carpiquet garrison was making the most gallant stand on the whole front. On the third day I went in to see the troops and get the story. I drove down to Bretteville and on to the Marselet woods where Major Geoff Boone of Toronto, the brigade major at Brigade Headquarters located in the woods, gave Captain Golding and myself some tips on how to negotiate the mile and a half over the open stretch of road from there to Carpiquet.

"Go like a rocket, for you're under observation from the machine-gunners in the hangars on the south side of the field," he said, "but watch the dust you kick up, for it is certain to draw fire."

Lieutenant-Colonel Freddie Clifford of Hamilton, whose field regiment was supporting the Carpiquet force, wasn't very cheerful. "The Huns are spasmodic in their firing today," he said. "They go for an hour and then they let up for one. How about staying around here for a cup of tea?"

I would have, but I knew Ralph Allen had been into Carpiquet in the morning and we didn't want to be beaten on the story. Ralph came back to our camp at noon, before I set out, with a story that Carpiquet was a village of hell. The fire was terrible. You could hardly get to the village and when you got there you wanted to get out right away.

I found out later that Ralph was spinning a tale to dissuade others from going to the village that day— which was, I suppose, ethical—but with what he had said still not doubted in my mind, I set off along the road in our jeep with Goldie. I was feeling very subdued and hesitant about this latest news-gathering expedition.

A couple of our tanks were on the edge of Marselet woods and they looked too ready for business to please me. The road, flat and straight, stretched out ahead of us and the driver put the gas to the floor.

Dodging the bomb craters in the macadam, we tore along for Carpiquet, keeping our eyes on the south hangars that looked so very close. Half a mile gone; another half a mile; we're on the last stretch. We wheeled into the Queen's Own sector among the ruined buildings, and I've never been more surprised in any front-line position. The riflemen were sitting around by the buildings, smoking, yarning, eating, even sleeping. Tank crews idled by their tanks alongside the hangars.

I had expected to spend my time in Carpiquet leaping from dug-out to slit-trench, but it was nearly as quiet as the base areas.

Luckily we had hit a lull. It all seemed magically

unreal. Germans were in the hangars to the south five hundred yards away; they were in the administration buildings and manning dug-in tanks at the east end of the airfield four hundred yards away; they were in Franqueville and Authie just over the railway tracks half a mile to the north. No, it was not a healthy spot, but these Canadian troops, inured to the bombardment and veteran campaigners, now took it right in their stride.

I went into a dug-out where Lieutenant-Colonel Sprague had made his Queen's Own H.Q. He was fast asleep in a corner, and one of his officers, Lieutenant Bob Rae of Toronto, was there keeping in touch with the companies and brigade over the field telephone and handling battalion H.Q. business which goes on even when units are smack on the front.

Bob Rae was a youthful officer, with an easy, infectious smile and he certainly put me at ease without saying a word. We sat and talked about the Queen's Own attack and I could not get a thought out of my mind: This is like a setting for "Journey's End". It had the dug-out, the timbers, the mellow light and casual talk of the front-line troops.

Lieutenant-Colonel Morton came into the dug-out. With him was his adjutant, Captain Jim Fraser of Altamont, Man. They told me about their tanks. What a job they had done! They were the Carpiquet garrison's mobile artillery, and the infantry thought the world of the tank crews. This wasn't unusual, though, for in the Canadian army there was perfect co-ordination between infantry and armour, probably as good as in any force in the world.

The eerie stillness that hung over Carpiquet was a sinister kind of atmosphere, and Rae said: "Don't let it kid you; we have a couple more rough days here and then it will be over."

I knew what he was talking about. In two days the big attack was to be made directly on Caen by British and Canadian troops, and Carpiquet would be relieved.

Outside the dug-out, I watched our artillery from over by Rots shelling Franqueville and Authie to the north, and clouds of brown dust and smoke billowed up as the shells pounded the towns.

Goldie and I walked down into the village and stopped to talk to some Chauds—a group of young lads digging a trench. We talked about the battle, and I felt I was holding them up. Suddenly I realized they were digging graves for a dozen of their men. Grey blankets covered these gallant men of the Chaudières, who had given their lives that Carpiquet might be held.

This was the terrible cost of war. Throughout the war I never got used to the sight of death. It made me shake inside to see our men lying sprawled on a fresh battle-field. Perhaps I was too sensitive to it, but there was tragedy in every body, in every wounded soldier.

We walked about the eastern end of the village, talking to troops, getting their stories. I was struck, as I always was, by the wonderful resilience of the Canadian fighting man. He can go through the worst terrors of war and in a few hours he is grinning, wise-cracking, complaining about the grub. That has been his strength. He is not so much a fatalist as a man who can find something, somewhere, to laugh about or make some crack about. He primarily has a sense of humour deeply ingrained in him. That has carried a lot of our men through a lot of fighting. And it is a real achievement to find humour in situations of war. It takes courage. The Canadians had plenty of that. Plenty!

Goldie and I left Carpiquet after we figured we'd learned enough about the fighting there and raced again along the straight, open stretch back to Marselet. One lone jeep was poor pickings for the Germans, I suppose, and they let us go by without interference. Then we looked back at Carpiquet. The area around the Queen's Own H.Q. billowed with yellow dust. The bombardment had started again.

It kept up spasmodically all the rest of the day and all the next day and then the trials of Carpiquet were over. The attack was made on Caen.

A three-division attack had been mounted by the Second Army to capture Caen, and it was as neatly executed an operation as any the army carried out in France.

The plan called for the 3rd British Division to attack on July 8 over its old D-Day battle-ground at Lebisey Wood and enter Caen from the north; the British 59th Division, which had been brought into the line secretly between the 3rd British and the 3rd Canadian, was to capture several towns including Galmanche and St.-Contest on the right of the 3rd British; and a brigade of the 3rd Canadian was to break through the German defence system at the three neighbouring towns of Buron, Gruchy and Authie on the right of the 59th.

The brigade was to link up with the Carpiquet garrison and then swing east to enter Caen from the west, while another Canadian brigade cleared German positions north of the highway running from Caen to Bayeux.

The operation worked out almost entirely as planned, and on July 9 Caen was captured by troops of the 3rd British and 3rd Canadian Divisions.

The attack was preceded by the bombing of

German defence positions immediately north of Caen just before dark on July 7. This raid was in the nature of an experiment to determine whether heavy night bombers of Bomber Command could be satisfactorily employed in direct support of ground troops, and the results proved so good that the heavies were subsequently used on every attack in France where a strong defence line had to be shattered.

In the late evening twilight, about eleven P.M., the Lancasters and Halifaxes streamed out from England. Flying through a spotty belt of flak in the Caen area and along the Orne, they droned over the target and, in the wake of the Pathfinders who marked the target with a shower of flares, they dropped their bombs north of Caen.

Six or seven hundred heavies plied methodically over Caen that evening and for the troops in the beachhead it was the most magnificent spectacle of Allied air power they had seen.

For the troops opposing the British and Canadians —the 12th *S.S.* Hitler Youth Division, the 16th German Air Force Division, an infantry formation formed from air force personnel, and the 21st *Panzer* Division—it was a devastating surprise and shock.

Before dawn, at 4.30 A.M., the two British infantry divisions began their attack. They made good progress from the start, with an unusually heavy artillery barrage helping them on their way. At 7.30 A.M. the Canadian brigade crossed its start line, heading for its three village targets northwest of Caen.

The formation was Brigadier Cunningham's Highland brigade which had held the Les Buissons area since D-plus-one. It had never come out of the line and now it took the offensive with a vengeance, knowing it was going against the bitterest foes the Canadians had on this front—the 12th *S.S.* Division.

The 12th *S.S.*, full of young Nazis who had been taught for years to kill, and knew little else, had been at grips with the 3rd Division since the day after landing. These *S.S.* troops wore loose knee-length battle smocks, dotted with a mottled camouflage, and the Canadians dubbed them the "zoot-suit boys".

Many of them were youths of seventeen and eighteen, steeped in the Nazi creed and trained through their boyhood for battle. Troops of this division carried out a criminal act on June 7, when they murdered nineteen members of the Royal Winnipeg Rifles whom they had taken prisoner. The incident was carefully investigated and later General Crerar officially informed his troops of this murder.

But many soldiers knew of this criminal act soon after it happened. The 12th *S.S.* was a marked division. Eventually it was annihilated in the Trun gap, but it first suffered extremely heavily at the hands of the Canadians in this attack on Caen.

As hundreds of shells screamed overhead to plough the fields around the three wrecked villages which the enemy had surrounded with intricate trench systems, the Highland Light Infantry, led as usual by Lieutenant-Colonel F. M. Griffiths of Niagara Falls, Ont., attacked Buron and the Stormont, Dundas and Glengarry Regiment went for Gruchy. "Chris" Christiansen had the Glens.

Tanks of the Sherbrooke Fusiliers, still commanded by Mel Gordon who led them right across France, supported the two battalions, while the North Novas, with Charlie Petch leading them in the same spirited fashion, followed up the attack to pass through the leading battalions and attack Authie.

Despite the artillery barrage, the Germans resisted the Highlanders' attack and fought for every trench and yard of ground. The H.L.I. came under particularly heavy fire and they had a terrible struggle for Buron. The village finally was captured but it took a tremendous effort on the part of the H.L.I. to do it. The Glens had a somewhat easier task at Gruchy but they too had heavy fighting. The village was captured and the Glens passed on to attack and capture the Château St. Louis, four hundred yards from Gruchy.

The North Novas, in their efforts to pass through the two leading battalions, were shelled and mortared even before they got moving. They did break through to Authie, however, and drove the enemy from its ruined streets and houses. The capture of Authie was sweet revenge for the North Novas and the Sherbrookes who helped them, for it was here that they had the big battle with the German tanks and infantry on D-plus-one, from which they were ordered back to Les Buissons.

The North Novas continued on to Franqueville and that night made contact with patrols from the North Shores which had come out from Carpiquet. The link-up had been made and the Carpiquet garrison was relieved.

Brigadier Foster's western brigade went into action as Buron, Gruchy and Authie fell, and advanced eastward through this area. The Canadian Scottish fought their way to Cussy, a mile east of Authie, and the Regina Rifles battled ahead to the ancient Abbey of Ardennes, a few hundred yards south of Cussy. Both were enemy strongpoints in this inter-locking Caen defence line.

The 1st Hussars fought with the Canadian Scottish and Reginas, and the Winnipegs also shared in the battle for Cussy.

British armoured cars and the 17th Duke of York's

Royal Canadian Hussars from Montreal, moved along the main Caen-Bayeux highway, but in St.-Germain, the western suburb of Caen, came under such heavy mortar fire they could advance no farther at that time.

On the left of the Canadians, the 59th and 3rd British Divisions had had splendid successes, and although there was fierce fighting all along the Caen perimeter, the enemy line had been pierced in half a dozen places, and the Germans were beginning to pull back to Caen.

The following day, July 9, the Glens and the Sherbrooke tanks went along the main highway towards Caen, followed by the H.L.I. In the late morning the Glens and the tanks entered Caen and against intermittent sniping went right through to the centre of the city, receiving a tumultuous welcome. The citizens of Caen, even bombed as they had been by our aircraft, welcomed the Canadians as their liberators and tossed flowers in their path.

The North Novas cut across the corner of Carpiquet airdrome and entered Caen from the southwest, while the troops of the British 3rd Division came into Caen from the north.

Opposition in the city was very light and it was soon cleaned up.

Hardly had Caen fallen, than the Carpiquet garrison took the offensive and after occupying the airfield, the three battalions and the tanks advanced southeast to take up positions on the Odon River.

*   *   *   *

The western brigade moved into Caen with the Highlanders and the Canadians took over the city completely. The Germans were holding the other side of the Orne at Vaucelles and some skirmishes took place along this river line as well as exchanges of shell-fire.

But after Buron, Gruchy and Authie, Caen was a quiet retreat for the Canadians.

Caen had suffered more heavily from our bombing than any other place we had seen in Normandy. Each street had its ruins and its desolation and thousands were homeless. Many bombed-out women and children had taken shelter in the fine church of St.-Étienne which contains the tomb of William the Conqueror.

They had been living in the church for weeks and we saw many touching, pathetic sights when we went to that edifice. Yet these people were not hostile. They talked of the bombings with fear in their eyes, yet they did not look at us with malice. They said it was the price of their liberty.

For more than a week, the 3rd Division remained in the Caen area as the next step forward was being prepared. The 2nd Canadian Infantry Division, which carried out the Dieppe raid two years before, had now arrived in Normandy, and on July 11 the Canadian Corps became operational. The two Canadian divisions and the 2nd Armoured Brigade were under its command, and the corps was led by Lieutenant-General G. G. Simonds. He had had a spectacular career in the Canadian Army during the war. In his first big show in Sicily, where he commanded the 1st Canadian Division, he had shining success which continued on into Italy. The preceding winter he had been brought back to England to command this invasion corps.

The Corps was at first in the Second Army but on July 31 it came under First Canadian Army when that formation, in turn, became operational.

General Simond's chief of staff was Brigadier Elliott

Rodger of Ottawa and his G.S.O. 1 was Lieutenant-Colonel Bob Moncel of Montreal. Among officers in the various operations branches were Major Tommy O'Hara of Montreal, Major Fred Wigle of Montreal and Hamilton, Ont., Major Bill Broughall of Hamilton, Major Ronnie Marks of Toronto, Major John Delamere of Toronto and Major Bill Carsley of Montreal.

Corps Headquarters was established in the wooded grounds of an estate near Vieux Cairon, immediately north of Buron and Gruchy, and each day we called there, for it now became our chief source of official information.

The 2nd Division troops took over the Odon River positions from Brigadier Blackader's brigade and it was a tough initiation into battle in Normandy. The Germans shelled and mortared the positions with little respite, and the 2nd Division's men could do nothing but sit there and take casualties, without getting the satisfaction of hitting back.

However, the plan for the new attack was nearly ready and soon the Canadians would be on the move again. Aggressive patrolling was done along the Orne and on the evening of July 15 the first Canadian patrols got over the river into Vaucelles. They met brisk opposition and later withdrew. On the same day the British 15th and 59th Division launched a new attack southwest of Caen and a few miles were gained in hard fighting.

The big attack, though, was to be made at Caen, east of the Orne.

While the British infantry fought southwest of Caen, three armoured divisions—the 11th, the Guards and the 7th—massed for this powerful drive.

Rolling over the cross-country tank tracks which

our engineers had created throughout the beach-head,
the armoured divisions concentrated along the Orne
north of Caen, and on the night of July 17-18, they
crossed the bridges over the Orne and the Caen canal,
going into the narrow bridgehead northeast of Caen
which had been held since D-Day by the 6th Airborne,
later supported by the 51st Highland.

We had wondered for many weeks about the purpose of this bridgehead. It seemed to have no great
value, yet General Montgomery and General Dempsey
insisted that it be held at any cost. Now we could see
its purpose. It was a spring-board for operations
against the Caen-Falaise hinge.

On a rose-flushed dawn on July 18, I sat in a trench
near Caen and watched the attack go in. The greatest
air show in history started it off. One thousand Lancasters and Halifaxes of Bomber Command winged
out from England, and they bombed German positions
at Colombelles and Vaucelles and a series of towns
four miles east of there—Touffreville, Sannerville and
Banneville.

The heavies were hitting the sides of the corridor,
through which the three armoured divisions were to
pass. Following up the Bomber Command planes,
came fifteen hundred daylight heavies of the American
8th Air Force. These Fortresses and Liberators
bombed German gun positions and defence lines south
of Caen and Vaucelles. Then six hundred American
mediums beat up the corridor with fragmentation
bombs, which do not crater but which have deadly
effect against personnel.

After a few squadrons had dropped their bombs, a
pall of smoke and dust clouded the entire Caen front.
Through the murk, I kept watching that stream of
bombers coming out from England like a fantastic sky

train. Several planes were hit. One Lancaster burst into flames and plummeted to earth like a torch.

The sky was crowded with aircraft, streaming in to the target or wheeling to the west and passing over the beach-head on the way back. While the bombing was taking place, masses of artillery in a ten-mile semi-circle around Caen fired without let-up. Of all the attacks I saw in France, this one was the most stagger-ing and the most deafening.

As the bombers finished their job, the armoured divisions rolled south from the airborne bridgehead. They went right down the corridor east of Colom-belles and Vaucelles, with the 3rd British Division following them up to clean up in their wake. The 3rd Canadian Division's job was to support the right flank. Two Canadian brigades moved down the east bank of the Orne, captured the factory district at Colombelles and then took Vaucelles.

The armoured divisions had spectacular successes at first, getting over the Caen-Vimont road and rolling south. German opposition had been paralysed by this bombing effort and no co-ordinated resistance was offered in the first few hours. But then it stiffened. As the British armour got about four miles south of Caen they ran right into a screen of enemy guns which had not been touched by the bombing. Every village in that area was heavily defended and had its comple-ment of guns. The armour ran into great difficulty and the attack bogged down. All the high hopes were not realized, for the tanks had not been able to shake loose through the open country leading to Falaise, twenty miles south of Caen. But a salient had been pushed south of Caen. This set the stage for further operations in this hard, bitter struggle to break the German's Caen-Falaise hinge.

While the 3rd Canadian Division's operations in the big attack were quite secondary to the armoured drive, it was vital that Vaucelles be captured. The Division achieved this by the night of July 18 with the lightest casualties it had had in any divisional action.

The Division's attack started badly when the Chaudières were held up by a strongpoint in a château outside Colombelles, but while the Chauds worked on the strongpoint, the Queen's Own and the North Shores carried on. The Queen's Own took Giberville, one mile east of Vaucelles, and bagged four to five hundred prisoners there. The North Shores fought for and captured the Colombelles factories.

Brigadier Cunningham's Highland brigade passed through the three battalions and entered Vaucelles from the northeast and at the same time Brigadier Foster's western brigade crossed the Orne from Caen to Vaucelles and linked up with the Highlanders. Opposition was scattered, for the bombing had demoralized the enemy throughout this built-up area.

The 3rd Division followed up its Vaucelles success by pushing south to Cormelles and several hamlets beyond there.

The 2nd Division was not idle during this intricate operation. The Royal Regiment of Canada, in its first offensive action since Dieppe, advanced from the Odon River positions and attacked the woods and the château at Louvigny, one mile southwest of Caen where the Odon flows into the Orne. Led by Major Jack Anderson of Toronto, who had won the Military Cross with the Royals at Dieppe, the Regiment fought for hours in the battered orchards and the tangle of scrub and woods around the château, but they cleared the area.

While this fight went on, other 2nd Division battalions crossed the Orne and advanced south on the flank of the 3rd Division and the British armour. The Regiment de Maisonneuve captured Fleury-sur-Orne, two miles south of Vaucelles; the Calgary Highlanders advanced towards Ifs; the Black Watch of Montreal and the Cameron Highlanders of Winnipeg went south towards St.-André-sur-Orne, five miles south of Vaucelles.

St. André was captured and the Camerons hung on to it grimly. The South Saskatchewan Regiment advanced over the fields to Verrières, east of St.-André and near the Caen-Falaise highway. Other regiments were spread out over the rolling cropland which rose gently to a hump of high ground. The Germans were on this high ground in strength and from their positions practically dominated St.-André, Verrières and May-sur-Orne, one mile south of St.-André.

Their 88mm. guns could pick off nearly anything in the area from St.-André to Verrières and over to the highway. The enemy mortar crews had a clear field for their deadly work.

The 2nd Division was in a dangerous position, exposed as it was to heavy enemy fire wherever it moved in the open fields. The S.S.R. suffered the first had blow in their advance on Verrières. They were attacked by German tanks and infantry in the wheat fields and some companies were overrun and scattered. The battalion had to fall back a mile to the positions of the Essex Scottish from Windsor, Ont.

The attacks kept up and the situation for days was grave. The enemy was proving terribly strong here and the 2nd Division in particular was suffering dangerously high casualties.

Looking at the situation hastily, it seemed that the loss of men on those open slopes did not make sense. But from the point of view of the broad plan, it made

all kinds of sense. The pressure had to be kept up
here. The German armour and infantry had to be
held on this pivot while the American and British
forces to the west broke loose.

VI

THE PUSH TO FALAISE

GENERAL MONTGOMERY gave the Canadian
Corps the first opportunity to take a hard crack at
these German defences which were blocking our
progress towards Falaise.

The plan was carefully worked out and in the early
morning of July 25 the Corps attacked, with strong
artillery support. The 2nd Division was on the right
and its task was to capture May-sur-Orne and Verrières
and go on from there to take the towns of Fontenay-
le-Marmion and Rocquancourt, a mile and a half
farther south. The 3rd Division was to capture Tilly
la Campagne, a village one mile east of Verrières.

Following this infantry attack the 7th Armoured
and the Guards Armoured Divisions were to go
through the Canadians and exploit southward as far
as possible in the direction of Falaise.

The operation turned out to be the most tragic of
any Canadian attack in the French campaign. The
only success achieved was at Verrières, where the Royal
Hamilton Light Infantry captured the village and held
it, while the Royal Regiment occupied ground to the
east of the village and also withstood all German
attempts to beat them back.

On the right flank, the Calgary Highlanders and
the Black Watch suffered terrible losses. The Calgarys advanced from St.-André to May-sur-Orne, but
in the low fields around the town they were lashed by
German fire. Enemy close around them and on the

ridge along the Falaise highway took a heavy toll of the Calgarys. From the west side of the Orne, German gunners poured down murderous fire.

The Black Watch tried to go forward to Fontenay and nearly the whole battalion was lost. Like the Calgarys, they ran into far stronger German defences than they had anticipated. Nobody knew exactly what happened to the Black Watch. They went over a slope in the night and very little was heard from them. Reports that did come back over the field wireless before it went dead, and what the few survivors were able to tell, indicated that the battalion fought a mad, tumultuous battle against fearful odds and under merciless fire, particularly from German tanks.

The Regiment de Maisonneuve was also involved in the fighting around May and Fontenay.

On the 3rd Division sector, the North Novas got into Tilly all right, but the Germans were in the town in greater numbers than had been thought and a see-saw battle went on, with the H.L.I. later engaged around Tilly too. Eventually, the Canadians were ordered out of both the Tilly zone and the May and Fontenay areas.

Canadian tanks of the 2nd Armoured Brigade shared in this brave but unsuccessful attempt to penetrate the German defence line but the two British armoured divisions which General Simonds had at his disposal were not committed for the exploitation which had been planned.

The attack clearly showed that the Germans had strengthened their defences, screening Falaise out of all recognition. Crack divisions were identified as opposing the Canadians and they formed the most potent enemy force on any one sector of the Allied front.

These defences emphasized the importance of this Caen-Falaise hinge. The enemy realized that he must hold at any cost on this hinge or his whole line in the west would fold up. His principal communications went through Falaise and Argentan, and they must be protected or else the battle of Normandy would be lost.

So the Germans kept a large number of *S.S.* and *Panzer* forces in this area between Caen and Falaise—kept them there until it was decided to rush armour into the Mortain salient on the American front to try and break through to Avranches and the sea, splitting the American forces. This wild German gamble, dictated by anything but sound military judgment and coloured with Hitler's own fantastic whim, failed completely.

The Canadians contributed to this failure by holding the German armour south of Caen for weeks. They hammered at the German line there; hammered at it many times when it looked like a useless expenditure of our troops. But the plan was working out—the long-range plan to liquidate the German Seventh Army which was opposing the Allied forces in Normandy.

By maintaining constant pressure south of Caen, the Canadians put the enemy in a dilemma. He had to hold the hinge and yet he also must send armour west to try to stop the American and British divisions there. The gallant sacrifices made by the Canadian infantry particularly, in this rugged fighting south of Caen in those bloody days, was a big factor in the final triumph in Normandy which was the victory for all France.

Take the attacks made on Tilly. The Calgary Highlanders were sent against Tilly one day and on the flat fields in front of the town they suffered heavily again. A few days later the Lincoln and Welland Regiment struck at the shattered village and they too could not break the defence.

Tilly was not that vital but the pressure had to be kept up, for the Germans, given any rest, would have been able to deploy their forces more to their own satisfaction. When they were being hit time and time again like this, they were baffled about our intentions.

Several local attacks were thrown in, too, against St.-Martin-de-Fontenay, immediately south of St.-André, and the Fusiliers Mont-Royal particularly distinguished themselves in heavy fighting in that village of death.

The German line extended from St.-Martin and May-sur-Orne eastward through Fontenay-le-Marmion and Rocquancourt, and then swung northeast to Tilly. This line crossed the Caen-Falaise highway and a screen of 88mm. guns, dug-in tanks, self-propelled guns, machine-guns and mortar positions was located on the slopes which rose southward from these villages. Five miles south of this first screen another defence line was being hastily thrown up.

From their positions, the Germans made several forays of their own after the Canadian Corps attack, and the R.H.L.I. and the Essex Scottish took the brunt of these attacks in their positions around Verrières. The enemy used their robot tanks against these two battalions, when they employed them for the first time in Normandy, and they did not make much of an impression on these stout-hearted Ontario troops. A dozen of these tanks, looking like Bren carriers, and carrying a big war-head of explosives on the front, were sent by radio direction against the Canadians and some blew up inside our lines. However, they seemed little more than an army toy, and after these few attempts, the enemy gave up using them here.

At the end of July, the 3rd Division was taken out of the line, being replaced by the 4th Canadian Armoured Division, which had recently arrived in France to make up the full Canadian complement of the Canadian Corps. It was an occasion when the 3rd Division left the front for a rest. For fifty-six consecutive days it had been fighting the enemy around Caen. Its record had been magnificent and now the troops went into the base area of the beach-head where there was no shelling and few air raids. It was their turn to sleep, eat and get re-equipped.

The tempo of the campaign was speeding up at this time. The British attacked at Caumont, west of the Canadians, and the Americans, still farther to the west, were breaking away for gigantic gains. But on the Caen front the fighting was still close and bitter.

On July 31, the Canadian Corps came under command of the First Canadian Army, which now took its place on the extreme left of the Allied front. In addition to the Canadian Corps, General Crerar also had the 1st British Corps under command.

Quietly and efficiently, the Canadian Army H.Q. had assembled itself at Amblie, in the base area three miles south of Courseulles, and here the staff prepared for this day when the army would become operational.

It was an historic day. Never before had Canada had an army formation in the field. In the First Great War the Dominion was represented by a corps. In this war, there was a two-division corps fighting with the Eighth Army in Italy and here in France there was a three-division corps in the army.

The British troops in the army gave it a composite character, but soon it became an international force.

The 1st Polish Armoured Division was put in the Canadian Corps, and Belgian and Dutch brigade groups were placed in the British 1st Corps under General Crerar. Later other nationalities fought under Canadian command.

Immediately on the Canadian Army becoming operational, we began to get briefings twice a day at H.Q. about progress of the fighting on our own front and the other Allied fronts in France. Our briefing officer was Lieutenant-Colonel H. E. T. ("Pot") Doucet of Montreal. "Pot" Doucet was the most able briefing officer any correspondents had helping them in France. Personally I have never known a better one anywhere. He gave us all the information we needed and gave it precisely, accurately and briskly. Every newspaperman who was ever with the Canadians in France, owed a debt to this young colonel in the Black Watch. With our own army functioning, we got the broad picture in proper perspective from him.

At the beginning of August the British and Canadians in the First Canadian Army were opposed by elements of at least eight German divisions along the semicircular line from the Bay of the Seine around Caen and Vaucelles, to the Orne River south of Caen.

Four of these divisions were fierce-fighting *S.S.* formations—the 12th, 1st (which was the crack Adolf Hitler outfit), 9th and 10th—and the others were the 16th German Air Force Division and the 711th, 346th and 272nd Infantry Divisions.

Doucet explained the situation in capsule form when he said: "We are holding down a very large proportion of armour on our front and this is facilitating the advance of the Americans and the British; there is no question of this."

During the first week in August, however, the enemy

started withdrawing armour from the Caen area and moving it west into the path of the fast-developing British and American advances.

While this was going on, the Canadian Army prepared to strike its first blow as an army. An attack was teed up to shatter the Caen-Falaise hinge once and for all; to break through to Falaise and make a big contribution to the defeat of the Seventh Army.

The attack was scheduled to begin late on August 7, but General Crerar liked it to be said that it was launched on August 8.

The date meant a lot to him and other Canadians who fought in the First Great War, for it was on August 8, 1918,—the day Ludendorff called the "Black Day" of the German Army—that the Canadian Corps attacked at Amiens and the Last Hundred Days of the war began.

General Crerar himself briefed the correspondents for the big attack and told us how his forces would be used. Five divisions were to be employed in this battle for Falaise. The 2nd Canadian, commanded by Major-General Charles Foulkes of London, Ont., and the 51st Highland, with the 2nd Armoured Brigade and a British armoured brigade, were to make a night attack, with heavy bomber and great artillery support. If they broke through the screen of German guns in the darkness and gained the slopes behind Rocquancourt and Tilly, then the 4th Armoured and the 1st Polish Armoured Divisions, backed by the 3rd Canadian Division, were to carry on the advance towards Falaise.

Brigadier Wyman commanded the 2nd Armoured Brigade, but this was his last action. He was wounded in the arm the morning of August 8 and he eventually had to return to Canada. The brigadier was one of

Canada's best tank commanders in action, probably the greatest and certainly the most experienced.

General Keller was still commanding the 3rd Division which came from its rest area to join in this Canadian Army operation but he too was wounded the following morning when American heavy bombers dropped bombs on his H.Q. at Vaucelles by mistake.

While this was to be a Canadian Army attack, it was Canadian Corps which was making it and General Simonds who would actually direct the operation in the field, and he and his staff were responsible for the novel methods used.

In the first place, the employment of tanks at night was unusual and had not been tried out very frequently. General Simonds believed it would work and he felt it was the only way to put his forces through the German gun screen.

Bomber Command was to come over in full strength with a thousand heavy bombers to give close support to the attacking force by bombing specific areas on the flanks. This was an exceedingly ticklish business, for the leading troops were going to be very close to the bombing.

The infantry were to be mounted in armoured carriers to give them full protection against small-arms fire. These carriers, later known as "kangaroos", were converted "priests", the American 105mm. self-propelled gun on a Sherman tank chassis. The gun was taken out to make space for the infantry. The armoured infantry carriers were one of the most ingenious inventions of the Normandy campaign and they provided the answer to the problem of getting infantry through fields of small-arms fire.

In the shuffle of the German forces opposing the Canadians, the 1st *S.S.* Division had been replaced by the 89th Infantry Division, which had only recently come from Norway. This division would be hardest hit. Zero hour was 11.30 P.M. on August 7, when the heavy bombers came over, and I watched the raid from a tall house in Caen as the earth quaked for miles around.

This was the third heavy bomber raid I had watched, and the Halifaxes and Lancasters drummed through the dark sky, passed over Caen and dumped their cargoes of bombs on the German positions to the south, marked by flare shells fired on the exact target areas by our artillery. The sky glowed with flares and with the red and yellow bursts of bombs, but soon the usual fog of smoke and dust thickened up the night. The relentless, devastating, breath-taking bombing kept up. One wave of heavies followed another and the Germans were pounded with an accuracy that they had never experienced before.

Searchlights fingered through the darkness and the smoke at low trajectories over the battle line, making artificial moonlight for our infantry and tanks that crossed the start line as the bombing mounted in *crescendo*.

Even before the bombers had finished their job, massed Canadian and British artillery opened one of the greatest barrages fired in the French campaign. The night was a mad, fantastic confusion of thunderous explosions, roaring guns and clamour of tanks. Occasionally you heard the clatter of a machine-gun and it sounded puny and out of place in this battle of the giants of the battle-field.

In addition to the 12th, 13th, 14th and 19th Field Regiments, R.C.A., of the 3rd Division, the 4th, 5th, 6th, 15th and 23rd Field Regiments fired until gun barrels glowed. These latter regiments had come to

Normandy with the army build-up as well as the 3rd, 4th, 7th and 15th Medium and the 1st Heavy, which were all in action this tremendous night. It was the Canadian artillery's greatest shoot of the war up to that time.

Other artillery regiments which rolled forward with the attack were the 6th, 2nd and 5th Anti-Tank, and the 6th, 3rd and 8th Light Anti-Aircraft, the 2nd Heavy A.A., the 3rd Anti-Tank and the 4th Light A.A., which had been on the continent since D-Day.

Leading the 2nd Division attack, commanded by Major-General Foulkes, were the Ontario regiments —Royals, Essex Scottish and R.H.L.I.—with the Sherbrooke tanks. In several long columns of tanks and "kangaroos", they thrust south along the Falaise road in the wake of the bombing and the barrage. The German gunners, manning the artillery which screened the road and the vital ridge behind Rocquancourt, had been hammered by the pre-attack bombardment. In the night they did not know what was coming straight into their lines as the tanks and infantry carriers crunched into their positions. This novel attack was a staggering surprise to the enemy. They never recovered from it.

By the end of the first hour, the Canadians and the Scots on their left had broken through the gun-screen with remarkably light losses and were up on the high ground they had been ordered to capture.

The rest of the 2nd Division infantry followed in the wake of the Ontario regiments, mopping up. By dawn the leading troops had gained about four miles and were slogging right ahead. The Germans were in confusion and their organized defence of this line had been thrown into a complete muddle. But groups of enemy stayed and fought at Rocquancourt, Fontenay-le-Marmion and May-sur-Orne, and it took hours of heavy fighting to oust them from these places, which were by-passed in the original night break-through.

The Camerons of Winnipeg and the S.S.R. cleared Rocquancourt and Fontenay and the F.M.R. threw the last Germans out of May-sur-Orne to settle a score in that town where so many young Canadians had given their lives.

The operation gathered momentum with terrific speed. In the morning, the 4th Armoured and the Polish Armoured Divisions were committed and they fanned out over the brown slopes and rolled south, kicking up a gigantic cloud of smoke that veiled the front for miles.

Everything was moving now. Along the roads and over the tank tracks, vehicles and guns flooded south on the heels of the tanks and infantry. The most inspiring sight in war is to see an army rolling, and here was the First Canadian Army, in its first operation, racing wildly south towards Falaise.

The American bombers came over, wave upon wave, to blast the Germans in daylight. Hundreds of them carpeted a path ahead of the advance with fragmentation bombs and the heavies smashed at gun positions and troop concentrations. The entire force of war's weapons was unleashed in this great night-and-day attack.

Some of the American bombers, however, missed their targets. They dropped their bombs on the Canadian lines at Vaucelles and in several little towns nearby.

I was driving back to the front and nearing Caen when the bombs came down. All Vaucelles seemed enveloped in smoke and flames. Bombs hurtled into our gun lines, into ammunition dumps and near troop concentrations. It filled me with terror to see this havoc even from a mile away.

Squadrons of Fortresses wheeled over Caen, and it looked for a moment as if they too would be misled by the error of the planes they were following. However, they realized the mistake and, taking their bearings, turned around and dumped their bombs on the Germans to the south.

In this bombing General Keller received wounds that put him out of the campaign. He was hit badly in the arm.

For a while we thought the mistake in bombing of our own troops and dumps might have had serious effects on the progress of the attack. But rapid adjustments were made, replacements for damaged vehicles and supply and ammunition dumps were rushed up.

The advance went on. The 4th Division, then commanded by Major-General George Kitching of Montreal, thundered down the highway and over the wooded fields, gaining another five miles, while the Poles, eager to get at the Germans, fanned out on the east side of the highway. This armoured fist broke through the second line of German defences, and with 2nd and 3rd Division infantry following them up, these two armoured divisions pushed ahead.

By the evening of August 9 Canadian tanks were northwest of Potigny, five miles north of Falaise, but were meeting stronger opposition. The Poles had made excellent gains but as they neared the Laison River valley they were held up.

Canadian infantry, though, mopped up the areas thoroughly behind the tanks, and prisoners from the 89th Division streamed in. The Division had been practically annihilated.

A break-through right to Falaise seemed to be on

the books but the Germans, showing incredible ability to throw up a new defence even when they had suffered a body blow, rushed guns and troops from Falaise to screen the city from the north. Somehow they got their guns into position in time and the 4th Division and the Poles were finally stopped in their wild surge towards Falaise. They were stopped north of Potigny and the Laison River valley.

Troops of the 12th *S.S.* Division were among the hard-bitten Germans who blocked this advance despite the courageous efforts of the 4th Division and the Poles.

North of Potigny, the enemy guns were thickest, and the British Columbia Regiment, a tank unit, and the Algonquin Regiment, an infantry battalion from northern Ontario, fought a bloody battle near Hill 195 —a battle which stands out as a Canadian epic of sacrifice and heroism.

Hill 195 was the plug in the bottle-neck leading to Falaise, and there the Germans made their most desperate stand in the battle for the town.

In a night attack the two regiments advanced to the hill in a thrust which carried them to within two thousand yards of the H.Q. of the 21st *Panzer* Division. At dawn the enemy hit back at the Canadian spearhead and for fourteen hours a furious battle raged near the hill, with the B.C.R.s and the Algonquins fighting back from a square they had formed on the shell-blasted slopes.

Thirty-eight Canadian tanks were knocked out, but the Canadians stubbornly fought on until they had nothing left with which to continue. Lieutenant-Colonel Don Worthington of Vancouver, commander of the tank regiment, was an inspiring figure as he moved around the fire-swept square encouraging the men and organizing the defence. In the afternoon he was wounded. He carried on. Late in the day he was killed. The square got smaller and smaller. In the evening the battle ended and the remnants of two regiments rejoined the main Canadian force north of the hill.

The struggle on Hill 195 had revealed the strength of the enemy and disclosed their dispositions.

The Poles, on the left of the 4th Division, ran into Tiger tanks and guns and they too could not continue the advance. By August 11 the attack had stopped entirely. At Army H.Q. and at Corps there was no pessimism, though. It was felt that one more crack would carry them through to Falaise, and a new full-dress offensive was prepared.

Meanwhile, American tank columns had swung far around to the south and Le Mans fell to them. The German armour which had been concentrated in the Mortain area was now in a big salient sticking out to the west, flanked by the Americans and the Second British Army. The chips were down for the enemy and they were beginning to realize the folly of committing their tanks in an attempt to split the Americans at Mortain and Avranches.

On the front there was rising optimism that the German forces in the west were seeing their last days. In our press camp a notice from 21st Army Group was posted reading: "In the event of the disintegration of the German forces you are reminded that war correspondents are strictly forbidden to advance beyond the zone of military occupation of the Allied armies."

The men at the top saw victory in the making. The troops just saw a lot of hard fighting ahead, and in the long run they were right.

The Canadians with the Polish Division had carried out the exploitation down the Falaise highway and the

British troops in the Canadian Army now faced east towards Vimont and Troarn. Their role was to strike east towards the Seine once Falaise was captured and the trap was closed on the Seventh German Army now struggling in the long salient which had its head still at Mortain.

The 2nd Division had made good gains while the 4th Division and Poles fought southwards, and the Calgary Highlanders, with the Black Watch and the Regiment de Maisonneuve, advanced through the Bretteville-sur-Laize area on the right flank of the main Canadian thrust. Followed up by the other regiments, they worked into the pine-clad hills along the Laize River valley, swinging around on a wide right hook on Falaise.

On August 13, the Americans moving up from the south were reported in Argentan, south of Falaise, and the stage was set for the destruction of the Seventh Army. The Second Army was pressing the enemy forces hard to the west of the Canadians.

The Canadians' second attack went in at noon on August 14, and the main effort was made over the Laison River valley, northeast of Falaise. The 3rd and 4th Divisions with the 2nd Armoured Brigade lunged forward in the greatest armoured and infantry attack the Canadian Army made in France.

General Crerar told his troops "hit him first and hit him hard and keep on hitting him". They did.

The artillery laid huge smoke screens on the flanks to block out the vision of the German gunners, and in the blazing sun of noonday on one of the hottest days of the summer, three hundred Canadian tanks, leading the attack, swept down on the Laison valley. It was a charge of armoured light brigades. The tanks thundered pell-mell into the valley, churned through it and lunged up on the slopes on the far sides. Straight into the German gun lines they roared, with guns and machine-guns blazing. The infantry followed them closely in their armoured "kangaroo" carriers which were doing noble service again.

This mass of tanks and infantry punched straight through the German gun-screen and swept up on the slopes northeast of Falaise. It was a rousing attack that has had few equals. Take the 1st Hussars from London, Ont. The order was given: "1st Hussars charge." And they charged like old-time cavalry, sweeping over the Laison and into the German positions on their Sherman steeds.

The attack was a devastating blow to the Germans, and in the late afternoon, with Canadian armour and infantry bursting into his lines, General Von Kluge, commander of the Seventh Army, sent this report to Berlin: "A break-through south of Caen has occurred, the like of which we have never seen."

Another thousand-bomber raid was laid on for the attack and Bomber Command was to send its Lancasters and Halifaxes over between two and four P.M. to bomb the German-held area on the right flank of the 4th and 3rd Divisions' thrust. Big bombs were to be used to knock out enemy positions and to crater the flank zone so badly that the enemy could not move up tanks from that direction in any counter-attack.

The ground advance was going well when the bombers streamed out from England to lend their support. They came in at about eight thousand feet and the first waves were right on their target, blasting the Potigny area and the Quesnay Woods, just off the highway four miles north of Potigny, where a force of enemy was holding out stubbornly.

Then some bombs fell short. Some pilots had mis-

(TOP): *Moving ahead under the protection of a tank, these Canadians advance through the streets of Falaise, looking for snipers hidden after other Germans had fled.*

(LOWER): *Amphibious Canadians at Nijmegen, Holland. In the Schelde Estuary, during the polder warfare, the Canadians perfected an original technique in the field. This won special notice from the British War Office, which requested the preparation of special reference records.*

taken landmarks and roads, and high explosives
showered down five and six miles behind the front.
For the second time within a week the Canadians suffered losses from supporting heavy bombers. Finally
the bombers were called off and fortunately the ground
attack did not suffer, for the troops involved were well
ahead of the areas in which the bombs fell. Troops
in the rear were hit, though.

It was a heavy price to pay for close support of
heavy bombers and criticism of the Air Force was rife.

A crisis in relations between Army and Air Force
would easily have arisen if General Crerar and his staff
at Army H.Q. had not taken a firm stand on this issue.
They did not cast a word of blame on Bomber Command.   Instead, they pointed out the tremendous
advantage, even with the risks involved, of the support
of heavy bombers to the ground forces in attacks against
strongly-held German positions.

Co-ordinating the ground and air attack was a ticklish business recognized by all, and when accidents did
occur they had to be accepted, particularly at this stage
when this system of close support was being worked
out. Much was learned in these attacks which later
guaranteed success without casualties to ourselves, in
the use of heavies close to our own troops.

Beyond the Laison valley, the 4th and 3rd Divisions
found that even when they got into and past the main
German gun lines there were still more guns located
farther back, and for two days they fought it out along
those slopes, gradually pushing the enemy out, while
the 2nd Division descended from the northwest on
Falaise itself.

The next day the Canadians were two and a half
miles from Falaise and 21st Army Group put a blackout on all news of movements of Allied troops east of

the Caen-Falaise-Argentan-Alencon-Le Mans line.
German communications were in a state of chaos and
nothing was to be given out in news dispatches which
would help them sort out the mess. They were left
completely in the dark during the next few critical
days when the jaws of the trap closed on the German
Army in Normandy.

The Polish Division had been swung around to the
left flank of the Canadian Corps and went over the
Dives River, heading for the town of Trun at the head
of the gap between Falaise and Argentan, which was
the only route of escape for the trapped German Army.

The 3rd and 4th Divisions also made good progress
cleaning up the area northeast of Falaise, but not a
word was said about these successes at the time.

It was the 2nd Division which sprung the surprise
that won Falaise. It swept down the road from the
Laize River valley supported by the Sherbrooke tanks
and by the afternoon of August 16 it had troops west
of the city. The enemy tried to muster tanks and
infantry for counter-attacks but they were nearly all
broken up, before they even started, by the phenomenal Typhoon rocket-firing planes, the great air
discovery of the Second Front and the most effective
plane devised up to that time for close support of
the army.

The night of August 16-17 the S.S.R. and the
Camerons, with the F.M.R. in reserve, fought their
way into Falaise with the help of the Sherbrooke tanks,
which gave them superb artillery support with their
guns.

On August 17, in the early afternoon, Army H.Q.
announced that Falaise had been captured.

The Caen-Falaise hinge had been completely broken
by this twenty-mile advance of the First Canadian

Army down the straight highway to Falaise, and now the disintegration of the Seventh Army began; the slaughter in the Trun gap began; the push to the Seine began. The fall of Falaise was a major contribution to it all.

VII

TRIUMPH AT TRUN—ON TO THE SEINE

THE FALL of Falaise was swiftly followed by the most momentous events of the French campaign, as the German Army, which had been charged with the defence of the west, was smashed completely.

The Polish Division and the 4th Division charged southeast to Trun, bumping and overcoming opposition as they rolled their tanks over the fields and through the woods to the base of the hills that fall back towards the Seine east of Trun.

As these tank formations broke away, the 1st British Corps operating between them and the Channel coast began to roll east. On the coastal sector, the 6th Airborne Division, along with Belgian and Dutch brigade groups, pushed out from their narrow bridgehead which they had held east of the Orne River and northeast of Caen since D-Day. The airborne division, which had longer continual service in the Normandy line than any other formation, took the bit in its teeth and even without normal transport for a pursuit, swept eastward along the coast.

South of it the 49th Division struck east to the Dives River and beyond, and the 51st Highland Division, south again of the 49th, conformed with the same spectacular rapidity.

The Polish and Canadian advance put Trun in our hands and the escape gap was reduced to a scant few miles. The weather was excellent for flying and our Typhoons and Spitfires worked havoc on the miles of

German convoys and thousands of troops milling around south of Falaise and in the gap.

Hundreds of trucks and scores of tanks were destroyed and damaged every day as the air force ran a shuttle service from the beach-head airfields to the gap. The day after Falaise fell, I stood on the road east of the town and watched the air attack spellbound. The rocket-firing Typhoons hurtled down on the German convoys, helplessly jammed on the road, and massacred them. The fighter bombers came over, squadron after squadron, whistling along the gap, and scattered their bombs up and down the roads and through the fields where the Germans scurried for shelter.

Medium bombers and even heavies droned steadily over the gap, showering high explosives like confetti. I was seeing the Seventh Army die. The plain south of Falaise and the narrow bottle-neck of the gap was dotted with fires, and pillars of black grey smoke billowed up from the battle-field. They were the funeral pyres of an army. The roads and fields were under air attack constantly. If it wasn't bombs that were hitting the enemy columns it was fighters winging low over the roads and strafing them relentlessly. The cannon shells and machine-gun bullets kicked up lines of dust.

Down by Trun our guns were in action. The Poles and the 4th Division artillery, with the gunners, too, of the 3rd Division which had joined them in the gap, were shooting over open sights into the chaos of men and material that they had trapped.

The Germans in their panic continued to try to force their way through the narrow exit left to them. They were slaughtered by the thousands between Trun and Chambois, particularly around the village of St.-Lambert-sur-Dives, half-way between the two towns.

The night of August 18 the correspondents were called to 21st Army Group H.Q., then at Bayeux, and General Montgomery's chief of staff told us, without mincing words, that the Battle of Normandy had been won by this tremendous victory, and that the enemy's power to resist effectively again in France had now gone.

Sketching a vivid picture of what was behind the German disaster in France, he said that the first reason was that the Germans lacked appreciation of Allied strategy.

"To begin with," he said, "the enemy had an army north of the Seine with which he could do three things: "1: Send it to reinforce his two commands in Normandy. 2: Hold it to man the Seine lines. 3: Send it to the Eastern Front if the Russian threat became too great.

"He decided to send it over the Seine to try to plug the holes which were developing in his positions. Owing to the lack of mobility of his army, it arrived too late. The second reason for his position was due to the fact that he was expecting a second landing on a stretch of coast closer to England. The result of all this is that he has no longer an army on the Seine.

"The American drive eastward caught him off his balance and swiftly severed sixty per cent of the lines of communications for his forces still operating in Normandy. Most of his dumps were overrun, and this left him only the Seine ferries as his main line of supply. The Americans, in a magnificent push, have seen off the German attempt to breach through to Avranches, and have sent troops to Argentan, sealed off Brest and Lorient and taken St.-Malo. It is a magnificent achievement.

"By trying to push to Avranches, the enemy himself

created a salient in which he is now struggling. This decision is at the seat of his present troubles. It gave General Bradley time to swing east.

"As these thrusts developed, the enemy was very slow to react—even when the Canadians came down from the north of Falaise. Owing to his total lack of tactical reconnaissance, he has never known where we were on his flank. Even his administration units stayed too long and had to hurry back.

"Finally it appeared he was using S.S. divisions in an effort to steer the infantry back in an orderly fashion and get them through the gap. Then the S.S. divisions realized they were in a bad spot themselves and dashed away, leaving the infantry.

"Last night we began getting new kinds of reports —assembly of large numbers of military transport and Seine ferries operating in daylight. Today it has been the same sort of thing, as thousands of M.T., tanks and artillery are trying to move southeast around Trun.

"In the Falaise-Argentan area are elements of these infantry divisions—84th, 85th, 89th, 271st, 272nd, 275th, 276th, 277th, 326th, 331st, 353rd, 363rd and three paratroop divisions. In addition, there are elements of four *Panzer* divisions. There was a steady seep out of the area until yesterday, and then the enemy made a sudden, convulsive effort to get the Hell out of it—especially the S.S. and *Panzer* divisions.

"Only one route was open—northeast to the Seine. He could not try for the Paris gap because he has no dumps that way. He must try to get himself where he can re-fuel. We are after the German Army wherever it cares to go."

I drove back to the front from Bayeux and the German panic in the gap was growing every hour. Our guns roared and our planes drummed and the doom of the Seventh Army was conclusively sealed on Saturday, August 19, when the Trun gap was closed. The Poles and the 4th Division linked up with the Americans and the French between Trun and Chambois. The enemy made wild, hopeless attempts to break this barrier, but every time tanks and infantry were hurled against it, the enemy losses were incredibly large. The Seventh Army—what was left of it—gasped its last under our guns and planes, and under the terrific small-arms fire of our infantry that closed in on the shambles and put the finishing touches on this disaster for German arms in the west.

A tidal wave of prisoners flooded the Canadian lines. By the thousands they came into Trun and the little towns around, and thousands more were taken into the American lines south of Chambois. One Canadian brigade alone took 7,000 in one day and nearly wènt crazy trying to handle this horde of beaten men. All the fight had gone out of them. They shuffled down the dusty roads, with only a handful of guards for a whole battalion. The prisoner-of-war cages overflowed and our interrogators went sleepless for days.

By August 21, men from thirty-four German divisions had been identified. These included twenty-one infantry divisions, five *S.S.*, five *Panzer* and three parachute formations.

The Mortain salient had been reduced to the Falaise-Argentan pocket and this pocket had dwindled to the Trun gap and then it had been closed. In this elimination the Seventh Army had collapsed into piles of dead in the ditches, wounded lying on the roads and fields, and exhausted nerve-shattered men in the huge prison cages.

The Americans had surged around to the south and

east with their tremendous force of tanks and infantry to out-manoeuvre the enemy and stagger them with the lightning speed of their advances and the audacity of their headlong thrusts through France towards Paris. The British Second Army had pummelled the enemy from the north and the northwest, hitting out day after day with infantry, tanks and guns and not letting up for a moment. The First Canadian Army had cracked down like a guillotine from Caen, to chop right into the German force as it fell back from the trap in which it had been caught in one of the greatest enveloping movements in any war.

This three-way pressure wrote finis for the Seventh Army.

As the final shots were being fired, I went into the gap. I drove down to Trun where more prisoners were crowding through the streets and up into the hills beyond the town.

Here the Poles and the Canadians had caught the Germans on the narrow, sunken roads and each road was a long open grave of men, horses, vehicles, guns and equipment.

The fetid stench of this mass of death filled the air and choked the senses. I saw the remains of the massacre of an army, a sickening, terrible, inhuman, gross spectacle. Yet in this slaughter I saw our victory in the west.

There were the Germans, lying grey-white and stiff in muddy ditches flowing red with German blood. There were the men of the Reich who had stormed through Europe and had pillaged and looted and forced endless disorder and grief on the world in their aggression from Warsaw to Athens, from Kiev to Brest. I hate the sight of death, but this afternoon I liked it. I got an insensate pleasure out of this disaster

to the men of the German Army. This was a fitting
reward for their labours on behalf of the *Fuehrer*.

This was a fitting end for men like these, corrupted
and motivated by a mad creed of power and weird
and warped Nazi principles. Misguided fools, dead in
the mud, slime and blood of the ditches.

They lay sprawled by still-smoking Panther tanks,
ripped open by our guns. They lay where they fell
when our machine-gunners cut them down, when the
Canadians and Poles went at them with bayonets. In
one eerie, silent stretch of road, there were hundreds
of them, slumped in the ditches as if they had fallen
into a deep sleep.

German trucks and cars, with their mottled camouflage of grey, yellow and green, stood wrecked on every
path and road. Documents, letters, newspapers, orders
and instructions littered the ground around them,
amid a mess of personal equipment, weapons and
ammunition. I picked up a machine-gun for our cook;
three rifles for some of our drivers; an *S.S.* pennant as
a souvenir; some Turkish cigarettes.

The havoc seemed endless. All afternoon I drove
along these roads of sudden death, past the heaps of
stinking dead horses, dead men and dead vehicles and
tanks. At St.-Lambert-sur-Dives the carnage eclipsed
anything I had ever seen.

Here the Germans had been caught in the most
terrible trap of all. The roads, fields and the woods
around were littered with the dead. Hundreds and
hundreds of Germans had been cut down like wheat
by a reaper, in their last mad, panic-stricken effort to
break through the gap and get east to the Seine.

The ground was grey-green with Germans in their
blood-stained field uniforms. Bodies had to be cleared
from the road to permit our transport to pass through

to the east and the Seine. Our bulldozers heaved vehicles off the roads, threw tanks into the ditch to make way for our convoys.

Our infantry marched through these lanes of destruction and along these sombre highways of death —marched to the east, for they had conquered what opposed them in Normandy. These macabre spectacles did not trouble them. They marched grimly east through the fields of dead, knowing full well the price of war. They had made the Germans pay in full here in the Trun gap. And this was just the beginning.

*   *   *   *

The Trun gap was closed completely at St.-Lambert-sur-Dives and it was there that Major Dave Currie of Moose Jaw, Sask., won the Victoria Cross, fourth of the war to be awarded to a member of the Canadian Army.

From August 18 to 20 the Major led a small force of tanks, infantry and anti-tank guns in a battle in and around St.-Lambert. He only had 175 men in all, yet they accounted for the destruction of seven enemy tanks, twelve 88mm. guns, forty armoured vehicles, five hundred wounded, three hundred killed and more than 2,100 prisoners.

Major Currie was in command of "C" squadron of the South Alberta Regiment, the armoured reconnaissance unit of the 4th Division, and he was ordered to advance on St.-Lambert from the Trun area. Under his command were put a company of the Argyll and Sutherland Highlanders from Hamilton, Ont., and one troop of 17-pounder anti-tank guns of the 5th Anti-Tank Regiment. Major Currie and his tanks, leading the force, reached the outskirts of St. Lambert where they were engaged by a strong enemy force.

The Major could not get permission to dismount his tank crews and attack as infantry, but during the night he made a personal reconnaissance of the village, passing through enemy positions, and at dawn the next morning he led an infantry-tank attack on St.-Lambert. The small Canadian force got half-way into the village when it was forced to consolidate in the face of increasing German resistance. The Major organized his defences and for thirty-six hours the Canadians were counter-attacked persistently. Major Currie's force stubbornly held its ground and threw back every attack on its positions.

At dusk on August 20, enemy infantry massed for an attack which proved to be the final effort to drive the Canadians from St.-Lambert. The Major, spotting the Germans forming up, personally sited a troop of tanks to shoot them up, and under his direction the gunners did this so effectively that the attack never was made. The Germans then began to surrender in hordes. Eight hundred of the infantry force which made the last threat came into the Canadian lines to surrender on the morning of August 21. The Canadians completed the capture of St.-Lambert and the Trun gap was completely closed.

The Canadians had suffered heavily and every officer in the force, with the exception of Major Currie, was killed or wounded. With only one hour's sleep, he led his little battle group through this tumultuous battle and showed tremendous personal courage throughout the fighting. He directed tank fire, he led the infantry, he worked with the anti-tank gunners, he personally knocked out one Tiger tank and all the time gave his men so much encouragement that they never weakened. "We knew at one stage that it was going to be a fight to the finish, but the Major was so cool about it, it was impossible for us to get excited," remarked one non-commissioned officer after the battle.

Major Currie fought with his regiment right through the summer and fall campaign until they got to Bergen op Zoom in southwest Holland. In November it was announced that he had been awarded the Victoria Cross. The war correspondents met him at Breda in Holland and a hand-out giving some background on the Major was given to the press. It said that he had been a garage manager in civilian life in Moose Jaw. Modest Dave Currie, the V.C. winner of the tanks, was worried about this. "There's one thing wrong with that screed about me," he said. "I wasn't any garage manager. I only worked there."

*   *   *   *

We entered the pursuit phase of the French campaign when Trun was mopped up. The orders were to get to the Seine without delay and General Crerar wheeled his forces east. Even before Falaise was captured, the 1st Corps had begun to roll east and it was in high gear when the Canadians started from Trun. On the Channel coast the 6th Airborne Division performed wonders, and, with the Dutch and Belgian brigade groups, subdued Houlgate and Cabourg, raced through the resort town of Deauville, crossed the Touques River to Trouville, and surged on to Honfleur, across the estuary of the Seine from the sprawling port of Le Havre.

South of this maroon-bereted force, the 49th and 51st Divisions kept up the momentum, driving the scattered German remnants before them. The 7th Armoured Division was switched from the Second Army to the Canadian Army, and it shared in the advance.

The British took Lisieux, on the River Touques south of Deauville, in heavy fighting, and Pont Leveque was captured on the same river. Crossing this water barrier, the British tanks and infantry surged on through the rolling, tree-clad hills to the River Risle, and Pont Audemer fell. At several points the German rearguards stood to fight. There were some severe actions in this seventy-mile advance which carried the 1st Corps into the valley of the Seine.

The Canadian Corps advance was led by the 2nd Division which left Caen and struck east at top speed. It passed through Vimoutiers, northeast of Trun, and fanned out over the network of roads and highways which run through the hills and the rich farming country to the Seine.

Occasionally there were some brisk skirmishes but nothing could hold up this avalanche of infantry and armour thundering east. Orbec was captured; our troops entered Thiberville and Bernay; they went on to Brionne on the Risle River. The Germans, fleeing now in disorder, blew bridges behind them and mined roads hastily, but they could not pull themselves together for an organized stand on even the river line of the Risle. They did not even try.

Behind the 2nd Division came the 3rd Division, fresh from the tremendous victory in the Trun gap. Near Brionne, it passed through the 2nd Division and, jumping the Risle, struck out on the home stretch to the Seine. The 4th Division rolled east too, and south of the Canadian Corps the entire Second Army was lunging ahead, its gains screened by a news blackout like that we had for those few days at Falaise.

The story of the drive to the Seine was overshadowed by the liberation of Paris on August 23, when the French Forces of the Interior announced that the city had been freed by its citizens rising in revolt.

Nevertheless, the thrust to the lower Seine was a dramatic phase of the French campaign and one of vital importance to subsequent events which cleared the whole of France of the Germans.

I had a fantastic time keeping up with the moving columns, which travelled day and night. Headquarters changed sometimes twice a day and you could never find out exactly where the next location was. Our press camp at the start of the pursuit was back behind Caen in a château in the tiny village of Villeneuve, and each night I would rush back there from the front, at one time a hundred miles away, to send my stories on the day's advance. The roads were clogged with traffic and burnt-out German vehicles hit by our incessant air attack, and progress was slow against the stream of our guns and trucks. Finally the press camp jumped forward to near Brionne, but by the time we got settled down in another château, whose most recent occupants had been *S.S.* troops, the Seine had been reached and the front was eluding us again.

On August 25 the leading Canadian troops linked up with American forces which had pushed north along the south bank of the Seine to Elbeuf, below Rouen. It was the 18th Armoured Car Regiment (12th Manitoba Dragoons) which first established contact with the Americans. The regiment, the Corps' long-range reconnaissance unit, had roared east from Brionne over uncertain roads and briskly carried out this task, the first of many notable jobs undertaken and accomplished by this fine outfit.

The 3rd and 4th Divisions were at the Seine the following day and the Americans withdrew to their own areas to the south as the Royal Canadian Engineers went to work erecting bridges over the Seine at Elbeuf and later at Pont de l'Arche, east of Elbeuf. The 3rd was then commanded by Major-General Dan Spry, and the 4th by Major-General Harry Foster, who had led the western brigade of the 3rd Division on D-Day.

The first Canadians over the Seine were rafted across the broad river on August 26, and the following day men of the 3rd and 4th Divisions went over in strength by the long bridges the sappers had rushed across.

The 1st Corps put troops over the Risle in the Pont Audemer area and they slowly swept the pocket along the lower Seine between the area west of Elbeuf and the mouth. At many points they found it heavy going but the 7th Armoured and the 49th Divisions finally cleared the district of Germans.

The 2nd Division had been ordered to push up the Rouen loop northwest of Elbeuf and immediately south of Rouen. It got into the forest of La Londe at the mouth of this loop and there the Division fought a bitter and bloody battle. A large German force, which had not been able to escape to Rouen, made a desperate stand in the woods and along the sunken roads, and heavy fighting ensued. The plan to push the Division through the loop to Rouen was abandoned and emphasis was placed on the successes the 3rd and 4th Divisions were having in their advances north from Elbeuf after they had crossed the Seine.

The German Fifteenth Army was north of the Seine and into it merged the troops of the Seventh Army which had been able to escape to the Seine. The job of the Fifteenth Army was to defend the Channel coast from Le Havre to the Belgian border. This involved defending the flying-bomb sites which dotted this district. We called it the "rocket coast". The Fifteenth Army had no armour to speak of. Its divisions were weak. It had few *S.S.* troops. It was the German second-rate army in the west and it was decided not to commit it in a show-down battle against the drive of the Canadian Army and the Second British Army which now had several divisions over the Seine between Rouen and Paris.

The German High Command decided to withdraw this army to the Somme, and then into Holland. Garrisons were left behind in vital Channel ports and the policy of delay was adopted. The enemy had decided to give up France completely, and we soon realized that this was the case.

The Canadians seized the opportunity of the German withdrawal and persistently pushed on. By the morning of August 30, one of the brigades of 3rd Division was nearly at the outskirts of Rouen, and in a drizzling rain late in the afternoon, the Stormont, Dundas and Glengarry Highlanders, with the Highland Light Infantry and the North Nova Scotia Highlanders—the regiments which were the first Canadian infantry into Caen—entered the city.

I was roaming around the sector with the Division and, buttoning up my scout car, I went in with the Glens. Only a little sniping marred the scene of jubilation as thousands of Rouen citizens greeted the Canadians with a wild demonstration of joy and relief. I had not been to Paris for its liberation, but I saw the whole incredible show in Rouen and that was enough for me. Paris might have been bigger, its liberation more important, but its welcome could not have been any more spontaneous or exciting than this one we received in Rouen, badly bombed as it was, along the banks of the Seine.

The scout car in which I had entered Rouen was quite an acquisition. Normally correspondents drive around the front in jeeps and I was the one on the Western Front with the good fortune to have my own private armoured buggy. It was nice and comfortable going into Rouen that day, with the hatches closed down tightly and immune from sniper's bullets behind half-inch steel plating.

The car had been given me during the Battle of Falaise by a young colonel of a Canadian tank regiment. I was at the front with him one day between Caen and Falaise and we were yarning about news coverage.

"You must have a hell of a time wandering around in an open jeep when the stuff is flying," he remarked.

"Some of our crowd have found it sticky at times," I replied diplomatically, eyeing a trim scout car parked nearby. "What one really needs is a little armoured job to keep up with the tanks."

"Well," said the colonel with a boyish grin, "we can probably fix you up. Tonight we are attacking, as you know. I think we can write off a scout car as being destroyed by enemy action. Keep mum about where and how you are getting this vehicle and come around in a couple of days to pick it up. It might add years to your life."

The colonel was as good as his word. The night Falaise was under attack, I called on the regiment and my scout car was ready.

I took it with me all the way to Germany.

*　　　*　　　*　　　*

The day after the Highland battalions liberated Rouen, the rest of the 3rd Division and all the 2nd Division passed through the fine old city. Thousands upon thousands of people jammed the streets as the convoys rumbled over the pavement. They cheered the passing troops for hours on end, and the streets were littered with flowers. Tricolours flew from every building in wild profusion. Rouen had never known a day like this in war, and I don't think any of the Canadians had ever seen anything like it, outside the reception the King and Queen received in the Royal tour of Canada.

For the Canadian fighting men it was a fitting reward for their long, arduous push from Caen.

General Crerar had several important tasks to carry out now. Le Havre had to be taken quickly and the Channel coast had to be cleared to the Somme and through the Pas de Calais to the Belgian border and beyond.

With a fine sense of justice and history, the General directed the 2nd Division on Dieppe, forty miles due north of Rouen.

The 3rd and 4th Divisions, without resting or re-fitting even after their seventy-mile advance from Trun, were ordered to go on to the Somme. The 1st British Corps was to swing around on Le Havre, but the 51st Division first was to return to St. Valery, west of Dieppe, where in the gloomy days of June, 1940, the original 51st was forced to surrender to the Germans after a gallant, fighting withdrawal from the Maginot Line.

VIII

RETURN TO DIEPPE

FROM morning to night on the last day of August, convoys of the 2nd Division whisked through Rouen and turned north on the long, straight highway leading to Dieppe, forty miles away. Columns of Bren-gun carriers and half-tracks, jammed with troops and weapons, clattered along the streets, followed by tanks and guns and hundreds of trucks filled with fighting men. They passed down lanes of madly cheering, ecstatic French people who packed the wide thoroughfares by the Seine to give this wild, prolonged welcome to the Canadians with the dark-blue battle patches on their sleeves. The 2nd Division could not tarry. It had a rendezvous with history.

Through the tricolour-waving, flower-tossing throngs, the columns raced to the northwestern outskirts of Rouen where the highway forks—left to Le Havre, right to Dieppe. The crowd at the fork watched the Canadians wheel to the right where the signpost said "Dieppe".

More excitement! The word ran through the crowd: *"Çà, c'est bien! Les Canadiens s'en vont à Dieppe."* And with faces sparkling, they waved and shouted all the more. The columns sped north up the long, straight road.

Leading the advance was the 8th Reconnaissance Regiment, the "recce" unit of the Division. It had not been on the raid of two years before, but some of its officers and men had. In this spearhead column was a squadron commanded by Major Dennis Bult-Francis of Montreal. He had been wounded on the beaches during the 1942 raid and by a miracle got back to England. Now he was going back—the first of the old Division to get into the port.

Behind the "recce" came the Dieppe regiments—the Essex Scottish who had faced the hell of fire on the main beach of Dieppe; the Royal Regiment, which had been practically wiped out in the inferno that raged on the narrow beach at Puits, a mile east of Dieppe; the Royal Hamilton Light Infantry, the famous "Rileys" who had fought on the main beach and got troops over the Esplanade into the centre of the town on that blazing August 19, two years before.

And behind them came the South Saskatchewan Regiment, those heroic Westerners who fought at Pourville, a mile west of Dieppe, and whose commanding officer, Lieutenant-Colonel Cecil Merritt of Vancouver won the Victoria Cross; the Cameron Highlanders of Winnipeg who passed through the S.S.R. at Pourville and penetrated three miles inland up the valley of the Scie River; and the fighting Fusiliers Mont-Royal, who as the reserve battalion were committed to the fiery main beach and fought with the Essex, the "Rileys" and the Calgary Tank Regiment there.

In the Division that sped north on that single highway were the Calgary Highlanders, which had contributed some men to the raid force, the Black Watch from Montreal, which sent a company and lost a company, and the Regiment de Maisonneuve, which had sent some men too.

The Toronto Scottish, which had machine-gunners at Dieppe, was coming back with the whole regiment, its Vickers and heavy mortar crews bouncing north in their Bren-gun carriers. The three field regiments, the Light Anti-Aircraft Regiment and the Anti-Tank Regiment rolled with the Division too.

Few thought that Dieppe would be taken without a battle. A plan for an assault was ready. The units had been briefed. Lancasters and Halifaxes of Bomber Command were to raid the port in great strength in the early evening of September 1, bombing every German position in the area. Warships of the Royal Navy were to appear off shore and shell coastal positions. The plan called for a large-scale combined operation to take the port.

The Canadians left the delirious crowds of Rouen and rushed on, grimly determined to settle an old score and destroy the enemy garrison in Dieppe. They expected a battle and were ready for it.

The 8th "Recce" got to Totes, half-way between Rouen and Dieppe, and had a sharp brush with a German anti-aircraft unit withdrawing eastward from Le Havre peninsula. The Germans scattered and the "recce" had another scrap at Longueville where they bumped a small packet of enemy.

By nightfall on that last day of August, the "recce" were just short of Dieppe, the rest of the Division stretched out a dozen miles behind them.

After dawn, the armoured cars covered the last few miles to the town. No shells screamed down the highway at them. No machine-gun bullets splattered against the armoured cars. There were few mines on the roads. At one point near the town, the road was cratered by a demolition, but the "recce" cleared this and at 10.30 A.M. entered Dieppe.

They expected anything to happen. They thought they might have to fight in the streets. But the German garrison had gone. A few men of the last demolition parties, firing charges in the harbour area when the Canadians arrived, fled east along the coast road.

Instead of bullets and blood, Dieppe gave the Canadians flowers and wine. The delirious population poured into the streets to tell the 8th "Recce" in a frenzy of joy that the Germans had gone, that the town was free.

Through the swirling crowd, armoured cars poked their way into the centre of the town. But, in truth, the enemy had fled. Dieppe had been hastily evacuated as the 2nd Division stormed up from Rouen.

The Canadians liberated Dieppe and won the first Channel port without firing a shot, without losing a man. It was completely unbelievable. Yet it was only as it should have been. Too much blood had been shed on those desperate beaches.

For those who had been on the raid two years before, this day of our return was the war's greatest triumph, and the whole of that fine Division shared it with us.

*   *   *   *

The advance from Rouen went so swiftly that I had a frantic time getting to Dieppe on time with the Division. We had expected that it would take several more days to get into the port and I was still cleaning up the story of the Canadians in Rouen and the advance on Dieppe when the word flashed back from the front that the "recce" were at Totes and the road to the port was practically clear.

I heard this amazing news at Army H.Q. near Brionne on the Risle River, thirty miles west of Rouen. The next morning, September 1, I climbed into my scout car, piloted by that superb little driver of mine, Gunner Norman Beattie of Mount Dennis, Ont., and we raced to the Seine, through Rouen and up the highway to catch the 2nd Division.

In every hamlet, crowds lined the roadway cheering on every Canadian. Prisoners taken by the vanguard of the Division in the few clashes on the road to Dieppe were marching back under a few guards. It was as clear and bright a day as it was two years before when we crossed the Channel.

We rocketed past the artillery and the tanks, went through Totes like a flying-bomb. We passed the Black Watch and the Regiment de Maissoneuve moving along in troop-carrying vehicles, we went through the South Saskatchewans and the rest and skidded to a stop with the "Rileys", five miles from Dieppe.

I was as excited as I was on the day of the raid. This was the day I had been waiting for ever since we had landed in Normandy. The whole 2nd Division had that same feeling. You could see it in the faces of those soldiers as they waited to go on into Dieppe. They had come down this victory road, cheered to the blue French skies, and now the climax was at hand.

I spotted Lieutenant-Colonel Graham McLaughlin of Toronto standing by his carrier. He was then commanding the R.H.L.I. "You'd better hustle," he said. "The 'recce' have just reported they're into the place."

Beattie rolled that armoured car as it never rolled before or since, and we flew down the highway. I sat on the turret and watched the fields and woods flash by, peering ahead for that first important glimpse of Dieppe. Around a bend the car screeched and there was the port spread out on flat ground between the two great headlands at the mouth of the Argues.

The eastern end of the town down by the harbour and in the lee of the east headland was smoking, but there was no other sign of war. Dieppe looked like the languid, quiet Channel resort town it should always be.

Yet I was awed by that first sight of Dieppe again.

I told Beattie to slow down and, as I looked at the place, my mind was flooded with conflicting emotions —I was thrilled, exhilarated and moved as I had been by few sights in the war. Yet I was moodily saddened and I had a dozen flash-backs to the horrible scenes on those beaches.

I thought of the men who died there, who were wounded, who were taken prisoner when they could fight no longer. I thought of old friends like Jack Prince, Art Hueston, Walt McGregor, Brian McCool, John Counsel. I thought of Lieutenant-Colonel Doug Catto of the Royals, the regiment with which I had gone into Puits and had somehow survived the massacre on that beach, of Brigadier Bill Southam of Toronto and Brigadier Sherwood Lett of Vancouver. This was a moment which they should have shared. I felt as if I were witnessing this drama almost alone, but there really were about twenty-five men in each of the six main battalions who were coming back.

I looked at Dieppe and cursed it for the Canadian lives it had cost before. I looked at Dieppe and saw lying below me the genesis of our mighty combined-operations victories from North Africa to Normandy.

My mind was a tumult of grim memories, of relief, of revenge, of thankfulness, but above all I saw the grey shadows of the men who had given everything they had on those bitter beaches two years and thirteen days before. I had a vivid memory of their folks whom I had seen and talked to in Canada after the raid— people in the seven cities from which the Dieppe regiments had come. The men and women of Windsor, Ont., of Toronto, Montreal, Weyburn, Calgary, Winnipeg and Hamilton. They had borne their grief as their sons and their husbands would have wished. At home in their loneliness and their bereavement they were, in their way, as gallant as their men.

And for the men of Dieppe, among the heroes of this war, I can never give to any a higher place than to those soldiers of the 2nd Division who rushed up the beaches on that day when we had not yet begun to win. They helped make the winning possible.

It may have been the wind that put tears in my eyes as I drove into Dieppe to the crowds and the flowers and the memories, to the acclaim of a town which had lived for the day the Canadians returned.

I went through the throngs on the streets to the central square and stopped near an armoured car of the 8th Recce. In ten seconds Beattie and I were surrounded by laughing, extravagantly happy civilians. An old lady tottered up to my scout car with a huge bouquet of flowers. A pretty girl pressed through the crowd and gave us another bouquet she had picked that morning from the gardens of the town. A hundred Dieppe people crushed around the car, wanting to shake our hands, to kiss us and to tell us how welcome we were. These demonstrations had embarrassed me all across France, for a war correspondent is not the person to whom such homage should be paid. We don't do any liberating: we just ride along with the troops who do. But in Dieppe, I accepted it all, for there were not many of the original 2nd Division who were coming back and I had an idea I was pinch-hitting for some of them at least.

Our scout car was decked with flowers. Even in Rouen we had not collected a floral display like this. I shook hands for half an hour and sputtered, *"Merci, merci, mes amis,"* in high-school French which had improved little in the rush across France.

It was the same with everyone who entered Dieppe that day. They were literally mobbed by the crowd, taken off to cafés and to homes to be plied with liberation wine and to be applauded like the victors they were.

I met General Foulkes in the town, grinning from ear to ear. He had just had a talk with the mayor and had walked on flowers in the streets. "I'm afraid I'm going to spoil your story a little, Munro," he said with a laugh. "I can't possibly bring the whole Division into town today for I really don't know what would happen in this tumult. I'll hold the infantry battalions back on the hills outside the town and we will have a formal parade later."

It was probably a sensible decision, for the 2nd Division might have been enveloped for a week in Dieppe hospitality.

So once the "recce" determined there were no Germans in Dieppe, no more troops entered. The battalions which had been on the raid waited outside the town and in the next few days, when the first liberation enthusiasm had died down slightly, they were allowed into a town a few hundred at a time. They did not lack the fullest hospitality even then. For a week Dieppe was Canada Town.

I wandered around the place all day like a man in a dream. First, with a French guide, I went down to the harbour. The enemy had carried out some demolition there and sown some sea mines but had not had time to destroy the installations completely. The army and navy were able to get Dieppe operating, as a matter of fact, within a few weeks of its capture.

I walked past the ruined tobacco factory on the Esplanade. The factory had been set on fire during the raid and it was only a skeleton. All the buildings along the front were fortified and my guide and I went through a concrete pillbox out onto the Esplanade where the fiercest fire had raged during the Canadian attack. The Esplanade was covered with thick barbed wire and was mined from one end to the other. The pier jutting out on the west side of the harbour was mined and criss-crossed with wire. The main beach was piled with obstacles and wire and every foot of it was mined. The Casino, which the "Rileys" had fought for and captured at the western end of the Esplanade, had been demolished to give a clear field of fire for the coast guns in the cliff face of the west headland.

Looking at the beach and the towering headlands on either side of it and the fortified houses along the front facing the beach, I was appalled at the target the Canadians had raided. Of course, two years earlier the defences had not been as formidable. Immediately after the raid, the Germans put the Todt organization to work on Dieppe and built as complete a defence system on the seaward side as there was on the Channel coast. The headlands were completely fortified with huge concrete casemates, sunk deep into the hard, chalky ground, linked with tunnels and trenches. Guns and more guns were added to the defences. The flanks were screened with mine fields and more huge casemates, but the Germans did not fortify the approaches from behind—from the south. This was the way the Canadians returned.

Nevertheless, Dieppe could have been defended for days and even weeks. A heavy battle would have been necessary to capture the port. Yet the Germans fled and it is a mystery yet to me why they evacuated so completely. Not even a rearguard was left. Two years' labour on the coastal defences went for nothing.

I suppose the Germans knew they had to cut their losses. But they probably also believed that the Canadians would have been merciless in their assault on Dieppe. It was wiser, far wiser, for them to give it up.

Everywhere on the Esplanade and in the town, I was moved to the depths of my feeling by what I saw. I think everyone from the old Division was too. I remember meeting Lieutenant-Colonel Eric Bell of Regina on the Esplanade and he could hardly talk. He had gone through the hell of that main beach and could not keep his eyes off it. The sight of that beach and that Esplanade nearly mesmerized us. Eric's jaw just tightened and I knew the memories he had.

He was seeing the Essex, the R.H.L.I., the Calgary tanks and the F.M.R. on that beach again. He turned and walked silently back into the town.

Major Bult-Francis was down near the Esplanade too. And it was there that he found the French girl who had bound his wounds in 1942 when he fell near the houses by the beach. She remembered him, and no woman of France was as surprised as she when he walked up to greet her.

All the civilians in the town seemed to have been there two years before. All they would talk about was the raid.

Wandering through the centre of town we saw the places where the infantry had fought it out. The stone of one of the churches was chipped by bullets and the buildings around it still were pitted with small holes.

The mayor pointed out a plot of grass near the church where he, then an air-raid warden, had talked with some of the Canadians during the heat of battle and they had given him cigarettes. "One of your men was hit right there," he said. "He lay on the grass and we could not reach him and he died there. We buried him with the other Canadians up on the hill behind the town."

The French people of Dieppe had buried the Canadian dead. They took their bodies from the beaches and from the Esplanade and the streets of the town, and made a cemetery for them on the hill behind the town. Over each grave they placed a plain, unpainted wooden cross and they gave their record of the names to the Division when it came back.

For two years, French caretakers tended those graves. Fresh flowers were placed on them by the town folk. The Canadians were not forgotten.

Passing through the new coastal fortifications, I went to the hill which overlooks Pourville. There was the bridge which Lieutenant-Colonel Merritt had crossed to lead his men of the S.S.R. There were the pillboxes on the hills he had attacked with his men.

Pourville was an empty shell and areas behind the town had been flooded as a defence measure. Half-finished casemates were scattered around the town and on the hills.

Then I made a pilgrimage—it was that to me—to Puits, east of Dieppe. Circling away around behind Dieppe because of blown bridges over the Argues River, I went along a lonely, desolate road which wound down to the Channel and to the village where the Royals had gone ashore.

I went through the lonely, grey-brown town of Puits and down the gulch towards the beach. The mines on the road had not been lifted. Beattie stopped the scout car and, picking my way cautiously through the mine field, I reached the beach. I wished I had not come alone. It was like walking into a tomb. I shuddered to look at the beach, at the twelve-foot stone wall across its top where so many of the Royals had been cut down before my eyes. I shuddered when I looked at the quaint houses still there on the cliff-top from which German machine-gun fire had poured into our boats.

Here one of the finest regiments in the Canadian Army had fought and died without much chance of living, for it had been caught in the daylight under murderous fire, and had been decimated.

The Puits defences were strong two years ago but now they were twice as formidable. Concrete casemates had been added to the sides of the narrow defile leading from the beach. Obstacles were littered on the beach. Mines were everywhere. No craft could possibly land in the face of the new defences.

Alone with my thoughts, I could not stay on the Puits beach a minute longer. The Channel wind eerily flapped the German camouflage on the casemates. Everything was ominous, grey and death-like and I hurried back through the mine field, past the houses where the Germans had shot at us at point-blank range right into our boats.

I had returned to Puits but it was a place of death and horror even two years after. We drove along the winding road back to the friendly crowds of Dieppe.

The following Sunday, September 3—the fifth anniversary of the start of the war—the entire 2nd Division formally paraded through Dieppe and General Crerar took the salute in the centre of the town. It was probable the most impressive and meaningful parade held by Canadian soldiers of this war.

A memorial service was held at the cemetery on the hill, and the veterans of the Dieppe raid, with the rest of the Division, paid their solemn homage to their comrades who had died.

IX

CHANNEL PORT BLITZ

WHILE the 2nd Division rested at Dieppe after its return, the other divisions of the First Canadian Army rolled forward to new objectives. A British Corps crossed the Seine and hooked around on Le Havre, with the 49th Division and the 51st Highland Division investing the huge port.

But before it went to Le Havre, the 51st returned to St.-Valery-en-Caux, west of Dieppe, where the original Highland Division of this war had been forced to capitulate in the débâcle of 1940, after making a gallant, fighting withdrawal across Belgium and northern France from the Maginot Line. The "Jocks" now had no opposition. They simply marched into the little Channel coast town, but for the Highland Division and for Scotland it was as historic a day as the return to Dieppe was for the 2nd Division and for Canada.

The pipes of the famous Highland regiments skirled in St.-Valery again and then the Division moved on to the battle for Le Havre.

Meanwhile the 2nd Canadian Corps, with the exception of the 2nd Division, struck out from Rouen for the Somme as the British Second Army on its right flank rushed over the roads towards Amiens and the American forces fanned out east of Paris.

The German front in France had folded up completely and the Fifteenth Army, charged with the defence of the flying-bomb coast from Le Havre to

(Top): *Canadian infantry flushing Germans from the mass of rubble which was once a thriving French city. Panzer troops fought stubbornly here.*

(Lower): *Western Canadians hitch-hiking to victory, on tanks that sank deep in mud as the spearhead of the Allied attack in the West pushed into Germany in the spring of 1945. It was a typical scene in the advance.*

Holland, was withdrawing as fast as it could, blasted from the air by Allied planes that raked the long columns of men, vehicles, tanks, guns and horse-drawn carts.

The 4th Canadian Armoured Division and the Polish Armoured Division, with the 3rd Canadian Division, pushed ahead day and night, hot on the heels of the retreating Germans. It was a straight pursuit, with the occasional skirmish with small rear-guard parties. Through St.-Saens, and on to Neuf-chatel went the Canadian Corps, armoured cars fanning out on the roads ahead of the divisions and sometimes catching up with the ends of the German columns. Down the broad highway from Neufchatel, the Canadians rolled through Faucarmont and cross-ing the Bresle River drove on to the Somme at Abbeville.

Blown bridges were repaired by Royal Canadian Engineers who rode along with the leading troops, and by September 3 troops of the 4th Division and the Polish Division were across the Somme and racing through the Pas de Calais. These armoured columns thundered through Hesdin and into St.-Omer. The Poles took the lead and swinging past the big St.-Omer airdrome went over Mount Cassel, from the top of which they could see Dunkerque, and rolled on into Belgium, going through Poperinghe and liberating Ypres by September 7.

The 3rd Division took the other road from Abbe-ville, the one which goes through Montreuil, where Earl Haig had his headquarters in the First Great War, and went due north towards Boulogne. The Division had been ordered to close in on Boulogne, Calais and Cap Gris Nez and capture them.

As it fell back into Holland, the Fifteenth Army

dropped off troops to strengthen the garrisons of Boulogne, Calais and Dunkerque, and it formed up on the Leopold Canal, south of the Schelde estuary, prepared to make a stand there. The 4th Division and the Poles got to the Bruges area with little fighting, but they found the Germans were holding the network of canals east of the ancient town.

On the coast, the 18th Armoured Car Regiment (12th Manitoba Dragoons) spurted past Dunkerque and occupied Ostend on September 8. The 2nd Division came up from Dieppe to join the Corps and it operated along the coast, encircling Dunkerque and relieving the armour at Bruges.

By then, however, it was clear that the pursuit across France and Belgium was over. The Germans were going to fight to hold the Schelde estuary as long as they could, and before the Canadian Army attacked on the Schelde, it was imperative to clear the enemy from the Channel ports.

Le Havre, Boulogne and Calais were to be stormed and captured. Supply ports comparatively close to the front were urgently needed and it fell to the Canadian Army to provide the ports.

In the long run, even these ports were not enough. The vast port of Antwerp, second only to Hamburg among the ports of northern Europe, was essential to keep the Allied forces supplied for the push into Germany. To open Antwerp, the Schelde had to be cleared. The port itself had been captured by the British 11th Armoured Division early in September in the Second Army drive through Belgium but it was of no use at all until the forty-five-mile estuary from the North Sea was free of the Germans, holding it in strength. This was another of the tough jobs carried out by the coast-hopping Canadian Army. It seldom had a sinecure in assignments during the entire campaign in the west. From Caen to Holland, on the left of the Allied line, it faced heart-breaking difficulties but it never failed in any task.

*   *   *   *

Its advance from the Seine to the Leopold canal through the flying-bomb-site area brought quick relief to London and southern England. At least three hundred V-1 sites were overrun—most of them having been blown up by the Germans as they fell back. In behind Dieppe there were a dozen sites which had been operating for months. All along the coast, there were scores more and through the Pas de Calais a hundred or more were located.

I must have seen fifty myself, as I followed the Corps on the wild advance across northern France into Belgium. Particularly in the Pas de Calais every wood of any size held its flying-bomb site. A few were intact but most of them were destroyed. I was impressed by the remarkable bombing job which had been done on these sites by the Allied air forces. Very few woods containing sites had not been attacked and in each case scores of gaping bomb craters were evidence of the accuracy of the bombing. Sometimes the bombs had landed right on the site, blowing it to pieces. At other places, the bombing had been so close that the launching-track had been knocked out of line and installations damaged.

Each site had a steel launching-track about a hundred and fifty feet long, rising on an angle of about forty degrees through a gap cut in the trees. Around the track were heavy concrete structures where the bombs were stored. In many there were elaborate dug-outs for the site crew. Bits of the flying-bombs could be seen lying around in the wreckage of the sites.

Members of the French underground had all these sites pin-pointed and it was on information passed by secret channels to England that the air forces carried out prolonged, relentless attacks for months on this "rocket coast".

We passed along the coast so rapidly, though, that we scarcely had time to bother with rocket sites. One lone officer at Army H.Q. was detailed to check on the sites and make a tally, while everyone else concentrated on the advance to the Dutch border and the attacks on the Channel ports.

It was the people of London and southern England who sang the praise of the Canadian Army, which in liberating northern France and northern Belgium eased the terrible burden they were bearing under fire of this flying-bomb weapon since mid-June.

*   *   *   *

The Second Army route to Belgium, Holland and the German border in that thrilling advance from the Seine took it through the belt of battle-grounds of the other war. As the Canadians reached the Somme at Abbeville, British tanks of the Second Army shot their way into Amiens, farther up the river. They roared through the old city of a million memories for a million fighting men of another conflict with Germany, and they rumbled up the roads to Arras, through rolling farmland reclaimed from the battle-fields.

A column of tanks and infantry pushed north on the Lens road and the British Tommies came to Vimy Ridge, graced by the gleaming white memorial to Canada's sixty thousand dead of the First Great War.

They paused for a moment by that heroic monument with its two white pylons reaching to the sky, and they passed on along the road to Lens, to Lille and to Belgium.

At Canadian H.Q. near Rouen we heard the news of the bloodless capture of Vimy Ridge on September 2, the day after the return to Dieppe, and Lionel Shapiro and I jumped into our weary jeep and headed for Amiens, for Arras, for Vimy.

From Rouen to Neufchatel we sped and then cut east through Aumale and Poix through an empty area where there was a gap between the two armies. I believe we personally liberated a few small hamlets, and as a mark of appreciation in one chaotic little village, a woman surrounded by a throng of children pressed a fried chicken into my hands. That topped all the amazing liberation gifts we ever received. We ate it that night in Arras.

At Poix we came into the British lines and the convoys were flooding to Amiens. Germans who had not been able to flee were marching back down the road to the prison cages.

Shap and I dodged in and out of the hustling trucks, guns and tanks and slithered into Amiens in the rain. I can remember old soldiers saying gloomily that it always rained in Amiens and it was raining true to form when we got there.

The city was not a stopping-point for the Second Army. The convoys zoomed down the boulevard and out on the roads to Arras, Doullens, Cambrai and Douai. Tommies gaped from the trucks and the tanks at the buildings and people of Amiens and tried to remember what their fathers had told them years ago about this city, but they could remember no better than we. Some old sweats with ribbons of the last war

on their tunics regaled the young ones with their tales
of Amiens as they bumped over the *pavé*, but nobody
seemed very interested. They were looking ahead to
Belgium and to Germany. In those hours it looked as
if the war might be over in a week or a month. It
would certainly be over by Christmas.

Here at Amiens, the Canadian Corps of the last war
had launched its big offensive on August 8, 1918,
which swept through the shell-churned fields to Arras
and to Vimy and took the Canadians back to Mons
when the Armistice was sounded. Here at Amiens,
the Last Hundred Days began. On August 8, 1944,
the First Canadian Army had attacked at Caen in what
was predicted might be the beginning of the last hundred days of this war. In Amiens on September 2, I
felt the end was drawing near.

I was not alone in that opinion. In the High Command, there were ranking officers who held the same
view, and certainly among the troops optimism was
running wild as they rushed north and east for the
Reich in pursuit of the German forces in the west.

We took a secondary road from Amiens to Arras,
past the well-kept cemeteries. On the plain headstones
were many Canadian names, each surmounted by a
maple leaf.

In early evening, we drove into Arras, crossed the
famous square and went to a hotel crowded with
British officers, taking an hour out from their pursuit
of the German Army. An artillery major, whose field
guns were on the road to Germany, said sincerely that
he did not think he would ever fire his guns again.
It was all over, he said.

In the morning the Second Army crossed into Belgium and from the vantage point of Vimy Ridge,
Shap and I watched the columns snake north past the

slag heaps of Lens and go on in the smoke and the ground mist to Belgium.

But the Second Army entry into Belgium almost seemed secondary to us as we stood there on Vimy. We were the first two Canadians to reach the Ridge in this advance, and for us it was a personal pilgrimage to this magnificent shrine of the Dominion.

I walked up the path to the monument as if I were entering a church. My army boots crunched too loud on the gravel for this hallowed place.

We stood and gazed at the splendour of the pylons towering against the blue sky. Slowly we went up the steps and slowly, without a word, we read the inscriptions carved in the stone—the battles fought long ago.

Opposite each one—Ypres, Cambrai, Passchendaele, Hill 70 and the others—I mentally placed Bretteville, Buron, Caen, May-sur-Orne, Falaise, Dieppe. This was a monument not only for one war, but for two wars of sacrifice by the men of Canada.

The monument was not damaged to any serious extent. There were a few chips here and there and a hand was missing from one of the figures. It had been knocked off, it was said, in scattered shelling around Vimy during the retreat of the British Expeditionary Force in 1940.

We were two solitary persons on the ridge. Then two members of the F.F.I. came along on bicycles, with rifles slung over their shoulders. They were part of a patrol scouring the area for scattered bands of Germans.

We talked with the wife of the caretaker, George Stubbs of Winnipeg who had been interned at St.-Denis near Paris by the Germans, and we returned to the war again. It was walking out of one world into another to leave the Ridge and the Memorial for the Canadian front on the coast.

*   *   *   *

Our attention was now focused on the operations against the Channel ports. Le Havre was to be attacked first and the 49th Division and the 51st were in positions north and east of the city. The fame of the 51st Division had spread the world over. It fought with the B.E.F., it was re-formed after St.-Valery and it served with the Eighth Army. The 49th was not as well known but it had served in the ill-starred Norwegian campaign in the spring of 1940; it had a tedious stretch in Iceland and it fought in Normandy with great distinction in the break out from the beach-head.

The attack on Le Havre was preceded by several large-scale raids by Bomber Command and massed British and Canadian artillery pounded the place for days. Following this softening-up, the two infantry divisions, supported by British tanks, stormed the outer defences. They broke through and fought their way steadily through line after line of concrete gun-posts and machine-gun pillboxes. For several days there was fierce fighting and then at 11.30 A.M. on September 12 the German garrison of Le Havre surrendered.

More than thirteen thousand German prisoners, in addition to two hundred wounded, were taken at Le Havre and British casualties were less than four hundred.

*   *   *   *

Some of the special assault equipment, such as the flame-throwers mounted on Churchill tanks and "flail" tanks which go through mine fields whirling great chains ahead of them to blow up the mines, had to be rushed from Le Havre to Boulogne before the 3rd Division could strike at that port. On September 17 at ten A.M., however, the attack went in, after Bomber Command had raided German positions around the town for four hours.

The heavy bomber attack was closely co-ordinated with the infantry assault and it was carried out in a masterly fashion. There were no mistakes like those made at Caen when our own troops were bombed on two occasions. This time, as at Le Havre, the Lancasters and Halifaxes were right on their targets and it was all carried out in text-book fashion.

The principal target in the first assault for both the bombers and the infantry was Mont Lambert, a five-hundred-foot hill east of Boulogne. The Germans had fortified this hill and it was the linchpin of the Boulogne defences.

A thundering artillery barrage from about twenty regiments of Canadian and British guns hit the German positions too. The guns were under command of the Division's artillery chief, Brigadier Todd, and he had the time of his life lathering Mont Lambert and other Boulogne defences with high explosives from his field, medium and heavy guns.

The Dover cross-Channel batteries also shared in this fight for Boulogne. Co-ordinated with the operation and corrected by artillery observers in the Canadian lines, the long-range guns shelled German gun positions at Calais and knocked out at least two batteries.

Aided by flame-throwing Churchill tanks, the Canadian infantry stormed up the slopes of Mont Lambert, while other infantry swung around north of the hill and went for Boulogne itself. All day and throughout the following night the struggle went on for Mont Lambert and the approaches to the port.

The town of Wimereaux, on the coast two miles north of Boulogne, was captured and the next day, September 18, the Germans on Mont Lambert gave up under pressure of the Canadians' attack. Eighteen concrete pillboxes had to be overrun before the enemy yielded. That day the infantry fought their way into Boulogne itself and the Germans in the citadel of the town surrendered. The Canadians rapidly cleared up the town but the Germans continued to resist in the belt of fortifications south of the town, particularly at Le Portel, and also on hills north of the port.

In dogged infantry fighting, the Canadians finally overcame the last garrison of Germans in Le Portel and at four P.M. that afternoon it was all over. Lieutenant-General Heim, the garrison commander, surrendered with the last of his men to Brigadier John Rockingham of Victoria, commander of the assault brigade.

In that brigade were three great Canadian regiments—the North Novas, the Stormont, Dundas and Glengarry Highlanders and the Highland Light Infantry. They had seen the heaviest fighting in and around Boulogne.

The Regiment de la Chaudière, the North Shores and the Queen's Own also shared in the six-day battle that won for the Canadian Army its second Channel port. Nine thousand German prisoners streamed out of battered Boulogne. The stage was now set for the attack on Cap Gris Nez and Calais.

*   *   *   *

Bad weather which cut down visibility for the air force delayed the start of the 3rd Division assault on Calais but on September 25 it opened. The heavies came over; Brigadier Todd unleashed his artillery fire again and the infantry went in. Within two hours the strong positions at Escalles on the coast, four miles west of Calais, were captured and the infantry were cutting into the defences between Escalles and the port itself. Meanwhile, more infantry units were attacking Calais from the southwest and by late afternoon they were within two miles of the outskirts.

Rocket-firing Typhoons streaked over the battle zone, hitting at the enemy positions as they had done at Boulogne, and on the ground flame-throwers, "flail" tanks and the rest of the assault paraphernalia were in action.

The next day heavy bombers again rained down a torrent of high explosives on the Calais defences and the Canadian and British gunners pumped thousands of shells into the enemy lines.

The infantry slugged their way forward and on September 27, Fort Lapin, a thousand yards west of the harbour, was captured. The infantry were also working into Calais from the southwest over flooded ground in attacks where they had to wear Mae Wests.

The following day, the infantry reached the west side of Calais harbour. They were also over the inundated area to the southwest of the town and had fought their way into the southwestern outskirts. Calais citadel on the northwestern outskirts was captured and the ancient moat skirting the built-up area was reached.

A lull in the fighting at Calais came on September 29 when a twenty-four-hour armistice was agreed upon to evacuate ten thousand civilians from the town. But while this was going on an attack was put in at Cap Gris Nez by Brigadier Rockingham and his Canadian Highland troops. The defences there were stormed and captured, the big coast guns which had fired on

Dover for years were silenced, and thirteen hundred prisoners taken.

At noon on September 30 the armistice of Calais ended and the battle was resumed. It roared through the afternoon and by six P.M. that Saturday night all organized resistance was ended.

Colonel Schroeder, the garrison commander, surrendered with his staff. The operation took only six days, as had the capture of Boulogne.

On Sunday in Kent, and particularly in Dover, they gave thanksgiving in the parish churches for the Canadians' victories on the cross-Channel coast from which the enemy had hit out at England since the summer of 1940.

The Glens, North Novas and H.L.I. had done the job at Cap Gris Nez, and at Calais western regiments— the Reginas, the Winnipegs and the Canadian Scottish —had fought with the Queen's Own, the Chaudières and the North Shores.

For the D-Day 3rd Division, it was its greatest triumph since the fighting at Caen. Since Caen the Division had been led by thirty-one-year-old Major-General Spry, who was rushed from an infantry brigade command in Italy to succeed General Keller after he was wounded at Caen.

X

THE *POLDERS* BATTLE—INTO GERMANY

WITH the capture of Calais, the Canadian Army marshalled all its strength for the complicated and difficult operation of clearing the Schelde estuary to open the huge port of Antwerp, forty-five miles up the Schelde.

This operation then had first priority on the Western Front, for on its success and on the opening of Antwerp to our shipping depended the new offensive which was planned to carry the Allied armies into Germany.

We had a string of ports as supply bases, but they were not sufficient for all offensive needs of the gigantic force mustered in Holland, Belgium and on the frontiers of the Reich. We had Cherbourg, Brest, Le Havre operating in addition to the miraculous artificial port off the beaches at Arromanches in Normandy. Ostend and Dieppe were being used as well, and Boulogne and Calais were being cleared of mines. But the supply lines from most of these ports to the Western Front were too long. The supply problem in relation to a new offensive was grave. Antwerp was the answer. This vast, undamaged dock area practically in the backyard of General Eisenhower's forces was the ideal supply base.

It was large enough to meet all the requirements of the armies in the west and now that the mid-September attempt by the Second Army and the airborne forces to cut a corridor through to Arnhem and into the north German plateau had failed in its final objective, the opening of Antwerp was more imperative than ever. Without the port, only limited operations could be carried out during the late fall and winter.

General Crerar had received the order to clear the Schelde. During September he and his army H.Q. staff worked out the plan. By the end of the month it was complete, but the General himself was not well enough to execute it. Under the weather for some time, he temporarily left his command to have a medical check-up in a Canadian Army hospital in England. He was suffering, the doctors found, from anaemia and dysentery, and although he came back to the front in November, fit as ever, it was General Simonds who fought the battle of the Schelde on the plan General Crerar had drawn up.

The three Canadian divisions all figured prominently in the plan and several British formations were to be brought in during the later phases. The Schelde operation also was to coincide with correlated pushes by both the Canadian Army and the Second Army to drive troops of the German Fifteenth Army from southwest Holland.

Fires were still burning in Calais when the 3rd Division was ordered to move eastward and take up positions south of the Leopold canal, in preparation for an attack over the canal into what became known as the "Schelde pocket". This was that strip of Holland south of the estuary and it was held by the 64th German Division, which proved in battle to be one of the best divisions the Canadians had met since they battled the S.S. divisions around Caen.

The 2nd Division was moved to the Antwerp area and sweeping around to the southeast and east, its infantry fought their way over the Albert and Escaut canals and pushed north to cross the Antwerp-Turnhout canal. This screened the right flank for an attack by other infantry of the Division to clean out the enemy in the northern suburbs of Antwerp itself.

The 4th Division remained along the Leopold canal and in the Bruges-Eecloo area until the attack by the 3rd Division went in.

This Division had fought a series of actions west and south of the canal during the latter part of September and it carried out the reconnaissance work for the attack by the 3rd. The Algonquin Regiment, for instance, advancing east from Bruges crossed the Leopold canal at Moerkerke and it bumped strong forces of the 64th Division. Massed enemy artillery hammered the Algonquins bridgehead and severe counter-attacks were made against the Canadians. The regiment was ordered back. The Canadian command now had definite information that the enemy was going to fight hard for the pocket.

The Argyll and Sutherland Highlanders and the Lincoln and Welland Regiment also had a canal battle south of Bruges when they forced a crossing over the Ghent canal at Moerbrugge. This bridgehead was held, the town was captured once the tanks of the South Alberta Regiment got across to support the infantry, and the advance to Eecloo was successfully carried out. Other units in the Division—the Lake Superior Regiment, the Canadian Grenadier Guards and the Governor-General's Footguards—also fought through this area, as the 4th tidied up the situation as a prelude to the assault into the Schelde pocket.

The Polish Division shared in this task too, operating to the east of the 4th Division. It went through Ghent and after fighting in the northern outskirts for several days linked up with the British Second Army forces which at that time were in the Antwerp area. The Poles helped clear the country northeast of Ghent to the Schelde.

Following this, the Poles were moved through Antwerp and took up positions along the Antwerp-Turnhout canal east of the city on the right flank of the 2nd Division.

So after a great deal of shuffling of forces and after much confused and scattered fighting, the Canadian Army was in a position in early October to launch the Schelde clearing operation.

This was the position of the divisions under General Simonds' command before the curtain went up on October 6:

The 3rd Division was located south of the Leopold canal with the assault brigade near Maldegem, on the main highway leading east from Bruges to Eecloo, parallel to the Leopold. Scattered along the Leopold also was the 4th Division, but it was preparing to move to the Antwerp area for the operations in southwest Holland. The 2nd Division was in the northern suburbs of Antwerp and also along the Antwerp-Turnhout canal. The Poles were on their right and the British 49th Division, brought from Le Havre, was in the same general area as the Poles.

Practically all the German Fifteenth Army had been able to withdraw successfully from northern France and Belgium, even though its main escape route through Antwerp had been cut in early September by the lightning thrust of the British 11th Armoured Division into Antwerp. The Germans evacuated, however, through the Schelde and by ferry and boat across the Schelde estuary from Breskens to Flushing on Walcheren Island. From there they fell back along South Beveland Island to the Dutch mainland.

However, the Fifteenth Army left two divisions and all the coastal garrisons behind on the Schelde to fight for the estuary. In the Schelde pocket, the 64th Division, which I have mentioned, was in position on the Leopold canal. North of Antwerp was the 70th Division, with about a dozen roving battle groups of infantry and self-propelled guns. The 70th eventually fell back to South Beveland and to Walcheren, which lie across the northern side of the Schelde estuary.

The Germans had strongly fortified the mouth of the Schelde with big coastal batteries at Flushing and at Breskens, covering the entrance completely. Other fortifications extended along the North Sea coast to Knocke and Heyst, twelve miles west of the mouth of the estuary.

The task of the Canadians was to destroy the 64th

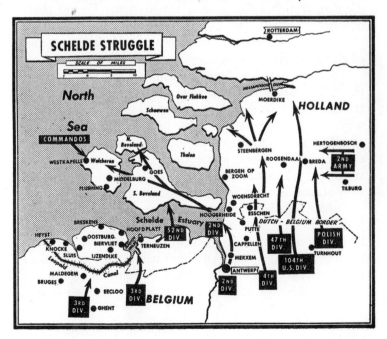

and 70th Divisions and to overrun the coast guns.

The enemy held every advantage of ground. To get into the Schelde pocket, the Canadians had to cross the Leopold canal, and it was covered by machine-guns, artillery and mortars. To get out to South Beveland Island and to Walcheren, the Canadians first had to drive the enemy back for fifteen miles north of Antwerp and then attack west along the narrow causeway connecting the Dutch mainland with South Beveland.

All this area over which the Canadians were obliged to fight was the flattest country in Europe—dead flat, soggy and flooded. Largely reclaimed from the sea, this Dutch *polder* country is criss-crossed with dykes about fifteen feet high. Each dike was a formidable barricade which the enemy could easily defend by digging trenches along it or through it. To aid their defensive system, the Germans could flood hundreds of acres as they wished. It was the worst battle-ground of the western campaign.

The weather, too, was abominable, far the worst of the fall campaign. Cold, sleety rain beat down on the troops, who went for days soaked to the skin and slimy with mud. Many times they had to wade knee-deep through water and mud as they advanced. Along the dikes was the only place they could dig their slit-trenches; when they started to dig them in the fields, they struck water a foot or two down.

Polder fighting was entirely new and the Canadians had to make their own tactical rules. By ingenious innovation and adaption, they mastered the problem of dike fighting. After the operation, they were asked by the War Office to prepare a manual on *polder* warfare to be the standard work for the British Army.

*   *   *   *

The early-September capture of Antwerp by British armour was a heavy blow to the Germans and they fully recognized the grave consequences it held for them. In the confusion of their withdrawal into Holland, they were not prepared for the sudden British sweep to Antwerp, and they had no time to destroy any of the harbour installations in Antwerp.

Anti-sabotage teams of Belgium's secret army also were a big factor in preventing the Germans from wrecking the port. Under a leader known only as *"Le Pélerin"* (The Pilgrim), the teams blocked many German plans to destroy port facilities. A special anti-destruction command of the Belgian underground was located in Antwerp itself.

When the first British armoured spearhead pushed into the city, the secret army went into action and helped hold off the enemy for five or six hours until the main British force arrived. In those five or six critical hours the Germans might have done great damage in the port area.

Caught entirely off balance, they simply could not carry out any demolitions. It seems inconceivable, but it was true. The port fell into our hands intact and only after the enemy force in Holland had pulled itself together miraculously was it able to deploy two divisions around the Schelde. They would hold the Schelde to prevent us using Antwerp. That was the broad policy, and the Germans launched a campaign to boost the morale of the sacrifice troops on the Schelde—the men left behind to die for the Fatherland.

Officers in the units on the Schelde had to sign pledges that they would fight to the end and never give up. They were pledged to lead their men to the death.

General Gustav Von Zangen, commander of the Fifteenth Army, issued a long order to his troops in an effort to bolster their spirit. In the order he spoke frankly.

I picked up the order from the 2nd Division which had captured it on South Beveland. It was dated October 7—the day after the 3rd Division struck on the Leopold canal, and it said: "The defence of the approaches to Antwerp represents a task which is decisive for the further conduct of the war. Therefore every last man in the fortifications is to know why he must devote himself to this task with the utmost strength. After overrunning the Schelde fortifications, the English would finally be in a position to land great masses of *matériel* in a large and completely protected harbour. With this *matériel* they might deliver a death blow at the north German plateau and at Berlin before the onset of the winter."

The Canadians were simply told they were going to clear the Schelde estuary of the Germans. The operation began.

*　　　*　　　*　　　*

Before the 3rd Division struck over the Leopold, the 2nd Division cleaned up the situation north of Antwerp.

The Ontario brigade commanded by Brigadier Cabeldu, who, as a lieutenant-colonel, had led the Canadian Scottish in the Normandy landing and the battles around Caen, was in close contact with the enemy in the northern suburbs of Antwerp, particularly at the factory town of Merxem. His troops also were scattered through the harbour area to the west.

On October 3-4, these troops put on the pressure at Merxem and other 2nd Division men pushed out from the Antwerp-Turnhout canal on their right. The Antwerp suburban front was one of the weirdest of the campaign. The city went about its normal business, with fighting going on on its outskirts. You could get on a street car in the centre of Antwerp and take the trolley to the front. It ran to Merxem and to the fighting.

On October 4, I went to this sector as the Royal Regiment and the Essex Scottish drove the Germans out of Merxem and pursued them up the highway to Cappellen and the Dutch border at Putte. The R.H.L.I. were in the harbour area and they cleared out that section and joined in the pursuit north.

I watched a couple of skirmishes and, as darkness fell, drove back to Antwerp. In half an hour I was in the lounge of the Century Hotel, listening to a string orchestra and having an *apéritif* before dinner, served by waiters in white tie and tails. It was fantastic! Some 2nd Division officers, given a breather from the front, were in the lounge too, fresh from battle that afternoon and goggle-eyed at the splendour half an hour from the shooting.

*   *   *   *

The advance of the 2nd Division relieved the pressure on the Antwerp sector, and on October 6 at 5.30, just before dawn, the 3rd Division hit out in what was really the opening blow in the battle for the Schelde.

A brigade consisting of the Regina Rifles, the Canadian Scottish and the Royal Winnipeg Rifles, which had stormed the Normandy beaches at Courseulles on D-Day, was the assault formation. Brigadier "Jock" Sprague was commanding the formation. From D-Day to beyond Caen he had commanded the Queen's Own Rifles, when he was given the brigade and led it through the battle at Calais.

These infantry crossed the 150-foot-wide canal in the area north of Maldegem where they had concentrated. Flame-throwers, mounted on carriers in position behind the southern dike, hurled sheets of fire right across the canal and behind this roaring, searing screen of fire the infantry went over in assault boats.

The Canadian Scottish and the Reginas led the way and under the Reginas' command was a company of the Royal Montreal Regiment. The company was the defence force at Army H.Q., but had pleaded for action, and was relieving a company of the Reginas at this time.

The Scottish scrambled up the opposite bank without much difficulty, close behind the flames which killed some Germans right in their slit-trenches on the north dike running along the canal. From the dike, the Scottish pushed inland for several hundred yards, over the flat, open fields to groups of buildings on the Dutch-Belgian border, north of the canal.

The Reginas ran into trouble on the crossing, their boats being laced by machine-gun fire from a pillbox to their left. But the R.M.R. company and the other companies made the north dike. They tried to push inland but the enemy fire was so intense that they were forced to dig in on the dike beside the canal.

By dawn, both battalions were under terrific fire. The Germans shelled and mortared the canal on both sides and machine-gun bullets whipped down the length of the canal. Shells from heavy coastal guns far back in the pocket roared into the bridgehead area like a freight train high-balling past. They dug craters in the soft soil large enough to take a jeep.

Into this inferno, the Winnipegs crossed to join the Scottish who held the deepest bridgehead. A gap existed between the Scottish and the Reginas and it was the Winnipegs' task to close this gap and firm up the Canadians' line.

For five days the battle raged on this perilously narrow Leopold bridgehead. I watched a good deal of the fighting, and it was only by sheer guts that the western units hung on to their positions. By all the rules of war the bridgehead should have been lost; the battalions should have been wiped out or forced to withdraw. But even though they suffered heavy casualties, they stayed there on the north side of the Leopold and slaughtered the Germans of the 64th Division who hurled scores of counter-attacks against them. When it was over, it was estimated that the Westerners had destroyed at least three German battalions—totalling about fifteen hundred men.

The fighting was as savage and unrelenting as the same battalions had seen at Bretteville and Putot-en-Bessin on the Caen-Bayeux highway in the first week of the Normandy campaign under attack day and night by German *S.S.* tanks and infantry.

The bridgehead was so narrow the engineers could not get a vehicle bridge over the canal. Several footbridges built under a torrent of shell-fire were always being knocked out. Frequently rations and ammunition had to be ferried over the canal in flimsy assault boats, with mortar bombs and shells exploding around them and machine-gun bullets zipping through the water.

The Reginas were in the worst position of all. They were nearest the highway leading to Aardenburg and it was down this highway that the Germans moved their troops into the attack, for much of the area north of the bridgehead was flooded. From their slit-trenches on the dikes right by the canal the Reginas were unable to move by day, only occasionally by night were they able to make forays over the open ground to the north.

They literally "hung on by their finger-nails", as Major Larry Dampier of Toronto described their position one afternoon at Divisional H.Q. at the height of the battle.

It was so hot on the Reginas' sector that the men could not leave their slit-trenches to eat. Tins of rations were heated up on the south side and ferried over to a dug-out. From that central ration dug-out, they were thrown like grenades to slit-trenches dotting the dike. One isolated rifleman, exasperated at the grub he was getting, finally yelled back: "Why the Hell do I keep getting marmalade?"

The Canadian Scottish on their sector got established in a cluster of houses about five hundred yards inland, but one company in particular had a vicious night battle. The Germans attacked the houses and for hours a close-quarters fight went on, with grenades being thrown in and out of the shattered windows of the houses and machine-guns ripping through the rooms and the doorways.

In the fight to close the gap, the Winnipegs had heavy going along the dike and over the marshes but they finally made the link-up.

The nights were the worst on the bridgehead, which became a "Little Arnhem" as the Canadians hung on against desperate German attempts to drive them back into the canal.

Under cover of the darkness, the enemy infantry would infiltrate into the bridgehead and fighting would rage among the slit-trenches. The Scottish fought with fists and knives one night in a bloody brawl when the Germans rushed into their positions.

For days and nights even the south side of the canal was stormy enough. The Germans on several occasions infiltrated across the canal and prowled through the gun lines, shooting up anything they could find in the darkness.

The south side of the canal was under a howling tumult of shell-fire when the battle was at its worst, and it was as much as your life was worth to go down to the dike and peer across the canal to the bridgehead area. I was terrified every time I went to the dike but on the fourth day I scurried over the fragile pontoon bridge during a lull and saw that grim battle-field. The dike was scorched black by the flame throwers and in the muddy trenches behind them were the Germans who had been caught in the fiery blast. The Scottish were in a line of water-filled slit-trenches, watching, waiting for the Germans' next attack. A gramophone they had found in one of the houses whined out a Dutch folk song from the depths of a trench.

By October 10, the Germans stopped trying to knock out the bridgehead. They were occupied with a new Canadian threat to their position in the Schelde pocket—a landing made from the sea southeast of Breskens on the south shore of the estuary.

Originally it had been planned to exploit the Leopold canal bridgehead and pass the other brigades through that breach in the German defences. But the enemy resistance was too strong. The bridgehead had held firm and the 64th Division had been drawn into battle but it would have been too costly an effort to put in more troops to break out to Aardenburg.

So the Highland brigade, commanded by Brigadier Rockingham of Boulogne and Cap Gris Nez fame, prepared to sail from Terneuzen and land at the back-door of the pocket, behind the barrier of the Leopold canal.

This was not part of the original plan drawn up by

General Crerar, although it was the only deviation from it. This was a master stroke by General Simonds, who, appreciating that there would be heavy losses if the Leopold was exploited, decided on a bold attack from the sea at this vulnerable spot on the Schelde.

Later, General Eberding, captured commander of the 64th Division, admitted to General Spry that this seaborne attack caught him by surprise. He was expecting an armoured thrust from the 4th Division, which he had identified as being along the Leopold. But the tanks of the 4th had moved to the area north of Antwerp in the interval for the attack through southwest Holland, and the job in the pocket was exclusively for the 3rd Division.

The landing was to take place in the early morning of October 8, but bad weather led to a postponement and it was not made until the following morning. The Canadian infantry were carried along the coast from Terneuzen in amphibious, tracked vehicles known as "alligators", used first by the Americans in the southwest Pacific.

The North Novas, the Glens and the H.L.I. landed on the dikes just west of the Savoy inlet, between Terneuzen and Breskens, and won a firm beach-head against comparatively slight opposition. But within a few hours, the Germans began to hit the beach-head, swinging their guns around and rushing up infantry to attack.

For several days there was heavy fighting on the beach-head perimeter but another brigade was passed into the area—the Queen's Own, the Chauds and the North Shores. Then the attack from the beach-head began. The Highlanders battled their way north over the dikes and the *polders* to take Hoofdplaat. The other units closed in on Biervliet and, capturing this road junction town, punched out for Ijzendike.

The 17th Hussars, the divisional "recce" unit, were put in as infantry and shared in the advance. The Germans could not cope with this attack. To add to the enemy's grief, the Argyll and Sutherland Highlanders of the 4th Division who had been holding the line of the Leopold canal at the head of the Savoy inlet, jumped across the canal and swept north to capture Watervliet and link up with the beach-head force.

The infantry slogged north and west through the bleak, flat, desolate Schelde pocket under terrible conditions and in frightful weather. Mist and fog rolling in from the North Sea reduced the support from the Tactical Air Force and the artillery had difficulty finding its targets because in this flat district there was little observation. The Auster planes, which are flying observation posts, did a fine job for the gunners and for the infantry, hovering over the battle area for hours at a time to correct the artillery fire.

The Canadians slogged ahead, however, and on October 22 the Glens captured Breskens after the artillery and the planes had beaten this town, at the mouth of the Schelde opposite Flushing, to the ground.

Fort Frederik Hendrik, north of Breskens, was subdued in bitter fighting by the North Novas, and the H.L.I. went for Schoondike, south of Breskens, and overcame the Germans there.

Ijzendike was captured by troops of the other brigade and they went on for Oostburg in the centre of the pocket. The pressure on the Leopold canal bridgehead was off now and the western brigade was relieved by British infantry, with the Westerners swinging around to the Breskens area where they went into the line again to drive westward along the North Sea coast.

While the 3rd Division was shaking the pocket to

pieces, the 2nd Division had advanced north of Antwerp to capture the towns of Woensdrecht and
Hoogerheide, just east of the entrance to the causeway
leading to South Beveland Island. Every 2nd Division
battalion was in action in the vicinity of those two
wrecked Dutch towns and finally the entrance to the
causeway was cut.

From Bergen op Zoom, north of this area, the Germans launched several determined attacks to re-open
the route to South Beveland, but they all failed.

The 2nd Division was to attack along the causeway
and get on South Beveland. However, before this
phase of the Schelde operation could take place the
right flank of the 2nd had to be protected fully.

The 4th Division had been all moved to a concentration area near Camp Brasschaet, six miles northeast of Antwerp where the highway forks to Roosendaal and to Breda, two of the principal towns of
southwest Holland.

On October 20, the 4th Division attacked up the
Roosendaal highway and along the railway line running from Antwerp to Roosendaal, three miles west
of the highway. The town of Esschen, six miles south
of Roosendaal and southeast of Bergen op Zoom, was
the initial objective. Once this place was taken, the
2nd Division's flank would be secure and the attack
could be made along the causeway to South Beveland.

General Foster split his 4th Division into two
columns for the advance on Esschen. On the right was
a column composed of the Algonquin Regiment, the
Lincoln and Welland Regiment, the British Columbia
Regiment of tanks, and tanks of the South Alberta
Regiment. This column was to follow the highway
to Esschen. In the left column were the Governor-
General's Footguards, the Canadian Grenadier Guards,

the Argyll and Sutherland Highlanders and the Lake Superior Regiment.

The British 49th Division was to make a simultaneous advance on the 4th Division's right flank and at 7.30 in the morning the attack began.

The Germans fought stubbornly against these two columns but on October 22 Esschen was captured, after a ten-mile advance through close, wooded country, over areas heavily mined by the enemy and along roads over which hundreds of trees had been felled as obstacles.

The felled trees were booby-trapped and mined and the Canadian sappers had to remove the explosives and then clear the trunks away with bulldozers or half-tracks. Much of this hazardous work was done at night when you could scarcely see an arm's length ahead of you.

The right column which captured Esschen, as was planned, was commanded by Brigadier J. C. Jefferson of Edmonton. He had commanded the Loyal Edmonton Regiment through Sicily, had fought with it in the heaviest actions at Leonforte, and later led the same battalion in the battle of Ortona in Italy. The infantry brigade in the 4th Division had been under his command throughout the campaign from Caen.

On the night of October 21-22, the Algonquins and the Lincs and Wellands closed in on Esschen in a night advance, going through the fields and woods and over the many streams and marshes, with both battalions strung out in single files, Indian-fashion. Lieutenant-Colonel Bill Cromb of Edmonton, who had fought with Jefferson and the Edmontons in the Mediterranean, led the Lincs and Wellands, and Lieutenant-Colonel R. A. Bradburn, also of Edmonton, led the scrappy Algonquins. The B.C.R.s' tanks rumbled through the darkness too, and at dawn a squadron commanded by Major G. O. Currie of Montreal, son of the late General Sir Arthur Currie, commander of the Canadian Corps in the First Great War, entered Esschen. The Algonquins got in shortly afterwards, following a stiff fight with an enemy rear-guard south of the town. The Lincs and Wellands took up position west of the town and the other column, led by Brigadier Bob Moncel of Montreal, who at twenty-seven was the youngest brigadier in the Canadian Army, also was in the area between Esschen and Bergen op Zoom, having successfully completed its advance. Bob was then commanding the armoured brigade in the Division.

The attack to Esschen and the area between there and Bergen op Zoom had been carried out with fine flourish and dash. It was a spectacularly successful operation, which played its part in the battle of the Schelde and brought a great deal of credit to the 4th Division.

Two days later, the 2nd Division, with its flank now protected, pushed out along the causeway leading to South Beveland Island. Brigadier Cabeldu's brigade began the attack, with the Royals, the "Rileys" and the Essex Scottish fighting their way along the open highway and over the flooded marshes to win a foothold on the eastern peninsula of the island.

The German 70th Division was defending every line of dikes across the peninsula and it was sticky going for the Canadians over country that was even more terrible for attack than in the Schelde pocket. The battle-ground was fogged in and the mud was Saskatchewan gumbo. The infantry slithered and slid from dike to dike, and the only way progress could be kept up was to keep jumping fresh brigades through tired ones. General Foulkes soon jumped the brigade composed of the Black Watch, the Calgary Highlanders and the Regiment de Maissoneuve through the Ontario brigade and these fresh units went through several small towns and neared the three-hundred-foot-wide ship canal which cuts the eastern peninsula of South Beveland from the main part of the island.

The third brigade of the 2nd Division, composed of the South Saskatchewans, the Camerons of Winnipeg and the Fusiliers Mont-Royal, then took the lead, and it was the S.S.R. which made an assault crossing of the canal under cover of darkness to win a bridgehead through which the Division passed to strike into the centre of the island.

The Schelde battle was racing to a climax. The 3rd Division was moving ahead rapidly in the Schelde pocket, sweeping west from the Breskens area. Cadzand and the coastal gun forts were captured. Oostburg fell. Sluis was attacked and taken. The Highland brigade was closing in on the last two German strongpoints—Knocke and Heyst on the North Sea coast where the last remnant of the 64th Division had fallen back to the West Wall fortifications on the beaches there.

British troops of the 52nd Lowland Division were now thrown into the battle, and on October 26 British infantry battalions crossed the Schelde from Terneuzen to land on the southeast tip of the main part of South Beveland Island. They went over in the amphibious "alligators" and this second Schelde landing was just as much a success as the first one made southeast of Breskens by the Canadians. The 52nd, trained as mountain troops and called the "Mountain Division", by a queer twist of war went into its first combined-operations action across Europe's flattest terrain.

This landing was an all-British show, with the exception of a company of Royal Canadian Engineers who went into the beach-head to cut roadways through the dikes, and some Toronto Scottish machine-gunners who crossed with their Vickers to support the British infantry.

The Tommies went over the big coastal dike and pushed inland over the *polders* against growing German resistance. But the enemy could not hold them. The Royals of the 2nd Division punched south after crossing the Beveland ship canal and linked up with the British as the 8th Reconnaissance Regiment of the 2nd Division ran wild along the roads and dikes going west across the island.

Goes, the principal town on the island, was liberated, and by October 30 South Beveland was entirely overrun. The 2nd Division did not stop for even a breather. On October 31, the Black Watch attacked along the mile-long causeway linking South Beveland with Walcheren Island. They were shelled and mortared all the way along the causeway but got to within twenty-five yards of the far end. The Calgary Highlanders passed through and a narrow bridgehead was established on the island, to which the 70th Division had retreated from South Beveland to bolster the Walcheren garrison.

The irrepressible 8th "Recce" was unemployed at this point and a squadron commanded by Major Dick Porteous of Montreal carried out some casual patrols along the north coast of South Beveland. Over a strip of water lay North Beveland Island.

In the best traditions of the "recce", whose job is to find out what is going on and to collect information beyond the main front, the troopers, who you would have thought had got enough excitement out of the

(TOP): *Canada in Germany. Past battered buildings but along well-preserved roads, traffic moves up the lines with the Canadians, in the Big Push. "Monty" held the first Allied investiture of Canadians on German soil.*

(LOWER): *A dream comes true! The sign tells the story, as Corporal Urban Mayo of London, Ontario, who has fought many a weary mile, reaches his primary objective.*

campaign already, climbed into a Dutch barge and invaded North Beveland Island.

The whole regiment followed up the landing, an off-the-record expedition which at first did not even have the blessing of Army Headquarters. The colonel was asked what this was all about and his reply was: "I'm waging a private war on North Beveland."

It turned out to be a quite successful private war. While the island was on the German escape route from Walcheren, it was not being defended and the 8th "Recce" overran it, taking several hundred prisoners. It was such a good show that they were reinforced with some Toronto Scottish machine-gunners. This was a comic side-piece to the Schelde operation.

The final drama of the Schelde fight was enacted on November 1 when two assault landings were made from the sea on Walcheren Island. These attacks ultimately finished the battle.

At 6.30 in the morning British commandos and 52nd Division Infantry crossed the mouth of the Schelde from Breskens, to land right at Flushing. They got ashore without a great deal of opposition, but in the streets of Flushing and in the areas of the coastal gun batteries around the town they had to fight hard. For several days the fighting went on in and around Flushing, but slowly and methodically the town was cleared and the guns silenced.

Three hours after the Flushing landing was made, a force of British commandos was landed by the Royal Navy at Westkapelle, on the western tip of Walcheren. They got ashore at the point where the R.A.F. heavy bombers had blasted great gaps in the coastal dike weeks before to flood large portions of the island. They won a foothold on the dikes, but the naval craft which brought them in and the ships which supported the landing came under terrific shell-fire from coastal batteries around Westkapelle. The navy suffered heavy losses in ships and personnel.

The two British seaborne forces linked up and after the Regiment de Maissoneuve had extended the Calgary Highlanders' bridgehead at the end of the Walcheren causeway, British infantry of the 52nd Division exploited the bridgehead. From the south and from the east, the British advanced on Middelburg, in the centre of Walcheren, and entered the flooded town in boats which took them over the inundated land around it.

The 70th Division was destroyed and all Walcheren was occupied by the end of the first week in November. General Desser commanding the Division was captured with thousands of his men.

While the curtain was being rung down on Walcheren, Brigadier Rockingham and his Canadian Highland battalions captured Knocke and Heyst, eliminating the last enemy resistance in the Schelde pocket. General Eberding of the 64th Division was made prisoner.

In less than a month's hard fighting, the Canadians, aided in the last phase by British troops in the Canadian Army, had cleared the Germans from the Schelde estuary. The navy went to work sweeping the mines from this approach to Antwerp and the port was made ready for the Allied convoys which would land masses of supplies on the doorstep of the western front for the offensive into the Reich.

*   *   *   *

Battles flamed through southwest Holland while the Schelde operation was rushing to its finish. After the 4th Division captured Esschen, its tanks and infantry

struck north and northwest towards Bergen op Zoom
and the highway linking Bergen with Roosendaal.
The 49th Division, the Polish Division and the 104th
American Infantry Division, which were all under
Canadian Army command, drove north on the right
of the 4th.

Attacking west from its salient into Holland at
Nijmegen, the Second Army advanced simultaneously
with the Canadian Army drive.

The Germans had tried to establish a line across
southwest Holland running from Bergen through
Roosendaal to Breda, Tilburg and Hertogenbosch.
The Second Army captured Hertogenbosch in short
order and also took Tilburg. They pushed west towards Breda and cleared the area south of the Maas.
The international force of the First Canadian Army
did the rest.

The 4th Division turned in the first success when
the enemy defences screening Bergen were battered
down. The South Alberta Regiment and the Lincoln
and Wellands fought their way up a trail, piled with
trees and sown with mines, to take Bergen as the
Germans pulled back hastily to the wooded area north
of the town. Other troops in the Division went over
the Bergen-Roosendaal highway and hooked around
to the northwest between Bergen and Steenbergen,
the only town of any size south of the Rhine estuary
at that point.

Good German troops from the Hermann Goering
Division and the 6th Parachute Regiment opposed the
Canadians there but they could not stand the pressure
and after a battle shared in by the Algonquins, the
Lincs and Wellands, the Lake Superiors and the tanks
south of Steenbergen, the Argyll and Sutherlands
passed through to capture the town. From there to the
Rhine estuary it was easy going.

The 49th Division meanwhile captured Roosendaal and went north towards the estuary and the Poles, with the 2nd Canadian Armoured Brigade under their command, advanced rapidly on Breda. They liberated this town and kept going north.

The American 104th Division, recently from home and the first American division to serve under Canadian command, learned its battle lessons rapidly and kept pace with the Polish advance north. Cutting the Roosendaal-Breda highway, the Americans fought their way over the awful *polder* country.

Forces of the German Fifteenth Army, under the weight of these devastating attacks, could not hold anywhere for long and evacuated its forces over the Rhine estuary towards Rotterdam.

The Canadians, British, American and Polish divisions reached the estuary along the Hollandsch Diep, and one lone pocket of Germans made a suicide stand at the southern end of the Moerdike bridges, a mile and a half long. The Germans blew the bridges—one for vehicles and the other for trains—and on November 9 the last action in the battle to clear southwest Holland was fought as Polish infantry and tanks captured Moerdike in the first flurry of winter snow.

On the fog-draped, bitterly-cold waterway, I watched the Poles write off the German suicide force of five hundred men. With seventeen-pounder guns, the Poles blew their way through six-foot-thick concrete walls which blocked the roads to Moerdike and the bridges.

Through the gaps tore the Polish tanks and infantry and in the blasted town of Moerdike they fired the last shots in southwest Holland.

*   *   *   *

As the Poles fought for Moerdike, the Canadians

engaged in the zaniest exploit of the campaign at the mouth of the estuary.

The Lake Superior Regiment and the British Columbia Regiment had prodded out to the end of the St. Philipsland peninsula west of Steenbergen, and from the end of the peninsula their lookouts spotted four German naval craft lying in a small harbour on an island half a mile away.

So they called up the mortars of the L.S.R., they called up some tanks of the B.C.R. and they opened a naval engagement between the army and the German fleet, as represented by the four vessels.

The mortars and tanks hurled high explosives at the craft and set them afire. A part of the L.S.R. crossed to the island and found the harbour empty of enemy and the ships sunk. The London *Daily Mirror* was so enthused that it headlined the story in big black type: "Monty's Men Sink German Fleet".

*   *   *   *

Royal Navy parties and army engineers worked in the dockyards throughout the Schelde battle preparing for the convoys which would sail up the estuary when the enemy were driven off the shore. When the Walcheren guns were silenced in early November, the mine-sweepers went into the estuary and within a few weeks a channel was swept right to the docks. By the end of November the first Allied convoy, led by a Belgian ship, sailed into the port.

For twenty-two miles, more than twenty huge docks sprawl along the Schelde in the Antwerp area, and in the outer river there are three and a half miles of quays. In peacetime 202 different shipping lines were based on Antwerp. Now it was the principal supply base for the Allied armies on the Western Front.

Napoleon had once referred to Antwerp as "a dagger pointed at the heart of England". In November, 1944, the dagger was turned towards Berlin.

*   *   *   *

In mid-November, the 2nd and 3rd Canadian Divisions relieved British formations in the Nijmegen sector. They took up positions south and southeast of the town, with the responsibility of guarding the vital Nijmegen bridge, seized and held in the September airborne landings.

The 3rd Division had had nearly a week in Ghent before it went into the line again at Nijmegen, and Ghent will never forget that week. The burgomaster invited the whole Division, fresh from its triumph in the Schelde pocket, to stay in Ghent as guests of the city and hospitality was showered on the Canadians during their whole stay. For the 3rd, it was its first real rest since the D-Day landing.

Then back to the mud and the cold of slit-trenches and front-line farmyards went the Division. Its troops were the first Canadians into Germany in this war, taking up positions inside the German border, southeast of Nijmegen.

Other Canadian troops and British formations under General Crerar also were put into the Nijmegen sector, which brought the First Canadian Army once more up on the left of the Allied line.

While the Canadian Army moved into its new area, the Second Army dropped south to clear the enemy from west of the Maas in an advance co-ordinated with the November attacks by the Ninth, First, Third and Seventh American Armies and the First French Army.

But the flourishing period of the campaign in the

west was over for the year. The weather was abominable and our gains could only be limited. A long winter of slugging struggles in mud and snow, with some heavy German attacks, was closing down on the Western Front. The Canadians were comparatively inactive, with only a few local tasks on their hands unless Germany collapsed—and then they would jump, with the rest of the Allied forces, right into the Reich. But that seemed a remote possibility.

The end of the big phase in the west had come and after six months on the front, I left for a leave—a leave, this time, at home in Canada.

There was Christmas shopping in the incredible stores in Brussels, packed with luxury goods you could not get in Britain or Canada, while Belgium cried for food; there was a visit to the First American Army in the Aachen sector of Germany and a few hours with our old friends the 104th Division, which had been with us in southwest Holland to get its battle inoculation; there was a two-hour plane trip to London with the R.A.F. Transport Command, the forerunner of British commercial airlines for the post-war years, I hope; another flight from London to Belfast by Transport Command and on H.M.C.S. *Forest Hill*, a bouncing, leaping corvette, I sailed for home. It took twenty days to get home.

Four and a half years before, I'd landed in Belfast on my way to the war. Then I'd come on the first flotilla of American over-age destroyers to go to Britain in exchange for Atlantic bases. I'd followed the Canadians since that time. It seemed strange to be leaving now, even temporarily on leave, but I seemed to have been at war too long.

I wanted to see our country again; to talk to its people at home; to see the lights, the expanse, the scope, the grandness of the Dominion, its cities, towns and farms, and then to go back to the war and its finish.

And on the same ocean in another ship were several hundred other Canadians with the same ideas. They were the first draft of long-service men going to Canada for home leave under the army's new policy.

*   *   *   *

In those first six months with the Canadian Army on the Western Front, one had an unique opportunity to study various aspects of Allied relations and co-operation. During that time, this co-operation was on as high and satisfactory a plane as Allied Command had known this war.

The situation within the Canadian Army itself was unusual, in that the army was a composite formation under General Crerar's over-all command. Yet throughout the campaign I do not know of a single serious clash between the forces making up this army. The British, Polish, American, Dutch and Belgian formations got along well together and worked in harmony with the Canadians. Contributing to this harmony, of course, was the diplomatic manner in which General Crerar dealt with the components of his army, with their varying temperaments and approaches to military situations.

The harmony was really something to marvel at. Another contributing factor was the competent fashion in which Canadian Army H.Q. operated. While the H.Q. had never directed battles before it took the field at Caen, it had existed for more than two years and in that time had been prepared for its duties with painstaking care. Despite its lack of actual campaign experience, the H.Q., with its young, keen officers drawn both from the Permanent Force and Non-Permanent Active Militia, proved extremely competent from the first.

It started out in Normandy under a psychological disadvantage in having sometimes half the troops under its command non-Canadian, but it did not take the formations under it long to find that it operated efficiently and that they could have full confidence in its direction of the campaign.

A splendid team ran the H.Q., and some of these officers were Brigadier Church Mann, the chief of staff, Colonel Ted Beament, Brigadier Jim Lister, Brigadier Charlie Fenwick, Brigadier Ernest Walford, Lieutenant-Colonel Bill Anderson, Lieutenant-Colonel Peter Wright, Lieutenant-Colonel Don McRae, Lieutenant-Colonel Doucet—and the list could include a score more who laboured hard and long on staff work from Caen to Germany.

Relations between the British and the Canadians seldom varied from those established during the long period the latter spent training in England. Each recognized peculiar qualities in the other, accepted them and found a workable basis. But to the British, the Canadians were always rough diamonds.

I remember when the 1st British Corps came under command of the First Canadian Army. The Corps had had the 3rd Canadian Division under its command for the first phase of the Normandy battle and I asked a senior staff officer at Corps how they liked working under the Canadians now, instead of having Canadians under them.

"We really don't mind it for we learned the Canadian system from the 3rd Division," he said. "You see, Lieutenant-Colonel Don Mingay was the G.S.O. 1 of the Division, and we would phone down orders to him. He would listen patiently and then say 'horse-feathers' and bang down the phone. So now when Canadian Army H.Q. passes orders to us we simply say 'horsefeathers'. It's all very simple."

Good humour predominated in Canadian-British relations on a staff level in the field, and although there was never much fraternizing between Canadian and British troops, they respected each other's fighting ability. After each had seen a couple of tough shows this respect was unshakable.

The Canadians did not get to know the Americans well, for they were generally on opposite ends of the Allied line. But when the 104th American Division fought in southwest Holland under the Canadian Army command, there were no hitches. As a matter of fact, the divisional commander, Major-General Terry Allen, who doesn't mince his words, went out of his way one day to tell me how pleased he was that his outfit had an opportunity to serve in the Canadian Army.

"My favourite story is this," he said. "The other day I needed some blankets for my wounded. I needed them in a hurry. I scribbled a note to Canadian Army H.Q., side-tracked all the proper channels and sent it direct to the supply chief. In three hours I had the blankets on my front. It is little things like that which count when you want to have good relations between forces of different nations."

On the High Command level of SHAEF, I feel that the Canadians always received fair consideration. General Eisenhower insisted above all that the Allied force operate as a team and the First Canadian Army, as an army representing a nation even though it was a composite formation, had full status with other armies. This status was always recognized.

We noticed this particularly in our press arrangements. Some of our facilities came from SHAEF and those of us operating with the Canadian Army never suffered from lack of facilities. Of course, our own public relations branch did a fine job for us all, but as Canadians we never found ourselves blocked because the Canadian contribution in man-power to the campaign was necessarily far less than that of the United States and Britain.

Canadians always felt they were an essential part of the Allied team—a feeling which General Eisenhower fostered and which Field Marshal Montgomery drove home at every opportunity.

*   *   *   *

In mid-February I flew back in haste to the war. The Canadian Army was attacking southeast of Nijmegen in the first move of an all-out Allied offensive to destroy the German armies in the Reich itself and end the war in Europe.

Under the original plan General Crerar was to have struck in early January to clear the west bank of the Lower Rhine for the forcing of the river when the floods subsided but Field Marshal von Rundstedt's December offensive in the Ardennes caused a postponement.

That threat removed, General Crerar launched his attack February 8. Most of the resources of the 21st Army Group were placed at his disposal for this extremely difficult undertaking. The weather was bad and the ground was worse—thawing, soggy and terrible for tanks. Large areas were flooded. Eight British divisions of the Second Army were put under General Crerar's command—two armoured and six infantry—along with the famous 30th Corps Head-

quarters. The Canadian Western Front force of three
divisions and the 2nd Armoured Brigade was in this
huge army of about 500,000 men, including corps and
army troops, the largest command a Canadian has
ever held.

The 30th Corps began the offensive, directed first
against the Reichswald Forest, through which ran the
northern end of the Siegfried Line. Into the Reichswald, torn by a 1,400-gun barrage, British troops
plunged and overran the entire forest. Cleve and Goch
were captured. The Canadian 3rd Division, temporarily under the 30th Corps, cleared the flooded
land between the Reichswald and the Rhine in
amphibious advances from dike to dike which won
for it the sobriquet "Water Rats".

Then the 3rd Division reverted to the 2nd Canadian
Corps under General Simonds and, with the 2nd
Division, captured woods and highways south of
Cleve on the way to Calcar. Field Marshal Montgomery's plan had called for the American Ninth
Army, then in the Twenty-first Army Group, to attack
on February 10 across the Roer River and strike northeast toward the Canadian Army. However, the
Germans blew the Roer dams and the flooding prevented the Americans from kicking off until February
23. By that time practically all of the German First
Paratroop Army on the Lower Rhine fronts had been
shifted north to the Canadian Army sector and was
strongly manning layback defences of the Siegfried
Line along the Hochwald Forest.

On February 26 the 2nd Corps attacked the Hochwald Line. The 2nd Division advanced southwest of
Calcar with the 2nd Armoured Brigade and the 4th
Division passed through them. Ploughing through
gumbo mud, the 4th captured slopes overlooking the

Hochwald, while the 3rd Division took the towns of Keppeln and Udem on its right. Infantry and some tanks of the 4th pushed into the Hochwald Corridor, a gap between two sections of the forest, and half-way through ran into terrific opposition. From three sides German paratroops hammered the Canadians and the quick break-out from the corridor which had been hoped for was impossible.

For several days the battle raged in the forest and corridor, with all the Canadian formations engaged at various times in some of the heaviest fighting they had known. Campaign veterans compared it to Caen and the Schelde.

The front began to loosen up on March 2. The Germans pulled out of the Maas River sector on the west and the 30th Corps rolled ahead to link up with the Americans at Geldern. The 2nd Division broke through the northern part of the Hochwald and the 3rd Division cleared the southern section.

The 4th Armoured Division came out of the corridor, hooked around the southern side of the Hochwald, fought a fierce engagement at Veen and closed in with other formations on the Wesel bridgehead. Xanten fell to British troops and the 2nd Division and by March 10 there were no Germans fighting west of the Lower Rhine.

In the battle of the Hochwald Line the first of Canada's home defence troops—"zombies"—were in action and without qualification commanding officers reported they fought well.

It took just over a month for the Canadian Army to clear its sector on the west bank and the High Command was elated. This victory at the northern end of the Allied line precipitated the break-up of the entire German front west of the Rhine. It was one of the major and decisive operations of the European war and the protracted and bitter series of battles fought by Canadian and British forces under General Crerar had direct relation to the Rhine crossing and the break-out into western Germany. If the Canadian Army had failed, the scope and speed of subsequent advances into the Reich would not have been possible.

The Lower Rhine itself was forced the night of March 23-24 by assault troops of the Second and Ninth Armies, followed by staggering airborne landings by British and American divisions and the 1st Canadian Parachute Battalion east of the bridgehead.

Never in this war had there been such a spectacle as we witnessed that morning. From the banks of the Rhine we watched it spellbound. For sheer concentrated power of attack the forcing of the Rhine eclipsed Normandy on D-Day.

The Canadian 3rd Division passed into the bridgehead in the morning with the Highland Light Infantry, commanded by Lieutenant-Colonel Phil Strickland, the first Canadian regiment over the Rhine. The North Nova Scotia Highlanders and the Stormont, Dundas and Glengarry Highlanders were next across and this Highland brigade, still led by Brigadier Rockingham, fought bridgehead battles northwest of Rees. The battle of Bienen, shared in by the North Novas and the H.L.I., was the bloodiest. At one time these two regiments fought four German paratroop battalions and a battle group of the 15th *Panzer* Grenadiers.

The attack from the bridgehead began and the 3rd Division captured Emmerich after fighting through rubble heaps. Outside the town the 3rd erected a sign:

COME IN AND LOOK AROUND
THE WATER RATS HAVE CLEARED THE TOWN.

The 3rd Division also captured dominating Hochelten, beyond Emmerich, and the 2nd and 4th surged into northern Holland, fought on the Twente canal. Then the 4th broke loose to cut back into Germany and cross the Ems River and the Dortmund-Ems canal at Meppen.

In the final phase of the war the Canadians were assigned the task of liberating northern Holland and advancing into Hitler's shattered nation along the northern flank of Allied armies which were knifing deep into the heart of Germany.

For the last hectic six weeks, the entire Canadian overseas army was together. During February, the 1st Corps, under Major-General Foulkes, began to move from Italy to the Western Front under the greatest secrecy. During March the transfer was completed and the troops were given the task of driving the Germans from West Holland.

In early April the Corps 5th (Armoured) Division, under Major-General Hoffmeister, with the British 49th Division, cleared "the Arnhem island" between Nijmegen and Arnhem, and the 1st Division, led by Major-General Harry Foster, went into its first action on the Western Front, April 11, in crossing the Ijssel River between Deventer and Zutphen, northeast of Arnhem, and attacking westward to capture Apeldoorn. Then the 49th crossed the Ijssel near its confluence with the Neder Rhine to capture Arnhem April 14, and the 5th Division went through it to break into the clear northwest of Arnhem. The 5th plunged through to the Zuider Zee, undermining every German plan for defence in that area.

The 1st Division pushed west from Apeldoorn and the German forces pulled west to the Grebbe line running from the Zuider Zee south to the Maas River.

This was the first defence line of "Fortress Holland" and the enemy threatened to unloose flood waters which would have been a catastrophe for the Netherlands.

However, there was a lull on the front. The Canadians did not attack. Instead, negotiations took place between the German and Canadian commanders which resulted in food being taken into Fortress Holland for Dutch civilians.

In the meantime the 3rd and 2nd Divisions with the 1st Polish Armoured Division, all under Lieutenant-General Simonds in the 2nd Corps, ran hog-wild through northwest Holland. Groningen surrendered to the 2nd Division and the Royal Canadian Dragoons reached the Dutch North Sea coast.

The 4th Division on the right flank in Germany advanced towards Oldenburg, largest German city between the Ems and Weser, and its infantry fought another grim battle on the Kusten canal where they established a bridgehead southwest of Oldenburg. The 2nd Division was rapidly switched from northwest Holland to the Oldenburg area and the city surrendered to the 2nd as the whole front loosened up.

The 3rd Division was then operating southeast of Emden with the Poles on the right.

On every battlefront the German army was writhing in the agony of its defeat.

*   *   *   *

The American First Army linked with the Russians at Torgau on the Elbe. The British Second Army captured Bremen. Hamburg surrendered and the British swept on to the Baltic. The Germans in northern Italy and southern Austria surrendered. The Russians captured Berlin.

At 8:15 P.M. on May 4 we heard the BBC announce

German surrender in Holland, northwest Germany and Denmark. At eight A.M. May 5 "cease fire" was sounded on the fronts of the First Canadian and British Second Armies.

During the afternoon of the same day in the lobby of a shell-smashed hotel at Wageningen, Holland, at the southern end of the Grebbe line, General Foulkes received a formal surrender from Colonel-General Blaskowitz, commander of all German forces opposing the Canadians in Holland and northwest Germany.

It seemed unbelievable the war in Europe was finally over for the Canadians. Yet there it was.

I watched tired old Blaskowitz sitting across the dusty table from General Foulkes and, blinking like an owl, agree to every surrender term.

The next night, Sunday, I was in Rheims, France, in a stuffy room in a barrack-like school which served as General Eisenhower's forward headquarters, Colonel-General Jodl and General-Admiral Von Friedelburg signed the documents of unconditional surrender for all German forces everywhere.

It was 2:41 A.M., May 7, 1945.

*   *   *   *

Back in Holland, the Canadians moved into Amsterdam, Rotterdam and The Hague to the acclaim of millions of liberated Dutch people. In Germany they took over Emden and Wilhelmshaven.

On two fronts the Canadians had contributed to the defeat of Hitler Germany. They had fought with shining distinction, with a valour that cost them a total of 79,774 casualties of whom 21,478 gave their lives — the bulk of the nation's 102,875 casualties, including 37,206 dead, in the three services up to VE-Day.

But now their job was finished. Their vigil was over, their victory won.

XI

ENGLAND AND THE LONG WAIT

BEHIND the exploits of the Canadians is the story of their preparations; the story of their long, weary wait in England where they trained month after month through endless manoeuvres for the battles they fought in the Mediterranean and on the Western Front.

On the farms and along the hedge-lined lanes of Surrey, on the South Downs of Sussex and in Aldershot and the English Camp Bordon, the Canadian divisions learned the technique of war. They learned their lessons well, as their battle record subsequently proved, but the waiting was almost unendurable. Yet the manner in which they met this test of patience is a remarkable tribute to their discipline and their leadership.

High-spirited, eager for the adventure and the uncertainties of battle, they came to England, division after division, to find that war for them, for months and even several years, meant endless training for vague actions that lay ahead.

This could have broken some troops. It could have made them slack, indifferent, slipshod, but this charge can never be laid against the Canadian troops who trained so faithfully over such a long period. They retained their buoyancy, their vigour, their enthusiasm through that long, dull time, and when they went into battle they went in trained to the height of perfection.

In the memory of every Canadian soldier overseas England will always spell "manoeuvres". It will recall marathon route marches, tedious exercises up and down Sussex and Surrey and into Kent, cliff-climbing in the quarries by the villages, assault landings on the south coast, artillery shoots at Lark Hill or Salisbury Plain and camp and barrack life from Brighton to Horsham, from Leatherhead to Littlehampton, from Reigate to Seaford.

They will remember the lovely summers and the bleak, cold winters in Nissen-hut camps. They will remember the scores of stately homes and spacious estates requisitioned for camps and barracks, and they will always recall Aldershot where every division went for its initial training overseas; grey, dull, uninspiring Aldershot where they lived in big prison-like barracks, drilled on the huge squares and were inspected by royalty and brass. Aldershot is as stiff and forbidding as a drill sergeant-major and in this oppressive barracks town the Canadians got their first impressions of England. They did not like it much, by Aldershot standards.

But Aldershot is far from being England. Those week-end leaves in London showed the Canadians part of real England, the throbbing, urban, wartime-capital part of it—and they were enthralled. Then they would move from Aldershot to the quaint towns of Surrey and Sussex, to the farm districts, the little villages, the Channel coast towns, and there they saw another part of England and got to know its people.

They were welcomed to the homes of the English, to the villages, cities and farms. They were greeted with as warm hospitality as people could extend, and through those dreary, waiting months and years this inexhaustible hospitality was one of the brightest features of the life of the Canadian soldiers.

After war was declared, Canada moved quickly to

get troops overseas and on December 17, 1939, the 1st Canadian Division landed from the convoy that brought it into the Clyde. General McNaughton was leading the Division and it went by train to Aldershot. There, in the bleakness and the dampness that only an English winter can produce, the Division went to work to get ready for battle. The British Expeditionary Force was in France and the original plan called for the 1st Division to go to the Continent and take its place in the line late the following spring or early summer. So through the winter, the Division trained and received its vehicles, guns and equipment necessary for field service.

The "phoney war", as Senator Borah dubbed it, went on on the Western Front, with the French armies and the B.E.F. on the frontiers and the Germans massing their strength for the spring. The Canadians pounded the training grounds of Aldershot in the slush and the rain, were inspected and applauded as the first contingent of Canada's volunteer army. The war seemed very unreal to them.

As winter ended, the Canadians were getting into fine shape and looking forward to a few large-scale manoeuvres in the spring to put the finishing touches on their training. Then came the first staggering surprise. By guile, deception and the work of the original Quisling, the Germans invaded Norway. The ill-starred British force was mustered and dispatched to Norway to stem the invasion, and with the Germans rolling up successes a Canadian force also was ordered to prepare to go to Trondheim. The 2nd Infantry Brigade was the formation selected and it was rushed north to a Scottish port. One disaster after another overtook Allied fortunes in Norway and before the Canadians sailed for Trondheim the situation had changed so much that the operation was cancelled. From the railway siding and the docks where they had waited for days in the rain to sail, the Canadians returned disappointed to their camps in southern England. It was the first of many false alarms for the 1st Division.

Norway was overrun by the Germans, and the British troops evacuated. The static war on the Western Front continued and on May 10 the German armies struck. The Canadians in England followed their advance aghast like millions of people the world over. Holland and Belgium were overrun, the *Panzers* broke through at Sedan and the French armies were rolled back. Huge German forces slashed into the B.E.F. and the retreat to Dunkerque and Calais was inevitable.

German armoured columns rolled around to Abbeville and Boulogne. Troops of the Rifle Brigade were put into Calais to delay the Germans at the port and help block their advance to Dunkerque. It was proposed to reinforce the Calais garrison with Canadians and General McNaughton went to Calais in a destroyer to make an appraisal of the situation. But it was obvious then that Calais would not hold for long. It would be a useless waste of men to reinforce the Rifle Brigade and the plan to use the Canadians there was not put into force.

Canadian infantry and gunners were at Dover ready to sail to Calais and they were ordered back to the Aldershot area. Meanwhile, as the Germans pushed along the roads towards Paris and closed in on Dunkerque, the 1st Canadian Infantry Brigade sailed to Brest with British formations in what has been called the "Second B.E.F.".

This force was sent to France in a last-ditch attempt

to bolster the fading French armies, but it was doomed to failure. The French front was crumbling. Leading Canadian elements, however, did get to within forty miles of Paris before they were ordered to withdraw. Back they went to Brest and under air attack they re-embarked for England and Aldershot.

The epic of Dunkerque was enacted and the B.E.F. was brought home, denuded of weapons and equipment. The world waited for the next blow.

Prime Minister Churchill roused England to its great and heroic efforts in the face of threatening German invasion, and thousands of Britons worked on the defences in southern England. Those were perilous, unnerving days, and through June and into summer the 1st Canadian Division was the only fully-equipped formation in the United Kingdom. From Aldershot it was rushed around southern and eastern England. Day and night its convoys rolled on the roads, giving an impression of far greater strength than existed in the island during that hectic period when the Germans could have won the war by airborne and seaborne landings.

Britain rushed ahead with defence preparations and the 7th Corps was formed in July, with General McNaughton as corps commander. A composite, British-Canadian force, it included the 1st Canadian Division, and this lone corps was the bulwark of the United Kingdom while the new British Army was re-mustered back to strength under the ever-present threat of invasion.

Troops of the Corps were deployed through Surrey and Sussex and around the southern outskirts of London.

The Germans were not ready to invade England. They did not come that summer and everyone breathed a little easier. British divisions were now being re-equipped and re-trained and in late August the 2nd Canadian Division, under Major-General Victor Odlum, arrived to join the 1st. Three of its units—the Royal Regiment from Toronto, the Fusiliers Mont-Royal and the Cameron Highlanders of Ottawa—were on duty in Iceland and they came to England later.

In August the German Air Force launched its daylight attacks on southern England and into September the battle of Britain raged, with the *Luftwaffe* trying to destroy the Royal Air Force as the prelude to an invasion attempt.

From the camps in the south, the Canadians witnessed the awesome spectacle of these gigantic air fights, as masses of German bombers and fighters were engaged by the "few" of the R.A.F. in the blue skies over Kent and Surrey. These were days of tense excitement and anticipation and the Canadians to a man thought their big test lay just ahead.

The Germans carried out invasion exercises on the coast of Belgium, Holland and France, and the Schelde estuary was lined with barges. The R.A.F. hit at these barge concentrations and smashed up many of them in suicide sorties in the face of heavy flak and fighter opposition.

Rumours ran through the Canadian camps of German invasion landing and half a dozen times during the fall I checked reports that raiding parties had come ashore, only to find they were utterly false. One prevalent story was that a German invasion force did sail for England but was attacked by the R.A.F. in the Channel. According to the story, oil was dropped on the fleet and then the oil was set ablaze, destroying the fleet and killing thousands of the enemy.

Later in Brussels and Antwerp I checked this story and although there seemed to be some truth in the report that a German fleet had met disaster by bombing, I could find no basis in fact for the story of the oil and the fire. I think it is more likely that the fleet was bombed while on an invasion exercise, rather than on a full-fledged attempt to land on the English coast.

From what I could learn in Belgium and Holland, there never was an actual German invasion attempt. Exercises were carried out, it is true, but no invasion force ever sailed with England its goal. Very elaborate preparations were made, though, and in France and Belgium we found maps for the invasion of England, as well as documents and pamphlets giving details of towns and districts in southern and eastern England, and in themselves revealing the general theme of the broad plan.

The defeat of the German Air Force in the Battle of Britain wrecked the invasion plan. Without driving the R.A.F. out of the sky, the enemy felt it could not land in England. So the plot to win the war in summer and fall of 1940 by overrunning England as France was overrun, failed when the first phase—complete air domination—did not succeed.

Yet, even with the Battle of Britain won, the ominous threat of a landing persisted through the following winter and spring.

During the fall, the 1st Division moved down to the Channel coast, taking up defensive positions in behind Brighton, Worthing, Newhaven and Seaford. Dawn and dusk patrols were carried out by reconnaissance troops and infantry on the rolling, muddy, misty downs, as a precaution against parachute landings. Pillbox and trench systems were erected along the coast and on the hills.

At best, the defences of the south coast were make-shift and scanty at that time. A division would be spread out for ten or fifteen miles, and the only immediate support they had was their own divisional artillery and a few coastal batteries on the beaches like those at Brighton and on cliff positions. Constant guards were kept on the coast, though, and the troops were alert to their responsibilities, but our forces were thinly spread out and our defences meagre.

Vital areas on the coast were mined, many roads were blocked with concrete and steel barriers, and the Home Guard formations trained diligently to fight in the streets and the hills. But, in fact, the defence of the invasion corner of England consisted principally of a few scattered divisions and Churchill's brave words.

The plan for opposing an invasion was defence in depth. It was acknowledged that the enemy could not likely be prevented from getting ashore. They would be hit after they had landed and too many precious men would not be expended trying to beat them on the beaches.

So the Canadians stood guard and continued their training in their operational areas. By platoons, com-panies, battalions and brigades they worked out their anti-invasion plans in the mud and the cold of the winter of 1940-41.

The invaders still did not come but the night bombers flew over in steadily increasing strength, hammering at London and the south of England. From dusk to dawn we heard the throbbing motors of enemy aircraft over Surrey, heading for London with its flaming anti-aircraft barrage. Searchlights latticed the skies over the Canadian camps and the guns roared in the fields and hills.

Within a few months practically every Canadian in England had been under the bombs at one time or another. Nearly everyone had his own personal bomb story to tell from some leave to London or some incident in the south.

During the fall, the Canadians made great strides in their training and on Christmas Day, 1940, the Canadian Corps was formed, composed of the 1st and 2nd Divisions. The composite 7th Corps was disbanded and the Canadian Corps under General McNaughton took its place as an all-Canadian formation and still one of the bastions of the anti-invasion defences of Britain.

That was a proud day for Canada. In the First Great War, the Dominion had had a corps in the field and now it had mustered another corps for this war. But this time, Canada was to go further. From the Corps developed the First Canadian Army.

As the training grind went on, the Canadian organization was gradually streamlined, the kinks were shaken out of it and the army policy took sure and certain shape. While the waiting period was a trial for the patience of the Canadians, it did give them a golden opportunity to prepare for future campaigns in a fashion which no other forces in this war have been able to do. Elaborate tests of organization, equipment, personnel, could be carried out in manoeuvres and alterations made when needed. Many technical developments were carried out. Lessons learned on distant battle-fields were applied in the Canadians' training which saved them from many mistakes when they took the field themselves.

But it was tedious work. I lived at Corps H.Q. at Leatherhead during these weary months and the most exciting story I had to write was of anti-invasion manoeuvres, which soon paled in interest. Larry Audrain of Winnipeg, who was then an army camera-man, and I probably covered more manoeuvres and inspections than any persons in the business. Week-end visits to London relieved the monotony but London in that full-bombing season was not the healthiest place to go.

Still, the great majority of Canadians headed for the city on leaves, short and long—at least until the hos-pitality of Scotland became known in the camps, and then thousands struck out for the Lowlands and the Highlands when their week's leave came around every three months.

We watched the war news with vague uneasiness in that second spring of the war and I was chary about straying far from the Canadian camps in the south. Many of us felt, at the time, that the Canadians would be given some task and I was haunted by the fear that I might miss the first Canadian operation unless I remained close to Corps H.Q.

However, in May I took two weeks off, with some doubts in my mind, and went to Scotland. I had intended to make it a leave, but the Canadian Forestry Corps was established then in the Highlands and I telescoped the leave into a tour of the Forestry Corps camps.

We drove through the magnificent Highlands in the crisp spring air and saw the amazing work being done by these Canadian lumbermen-soldiers, who were using advanced Canadian timber methods to provide much-needed lumber for Britain's war effort. It was an extremely worth-while trip, arranged by Brigadier-General J. B. White of Montreal, commander of the Corps.

Another Canadian organization which did unusual

work outside the army itself was the Tunnelling Company of the Royal Canadian Engineers, led at the time by Lieutenant-Colonel Colin Campbell of Sault Ste. Marie, one-time Minister of Public Works for Ontario.

Tunnelling Company troops, which included many hard-rock miners, did many secret jobs in England connected with defence preparations and later several hundred worked on Gibraltar when the fortifications of The Rock were being improved.

For the Corps, the training dragged on and on, and after Germany attacked Russia in June the operation against Spitsbergen was ordered, with a Canadian force carrying it out. By the fall, even the most pessimistic were conceding that Germany would not now invade England and the fundamental principles of army training in Britain slowly altered. Emphasis was switched from anti-invasion to offensive preparations and subsequent manoeuvres veered gradually from defence.

The new British Army was taking shape in Britain too. New divisions were being formed every few months and even with the drain of men and *matériel* to the Middle East, a formidable force was being mustered in Britain.

The Canadian overseas force also was being built up steadily to its full strength of five divisions and two independent armoured brigades. The 3rd Division, commanded by Major-General Price, the 4th Armoured, led by Major-General Worthington, and the 5th Armoured, commanded by Major-General Sansom, all arrived in England.

While these generals did not take their formations into action, they performed a lasting service in those important training days in England, and the same is true of Major-General Pearkes, who was given command of the 1st Division when General McNaughton became Corps Commander, and Major-General Odlum of the 2nd Division.

Backing up the build-up of the army in England was the training given new recruits in Canada to fit them for overseas service.

All soldiers received a minimum of four months' training in Canada—two months' basic training and two months' advance training. In camps in every province, infantry, gunners, tank crews, and soldiers in the service branches were taught their jobs.

*   *   *   *

On the other side of the world, at the end of 1941, Japan struck and two thousand Canadian soldiers, sent to Hong Kong that fall, engaged in a hopeless struggle alongside British and Indian troops to hold the colony.

The Winnipeg Grenadiers and the Royal Rifles from Quebec City, in a Canadian force commanded by Brigadier J. K. Lawson, were in heavy action. The Japanese hurled overwhelming forces against the defenders and hammered the island with artillery fire and bombs.

For more than two weeks the Canadians fought. Brigadier Lawson and his chief of staff, Colonel Hennessy, were killed by shell-fire. Casualties mounted and by Christmas Day further resistance was impossible. The Hong Kong operation was over. It had been the first Canadian action of the war.

*   *   *   *

Canadians shared in a second Pacific operation in August, 1943, when a force of Home Defence troops under Brigadier Harry Foster, who later commanded divisions on the Western Front, and in Italy, landed unopposed on Kiska in the Aleutians. The island had been evacuated by the Japanese before the attack.

*   *   *   *

In England, the spring of 1942 saw the creation of the First Canadian Army—the first army formation in the Dominion's history.

The offensive training was extended into the field of combined operations, along commando lines. Obviously, seaborne attacks were the principal method to be used to get back on the Continent, and manoeuvres took on a "web-footed" character.

Several assault forces were formed and in the spring of 1942 one in particular looked as if it were going on an operation. It was called "Viking Force" and was commanded by Major Brian McCool of Toronto, who later was taken prisoner at Dieppe.

About two hundred men made up the force, and after commando training on the cliffs and beaches at Beachy Head, the force moved mysteriously to Scotland. I went with the force and we sailed from the Clyde under great secrecy. Our combined-operations ship, which had been on some Norwegian raids, took us to the Isle of Mull off the west coast of Scotland and for a week we made practice landings on isolated *lochs*. The training concluded with a skirmish against British commandos in a practice landing near the mouth of the Clyde. Back to Gourock we went and then we returned to the south. The rumour was that we had been training for a raid on the Norwegian coast but nothing ever came of it.

To add to this bitter frustration, a small group from the Carleton and York Regiment had gone on a raid to Boulogne with British commandos while we were training on Mull.

The Carleton and Yorks ran into trouble on the way in to the beaches, when their craft stranded on a sand bar, but although they did not land they were on the raid and got credit for it.

A few months later—in August—the 2nd Division went to Dieppe and the Canadians, at last, were in the war. The North African landings by American and British forces followed in the fall but the Canadians kept training in England, with no part in those operations. The plan still was to use them in the west—to use the whole army there as one compact striking force.

But several groups of Canadian officers and non-commissioned officers—about four hundred in all—were sent to Tunisia in the early part of 1943 to get battle experience with the First British Army.

The Germans were driven from Tunisia by May and the next move in the Allied plan was to invade Sicily. The 1st Canadian Division was assigned to the Eighth Army for this task and in this decision to dispatch the 1st Division to the Mediterranean is the genesis of the controversy over the deployment of the Canadian overseas forces.

The full story of that controversy will only be told when official papers and memoranda are published, but briefly the broad picture, as I saw it, was this:

General McNaughton believed that the army should be kept together as an entity for the West Front campaign. That was the intention when the Canadian forces were given army status overseas. While the dispatch of the 1st Division to the Mediterranean was not in line with this view, he approved it under the circumstances, but it was intended to bring the Division back to England in the fall to rejoin the Canadian Army for the Normandy invasion.

But the Division stayed in the Mediterranean. Another division was sent out too and the 1st Corps took the field in Italy. It was argued that the time had come when Canada must make a considerable contribution to a fighting front, at the price of splitting the army, rather than wait for the Second Front to open.

The Army Commander's opinion was at variance with this plan. He opposed it and was overruled. The disputes over this issue were at times extremely acrimonious. In the fall of 1943 the Army Commander, whose health was never very robust, was taken ill and at Christmas it was announced that he was leaving his army command because of ill health.

There are many angles to the controversy which raged around General McNaughton, but I believe the fundamental reason for his retirement was the difficulty which arose between him and members of the Canadian Cabinet, particularly Defence Minister Ralston, over the question of splitting the Canadian Army.

The two men clashed practically every time they met. The climax came when it was decided to send the 1st Corps to Italy. Then the differences between the two burst wide open.

At the time, it was rumoured that a dispute between General Montgomery and the Canadian Commander was a basic reason for the latter's retirement. That story has little basis in fact. It is true the two Generals never saw eye to eye. They seldom agreed on anything and the schism between them was emphasized shortly after the Sicily landing when General Montgomery refused General McNaughton permission to land on the island to see the Canadians and study the campaign first hand. It was a sharp rebuff. The Canadian

(Top): *Canadians take over a German town. They are here seen in Cleve, a Rhine-land village captured in the advance.*

(Lower): *Lieut.-General A. G. L. McNaughton greets officers of a Canadian Machine-Gun Reinforcement Unit. An especially favoured army mascot is lying at the General's feet. There were many such dogs with the Canadians.*

General had to remain in Malta and finally returned to England. He did not get to Sicily until the campaign was over.

But despite this, there has been no convincing evidence that General Montgomery had anything to do with General McNaughton's retirement. The former was running his Eighth Army and he had no time or inclination to meddle in the affairs of the Canadian Army.

The issue, as I saw it develop, comes down to the acrimony which grew up between General McNaughton and the exponents of the plan to split the army.

It will be for history to decide who was right.

Apart from this domestic fight over army policy, subtle criticism of General McNaughton had been developing for eight months prior to his retirement.

The criticism—never very outspoken but heard in high places—sprang from the General's leadership of the Canadian Army on "Spartan" manoeuvre in March, 1943. This was the biggest manoeuvre ever held in Britain and the Canadian Commander was leading his army in an advance from a hypothetical beach-head in southern England. It was a work-out for the Second Front attack.

This was the first full-scale test for the army and although the 1st Corps under General Crerar did well, the 2nd Corps under General Sansom boggled its opportunities.

The responsibility was placed on General McNaughton, who up to then had been considered among the top-flight commanders in Britain.

The fact is the 2nd Corps could not have been expected to do very well at that time. It had not been functioning for very long as a complete formation and it did not have all its equipment. The armoured units were particularly short of wireless equipment.

But the critics got to work. Even the official report on the manoeuvre made some harsh comments about the General's tactics, without considering the unprepared state of the 2nd Corps. Through some error, the report was distributed to the various headquarters in Britain before General Paget, Commander-in-Chief, Home Forces, had read it carefully. When he saw the criticism he had it deleted.

But the damage was done. This sort of thing went on behind the scenes while the dispute over the disposition of the Canadian Army was boiling up.

General McNaughton's prestige was damaged and his standing the War Office and in Whitehall suffered. This probably was a contributing factor to his retirement, but the chief reason he left was the battle with the Cabinet and principally with Colonel Ralston.

General Crerar succeeded him, coming from command of the 1st Corps in Italy to assume this new responsibility. In taking General McNaughton's place, General Crerar faced one of the most difficult tasks of his career. He was not particularly well known outside Headquarters, for he always had been an unostentatious, quiet commander in the formations he led. But he took over with a firm hand and the proof of his success was the showing the Canadians made in the West under his sane, sound leadership.

For the Canadians who remained in England until the Normandy landings, life was a continuation of manoeuvres, but manoeuvres which grew larger, more impressive and more hopeful each month.

They were practically fully accredited citizens of England now and London was almost a Canadian city to them. On Cockspur Street, running off Trafalgar Square, was Canadian Military Headquarters, which grew from a few offices to a huge establishment, gen-

erally ridiculed as a red-tape factory by field formations but actually an organization which had important functions, including maintaining full liaison with
National Defence Headquarters in Ottawa and with
the War Office on Whitehall. Major-General Price
Montague was senior officer at C.M.H.Q. for several
years.

Across Cockspur Street was the Beaver Club, favourite rendezvous for Canadian other ranks in London.
Rt. Hon. Vincent Massey, Canadian High Com-
missioner in London, and Mrs. Massey were principally instrumental in organizing this fine club in the
early months of the war.

As more Canadians arrived in England, hostels and
leave centres were opened in London, most of them
operated by the Canadian Auxiliary Services, which
performed commendable work for the troops in England and on the fighting fronts.

For officers, the Park Lane Hotel on Piccadilly was
a rendezvous for the first few years crowded with Canadians on week-ends. Later, they drifted off to other
hotels, but every Canadian officer in England remem-
bers the Park Lane. The Haymarket Club on the
Haymarket was another popular hangout, but the
Canadians were always discovering new clubs and new
pubs as they came to know London.

Their knowledge of the United Kingdom was not
confined to London and the areas where they were
stationed in the south. On leaves they travelled far
and wide, and few counties in England, or few parts
of Scotland, Wales or Ireland—north and south—were
not visited by Canadian soldiers.

Many found brides in Britain and the total went
into six figures.

The Canadians were probably the most popular

overseas troops in Britain during the war. There were cases, which were inevitable, of misunderstandings and difficulties, but looking at the broad picture, the Canadians got along well with the British and the British with the Canadians. They had more in common than British and Americans, apart altogether from the Empire bond.

Many young Canadians went to Britain with swaggering intolerance, wrapped in their new uniforms and scorning the British mode of life; after a few months they realized the stuff the British were made of. They respected the British courage and steadfastness, marvelled at British hospitality, and forgave the British reservation, ubiquitous Brussels sprouts, bone-chilling, unheated houses and tasteless food.

XII

ARCTIC FORAY

THE days lengthened until there was no night and the damp Arctic air was cold and penetrating, even though it was summer, as we sailed northeast of Greenland through grey seas. The *Empress of Canada,* carrying Force 111, consisting of Canadians, with small British and Norwegian detachments, plodded steadily along, flanked by two cruisers and three destroyers of the Royal Navy.

Yesterday we had seen the last of our air escort from Iceland and now we were on our own, going north to land on the German-dominated island of Spitsbergen, six hundred miles from the North Pole.

It was late August, 1941. Two months earlier the Germans had launched their big attack on Russia. Prime Minister Churchill had made his stirring speech announcing that Britain would ally herself with the Soviet and now this force was on its way, the first military evidence of the alliance. We were going north in aid of Russia, to deprive the Germans of valuable coal mines on the bleak island and to neutralize Spitsbergen as a base for German naval and air attacks on the Arctic convoy route to Archangel and Murmansk.

Spitsbergen was Norwegian but the Germans in Norway, from headquarters in Tromso, were easily dominating the island and getting the coal from the extremely modern mines. There were two thousand Russian miners working one huge mine at Barentsberg and eight hundred Norwegians at Longyear City operating another. They had been running the mines for years and the war had caught them there.

The British and Russian governments, in consultation with the Norwegian government in London, decided to deny these profitable coal sources to the enemy, and troops of the 2nd Canadian Infantry Brigade, under then Brigadier Arthur E. Potts, were chosen under the original plan to make up the main part of Force 111, as it was officially designated.

So, early in August, the Princess Patricia's Canadian Light Infantry and the Edmonton Regiment, with a field company of the Royal Canadian Engineers, a battery of twenty-five-pounder field artillery, a detachment of machine-gunners from the Saskatoon Light Infantry, a Royal Canadian Army Medical Corps unit and some miscellaneous detachments, went to Scotland to embark on this expedition. Combined operations were in their infancy then and this was an ambitious task for 1941.

The Patricias and the Edmontons were to have attacked Trondheim during the Norwegian campaign a year and a half before but that operation had been cancelled before they sailed and it was just as well. This was their second chance and they eagerly anticipated it.

We boarded the *Empress* at a Scottish port and sailed to a west-coast *loch* for manoeuvres before the real job. There was no assault equipment available (since combined-operations developments were only beginning) and practice landings were made in ordinary lifeboats and whalers from the *Empress*. Civilian motor-boats, which had seen far better days and now had been taken over by the army, were put in the hands of Army Service Corps motor-boat companies, to their complete disgust, and were used to land supplies and ammunition.

There were comic scenes every day along the beaches of the *loch* as the Canadians tried to handle the awkward lifeboats. It would have been perilous indeed to attempt an opposed landing with such unsuitable craft.

At the time, it was thought that a German force might already have occupied Spitsbergen and that Force 111 would have to fight its way in. But some doubt about the German occupation arose and last-minute conferences were held in London and Brigadier Potts went down to attend them as the training continued.

Under the original plan the Canadians were to land, defeat any German force on the island, occupy the towns and the mines and remain on Spitsbergen for an indefinite period after the mining population had been evacuated. I had planned to go with the force, covering the landing and occupation and return with the Norwegian miners being brought back to Britain.

However, the plan was drastically altered. A British warship on the Arctic run made a reconnaissance of the island about mid-August and reported that no German force was yet there. It was then decided to reduce the force and rush it north immediately, take over the island, wreck the mines, take off the miners and then clear out. A plan for an indefinite operation was cut down to a quick raid. It was believed that the Germans were intending to land a force on Spitsbergen very shortly and speed was imperative.

In the reduction of the force, the Patricias were sent back to their camps in southern England, disgusted and frustrated. Only about two companies of the Edmontons were retained, with a detachment of Saskatoon Light Infantry, a field company of the R.C.E., a Norwegian platoon and some British R.A.S.C. personnel.

The navy alone provided the strength with its two cruisers and three destroyers. Our small force lived in luxury and comfort aboard the *Empress,* ate three whopping meals a day and had nothing much to do but keep anti-submarine and anti-aircraft watch on the top decks as we sailed inside the Hebrides, past Scapa Flow and north to Iceland, with an air escort all the way.

For several days we had the old aircraft carrier *Argus* with us, her flight deck jammed with Hurricanes. We thought for a while she was going with us but she left our convoy and headed northeast before we got to Iceland. She was taking the first Royal Air Force squadrons to Russia. When the *Argus* got within flying distance for Hurricanes from airdromes on the north Russian front, the planes took off and flew to the Soviet lines. Several Canadians were with those pioneer squadrons that did so well with the Red Air Force.

We got to Iceland on August 21 and even at that time there were United States warships in the harbours and American planes were flying operational patrols. We didn't dally and sailed again the next morning.

Once clear of Iceland, the brigadier briefed all the troops himself and told them the whole story. He was confident there were no enemy troops on the island yet.

The expedition heaved through the Arctic Sea without interference. Walrus flying-boats took off on patrol each day from the cruiser *Nigeria,* flagship of the naval commander, Admiral Sir Philip Vian, who won fame in the destroyer *Cossack* and later commanded the naval force which carried the Canadians in the invasion of Sicily. We sailed on serenely, day after day.

On August 24 we circled north of Bear Island and

married up with trawlers and an oil-tanker which were part of our raid force. Tomorrow was landing day (at that time in the childhood of combined operations the term D-Day was not used) and the troops got ready their weapons, ammunition and supplies.

A cruiser pulled ahead of the convoy and sent its flying boat over Spitsbergen. It reported that everything was quiet on the island and it did not appear that German forces had landed. That information buoyed up confidence but we would not know definitely until we tried to land—and we knew that if we tried to go in against opposition in the lifeboats it would be a bloody event.

The cruiser, destroyers and even the *Empress* sailed right up Green Bay, one of the *fjords* on the west side of the island, at seven o'clock the next morning, August 25, and there wasn't a sound from the shore. Barentsberg, with its two thousand miners, lay quiet. White smoke from the chimneys of the unpainted, squalid houses, clustering on the hillside above the docks and around the gaping black mouths of the mine shafts, was the only sign of life.

The ships sailed up the *fjord* and the troops stood by their boat stations. The warships trained their guns on the town in anticipation of any German fire from the shore.

Nothing happened. We might have been a coal-boat coming in to take off a cargo for the Germans in Tromso. Our ships anchored a mile past Barentsberg. The mist which clung like a fleecy rug over the *fjord* lifted and the sun shone brilliantly and warmly by ten A.M. when the brigadier and his staff, with a Russian government representative from the London embassy whom we called the "ambassador", as well as some British liaison officers representing the War Office and the Foreign Office, decided to go ashore.

We all climbed into the least decrepit of our motor-boats and nobody was certain what was going to happen when we landed. Perhaps the Germans were lying doggo in the town. The prospect did not daunt rugged Brigadier Potts. He wore his serge uniform and his British warm, with his scarlet-banded general staff officer's cap, and carried a swagger stick.

Our motor launch chugged alongside the tumble-down wharf and the brigadier was first out, followed by the rest of us who were trailed by a company of heavily-armed Edmonton riflemen aching for a scrap. On the dock stood a dozen scowling, silent Russians, very suspicious and extremely doubtful of our intentions, though they had been advised from Moscow we were coming.

They wore dark caps and blue padded tunics with black drill trousers, a sinister-looking group. One came forward sullenly and our Russian liaison man, a thirty-five-year-old persuader, spoke to him. Still there were no smiles of welcome. The miner beckoned to the brigadier and his staff to follow him up the long flight of stairs past the red flag, with its hammer and sickle, to the administration building up the slope.

As we got into the town our senses were assailed by a sweet, sickening smell—the scent of *eau de cologne*. No liquor was permitted on the island for the miners, so they imported great cases of *eau de cologne* and drank it wholesale. The whole town reeked of the stuff.

The Russian "ambassador" had partly convinced the miners by the time we reached the administration building that the Canadians were not going to loot the town and kill the inhabitants. We were ushered into a large conference room, which also smelled highly of *eau de cologne* and had large paintings of Stalin, Trotsky, Lenin and Molotoff on the walls.

The Russian leaders in the town passed around boxes of their long, strong cigarettes and sat around the table with the brigadier to parley through the interpreters. The brigadier told them the plan and the Russian liaison went to great pains to inform the head men of Barentsberg that this operation was sponsored by the British and Russian governments.

The consul, top man in the town, did not appear particularly impressed but the meeting wound up in an amicable spirit and it was agreed that the evacuation of the two thousand miners would take place the following day. The *Empress* was to take them to Archangel, escorted by a cruiser and two destroyers, while the Canadians remained to carry out the mine demolitions and to guard the place until the return of the troopship.

The evacuation was a weird affair. All night long, Russian men, women and children packed their belongings and by breakfast time were trudging down to the wharf with bulging bundles, suitcases, bags and boxes. Women wore kerchiefs over their heads, peasant style, and men were in their dark miners' clothes or their best suits, with clean shirts and collars.

Children wailed, parents cajoled and dogs howled. The babble of the evacuating horde echoed over the still *fjord*. It was a dismal and dejected community that was leaving its barren home at the foot of snow-capped mountains on this forbidding, treeless island. They had no idea what the future held. They were not optimistic. They always listened to the Moscow radio and its grim news of the Russian front and they knew their country was in deadly peril. The young men wanted to get back to join the army at beleaguered Leningrad. They alone seemed anxious to leave.

The crowd milled around the wharf, waiting their

turn to embark on the lighters or destroyers which carried them out to the *Empress*. Canadian officers who could speak no Russian tried in vain to maintain a semblance of order, but there was confusion for hours. At the last minute a score of Russians at a time would decide that they didn't want to go: or wanted to pick up some more belongings. One group insisted on trying to hoist a heavy gasoline engine aboard a destroyer. It was worse than any Christmas rush in a metropolitan station at home.

Women and children crowded the wardroom and mess decks of the destroyers. Babies cried on the wardroom tables and naval officers looked aghast at the turmoil in their quarters. By late afternoon the two thousand were aboard the *Empress* except for a small clique including the Russian consul of Barentsberg who were determined not to leave. It appears that after selling coal to the Germans they feared what would happen to them in Archangel.

The consul, living in a cottage on the edge of the town, began to drink bottle after bottle of fine champagne he had hidden away in his cellar. No *eau de cologne* for him. The drunker he got, the firmer became his determination to stay in Spitsbergen. A ticklish situation was developing fast. The admiral sent a message trying to persuade him to leave. The Russian envoy talked for an hour. The liquor-befuddled consul would not budge. Then Brigadier Potts took matters into his own hands.

The *Empress* had to sail that night, with all the Russians including the consul and his group of dissenters, but the brigadier did not want to use force unless necessary. He decided he would try some rugged diplomacy and went to see the consul in his cottage. The brigadier, smiling and affable with many good jokes, had a drink with the consul. They had another and then the consul himself finished that bottle and began to work on another. The Russian glowed with good fellowship as he sank lower in his cups and the brigadier, acting his role magnificently, saw the inevitable approaching. Finally the consul passed out on the floor from the effects of his own indulgence and a half-dozen of his henchmen carried him, like a bag of potatoes, down the long flight of stairs to the wharf. Dead drunk, he was taken aboard the *Empress* under a blanket and the rest of the dissenters followed him without further protest. I never found out what happened to the consul and his colleagues in Archangel.

The *Empress* with its warship escort sailed at midnight in the broad daylight of the Arctic night and we felt like a lost battalion on Spitsbergen, occupying this Communist town.

If the Germans attacked us by air or sea, we knew we couldn't last long. And we could not all have been evacuated on the cruiser and destroyer left with us. If the *Empress* and its escort going to Russia was attacked and was unable to return we might have been stuck there for weeks, with early winter coming on.

It was a dim outlook if anything went wrong with the main plans, but the Canadians' luck held. One lone German plane came over the western edge of the island but did not spot us, and nothing happened in the way of enemy interference during our ten days on Spitsbergen.

The Edmontons took over Barentsberg almost before the Russians left and had it running in a few days like a well-organized lumber camp. These ingenious Alberta soldiers could do anything. Men who had worked in Edmonton packing-plants before the war slaughtered and dressed hogs and cattle. We had fresh meat daily. Others started a livery stable with horses and carts the miners left behind. They got the Russian movie theatre going and played Russian music on gramophones all day long.

The engineers went to work on the mines, blowing up machinery and vital installations, but not wrecking the mine shafts because at the time it was considered possible that the British or Russians might want to re-open the mines later. They could replace the equipment but the Germans would not be able to do this easily. This long-sighted policy made the work of the sappers a ticklish one. They had to smash so much and no more.

Great dumps of oil in drums lined the shore and these were destroyed in gigantic fires. It seemed wanton destruction but it was ordered because no suitable ships were available to take these supplies back to Britain. They must not be left for the Germans.

The radio stations on the island were demolished with one exception, the Norwegian link from Longyear City to Tromso. This was kept open for deception.

Loyal Norwegians, working with Canadian signalmen, sent the regular weather reports and commercial messages which the Germans expected to receive daily in Tromso. The station carried on as if nothing had happened on the island and the enemy was completely duped. Fake weather reports were sent saying skies were overcast and visibility poor. There is no question that these reports misled the Germans and probably prevented planes coming while we were there.

When the navy captured three ships, come from Norway to load coal at Longyear City, Tromso was informed in routine fashion that the ships had arrived and had sailed again. But they sailed for Britain with prize crews aboard—not for Norway.

I stayed in a flea-ridden house in Barentsberg for a few days and then took a motor launch to Longyear City, fifteen miles down the *fjord*. It was a spotless, neat and efficient Norwegian town, much in contrast to the grubby, filthy Barentsberg with its stench of *eau de cologne*. Several detachments of Canadian troops, with a Norwegian staff officer from London and a token platoon of Norwegian infantry, had landed there from a destroyer the same morning the main landing was made at Barentsberg.

The Norwegians at first were indifferent to the proposal that they leave their town and island. Life was not unkind to them there on Spitsbergen. They had their own community centres; the miners played soccer on a good field by the sea and incidentally gave a Canadian team a trimming in a game later on; their houses were comfortable and they had their own church and stores, with plenty of food. Cigarettes and semi-luxuries came from Norway every few months. The Norwegian community was fairly self-contained. They had had no dealings or relationships with the Russians at Barentsberg.

But the great majority hated the Germans and spoke heatedly of the German occupation of their homeland. They talked over the whole question of evacuation in their meetings and agreed to the plan to go back to Britain with the raid force as soon as the *Empress* returned from Russia. Methodically they began to pack their things.

The Norwegians became very friendly and there was only one small group on which the Canadians had to keep their eye. They hoped to sabotage the power house, which was under a Canadian guard, in order to cut off electric power which operated the wireless station. If the station folded up the enemy might become suspicious and investigate this curious situation on Spitsbergen. The plots failed.

Then there was trouble at Barentsberg, not with the enemy but with fire. The sappers' careful plans were snarled up completely when a demolition to wreck machinery in a tinder-dry building at a mine shaft set fire to the structure.

I had flown down to Barentsberg from Longyear City in a Walrus off one of the cruisers when the fire broke out. Every soldier in town turned out and after a few hours it was brought under control. The next day, though, a fresh wind fanned the fire into life again. This time it could not be stopped. It ate its way from building to building until all Barentsberg was engulfed. The Canadians moved their kit and equipment down to the edge of the *fjord* and had to stand by helpless.

The next day, September 2, the *Empress* came up the *fjord*, safely back from Russia, and the Canadians from Barentsberg went aboard.

That night, back in Longyear City, the Norwegians held parties in practically every house. The Canadians were invited and the soldiers danced with the pretty Norwegian girls and everyone had a boisterous time. The Norwegians by this time were completely reconciled to going to Britain. They clearly saw the anomaly in their working the mines—for the Germans —and many of them were now anxious to get to Britain to join the Free Norwegian forces there.

The next morning the eight hundred clambered aboard destroyers and we sailed up the long *fjord*, flanked by mountains falling sheer into the water, and joined the others on the *Empress*, still lying off burning Barentsberg. Stray trappers who had their lines along distant *fjords* had been collected by destroyers previously. On the evening of September 3, the second anniversary of the start of the war, the convoy cleared from Spitsbergen.

The last of the force off the island was a detachment of Canadian signalmen and sappers, who kept the wireless station going until the convoy was well out to sea. Then the Canadians blew up the station and the power house and came away in a destroyer which caught up with us later. Not a soul remained on Spitsbergen.

During the ten days we had been on the island, the *Empress,* with thirty Canadians aboard, had gone to Archangel to repatriate the two thousand Russians. For days the Canadians had a chaotic but amusing time looking after the stalwart Russians, who knew how to exist on their barren Arctic island but had no idea how to live aboard a troopship. To complicate matters even more, several babies were born en route and the Canadian medical officer delivered them.

At Archangel, two hundred French officers and men had been put aboard the *Empress* by the Russian authorities. They were soldiers of the French Army captured by the Germans in May and June, 1940, who had escaped from Nazi prison camps and then been interned by the Russians.

Their liberty came unexpectedly. When they came alongside the *Empress* in a rainstorm in the river at Archangel and realized she was a British ship, they touched her sides with their hands and choked up with emotion as they tried to sing "God Save the King".

The Canadians brought them back to England, supplying them en route with battledress and other clothing. No men could have been more grateful to the raiders than those French soldiers. Later they joined the Fighting French.

We landed in Britain again on September 8. The expedition had been rather a strange one. There had been unexpected developments, like the accidental destruction of Barentsberg, but generally the Canadians had carried out the plan to the letter.

The *Empress* had sailed more than seven thousand miles on this voyage and it was a wonder something had not gone seriously wrong during the long odyssey through the Arctic Sea. It seemed almost miraculous that we had not been attacked from air or sea some time during the trip.

Spitsbergen was one of the less important combined operations of the war and it was disappointing to the Canadians, who had expected some kind of action. But it was their first successful operation and it was a triumph of surprise and secrecy. And it did make its contribution in the long run to protecting the convoy route to Russia and weakening the Germans on the far north flank.

XIII

DIEPPE—KEY TO INVASION

WEDNESDAY, August 19, 1942—Dieppe. For thousands of Canadians, that was the day stark memory and deep grief were born. It was a day also of full-hearted pride. It was a day on which one of the greatest adventures in war's history flared to its height in battle on the French beaches. It was a day that saw tried out the first complete modern experiment in combined operations—which became a fundamental requisite to Allied victory.

Dieppe was a disaster and a triumph. It was a defeat and a conquest. It was tragic; yet it brought forth such shining gallantry from five thousand Canadians—new to battle—that their courage and audacity electrified the world's free people. Dieppe became a watchword for gallant conduct on every Allied war front.

You can never assess the Dieppe raid bluntly by calling it a success or a failure. At the time it seemed a terrible reverse; casualties were tremendous for eight hours of battle. But even then, many compensating factors were evident. There were few to condemn it outright.

The pay-off for Dieppe came later. It came in brilliantly successful landings in North Africa three months afterwards, and in the Allied assault on Sicily and Italy.

Dieppe paid off in the assault against strong German positions on Salerno Bay; and in the walk-in landing which initially took place south of Rome on the Anzio-Nettuno bridgehead.

Dieppe was the test-tube for combined operations. This one costly raid on the French coast saved thousands of British, American and Canadian lives in the landings that followed. The men who went to Dieppe —those who were killed, were maimed, who were captured and those who came back—were the men who showed the way to success in the Mediterranean; and their sacrifice found its greatest reward in the Allied landings on the Normandy coast which opened the Second Front.

The chief secrets of successful combined operations were learned in that bitter battle at Dieppe. The army took the brunt of the shock but the navy and the air force shared the attack in full. Military leaders are sometimes too inclined to excuse failures by saying "lessons were learned". But in the case of the Dieppe raid this was not a fatuous statement. Lessons *were* learned at Dieppe—and emphasized in blood—lessons which gave the Allied Command the key to invasion.

Without condoning any of the mistakes made at Dieppe, I'm convinced that if the raid had not been carried out as a prelude to the North African landings, the combined operations in the Mediterranean and the Normandy invasion, these might have been so badly bungled that the war there could have been prolonged for years.

The Dieppe raiders performed a tremendous service in the anguish of battle on the beaches; and if sacrifice can be greater in one battle than another, then the men lost at Dieppe served the Allied cause with as high heroism as the war produced.

For more than a year the High Command had been working on combined-operations plans, seeking to devise new methods of amphibious warfare, the only way to get back into Europe on the offensive. The system had been worked out, but a trial for the new ships, tanks, guns and the troops themselves had to be run.

Dieppe was chosen as the target and men of the 2nd Canadian Division, commanded by Major-General J. H. Roberts, were given the assignment. They were not sent to Dieppe, however, as sacrificial guinea pigs in the Combined Operations Headquarters' laboratory. It was honestly believed there was a strong possibility of learning what was necessary without heavy losses.

Several mischances, some errors in timing in the landing, and sterner German opposition than had been foreseen, made the raid go sour and prevented attainment of most of the immediate material objectives. The story of the Dieppe raid has been told as completely as that of any operation in the war. There is also the story behind Dieppe—the story of the raid that was supposed to take place more than a month earlier but was washed out by bad weather. This background had to remain secret then, but knowledge of it is necessary to any complete understanding of the raid itself.

*   *   *   *

It was late spring and there was a new mystery in Sussex. From their camps south of the pleasant old town of Horsham in Sussex the majority of the 2nd Canadian Division had suddenly disappeared. The local folk were accustomed to troop movements and it was nothing new to see the Canadians moving in and out of the Sussex camps on one manoeuvre after another. Frequently roads would be jammed for a week with army traffic and troops "striking" at the invisible enemy on the South Downs behind Brighton and in the hop fields and farm lands of Kent. But the manoeuvres would end and the Canadians would come back to The King's Head and The Black Horse for beer on Saturday night.

This time they didn't come back. They were gone for two weeks that stretched into a month and by June the country people had concluded the Canadians had gone to the Middle East.

The war news wasn't particularly good. There seemed to be no momentum in our effort. Our aircraft were flying over France every day but this didn't seem to make much difference. The Germans were doing well in the Western Desert. There was a good deal of loose talk about a Second Front in Europe but we knew there weren't enough British and Canadian divisions in England to make much more than a dent on the Continent. We could never have gone to France to stay. General Montgomery headed Britain's Southeastern Command. Thus the Canadians came into contact with this new personality in the British Army with his many radically new ideas. They wondered how far he would go.

All the Canadian troops, with the exception of the 2nd Division, had just finished a manoeuvre directed by General Montgomery in which the infantry marched nearly three hundred miles in two weeks. It was a rugged exercise but what did it mean? The troops wondered. All this was becoming more and more monotonous and any opportunity to campaign seemed to be as far away as ever. There had been many high hopes that 1942 would certainly see the Canadians in action. But as May ran into the warmth of June the troops were getting discouraged at the year's prospects. In the camps nobody seemed to have much exhilaration about the war. Discipline was good, however, and training was carried out as usual. Still, you could sense the lethargy. The most exciting thing that could happen was a week-end trip to London and a round of clubs and pubs. London was well Canadianized in those days before the tide of Americans swept them back into the back eddies.

It was the whereabouts of the 2nd Division that puzzled me. On June 5, as these things always happen, I was told quietly to get my kit packed and drive to a certain map reference where I'd be met. At 1st Canadian Corps headquarters, to which I'd been attached for so long that I was becoming a permanent fixture, I could sense that something was in the wind. But it is a cardinal rule in this business never to speculate even in your mind about operations until you're briefed; so I just climbed into the station-wagon and whirled through Sussex.

In a quiet Channel town we joined Canadian troops with the dark blue battle patch of the 2nd Division. For several weeks these troops had been training here, occasionally working at sea in assault boats, and it was obvious to me that this was something more than mere manoeuvres. At Divisional Headquarters most of the officers knew that an operation was being prepared, but the work was always referred to as training and several big sea-going manoeuvres were in the offing. Ostensibly this was what I had come to cover.

Throughout June and into July this training went on, and in mid-July I was able to write some stories about great combined-operations landing practices, the largest held up to that time in British waters.

Because of obvious security considerations, that was all I was able to say. The full story is this: The force of Canadians, with British paratroops, Royal Marine

Commandos and some special troops, had been going through this training with the specific intention of raiding Dieppe on July 4. It was to be an eight-hour raid, nothing more, and the plan, with the exception of the use of the paratroops, was the same as for the operation eventually attempted on August 19, when British Commandos were assigned to tasks on the flanks previously allotted to the airborne troops.

Bad weather conditions forced a twenty-four hour postponement of the raid scheduled for July 4 and it was again postponed each day until July 7, when it was cancelled. The tides were suitable only for that short period and it was impossible to wait even a few more days for the Channel to calm and the wind to drop.

But I am getting ahead of my story. The Dieppe raid force included the Essex Scottish from Windsor, Ont., the Royal Regiment from Toronto, the Royal Hamilton Light Infantry, the Cameron Highlanders of Winnipeg, the South Saskatchewan Regiment and the Fusiliers Mont-Royal. The Calgary Tank Regiment, with forty-ton Churchill tanks mounting the then new six-pounder gun, was in the force, and there were some detachments of the Black Watch from Montreal, the Calgary Highlanders and the Regiment de Maisonneuve.

For the role they had, the Royal Canadian Engineers in the Dieppe force were as important as any troops that crossed the Channel.

There was also a considerable detachment from the Toronto Scottish with Vickers guns. Light anti-aircraft gun crews manned the Bofors guns on the tank-landing craft.

Divisional signals had vital jobs to do and there were small units of the Royal Canadian Army Service

Corps and the Provost Corps as well as a Field Security Section. Officers and men of the Ordnance Corps went along as well.

Royal Canadian Army Medical Corps units were with each brigade and medical officers served with every regiment.

A force of Royal Marine Commandos was under the Canadian command and also a force of British paratroops.

Throughout June I kept moving through the camps watching the training. It was a revelation. Nothing as advanced as this had ever been done in combined operations. The massive Churchill tanks lumbered off the tank-landing craft, fired their guns, and then clanked back to the craft nosing into the beaches. The base areas rocked with test demolitions.

The infantry were out every day, practising street fighting through a blitzed part of a built-up area; Sten guns chattered and grenades banged from morning to night.

A fleet of invasion craft gathered off our port and several hundred landing craft and ships were moored in the inlets and the roadsteads. The BBC warned the French people to evacuate the coastal areas.

Finally big, sturdy, heavy-set General Roberts called me into his office and told me an operation was planned. "There's going to be a party but that's all I am telling you at the moment," he said. "Later on you will be briefed fully. Before the force sails on the operation there will be several landing exercises."

On June 11 the whole force went aboard the assault ships for the first full-scale practice assault on a broad beach thirty miles west of our base. I was attached to the R.H.L.I. and we sailed into the Channel with escort vessels of the Royal Navy hovering around our invasion fleet, the largest assembled in European waters up to that time. It was small compared to the mighty armadas which later carried the troops to North Africa and to Sicily but in June, 1942, it marked a long step forward in Britain's preparations for the big offensives to come.

For some hours we sailed southwest in the direction of the French coast and wild rumours went around the ship that we were going to attack Cherbourg. By midnight the rumours died and the sea rose. Our large infantry ships rolled and pitched, but there was no postponement and we went over the side into the wild sea in the small assault-landing craft which carry thirty men.

We tossed about madly, released the davit cables and surged away from the mother ship. In a few minutes practically everyone in the force of five thousand men, rocking about now in these tiny craft, was violently sick.

It was a miracle there wasn't a disaster that night. But not a single boat capsized and not a man was lost. A year later when we were plunging through another tremendous sea in the landing craft going in to the beaches at Pachino in Sicily, I had a vivid recollection of this weird night in the English Channel.

The flotillas clumsily bobbed into position and we headed for the English beaches ten miles away. We were more than an hour late landing but the infantry and the tanks and supplies were put ashore rapidly.

For a start it was a good test run and nobody expected everything to click right along without a hitch.

The force stayed ashore eight hours and withdrew to the boats again to return to the base port, where the troops resumed their shore training. General Mont-

gomery visited the Division. It was he who originally
suggested that the 2nd Division be chosen for this
operation. Later, General Crerar, then commanding
the 1st Canadian Corps in Britain, came to headquarters and there were more high-powered conferences held in greater secrecy than ever.

A number of things were worrying the staff and
among them was the uncertainty of getting the force
on the beaches at the right time and at the right places
and the complicated problem of navigation facing any
sea-going force in the Channel, with its currents and
tides, some of them quite unpredictable.

A British paratroop unit joined the Canadians and
after a few days in our area disappeared again. The
town people were much puzzled about these movements and the field security police watched everyone
like hawks.

The security film "Next of Kin" was shown to all
the force as a grim warning. Most of the troops in the
film are killed in a combined-operation raid about
which the enemy learns because of careless talk.

The training and planning dragged on. Then on
June 23 I joined the Essex Scottish for the second big
practice landing. There was a calm sea in the Channel
this night, but again the navy erred in navigation and
besides being late, our battalion arrived off shore six
miles to the west of its beach. The whole infantry
assault was delayed and the tanks landed ahead of us,
which was wrong.

A group of top British, Canadian and American
officers watched the landing from the beach, and there
I saw General McNaughton, the Canadian Army Commander. He looked extremely worried and I remember his words: "These are anxious days. There is great
peril when the Navy does not land our men on the
right beaches at the right time."

Personally, I was not very confident after these practices. I had probably been on as many landing exercises as anyone in the Canadian Army during the previous year or more, and they never seemed to go according to schedule. Difficulties always cropped up during the run-in to the beaches and put the troops at a disadvantage from the start.

Later I found it was the same on actual operations. Seaborne attacks are among the most difficult in warfare.

The troops returned to the base once more and on June 27 General Roberts called all the officers in the force to a dramatic conference. Speaking to several hundred at a time in a stifling room which had its windows blacked out and was guarded by armed sentries, the general told them all that a raid was to be carried out shortly. He outlined the complete plan.

I was in the room for the briefing as General Roberts stood behind the big plaster model of a stretch of coastline and a port. He launched right into his talk without preliminaries and in short, clipped sentences, told them how the force would raid this target, and he specified the tasks of each battalion and unit.

He gave them every detail but did not name the target as Dieppe. There were not many officers who could tell from the model what port it was.

The German defence force in and around the port was estimated at about three thousand, some of whom were labour battalion troops. The 10th *Panzer* Division was believed to be at Amiens, sixty miles away, and it would probably be ordered to Dieppe after the attack developed.

General Roberts laid most stress on the air strength which would support the raid force. He said there

would be heavy air bombardment of many of the
targets, and Fighter Command would put up everything it had to give air cover for the operation. There
was no question that the officers were impressed by
the briefing. It looked like a good thing and I heard
one of them say: "This will be a piece of cake." Canadian casualties were estimated at about five hundred
killed, wounded and missing.

Everyone left that room with a feeling of high
elation. Here was the big job at last; all this training
was now to be put to use as the real thing on a daring
operation.

In my Dieppe diary I made these notes at the time
to tell the story of the next few heart-breaking days.

July 1: The other war correspondents arrive. There
are British, American and Canadian writers—the top
men in the business. Up till now I had been the only
correspondent with the force. I guess the job is imminent. Roberts did not give any date in his briefing
nor has any date been mentioned so far. At midnight
all the correspondents crowd into one tiny room on the
top floor of Divisional Headquarters building and
Church Mann sits on the back of a chair before the
plaster model and briefs the writers completely.
(Mann was a lieutenant-colonel then and Roberts'
principal staff officer). In typical breezy fashion, Mann
gave us all a crystal-clear understanding of the plan.
He made a big hit with the correspondents with his
clear-cut approach and his good humour, which persisted even at midnight after weeks of night-and-day
work, planning this show.

July 2: We go aboard our ships. I'm on the *Prince
Charles*, a Channel boat which ran from Dover and
Folkestone to Holland in peacetime. An assault com-
pany of the Essex Scottish is aboard. This is my regi-

ment for the attack. In the afternoon, Colonel Jasperson of the Essex has a great personal triumph when he comes aboard to tell his troops they are going on a raid.

The troops cheer the colonel to the echo. They are in tremendous spirits. By now they even know the target, for the maps and photographs of Dieppe have been issued all around. Security has been splendid so far and now there is no need for precautions with everyone aboard ship. The force has trained hard for this raid and the men know their job. It is just a question of making it a surprise attack and getting them ashore without too much opposition.

In the evening General Roberts boards the *Prince Charles* and talks to the troops. He understands his men and they admire him. There is more tumult and shouting. It is the boisterous enthusiasm you get on a college campus the night before a football game.

July 3: Our ships are scattered in the bays and inlets around our port. It looks as if H-Hour (which is this war's term for zero hour) will be 4.15 A.M. tomorrow, Saturday. It all depends on the weather. We need calm seas and little wind. Lord Mountbatten, the chief of Combined Operations, and General Dwight D. Eisenhower, the American Commander in the European Theatre of Operations, come aboard. Lord Louis gives the troops a pep talk on the deck but he doesn't make the same impression as Jasperson or Roberts. The Canadian soldier likes to listen to his own leaders. Eisenhower chats with half a dozen American Rangers attached to us for experience. I buttonhole him as he leaves and he says: "These boys of ours are just the first of thousands who will eventually go into Europe." That sure is Second Front talk.

The troops are all briefed now, right down to sections. The officers have been working like beavers putting them in the picture ever since we came aboard. Everyone has maps and knows the target area well. They know every street in the port by name. The intelligence maps have machine-gun positions and all strongpoints clearly marked.

Then we get a message: "Operation postponed twenty-four hours due to weather conditions."

We up anchor at 11.30 and begin to move down stream to join the other ships. Everyone's spirits soar for we are on our way. But we scarcely get to the submarine boom before we get another twenty-four-hour postponement. This is one of the toughest things about any operation, this waiting. Nerves are becoming ragged. The confinement and boredom are appalling.

July 5: The weather is breaking a little now but it is still not good. The difficulty is that there is a sea running in the Channel which may make it tough for the small boats to hit the beaches; and also there is too much wind for the paratroopers to land to attack the coastal batteries at Berneval and Vangreville on our flanks.

We can have only two more postponements because after Tuesday the tides are wrong for the landing.

In the wardroom the barometer is our idol. We worship before it every hour of the day and wear a patch on the carpet to it, praying that the weather will break. An officer has dubbed us "the wardroom commandos". Another postponement.

July 6: A fourth postponement. We go ashore for a route march. We return to the ship and everyone is in a better mood after the physical exercise.

July 7: The heart-breaking news comes at 10.30

A.M. "The operation has been cancelled, repeat cancelled, because of unfavourable weather conditions." God, what a blow to these troops! Men break down and cry on the troop decks, they take the disappointment so hard. In the wardroom the officers drink innumerable double scotches (at eight cents a glass—navy prices). "Let us hate," is the toast. In mid-afternoon I say *au revoir* to my Essex friends and leave the ship with Colonel Jasperson. I have never been more depressed in my life. Here was the opportunity for which Canadian troops had waited so long and it has been fouled by weather.

I get a train to London and moodily watch the lush English countryside flash past, reflecting on this twist of fate that has prevented the Canadians raiding the French coast when everything but weather favoured them.

*   *   *   *

Going to Combined Operations H.Q. we met Lord Louis Mountbatten at midnight but he told us little that we didn't know already. These disappointments of cancelled raids were nothing new to him. Others had been cancelled because of this unpredictable Channel weather. But none as large or as important as this has been prepared before.

He did say, though, that the top meteorological brains of Britain had worked on weather predictions for the Dieppe raid and they had believed it would be suitable for the operation. Freakish winds that blew up unexpectedly saved the German garrison in Dieppe in those days of early July.

I went down to our office in Fleet Street and confessed I had come back empty-handed from what would have been one of the great stories of the war.

(TOP): *At Dieppe, the plan called for an unopposed surprise landing at dawn, to gain the headland overlooking the harbour, knocking out the guns there and eventually circling back to re-embark in early afternoon. (These pictures are from captured German films.)*

(LOWER): *The main attack was to go in on the main beach. It was good for landings but loose shale and pebbles prevented tanks from getting a grip, and some foundered.*

That's the story of "practice Dieppe", the raid that didn't come off.

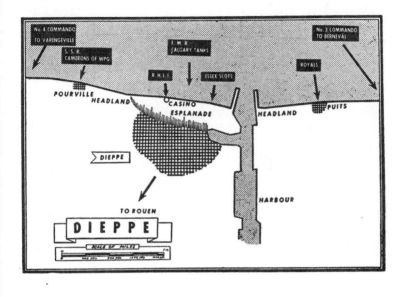

*   *   *   *

The maps and photographs and plans of Dieppe were collected and the troops disembarked to return to their camps.

For the next month they went back to the old routine of their training camps. Then early in August the High Command decided to make another try at carrying out the raid. From all information I could gather, it was a sudden decision dictated by the necessities of the North African landing which was being planned at the time, and scheduled for early November. Later I'll enlarge on that important background to the Dieppe operation.

On August 16 and 17 the same troops which made up the original main attacking force were piled into trucks and rushed secretly to various ports along the south coast. Only the senior officers knew that the raid was on again and reasons for the sudden move were carefully disguised.

With a group of correspondents I went down to Bath on a mysterious trip and there we hung around for two days playing billiards, wandering around the old town and getting more on edge every hour. Most of us had been on "practice Dieppe" but didn't know for sure whether it was the same job again or some new raid drummed up in the meantime. Finally, on August 18, we piled into trucks and buses and rolled south towards the main Channel ports.

In a quiet corner of a park near one of the ports, we sprawled on the grass. The then Major C. S. (Cliff) Wallace, our public relations officer who made the press arrangements to take about a score of correspondents on the operation and got them all back with only two wounded, told us we would be going on a raid to France that night with the 2nd Division. It was the same job again.

We dispersed to various ports to join the units to which we were assigned.

In a last-minute switch I had been assigned to the Royal Regiment and wouldn't be going with the Essex Scottish whom I had come to know and admire so much in training. My best friends in the force were in the Essex, but we were to be on their flank; and anyway, I thought, I'd join up with them in the town of Dieppe when things settled down a little.

The port at six P.M. was a busy spot. The last truck-loads of Canadians and their ammunition and equipment were arriving. It caused no particular stir and the workers paid scant attention to the troops, whom they had seen many times before, going and coming on manoeuvres.

By seven P.M. I was aboard the *Queen Emma,* another peacetime Channel vessel turned into an infantry assault ship for combined operations. The *Emma* carried the headquarters of the Royal Regiment as well as several hundred assault troops, mortar crews and miscellaneous detachments.

There were sealed envelopes distributed to us all there—the same maps of Dieppe and the same photographs and plans we had hopefully learned to know in every detail in July.

The officers and men had been told by now that they were going to Dieppe tonight and there were hurried conferences aboard the ship, refresher briefings and eleventh-hour preparations. Few of the Royals seemed to be in as confident a mood as I had known them in "practice Dieppe". The rush to the port and the mass of detail, which had to be crammed again in a few hours, left everyone rather ragged.

Even before we put to sea some had an ominous feeling about what was ahead of them on the other side of the Channel. Nobody said anything but many were wondering how the security had been in the time since July 7. Did the Germans know the Canadians were going to France and were they waiting? This was the question being asked in many minds.

They were puzzled, too, why the raid had been decided upon so suddenly. They would have liked more time to adjust themselves.

I shared most of their mental discomfort. For the first hour or so I ran over the plan and studied my maps and photographs and was surprised I had forgotten so much of the detail. I found misgivings

growing in my mind. This seemed somewhat haphazard, compared with the serene way in which the
cancelled raid was mounted.

The final Dieppe plan was altered only slightly
from the one prepared for July. British Commandos
were assigned to tasks on the flanks previously allotted
to paratroopers.

After the raid many people were anxious to know
why airborne troops were not employed. In the first
plan they were to be dropped near the coastal batteries
at Vangreville, six miles west of Dieppe, and at
Berneval, five miles east of the port, to destroy the guns
and prevent them firing on the ships lying off the main
beaches or on the beaches themselves.

There was too much wind for the airborne force in
early July, however, and this was one of the big factors
causing cancellation of the raid. The difficulties were
emphasized by employment of airborne troops, which
require almost perfect weather or they lose much of
their effectiveness by being blown off the dropping
zones in landing.

If it had been entirely a sea-going raid in July, there
is a strong possibility it would have been carried out
as planned, but tasks of the airborne force were such
vital links in the whole plan that once they were
removed from the picture, because of the weather, the
rest of the force could not sail.

So in August it was decided to make it an all-
seaborne landing, with commandos replacing paratroops.

The Commandos were to land in the darkness
shortly before the main landings, with No. 3 Commando attacking the Berneval battery and No. 4
Commando taking on the Vangreville guns.

Then the Royals were to land at Puits, a mile east

of Dieppe, and the South Saskatchewan Regiment was to go ashore at Pourville, a picturesque little seafront town a mile west of the town. This covered the flanks.

The beach at Puits should hardly be given that name. It is only a narrow strip of sand and small for a whole battalion to land on, even in relays. But the plan called for the Royals to make an unopposed, surprise landing there at dawn, go up the slope which led from the beach through a break in the cliff and occupy the hamlet of Puits, a short distance from the cliff-top. This was one company's assignment.

Other Royals were to gain the headland overlooking the harbour of Dieppe on the east and knock out any guns on that headland. This would dominate the whole town once it was captured. Following this the Royals would fan out over the farmland east of Dieppe and eventually would circle back through the southern outskirts of the port and re-embark in early afternoon from the main beaches.

The S.S.R. were to capture Pourville, make the bridgehead there firm and occupy high ground dominating the town, as well as destroy machine-gun posts and some artillery batteries in the vicinity. Eventually they were to circle around during the evacuation into Dieppe itself and also leave from the main beaches in front of the town.

Through the S.S.R. bridgehead, the Cameron Highlanders of Winnipeg were to pass. Their task, under the plan, was to strike inland immediately, marry up with some of the Calgary Regiment's Churchill tanks on high ground southwest of the port, and advance on a landing ground about two miles south of the port. They also were to attack what was believed to be a German headquarters in the village of D'Arques

behind Dieppe and to try to capture German staff
officers and documents there. In the final phase the
Camerons, too, were to move out via the main beaches.

The main attack was to go in on the mile-long main
beach in front of Dieppe. It is a good beach for landings, broad and sloping, but loose shale and pebbles
cover it and this was not foreseen. The tanks could
not get a good grip on the shale and some of them just
dug in and foundered before they had much chance
to fight.

The Essex Scottish were to land on the eastern
sector of the beach and the Royal Hamilton Light
Infantry were going in on the western sector, with the
Fusiliers Mont-Royal in reserve. The Calgary tanks
were to land with the Essex and the R.H.L.I. on the
main beach in the principal assault.

The two leading infantry battalions, with the
engineers, had complicated orders. Every platoon had
a series of specific things to do. The Essex generally
were to work into the buildings on the west side of
the harbour and clean out the enemy as rapidly as
possible. They were to attack a German naval headquarters building on the wharf and make an effort to
grab the German naval code book before it was
destroyed. They were to attack small craft and E-boats
moored in the harbour, and if they could not handle
them the tanks were to come up and sink them with
their six-pounders.

Looking back on it, this now seems a fantastic plan
for the Essex. When I was with them for the first raid,
I was completely naïve about street fighting, for I
attached myself to the platoon which was to lead the
way into the town and attack the naval headquarters.
I even made a date to meet one of the sergeants at the
corner just outside the naval headquarters and get the

latest dope from him there. Then I planned to get into one of the buildings by the wharf and watch the tank-versus-ship battle.

Everyone was so confident, in those July days, that it would be a nice easy raid. One found oneself thinking wildly like that—and even making complete plans to run around Dieppe, as if it was a manoeuvre in Brighton. Possibly there was too much manoeuvre-thinking.

The R.H.L.I. were to work their way into the west and central part of the town and with the Essex were to clean the port out street by street. Only a few hours were allotted for this task—an incredibly short time. It all depended on surprise—surprise that would catch the German garrison off guard and enable the Canadians to break into the town and overcome resistance before the enemy could get organized properly for any stout defence.

The Royal Canadian Engineers first were to check the beach for mines, mark it with white tapes, then blast sections out of the wall which ran the length of the main beach to enable tanks to get up on the Esplanade. The next task of the sappers was to tackle the twelve-foot concrete barriers blocking the entrance of the streets leading from the Esplanade into the town proper.

There were a score of targets for the infantry in the town itself—the post office, a chemical plant, the tobacco factory on the Esplanade, the railway centre and the warehouses, and a gas house at the docks.

Altogether it was a tremendously ambitious raid, as conceived in this plan. The R.C.E. were to do a number of important demolitions and the infantry, as the plan was described to me, were in the first instance to be the protecting force, with the tanks, for this work of the sappers.

A main girder-bridge over the harbour, linked to the main roads to Abbeville and Amiens, was to be blown up, and the engineers carried a mass of charges for various sections of the bridge. I remember seeing the plan for the bridge demolition and it looked like a Goldberg cartoon invention in the blueprint. The railway station was to be severely damaged with demolitions and the Rouen railway line, which enters a tunnel on the outskirts of Dieppe, was to be wrecked. The plan for this was to have the sappers take a locomotive, load it and some flat cars with time explosives and send it chugging into the tunnel. The explosives were to go off in the tunnel, which would have blocked the main line for months.

Apart from damage to be done in the town, the Royal Marine Commandos had a big job in the port. They were to sail right into the mouth of the harbour as the infantry cleaned out the town, attack craft, land on a quay in the centre of the harbour installations and hold it until the situation was under control in Dieppe itself. Then the Marines were going to take a number of German invasion barges from the lower basin of the harbour and tow them back to England. It was audacious. It would have made great propaganda.

But the biggest explosion of all was to have taken place under the eastern headland. Shortly before the raid, British agents reported that the Germans had stored three thousand torpedoes in caves in the cliff.

The raiders planned to set time fuses to that great pile of torpedoes, which were being used for German Channel E-boats, and as the force was returning to England the torpedoes would blow up. It would have been an explosion the like of which France or the Germans had never seen before. A torpedo expert from the navy had even been detailed to carry out the job.

Several hundred yards from the southern extremities of the town there was a race-course and some troops were detailed to mark this course with white strips indicating the direction of the wind. This would enable British aircraft in trouble to use it as an emergency landing field. In my ignorance of actual battle, like many of the troops, I planned at one time to make my way to the emergency landing field and get some copy flown back to England for me by an R.A.F. pilot. What a chance in the turmoil of the actual raid! Only a handful of troops, if any, got anywhere near the race-course.

In the raid force were representatives of the Ministry of Economic Warfare who were intent on getting samples of clothing, food and anything else they could lay their hands on. They had hopes of determining in a few short hours ashore just what the enemy situation was regarding consumer goods.

We were told that a counter-attack was to be expected from the 10th *Panzer* Division, resting at Amiens after the service on the Russian front. Several companies of the Essex with squadrons of tanks were to move through Dieppe and then swing to the east and take up positions on a shoulder of land giving observation along the road to Amiens.

These Essex Scots were to be our suicide troops, the boys who were going to fight as rear-guard while the rest of the force got away to the boats around noon. They were to fight a withdrawal action to the eastern headland. Then they were to clamber down the steep cliff and boats would be waiting for them in the harbour mouth to take them off—the last men to leave France.

The signals system was very intricate, and the two brigade headquarters were to be near a church off the Quai Duquesne, which ran along the west side of the harbour. This would put the headquarters three blocks into the town from the Esplanade. Brigadier Bill Southam of Toronto and Brigadier Sherwood Lett of Vancouver led the infantry brigades. The former was made prisoner, the latter came back badly wounded. Brigadier Lett returned to the field later, leading the same brigade at Caen, but was wounded in his first action.

Divisional Headquarters was not coming ashore, but was to remain afloat on the destroyer, although General Roberts and some of his staff planned to land during the morning to get first-hand information.

Dieppe was an intricate operation, to put it mildly, and hinged so much on initial surprise and overwhelming success both on the flanks and in the town, that when the bare plan was first outlined there must have been many Canadians, inexperienced as they were in actual warfare, who had some grave doubts, based on their own inherent common sense.

What convinced them it was a good plan was Intelligence information showing the defences to be comparatively thin and estimating the German garrison in the area to be only three thousand with not many first-rate troops.

This and the tremendous air support to be provided sold the idea. Not that "selling" was involved, for the Canadians were soldiers who followed orders and once the senior officers decided upon it, it was the duty of everyone to carry out the plan.

In the air we were to be supreme—as we were, or at least we had as much supremacy as you can attain in such circumstances—even if the Germans decided to take great chances to destroy the fleet and smash the landing.

Fighter Command was to give us everything—and did. Their share in the raid was a notable success. Medium bombers were to attack military objectives in and around Dieppe just before the landing and the navy was to shell the town with four-inch guns from seven Fleet-class destroyers. Hurricane cannon-fighters were to strafe the waterfront positions and aircraft were to lay smoke when necessary. Intruder aircraft were to drop tons of bombs on field-gun positions at several points behind Dieppe to prevent them ranging on the landing craft.

*   *   *   *

I was curious about the fundamental reasons for the raid and before and after the operation I talked with a number of high officers about this.

There seem to have been two purposes. The first was linked intimately with the North African landings which were made the following November. The second was part of the main Second Front planning, which was being started even at that early date.

Personally I believe the Dieppe raid was more closely associated with the North African operations than with anything else. The great American expedition to Casablanca, Oran and Algiers was being mounted in the spring and summer but combined operations of that magnitude were something entirely new.

A test for the new types of landing ships was necessary. It was important that co-operation between air force, navy and army be put to trial under difficult conditions.

The commanders in charge of the North African planning evidently were extremely anxious that combined-operation equipment and the new technique should be tried out before they attempted their vast and delicate operation.

Experience was urgently needed before North Africa and it appears that one of the principal reasons for the Dieppe raid was to gain this experience.

Any number of practice landings on the English coast would not provide this experience. It could only be gained on a large raid against fairly strong enemy coastal positions where the test would come in actual battle.

Dieppe was chosen as the particular target because of the long sweep of sloping beach there, where masses of infantry and tanks could land.

It also appears that an important purpose was to deceive the Germans as to where the main blow was to be struck the following fall. Dieppe thus was a decoy for North Africa. Following this raid the Germans moved seven or eight divisions from their strategic reserve to positions where they could cover the French Channel coast. The ruse had its desired effect of deluding the enemy.

This close relationship of the Dieppe operation to the North African landings helps explain why the raid was suddenly carried out in August after its cancellation in early July.

Following the cancellation there was no immediate intention that it should be attempted later. Something else would be teed up for the Canadians. But about August 1 the senior officers of the Dieppe force were called together and the planning was resumed.

Shortly afterwards the High Command decided it was imperative that the raid be made and the British War Cabinet, after pondering the problem, agreed that the operation should be carried out. The North

African preparations were reaching their final stage by this time and the Dieppe job, as a test and as a decoy, was considered of the most vital importance.

On August 19 the tides would be right again and that date was chosen. If there had been bad weather on the 18th-19th, the tides would still have been suitable for five more days as they were in early July.

In addition to these reasons for the raid, the British war leaders were anxious to hit the German positions on the French coast and find out exactly what was there. Intelligence reports only go so far. The Canadians found out that bloody morning that they do not go the limit and that there can be hidden defences about which they know nothing beforehand.

It was fundamental to British and Allied offensive planning that a landing be made in the summer of 1942 to provide accurate, first-hand information for future operations in western Europe.

A Second Front was impossible at that time and everyone on army staffs in Britain knew it. But the foundations had to be laid and Dieppe, as a "reconnaissance in force", was the start.

Shortly before the raid, an officer who had been close to the planning staff told me: "This operation will determine the course of the war; there has been nothing attempted with such importance for the future as this one job."

*   *   *   *

As the *Queen Emma* pulled away from the dock on that quiet evening of August 18, my mind wandered back over the months which had passed—months of hard training, of soaring hopes, disappointments and frustrations. And I pondered what was ahead. I was confused and baffled by the suddenness with which the operations had been resumed.

The barrage balloons tugging from the sterns of our ships sparkled in the soft evening sunshine and our fleet put to sea without a signal or a cheer from a single soul. We were on our way to France.

It was one of the finest evenings of the summer. The sea was smooth, the sky was clear and there was the slightest of breezes. The ships cleared and the Royals went to dinner before making their final preparations. In the wardroom, the officers sat around the tables and dined in navy style as the last sunshine poured through the open portholes. We had a good meal and everyone ate hungrily, for on the way to the boats all we had had was haversack fare—a few bully-beef sandwiches.

The Royals officers were in good spirits at dinner. Looking around the table you would never have thought that they were facing the biggest test of their lives. They joked and bantered across the tables and renewed old friendships with the naval officers whom they had known in "practice Dieppe" training days.

Dinner finished, there was plenty more to do as we sailed through the Channel to the beaches of France. The colonel, Doug Catto, set up his office in the wardroom after dinner and in a weird blue blackout light worked over his maps and his orders and photographs, with officers coming and going from the room every few minutes. In every cabin on the ship other officers were running over their orders and scanning their maps once again. It was the same on the troop decks. Platoon commanders, company commanders, sergeants, corporals and privates were going over the details of the plan and their part in the attack.

Weapons and ammunition were checked and then the soldiers just lay down on the decks or on their own kit and dozed. Through the darkness the *Queen Emma* pounded to the rendezvous with the other ships of the fleet, including seven Fleet-class destroyers, escort vessels, beach support craft and naval motor launches.

A sprawling, floating mine field protected the Dieppe coastline and trawlers swept ahead of us, clearing paths in the darkness for the attack fleet and marking the Channel through the mines with floating buoys. We sailed through them without loss of a ship.

From the bridge of the *Emma* you could vaguely distinguish shadows of other ships around us. A helpful haze settled over the Channel. The sea remained calm and the sky sparkled with stars. Later the moon appeared.

At midnight we were ordered to prepare to take to our boats. The *Emma* carried landing craft and in these the Royals would make the final run-in to the beach at Puits.

There was a drill for going to the small boats in the dark and the soldiers knew it well from long practice before this voyage.

By one A.M. the troops had filed up the gangways and out on the decks to their allotted spots in the craft which were swung out from the deck, ready for lowering.

We were about ten miles from the French coast and until now there hadn't been a hitch in the plan. The mine field was behind us. The boats filled with infantrymen were lowered as the *Emma* stopped and anchored. Nobody spoke. Silence was the strict order but as our boat, which was the largest of the landing craft and was jammed with about 80 soldiers, pushed off from the *Emma,* a veteran sailor leaned over and in a stage whisper said: "Cheerio, lads, all the best; give the bastards a walloping." Then we were drifting off into the darkness and our coxswain peered through the night to link up with the rest of our assault flotilla.

We had done all this so many times before in training that it was hard to bring one's mind around to the
realization that this was an operation, that men would
be killed and wounded, that it wasn't being ruled by
army umpires with white arm-bands, that Germans
were ahead of us in Dieppe.

But we hadn't gone far before we knew the reality
of the job. Our landing craft, joined by others from
other ships carrying more Royals, formed into two
columns of about nine craft each, sailing line astern.
There was a support craft with heavy machine-guns
on our bow.

Eyes were accustomed to the darkness now and we
could discern practically all our little craft; the sea was
glossy with starlight.

The boats plunged along, curling up white foam at
their bows and leaving a phosphorescent wake that
stood out like diamonds on black velvet.

We were about seven or eight miles from Dieppe
when the first alarm shook us. To our left there was a
streak of tracer bullets—light blue and white dots in
the night—and the angry clatter of automatic guns.
This wasn't according to plan and everyone in that
boat of ours tightened up like a drum. We kept our
heads down behind the steel bulwark of our little craft
but it was so crowded there that even to crouch was
crowding someone beside you. I sat on a cartful of
three-inch mortar bombs. More tracer bullets swept
across ahead of us and some pinged off our steel sides.
A big sailor by my side rigged his Lewis gun through
a slit at the stern of our boat and answered with a few
short bursts. A blob in the night that was an enemy
ship—an armed trawler or more likely an E-boat—
was less than two hundred yards away. It was firing
at half a dozen craft including ours, which was in the

lead at that time. From other directions came more German tracer. There might have been four ships intercepting us.

There wasn't much we could do. There isn't any armament on these assault craft to engage in a naval action against E-boats or trawlers. Our support craft didn't seem to be about at that particular time. It looked as if we were going to be cut up piecemeal by this interception; our flotilla already had been broken up from the close pattern of two columns we had held before the attack.

I blew up my lifebelt a little more. A few more blasts of tracer whistled past and then there was a great flash and a bang of gun-fire behind us. In the flash we could see one of our destroyers speeding up wide-open to our assistance. It fired a dozen rounds at the enemy ships and they turned and disappeared towards the French coast. They probably went right into Dieppe harbour and spread the word that British landing craft were heading in.

Farther to the east, the flotilla of No. 3 Commando which was to attack Berneval also was engaged, more heavily than we were. The small boats were dispersed and the landing there was a failure apart from the gallant work of one small boat-load of British commandos. These went ashore, knowing they were alone, and sniped at the Berneval coastal battery for hours, preventing it from firing accurately on the fleet at Dieppe and thus carrying out the plan under tremendous difficulties.

The interception slowed our flotilla up a great deal and it was soon apparent that we were going to be late getting to the Puits beach. We had to try to make it before daylight or we wouldn't stand much of a chance. Surprise was so important.

British bombers were now flying overhead to begin the bombing of Dieppe area. They flew high with the steady drone that is the distinguishing feature of the R.A.F. machines. In a few minutes the German flak began to spout from anti-aircraft guns at Dieppe. The tracer latticed a ceiling over the town, coning over the areas where the bombers concentrated their run. From the sea it was a spectacular sight, with this flaming chandelier of coloured lights and flashes. Searchlights fingered the sky. We heard the crash of bombs above the gun-fire, which rolled out into the Channel. There were a dozen sharp flashes of bursting bombs. Now I could see the long stone pier in the light of the flak and the bomb bursts and searchlights. It stretched out from the harbour and there was a red navigation light burning on the end of the pier.

Our flotilla was off its course three-quarters of a mile to the west and we took a bearing from the pier and shifted to the east to hit Puits beach. As we did this some of our craft had to pass through a column of boats carrying the last two companies of the Essex Scottish. There was some confusion, but we crisscrossed the Essex and curved in to Puits.

From my mortar-bomb seat I watched the flaming main beach where the guns were going now right in front of the town. It was still dark, although the dawn we feared before landing was coming up fast. The seven destroyers were pumping hundreds of shells into the buildings along the front of the town. Several squadrons of Hurricane fighter bombers, with cannons blazing, dived into the inferno just over the landing craft nearing the main beach and fired their cannon and dropped their bombs, sweeping the Esplanade. Brave men, those boys in the pilot seats; some of them had lowered their wheels to slow them up and give them a better aim at their targets.

The attack was rising to its climax on the landing and before we got to Puits I could see dimly, from five or six hundred yards out, assault craft touching down on the main pebble beach. Then the scene was blotted out by smoke. Our destroyers were still firing.

The Royals were very late. They should have been on the beach before dawn but it was grey light of morning by now. The air force, spotting our trouble, dropped a ton of smoke bombs on the headland east of the harbour. This smoke curled down to the sea and covered us temporarily for the run-in.

The story of that blood-stained beach at Puits is a nightmare. Our boat was one of the last to make the beach as we passed close by the eastern headland, with the austere French church with its high steeple on the crest. We sailed in a cloud of smoke under the guns on the cliff-top, most of them anti-aircraft guns that crashed endlessly at our fighters and bombers carrying out more attacks.

Our coxswain tried to take us in to one section of the beach and it proved the wrong spot. Before he grounded he swung the craft out again and we fumbled through the smoke to the small strip of sand which was the Puits beach. The smoke was spotty and the last thirty yards was in the clear. Geysers from artillery shells or mortar bombs shot up in our path. Miraculously we weren't hit by any of them. The din of the German ack-ack guns and machine-guns on the cliff was so deafening you could not hear the man next to you shout.

The men in our boat crouched low, their faces tense and grim. They were awed by this unexpected blast of German fire, and it was their initiation to frightful battle noises. They gripped their weapons more tightly and waited for the ramp of our craft to go down.

We bumped on the beach and down went the ramp and out poured the first infantrymen. They plunged into about two feet of water and machine-gun bullets laced into them. Bodies piled up on the ramp. Some staggered to the beach and fell. Bullets were splattering into the boat itself, wounding and killing our men.

I was near the stern and to one side. Looking out the open bow over the bodies on the ramp, I saw the slope leading a short way up to a stone wall littered with Royal casualties. There must have been sixty or seventy of them, lying sprawled on the green grass and the brown earth. They had been cut down before they had a chance to fire a shot.

A dozen Canadians were running along the edge of the cliff towards the stone wall. They carried their weapons and some were firing as they ran. But some had no helmets, some were already wounded, their uniforms torn and bloody. One by one they were cut down and rolled down the slope to the sea.

I don't know how long we were nosed down on that beach. It may have been five minutes. It may have been twenty. On no other front have I witnessed such a carnage. It was brutal and terrible and shocked you almost to insensibility to see the piles of dead and feel the hopelessness of the attack at this point.

There was one young lad crouching six feet away from me. He had made several vain attempts to rush down the ramp to the beach but each time a hail of fire had driven him back. He had been wounded in the arm but was determined to try again. He lunged forward and a streak of red-white tracer slashed through his stomach.

I'll never forget his anguished cry as he collapsed on the blood-soaked deck: "Christ, we gotta beat them; we gotta beat them!" He was dead in a few minutes.

The Germans were in strength on the top of the cliff and poured their fire into the gulch and on the slope which led up to the tops of the cliff crest. A high stone wall, topped with barbed wire, crosses the slope and Royals were dying by that wall.

From our battered craft lying in the centre of this wild concentration of deadly fire I could see sand-bagged German positions on the top of the cliff and a large house, with rows of windows, on the left side of the cleft in the cliff. Most of the German machine-gun and rifle fire was coming from the fortified house and it wrought havoc on the tiny beach. They were firing at us at point-blank range.

There was another smaller house on the right side of the break in the cliffs and Germans were there too.

Some of the Canadians were able to return the German fire and they knocked off a number of the enemy. One German in his grey-green uniform toppled from one of the windows in the big house. Some of the less-well fortified positions were hit by fire from anti-tank rifles and Bren guns and Germans there were casualties.

Into the terrible German fire ran the men from our boat and I doubt if any even reached the stone wall on the slope, for mortar bombs were smashing on the slope to take the toll of those not hit by the machine-gun bullets that streaked across the whole beach almost continuously. Now the Germans on the cliff were turning their flak guns down on the beach. Our craft was the only one left.

Somehow, the Royals got the two heavy three-inch mortars in our craft down the ramp, as well as the ammunition, but they were never fired. They fell in the water as the crews were hit. The bottom of the boat was covered with soldiers who had been machine-gunned. The officer next to me, Jack Anderson of Toronto, was hit in the head and sprawled over my legs bleeding badly. A naval rating next to him had a sickening gash in his throat and was dying. A few who weren't casualties were firing back fiercely now from the boat. It was useless for them to try to make the beach. The way those men stood up and blasted back at the Germans, when they could feel even then that the attack at Puits was a lost cause, was one of the bravest things I've witnessed. Most of them received decorations later and well earned they were.

The naval orders were to land the troops and then pull off back to the sea, and the naval officer with us rapidly sized up the situation. It was useless to remain a sitting target on the beach. Everyone who could be landed had tried to leave the boat. They had been cut down in front of our eyes. So the officer ordered the craft off the beach.

The hand of God must have been on that little boat, for we were nosed up hard on the sand and yet when the engines reversed it slid back into deep water as if it had been pulled by something out to sea. In training, many boats used to stick on the beach and we had to get out and push them off but this time by a sheer miracle the craft cleared and slowly, ponderously swung around. There was an opening at the stern and through it I got my last look at the grimmest beach of the Dieppe raid. It was khaki-coloured with the bodies of boys from Central Ontario.

We limped a few hundred yards out to sea in the brilliant morning sunshine. The few of us in that boat still unwounded were numb with the shock of that fateful period on the beach. Of the eighty we had taken in there were about twenty of us left and more than half the survivors were wounded. A few Medical

Corps lads with us were working on them and we all tried to help. There were shocking wounds. Some boys had been hit a dozen times with bullets or shrapnel.

Nobody had counted on casualties like this. We didn't know where to take the wounded. At first we thought we should land on the main beach and get them quickly to a dressing station we knew was to be set up in the town. But our wireless operator tried to check the main beach wireless station and there was no answer. That was the first hint we had that the attack on the main beach had gone badly too.

We did circle around to a point just off the jetty but came under machine-gun fire again and pulled back towards two destroyers lying about three-quarters of a mile from the main beach. We carefully got the wounded boys aboard one of them and into a doctor's hands.

For the rest of that morning one lost all sense of time and developments in the frantic events of the battle. Although the Puits landing had obviously failed and the headland to the east of Dieppe would still be held by the Germans, I felt that the main attack by three infantry battalions and the tanks had possibly fared better on the beach in front of the town.

Landing craft were moving along the coast in relays and the destroyers were going in perilously close to hit the headlands with shell-fire. I clambered from one landing craft to another to try to learn what was going on. Several times we were bombed too closely by long, black German planes that sailed right through our flak and our fighter cover.

Smoke was laid by destroyers and our planes along the sea and on the beach. Finally the landing craft in which I was at the time, with some naval ratings, touched down on the sloping pebble main beach which ran about sixty yards at that point to a high sea wall and the Esplanade, with the town beyond.

Smoke was everywhere and under its cover several of our ratings ran onto the beach and picked up two casualties by the barbed wire on the beach, lugging them back to the boat. I floundered through the loose shale to the sea-wall. There was heavy machine-gun fire down the beach towards the Casino. A group of men crouched twenty yards away under the shelter of the sea-wall.

The tobacco factory was blazing fiercely. For a moment there was no firing. It was one of those brief lulls you get in any battle. I thought our infantry were thick in the town but the Esplanade looked far too bare and empty.

There was no beach organization as there should have been. Some dead lay by the wall and on the shale. The attack here had not gone as planned either. A string of mortar bombs whanged on the Esplanade. The naval ratings waved and I lunged back to the boat as the beach battle opened up again. In choking smoke we pulled back to the boat pool.

Some other boats that had gone in to the beach were blown up. One tank-landing craft lay burning near the beach. The hulk of another floated aimlessly and deserted just off the beach. It had been bombed.

It was unbelievable to me even then that disaster had overtaken the units on the main beach. But the Essex, led by Lieutenant-Colonel Jasperson, had run into heavy fire as soon as they landed. They had got through the wire and to the sea-wall all right and there most of them were stopped. Some did make their way around the edge of the harbour and got into the town but the main force had to fight it out from the sea-wall. They were murderously mortared there and strafed and machine-gunned throughout the morning. But they fought on and on, until they had nothing left with which to fight. A handful of them got off in landing craft at the last minute but few craft got in to them.

The Royal Hamilton Light Infantry, commanded by Lieutenant-Colonel Labatt, were on the right side of the beach (the Essex landed on the left) and were also heavily opposed as soon as they landed. They got to the sea-wall and after heavy fighting drove the Germans out of the Casino on the western extremity of the beach. From there platoons worked into the town, fighting through the streets. Similarly with the F.M.R., who were put in on the main beach after the others had landed. Some of their platoons fought through the town too and some came back from those fiery streets. Lieutenant-Colonel Dollard Menard led the F.M.R.

The Calgary tanks, under Lieutenant-Colonel Johnny Andrews, had a bad time from the start. The tank-landing craft were large targets and German shell-fire blasted them as they beached. More than a squadron was landed and immediately the tanks struck the heavy shale. Some sank into it and were stopped right on the beach. Others wallowed through it, worked around by the Casino, got over the sea-wall, which is only a foot or two high there, sloping from about ten feet on the Essex beach. They fought on the Esplanade and at least a few of them broke into the streets of the town.

But German guns in the hotels and houses and entrances to the streets fired point-blank at them. The other squadrons were not landed but lay most of the morning off the main beach in their landing craft.

To the west of Dieppe at Pourville the landing fared better. The S.S.R. got ashore there without any opposition, climbed over the sea-wall and went into the town. They surprised the Germans in Pourville and established their little bridgehead before the enemy knew what was up. While the Germans were waiting for the Canadians at Puits and on the main beach, here at Pourville surprise was attained.

The S.S.R. got well established before the Germans began firing mortars on the town and the machine-guns on the hills on each side of Pourville opened up. The Cameron Highlanders, led by Lieutenant-Colonel Gosling, were coming in now and they had to run a gauntlet of fire in order to cross the beach and get into the town itself. They then made their way up the valley beyond, advancing along paths and a road nearly three miles inland towards the landing field, their objective. Meanwhile the S.S.R. carried out numerous attacks on pillboxes and machine-gun posts in the Pourville area that kept firing on the bridgehead. It was here that Lieutenant-Colonel Cecil Merritt, commanding officer of the S.S.R., showed such supreme gallantry in leading his regiment and personally attacking German posts that he was awarded the Victoria Cross—Canada's first V.C. of the war. He stayed on the beach after his regiment had withdrawn to the boats and fought alone until he was captured.

The two Pourville battalions realized that the main Dieppe plan had misfired in other sectors and late in the morning the withdrawal was ordered. The Camerons had done a magnificent job in going inland as far as they did. But without tank support and faced with the knowledge that the main landing in front of Dieppe had not been the success anticipated there was no purpose in their striking off towards D'Arques.

Neither would they be able to withdraw as they were supposed to through the town of Dieppe. So around eleven A.M. they fell back on Pourville again, retracing their steps along the valley. Lieutenant-Colonel Gosling had been killed in the landing.

The S.S.R. were having a rough time by now, with the enemy mortar fire becoming more accurate and some machine-gun posts still belting bullets into the streets of the town.

The landing craft now were moving in on Pourville, scores of them circling slowly off shore and then turning in to the beach, many of them grounding before they got there. The S.S.R. and Camerons came across the beach through the machine-gun fire and raced for the boats. They brought all the casualties they could. They even brought some prisoners.

I was in an assault boat which tried to go into Pourville; we got within three hundred yards of the beach when we were ordered along the coast to try to make the main beach and take off troops there. But I did get a glimpse of the Pourville evacuation.

It wasn't any nice ordered sight. The boats were having trouble. Many of them were under direct machine-gun fire. Some were sinking, with troops leaping back into the water. Batches of Canadians were on the fringe of the town among some trees on the inside of the sea-wall. Small groups of them hesitated there for a while; then they would leap over the sea-wall to the beach and scatter for the run over the pebbles to the water and the boats. There was the hammering sound of German machine-guns, the occasional sharp whang of the mortars and the knock-knock of the Brens. Smoke drifted over the beach in a long wispy trail as our craft turned for the main beach.

Then the German air force struck with its most furious attack of the day. All morning long, British and Canadian fighters kept a constant patrol over the ships and the beaches, whole squadrons twisting and curling in the blue, cloud-flecked sky. Hundreds of other planes swept far over northern France, intercepting enemy fighters and bombers long before they reached Dieppe. Reconnaissance planes kept a constant lookout on the roads from Amiens and Abbeville and Rouen where reinforcements could be expected. There were air combats going on practically all morning long. It was the greatest air show since the Battle of Britain in the fall of 1940, and the R.A.F. and R.C.A.F. had overwhelming superiority. The High Command had hoped the German air force would be lured into the sky and most of the enemy strength in western Europe came up.

They were given a thorough shellacking and the air victory at the time appeared to be the chief compensation for the raid.

But Fighter Command's powerful air cover did not prevent German planes racing in over the ships and even strafing the troops on the beaches. Many of those aircraft that did make these daring sorties were shot down but they made it hot for those in the landing craft and on the destroyers.

Practically all morning long I cruised along the French coast gaping at this air battle, at the fantastic spectacle of our fleet in possession of these enemy waters without surface challenge, and watching and listening to the battle ashore. And we were not invulnerable to bombing. Half a dozen times fighter bombers whirled past us with guns spouting and then twin-engined bombers—they were black-painted night bombers called up for the emergency—came in very low and dropped their bombs on the ships, aiming principally at the destroyers. Then more fast silver fighters screamed in out of the sun and attacked everything in their gun-sights.

But the final air attack around eleven A.M. was the wildest of them all. I've no idea how many planes were in the force that tried to knock out the fleet with one last blow. But at least seven bombed our tiny assault boat and it leaped madly in the bomb-made tempest of waves. For ten breathless minutes the air seemed full of diving German planes, screaming bombs and the awful noise of machine-guns and cannon.

Hundreds of guns in the fleet were hitting back; some of the soldiers in the boats even opened up with their pistols. The destroyers' pompoms and high-angle guns worked on the daring enemy. One destroyer laid smoke and the R.A.F. planes snarled down on the Nazi aircraft.

We were a scant few hundred yards off the eastern end of the main beach by this time. I could see the harbour jetty on my left.

Bullets screeched in every direction. The whole sky and sea had gone mad with the confusion of that sudden air attack and a dozen times I clung to the bottom of the boat expecting that this moment was the last as we were cannoned or another stick of bombs churned the sea.

Several landing craft near us blew up, hit by bombs and cannon shells. There was nothing left. They just disintegrated. These craft had been trying to make the main beach again, as we had been, to take off troops on the withdrawal.

As suddenly as it came the air attack stopped. The guns ceased their infernal stuttering. We caught our breath again but by now our craft, with scores of others, bashed and battered, was half a mile from the beach.

We circled around and around, and the worried young naval officer in my boat puzzled over whether he should try again to make the main beach and take off troops. It was getting late now, crowding on noon. The evacuation should have been in full swing on the centre beach by now. But there were only a few craft on the beach and they were under intense fire, having great difficulty clearing away. A destroyer was in close to the west headland pumping shells into unsilenced German gun positions.

A motor launch came alongside and we parleyed with the crew about what to do. We had no wireless to pick up orders from Headquarters Ship.

The beach was gradually becoming quiet. A pall of smoke hung over Dieppe itself. The tobacco factory was still flickering from its fire. The flak guns on the headlands had practically all ceased fire, although our planes were continuing sorties over the town.

The raid was dragging to a tragic finish. I didn't know how to feel about it. I had the natural relief that one gets at the end of any ordeal when he senses it is over, as I did at that moment. We were still lying off Dieppe, one of the last of the small boats still there and in a stunned way I tried to recollect just what had happened.

The landing at Puits had been a failure. The landing on the main beach had run into grief as well. The Pourville beach-head seemed to do better than the others. Our air support had been excellent, despite the last fierce attack, but now it was all over. The navy had not been able to get in to the centre beach to take off troops in any numbers. The troops at Pourville had had a fighting chance to get away. No craft at all had made the Puits beaches after we had left, following the initial landings.

Certainly the raid had gone all wrong as far as the detailed plan was concerned.

On towards one o'clock our craft turned north for England. There was nothing we could have done, for about the only ship left near the French coast was the Headquarters destroyer making one last effort to pick up some troops.

We ploughed along through the break in the mine field back into the Channel and overtook scores of other craft. I leaned on our bulwark and looked them over carefully for friends I might know, but craft after craft was nearly empty. I watched those boats in the warm sunshine going back to England empty when they should have been filled with the thousands of soldiers they'd taken to France. I had no stomach for food the naval rating cooked on a portable heater.

It was all too evident that this great adventure to Dieppe had turned out badly and that a large part of the force had been left on the beaches, either casualties or troops that would have to surrender because they couldn't be evacuated.

The trip back took us all afternoon. As we sailed north squadron after squadron of fighters and medium bombers skimmed over the sea on their way to France to keep up the air attack.

On the way our assault craft picked up a disabled support gun-boat which had been badly shot up. Its crew buried two men at sea and we towed the gun-boat into port.

We hobbled into the small port in the early evening —two battered craft, our sides splintered and chipped by German cannon shells, machine-gun bullets and bomb blast. Slowly we edged alongside the pier. The men of Lord Lovat's No. 4 Commando were there, grimy stalwarts who had done a completely successful job at the Vangreville battery—the only fully-accomplished part of the Dieppe raid. On the dock the commandos told me their story, and it was a bright light in the darkness that clouded us all on the dock that evening.

They had landed on their correct beach and thrust inland after going up the narrow cliff path. From there they attacked the battery and destroyed it, wiping out the gunners.

Up at the reception camp where officers checked everyone who returned to port, several hundred Canadian raiders were waiting for trucks. They were still stunned and shocked from the harrowing hours on those beaches and they had no coherent idea of how the battle went.

Some said Dieppe had been captured. Others said they never got past the beach. Some had to remain on landing craft off Dieppe throughout the raid and never got within rifle shot of the beach. Some had been three miles inland and others had fought in the streets and in the Casino. They had terrible stories to tell, and brave ones. Many reported gallant deeds. It was from a battle-dazed soldier that I first heard of the heroism of Lieutenant-Colonel Merritt—from one of the men who had been with him.

A handful of German prisoners was there as well and they seemed as stunned as the raiders themselves.

I drove along the coast road in a borrowed car, hopped the last train to London and in the blackout stumbled from the station to Combined Operations Headquarters. The German communique had just been monitored and it termed Dieppe a German victory.

(Top): *The beach at Dieppe after the raid. The Royal Canadian Engineers were to blast the length of the main beach to enable tanks to get up on the Esplanade, visible here in the background. (From a captured German photograph as is the lower picture.)*

(Lower): *Wounded and captured Canadians in front of a building in the town proper. "They fought on and on, until they had nothing left with which to fight."*

The correspondents who had gone to France with the Canadians wearily sat down to write their stories. There were many things we could not tell.

*   *   *   *

The raid raised questions about security. Was there a leak about the operation? Did the Germans in northern France know beforehand that a force was going to attack Dieppe?

I believe that security on the first project—the proposed raid in early July—was absolutely air-tight. I don't believe the Germans had any idea we were going to Dieppe then, although they must have known that a sea-going force was training on the south coast of England. They had reconnaissance planes over the area every day for weeks and you could set your watch by them flying high about noon.

However, other forces had trained in the same area before. It wasn't unusual for troops to be making practice landings and doing assault work in that district.

If there was any breach in security it came between July 7 when the troops left the ships and dispersed to their old camps in Sussex and August 18 when they boarded the ships again to go to France.

Something prompted the Germans to strengthen the Dieppe defences by August 19 and this was acknowledged in the official army account of the raid, which did not go beyond the barest facts, but which said French coast positions generally were strengthened as a consequence of the avowed Allied aggressive policy.

It is probable that the Germans became windy at the preparations they spotted in air reconnaissance and bolstered garrisons along the coast from Calais to Le Havre and Cherbourg.

Resistance in Dieppe was certainly stronger on the raid than Intelligence reports indicated when we were briefed originally before the July show. Mishaps in the Channel and late landings don't account for all the difficulties.

As far as the force itself was concerned you had this situation, which was precarious for maintaining security. You had the five thousand Canadians, all the naval crews, all the air force squadrons, paratroops and the marines who had been completely briefed for the July raid scattering to scores of camps and towns all over southern England after it was cancelled. They knew the target and every detail of the plan—every single man in the force knew these things.

It was a highly dangerous situation, even though they had all been warned to keep every detail to themselves and not mention Dieppe or anything about the operation to a soul. I know, however, that there were some loose words spoken in pubs in the south about the cancelled job and that Dieppe was named.

After the raid, with rumours flying about that there had been a breach in security, I made a number of inquiries and was never able to find any convincing proof that the Germans knew Dieppe was to be the target.

When I went back to Dieppe with the Division during the Normandy campaign, I asked many civilians in the town about this. They all told me that the raid had been a complete surprise to the garrison. Only the normal guards were on duty on the Esplanade that night and these men gave the first alarm.

The chance interception in the Channel of the flotillas carrying the Royals and No. 3 Commando gave the Germans along the French coast some tip-off that something was up, it is true, but the surprise achieved at Pourville by the S.S.R. who landed on time without a hitch showed the enemy was not in position and waiting through the night with all the guns manned, as they would have been if they had known that this force was striking at the Dieppe area. I remember, too, the red harbour light at the end of the jetty glowing full-on when we arrived.

On the other flank the situation was entirely different. The whole of the Dieppe garrison was aroused by the bombing and the naval shelling by the time the Royals got to Puits—very late and in daylight—and the enemy had time to man the fortified houses and the pillboxes there. The opposition at Puits under the circumstances was not unusual. That break in the cliffs and the small beach was a logical one to defend on the flank. If the Royals had been put ashore on time and in the darkness I think they could have attained the same landing success as the S.S.R. They would have scrambled ashore, gone up the gulch, captured Puits and the eastern headland and won their chief objectives before the German defenders had got out of their barracks.

The main beach assault by the Essex, the R.H.L.I. and the tanks missed success by the narrowest margin. The infantry were only slightly behind schedule on landing but the tanks which were supposed to be landed at the same time to give covering fire to the attack over the sweeping Esplanade, did not land until ten minutes later.

The delay for the tanks was caused by a navigational error made by a destroyer which was leading the tank-landing craft into the beaches.

That ten minutes was important and may have been the difference between success and failure. While the preliminary bombardment from the air and sea would arouse the garrison, very few of the positions were manned when the first wave of infantry crossed the beaches and got to the sea-wall. They still needed gun-fire from the tanks for the next hop over the Esplanade, and it didn't come until too late. Even tanks which did bog down on the shale could have fired and helped the infantry over the open space in that critical period.

But by the time the tanks were landed it was too late. The Germans were manning practically all their positions in the fortified houses and pinned down the majority of the main beach infantry behind the sea-wall.

The frontal attack was the most hazardous enterprise of the entire raid and success hinged on surprise and immediate fire support for the infantry. Surprise was practically attained but support not only came too late but was not nearly effective enough, or in sufficient strength, when it did arrive, with the tank-landing craft and the tanks themselves being bludgeoned by German artillery when they came in and landed.

*   *   *   *

Combined Operations Headquarters and the War Office were responsible for the broad plan. The Canadians had been selected for the operation; and it was difficult to press arguments against the accepted plan, since there was more behind the job than just the raid. To back out would have been very damaging to the Canadians' prestige in Britain. They had to take the risk and no operation is without risk.

The High Command in Whitehall was extremely anxious to determine whether heavy tanks could be landed in such an action, and the main beach at Dieppe was one of the few in northern France where the test could be carried out at that time with the tremendous fighter cover the plan called for. We did not then have the long-range fighter planes which gave the air cover for the Normandy landings, enabling us to strike at Channel beaches farthest from England. Dieppe was just about the right distance for Fighter Command in 1942.

To use the main beach meant a frontal attack on the town, with the principal attacking force striking on that beach. Tanks could not have landed at Pourville or Puits.

Even the frontal attack might have succeeded if there had been heavier bombardment from the air and the sea. Of all the lessons learned at Dieppe, the top one was this necessity. It has been followed in every landing since.

Bombers did strike at Dieppe but there was no attempt at a saturation blitz to knock the town down. The British War Cabinet opposed heavy bombing because of possible French reaction to killing civilians in the town. And the R.A.F. was not prepared at the time to handle a complete obliteration assignment.

For the first raid there was to be much heavier bombing, however, than the Canadians had supporting them on August 19. General Roberts had to accept a compromise on even the original plan because of other R.A.F. commitments.

The alternative was to have ships with heavy guns support the raiders from the sea, but here too the navy would not risk cruisers, monitors or battleships at that time off the French coast.

So the Canadians had to go in with the meagre support of seven destroyers. That wasn't enough; not nearly enough.

Heavy bombardment could have blasted the defences of Dieppe wide open and cleared a path for the infantry, even after they were pinned down by the sea-wall. Dieppe would have been wrecked and set ablaze, and probably the studied plan for engineer demolitions and capture of documents and materials in the town could not have been carried out. But anything would have been better than the half-measure of support provided the Canadian assault force.

There was the spectre of the possible loss of a valuable ship by air attack. This balanced the scale against using heavy naval strength, although Dieppe proved that it had to be risked on landings.

At Dieppe the headlands rearing up on both sides of the port were the toughest obstacles for the Canadians all morning. The headlands were not captured and German guns on the cliffs and in the face of the cliffs swept the beaches and the boats. If the headland defences had been silenced, the raid might have taken a new turn even an hour or two after the assault. Fifteen-inch guns firing at close range probably could have blown the cliffs into the sea or at least blasted the guns out of their positions. All this was lacking.

*   *   *   *

I was surprised when I talked with Dieppe people in the port two years afterwards that they had comparatively little new information to add to what already was known about the raid.

The new mayor of the town, who took office when the Canadians returned, said the raiders came very close to breaking the enemy resistance. "There was a terrible lot of confusion among the Nazi garrison and for several hours they did not know what was happening. They did a lot of firing but there was little

semblance of order in the town. Guns on the headlands on either side of the beaches, though, were in
action steadily and they seemed to be the worst thing
for the Canadians as they covered the beaches."

George Guibon, president of the Dieppe Historical
Society, agreed the raid was a surprise and said "if
more troops had been able to land in the morning
when the raid was ending, you could have gone far
inland, for the Germans were ready to quit, I think."

The best sources in the town said also that German
casualties were as high as Canadian in killed and
wounded.

The only other new bit of information I gleaned
was that German reserves from Rouen and Amiens
did not begin to move towards Dieppe until four P.M.
that day.

*   *   *   *

The outstanding immediate triumph at Dieppe was
the air victory of Fighter Command. For months on
end the R.A.F. and R.C.A.F. had been on the offensive
over France with little success in luring up German
fighter strength to battle. During the Dieppe operation they got what they were after. The German air
force surged into the air to beat off the attack and
Fighter Command had a field day.

Air Chief Marshal Sir Thomas Leigh-Mallory, then
chief of Fighter Command and running the air show
that day, said this: "That was where we had a real
chance—a large force, well-trained, good machines,
good weather. On that day I put all we had learned
into practice. The enemy admits we shot down 170
aircraft, more than a third of his whole force in the
west at that date."

The air victory was a tangible one. We could see

it on the spot. The achievement of the army force was an intangible one at that time. The casualty figures were staggering—667 killed or dead of wounds, 218 missing, 1,894 prisoners-of-war; a total of 3,371 casualties in a force of 5,000 Canadians. This heavy loss at first overshadowed other considerations and it was difficult to understand that anything could have been gained from the raid with the sacrifice of so many soldiers.

Still, the pattern for invasion landings was fashioned by those 2nd Division Canadians on that terrible August morning. In 1943 and 1944 the dividend from Dieppe was paid off in the successful landings in the Mediterranean, climaxed by the D-Day assault in Normandy.

XIV

DETOUR VIA NORTH AFRICA

T HE North African campaign was nicely under way
late in 1942, following the landings of American and
British forces, when the first group of Canadian
officers and non-commissioned officers from the army
in England was chosen to go to Tunisia to serve with
the First British Army and gain much-needed battle
experience.

I went to North Africa with this first group of about
one hundred and fifty. After spending the dreariest
Christmas imaginable on a troopship in the Clyde, we
arrived in Algiers on the second day of the New Year.

Algiers was a wild city to walk into to begin one's
first campaign in the field. It was a clattering, smelly
place, boiling over with intrigue and boom business
brought to it when overnight it became the principal
Allied supply base for the new front in Tunisia. Allied
Force Headquarters, headed by General Eisenhower,
was struggling with the tangled French political
situation, and feelings were at fever pitch following
the assassination of Admiral Darlan. The military
situation also had taken a turn for the worse. All
hopes for a snap victory in Tunisia were dashed when
the Germans blocked the British columns which rushed
across North Africa to the gates of Tunis, only to be
thrown back when they were within sight of their goal.
Now Germans were packing troops into Tunisia and
a hard winter campaign in the rugged mountains was
inevitable.

I was completely baffled by Algiers. The political squabble made little sense. It was difficult to get anything like a clear picture in Algiers of the military situation four hundred miles away. I had come to write about the war, so after paying several visits to the Canadians, who were living in picturesque villas on the shores of Algiers Bay, I headed east to Tunisia in the first available car, driving for two days along the fine roads winding through the magnificent Atlas Mountains. To get out of Algiers was like leaving a gas chamber.

At the front, it did not take long to find out what was going on. To my astonishment, I found there was no First Army in the line. To call the British force in Tunisia the First Army at that time was a misnomer. In fact, a lone corps was holding a long line running from the Mediterranean south through the mountains and the valleys about thirty-five miles west of Tunis. The wonderful 78th Division, a Brigade of the Guards, some commandos and some paratroops were the backbone of the force. The 6th Armoured Division was its chief support.

Under terrible weather conditions—cold, mud and rain—this slim force of British Tommies was doing a terrific job, but more troops were needed, many more. The outlook was depressing and the weather foul. I moved into a one-room billet with three other correspondents in a muddy French farm near Beja and for two months roamed that frightful front.

The first morning at the front I went to an airfield at Souk el Arba in the Medjerda valley to see some Canadian Spitfire pilots, and I had scarcely set foot on the field before a dozen German aircraft whipped out of the sun and beat up the landing strips and the dispersal areas as our ack-ack guns showered shells and tracer bullets around like a July 1 celebration. That was a spirited introduction to the front, and John Clare of Saskatoon and Toronto, the R.C.A.F. public relations officer on the field, didn't raise my spirits any when he grinned and said this strafing was part of the daily routine. John became a strafing and bombing veteran over the months on those fields at Souk el Arba and down the road at Souk el Khemis.

The *Luftwaffe* had air superiority at that time in Tunisia and it was a ticklish business driving on the roads along the front. We drove around in a lumbering Humber station wagon, the type generally used by staff officers, which made us fair game for low-flying enemy planes. The result was that one of us always was delegated to be lookout man—spotting for German aircraft with his head poked through a hatch in the roof of the car. I can't count the number of times we stopped the car with brakes squealing, and hit the ditch or scattered in the open fields. We imagined we were getting a new occupational disease out of this nervous watch and dubbed it "Tunis twitch".

A gallant band of Spitfire pilots battled the powerful German air force and in every R.A.F. squadron were Canadians. They were outnumbered by the *Luftwaffe* and they fought a Battle of Britain in miniature over those tremendous mountains and sweeping valleys. Their living conditions on the mud-covered fields were almost as bad as for the troops on the front and yet the pilots, flying sortie after sortie every day, were a happy-go-lucky crowd. Evenings with them in their tents, with the slit-trenches dug deep and narrow alongside them, were as enjoyable as you would want. But next day Tom or Joe would have "bought it" and some new lad would come up to take his place.

Every few weeks I spent some time with the fighter

squadrons, but generally I was with the army. I would go up to Medjez el Bab, a pivot point of the front from which you could see famed Longstop Hill, held by the Germans.

Skirmishes, patrols and the odd battalion action would enliven the front there but the British did not have the strength to hit the enemy hard. The Germans were preparing, though, to strike out.

The first real blow came at the front-line town of Bou Arada, south of Medjez, where the enemy, anticipating a foray by the tanks of the 6th Armoured Division, sent their *Panzers* down the long valley against the thin British line.

I had gone to Bou Arada to watch the British attack and instead saw the German tanks take a beating from the British field-gunners. I hadn't much battle-front lore under my belt at that time and I strayed into the front-line trenches outside the town, creeping in with some French colonial troops as thirty German tanks came trundling towards the town.

Like squat, black beetles they moved up the valley, and when they were five hundred yards from us the British gunners let go and three field regiments pummelled the enemy armour. The tank formations split up rapidly and small packets weaved about to escape the hail of shells. For two hours the battle of tanks against guns roared and German fighter bombers pasted Bou Arada. This small sector of the front was a flaming bedlam but the British gunners, sweating and toiling in the first warm day we had had, turned back the *Panzers*. The hulks of eight tanks were left on the battle-field and British Valentine tanks rushed up and chased the remainder of the German force back into the hills by Pont du Fahs.

Considering the scale of the Tunisian war during

that phase, it was a notable British victory and persuaded the enemy that they would have to try elsewhere than at the sad little town of Bou Arada, with its twenty battered white houses, to break the British line.

This had been a graphic battle to watch at such close range under precarious front-line circumstances and I drove to El Aroussa, seven miles behind Bou Arada, to write my story that night in the flickering flame of an oil lamp in a verminous Arab shack. El Aroussa was another small French colonial town and we had some dumps there. Our convoys collected there. In the morning at breakfast time the German air force raided the town. I saw the planes coming—a dozen or more *Stukas,* the original dive-bomber. They wheeled out of the sun and before the flak guns opened up on them they were going into their long, screaming dive. Half-shaven, I leaped instinctively into a shallow ditch and watched them plummet from the sky. When they seemed just over my head they let their bombs go and two dozen black bombs hurtled into El Aroussa. The town was convulsed like a live thing. Explosions rocked the ground and every house. Fires blazed and smoke poured from burning trucks, houses and dumps. Ammunition began to explode and the *Stukas* wheeled eastward into the sun.

The attack was an audacious one, yet the Germans knew we were so weak we could not keep standing patrols over the front and took advantage of this situation to do all the damage they could. This was not an important raid—it was one of many by the *Luftwaffe,* with probably about the same results—but it was the last time I saw *Stukas* in action. These dive-bombers had been a big factor in the German break-through in France in 1940 and as far as I know their swan-song raid was on the hamlet of El Aroussa.

The winter war in Tunisia became a battle of the passes in the mountain range along which the front line ran. After the failure at Bou Arada, the Germans sent another tank column down a valley to the south, aimed at the village of Robaa. Tiger tanks were used for the first time against the British in this valley action and I was in Robaa when the British infantry—the regiment was The Buffs—turned back the armoured monsters and proved that Tigers could be knocked out.

The action swung still farther south, the enemy prodding at the British line through the passes, trying to find a weak spot through which they could put strong forces of armour to get in behind the British and cut the long supply lines.

At Ousseltia, in a valley west of the holy city of Kairouan, the Germans made another attack and here they bumped troops of the 2nd American Corps, which had taken over the southern sector of the line and was based on the city of Tebessa.

From a lookout on the crags overlooking the valley and the town, I watched several actions and the Americans blocked the German armoured thrust and pushed the enemy back into the Kairouan Pass.

The Germans were held in every attempt they made to break through, but our own lines were so thin that we could not do much better than hold what we had.

The Canadians attached to First Army units were scattered along the entire front and a handful at least were in nearly every British action or serving with some formation headquarters during the fighting. I frequently bumped into some of them. "Snuffy" Smith of Dauphin, Man., was with a tank regiment and fought in most of the actions of the 6th Armoured Division. Don Worthington of Vancouver was another who fought in tanks. With the Grenadier Guards were Peter Lane of Winnipeg and Don Forbes of Sydney, N.S., and I met them down at Siliana when they were back-stopping The Buffs at Robaa and the Americans at Ousseltia. Strome Galloway of Toronto, Frank Klenavic of St. Catharines, Ont., Laird Bovaird of London, Ont., "Spike" Sprung of Winnipeg and Orville Gamble of Toronto and Ottawa were other Canadians I remember particularly from North African days.

The plan which called for these officers to get battle experience in Tunisia worked extremely well. They returned to the army in England and passed on their valuable knowledge to units preparing for campaigns in Sicily, Italy and on the Western Front. Most of those who went to Tunisia rose rapidly when they returned and served conspicuously in subsequent campaigns.

About the only British units which did not have Canadians serving with them were the Commandos and after going on one exhausting overland raid with them I concluded anyone on attachment was smart if he went to regular infantry battalions instead of linking up with anything as wild as the commandos.

One afternoon, on a good tip, I made my way with a British correspondent, J. D'Arcy Dawson, of the London *Daily Sketch* and the *Sunday Times,* up the lonely roads from Beja to Sedjenane in the Mateur Valley and there in an old iron mine belonging to the Bey of Tunis we found the headquarters of No. 1 Commando. These troops had taken part in the initial North African landings and had been fighting for months as infantry in the quagmires of the green Mateur Valley.

The colonel, a big, rugged man with a gigantic moustache, informed us briskly that his unit was carrying out a raid that night into the country to the northeast in the direction of Bizerte. Would we come along? He evidently took our hesitancy at making a snap decision to be acquiesence and immediately unrolled some well-thumbed maps and outlined the plan in detail. We had to go along then for we were briefed.

At midnight, three hundred commandos, the colonel's mule and two correspondents who had not walked five miles at a stretch all the campaign, walked down the steep hill from the mine head, passed through the wrecked village of Sedjenane and slogged north along tracks in mud sometimes knee-deep.

The commandos were trained for such heavy going and all were veterans of this front. Hour after hour they marched steadily on in darkness and rain, with the two reporters getting farther and farther behind in the column.

The only real opportunity we got to get a breather was when a skirmish broke out. The leading troops were fired upon and the column scattered into the bushes and rocks along the trail as bullets whipped over us. It developed that French troops holding this sector had fired on us by mistake. The message telling them we were coming had not reached them and it took some time for the commandos to establish their identity with the trigger-itchy Frenchmen.

They then showed us the path through a mine field and we pushed on into the night through a section of No Man's Land where Italian and German patrols were accustomed to make their forays.

We did not encounter anyone and at dawn we took cover in a big patch of shrubs and stunted trees, to wait until nightfall before making the attack into the enemy lines a few miles away.

We had marched about fifteen or twenty miles

during the night and I collapsed in the wet shrubs
and slept exhausted.

Bully-beef, hardtack and steaming sweet tea was the
commandos' recipe to revive me when I woke hours
later. The raiding force was now splitting up and
eighty men were going to Cap Serrat on the Mediterranean coast to embark in landing craft, which would
carry them at night down the coast and land them
behind the Italian lines. The main part of the force
was to go east into enemy territory, to attack Italian
positions and to burn a series of straw villages of Arabs
who had been dealing with the enemy and had been
causing us a lot of trouble on this sector. The purpose
of the raid was basically to make a show of strength
and give the impression we had much larger forces on
this sector than actually were there.

I could never have kept up with the foot-slogging
raiders so I went to Cap Serrat to go with the seaborne
party. The landing craft broke a propeller in the
heavy surf as we were taking off that night and the
landing was cancelled, but there was enough excitement at Cap Serrat to last us all for weeks. We had
scarcely got into the big fort-like lighthouse there,
defended by some R.A.F. Regiment troops, before
German fighters returning to the Bizerte and Tunis
fields beat it up with cannon and machine-gun fire.
Every few hours returning planes fired off their
remaining ammunition at our lighthouse and we
crouched behind the thick walls and prayed the
bombers would not take us on.

The bombing came at dawn, as we feared. Following the failure to sail for the landing, I returned to
the lighthouse and rolled up on a concrete floor in a
blanket. At eight in the morning I was thrown across
the room by an explosion that seemed to lift the light-

house off its base. A fighter bomber had dropped a five-hundred-pounder right beside the building and it was a wonder the whole place did not collapse. Before other raiders came, we were out of the lighthouse and on the road leading back to the rendezvous where we were to meet the other commandos.

From the hill-top we saw clouds of smoke rising from the areas to the east where the pillaging party had burned the Arab villages. The raid, even without the landing, had been a big success and a thoroughly good scare had been thrown into the Italian force.

We linked up with the other commandos and marched for many more hours back down the trails to the Sedjenane iron mine. In thirty hours the commandos probably covered fifty miles, carried out their raid and then faded away to their hideout.

The long hill leading to the mine head was a killer for me but there were rum, hot tea and warm blankets at the end of it. I slept like a dead man. I had learned about the Mateur Valley Commandos—and my feet ached for days.

After this sortie on the northern sector, I went to the extreme southern end of the front—down to Tebessa and Kasserine, where the Americans were operating. Something big was brewing there.

This was in February and the Eighth Army was moving up slowly to link with the Tunisian forces. The Germans were going to put forth every effort they had to prevent this link-up and one of the big battles took place on the Tebessa sector.

It started with a disaster to the American tank formations when the Germans drew them into a trap between Sbeitla and the Faid Pass. A screen of enemy 88mm. guns massacred the Shermans on the plain and at least seventy tanks were destroyed. That area had to be evacuated and the Americans fell back on the Kasserine Pass, east of Tebessa.

I drove down into the Pass on the afternoon when the crisis occurred and Headquarters talked gloomily that if Kasserine was not held Tebessa and the huge American supply dumps would be overrun.

The German guns were shelling Kasserine gap heavily and we crouched in fox-holes with the American infantry and engineers as the shells shattered the granite rock and showered us with stone fragments. The shelling grew worse and the troops in the gap were getting uneasy. Machine-gun fire could be heard on the hills around the gap—some of it German—and the enemy infantry and tanks were known to be advancing into the mouth of the gap through a thick mist that veiled the plain beyond.

A veritable barrage of shelling slammed into the gap and we went back to a hill with some American tanks. They were lining up in battle formation around the western end of the gap and all around us were signs of imminent retreat. In late afternoon we saw the infantry and engineers coming back. In straggling groups they withdrew to the plain and the low hills to re-form.

We could scarcely realize that we were spectators to a major disaster. Right before our eyes Kasserine Pass was being taken by the enemy. They had gained high ground on the sides of the gap and by nightfall it was in their hands. American fighters and fighter bombers streaked down the valley over our heads to hit the Germans but the Kasserine had fallen.

The reverse was a terrible blow; but instead of driving straight for Tebessa, large formations of German tanks rolled northwest from Kasserine towards Thala. General Alexander, who was directing the over-all operations of the Eighth and First Armies and also the Americans, had rushed British troops down from the north, and near Thala they took the full brunt of the enemy attack. For several days, heavy fighting raged over the muddy, brown fields as the British prevented a break-through. Meanwhile, the resilient Americans swiftly gathered their forces and prepared to strike back and revenge the Kasserine defeat.

North of Thala, other British forces had broken another German armoured thrust and at Thala a second big victory was won. After suffering heavy losses, the enemy pulled back and the Americans pressing the retreating Germans turned the withdrawal into a rout.

From March to the finish in early May, a succession of brilliant manoeuvres by the Allied forces brought the Germans in Tunisia to their knees. The link-up was made between the Eighth Army and the Tunisian forces and the enemy was cooped up in the northeast section of the country. In a smashing attack from the west, British armour and infantry broke through to Tunis while the Americans stormed down the Mateur Valley towards Bizerte. The long African campaign was over.

XV

SICILY'S THIRTY-EIGHT DAYS

SHORTLY after midnight, as the moon waned, the assault fleet carrying the Canadian 1st Infantry Division anchored seven miles off the beaches of Sicily. For an hour I had stood on the deck in the darkness watching the bombs from our aircraft bursting on the distant shore targets. The bursts glowed momentarily like cigarettes in a blacked-out street. Explosions rumbled out to sea, and occasionally red and green tracer shells threaded slowly into the inky sky at the unseen planes. A battery of enemy searchlights to the west peered inquisitively into the night.

A heavy swell slapped against the side of our twenty-thousand-ton troopship, wind sang through the rigging and wireless masts. It was clear and starlit. It was the first hour of July 10, 1943—D-Day for the invasion of Sicily.

Ships carrying the British Eighth Army, including the 1st Canadian Division, which had come direct from Britain to join the invasion convoys, were massed around Pachino peninsula on the southeast tip of Sicily. Ships with the Seventh American Army aboard lay off Gela on the south coast, west of the Eighth.

Twenty-five hundred troopships, landing craft and warships were in this invasion armada, the largest ever assembled up to that time. This was a large percentage of Allied shipping in the summer of 1943.

On one ship, men of the Royal Canadian Regiment, one of the four Canadian assault battalions, were ready

to transfer to landing craft for the run-in to the
beaches, and over the ship's loudspeaker system came
the level voice of an officer calling groups by serial
numbers to their boat stations. The padre held a brief
service in the mess decks and in the lounge the commanding officer, Lieutenant-Colonel Ralph Crowe of
Guelph, Ont., spoke to his officers.

"We are on the eve of a night in the history of the
world that will never be forgotten," he told us as we
stood in a group around him. "We'll look back on this
night, and so will our children. We will look back on
it as the night we started to put the skids to the
enemy."

We repeated the Lord's Prayer after the padre,
shook hands, and solemnly lined out of the lounge
which had been our mess for nearly a month. My
mouth was dry and my stomach felt squeamish.

The day before, the Canadian flotilla had taken its
station with the rest of the fleet in the Tunis-Malta-
Tripoli triangle which was the invasion rendezvous
zone for ships from Algiers and Cairo, from Bengazi
and Bizerte, from New York and the Clyde, from
Gibraltar, Oran and Casablanca.

On that pre-invasion day in the rendezvous triangle
the sea was stiff with ships of every variety that has ever
seen action in this war. There were hundreds of grey
troopers which had carried Allied troops to battle for
two and three years, including many veterans of the
North Atlantic convoy run. There were hundreds of
tank-landing craft jammed with tanks, vehicles and
troops, and there were the larger tank-landing ships,
heavily loaded with vehicles and men and riding low
in the blue-green water of the Mediterranean. Smaller
landing craft fussed about the big ships. The Mediterranean fleet of the Royal Navy, as well as a giant

American fleet of warships, was out to protect the invasion force.

Aircraft carriers churned along and on the horizon were battleships, cruisers, monitors and scores of destroyers, corvettes and other escort vessels. From horizon to horizon the ships were straggled, and fighter patrols from Malta and Tunis sang overhead, dodging through the drifting snow-white clouds, with the warm sunshine sparkling on their wings.

It had been calm all the way from Britain but on the morning of July 9 one of those freak Mediterranean winds blew up. It was the tricky *sirocco,* which worked havoc with Roman and Norman expeditions on this same sea centuries before.

Such a vast combined operation demanded good weather and particularly calm seas if it was to be an opposed landing at Pachino and Gela. There were worried commanders on the ships and at headquarters in Malta as the wind kept blowing. In the afternoon the ships, which had been idling at the rendezvous, turned north and we passed Sousse and Sfax and saw Cap Bon, where the German African Army had surrendered just two months before. Through the white-capped sea we plunged past the cliffs and crags of Malta in the early evening. The American convoy broke off for Gela, while we continued northeast towards Pachino.

The troopers rolled and pitched, and the escort craft and small landing vessels buried their bows in the waves. We thought the invasion would certainly have to be postponed, dogged as it was by this bad break in the weather; but we left Malta behind and kept on our course. The commanders, versed in the idiosyncrasies of Mediterranean weather, were gambling that the wind would die down; as darkness closed in on the fleet, it did diminish but a heavy swell remained. With the darkness came safety from air attack. It seemed a miracle that the great fleet had not been raided once by enemy aircraft during the concentration in the rendezvous triangle or the last-lap voyage north in daylight towards Sicily.

At one A.M. I got into an assault landing craft, slung on davits over the reeling sea, with the naval commander who was to guide the assault infantry to the right-hand sector of the curving beach.

We were the first away from the ship, and, hitting the sea with a bang, our craft crashed into the side of the trooper, steadied on the swell and then was swept off into the darkness. The sea was running heavier than it had appeared from the deck and my spirits sank. It looked as if the infantry might founder on the way in.

Our craft jockeyed into position and we transferred to a naval motor launch, making wild leaps with our packs as the craft pitched together. It was the wrong one. We found the right one and made another fearsome leap. I had had enough excitement for one night already. Landing craft were coming off the troopers around us and the Royal Marine Commandos passed us heading for coastal batteries on our left flank.

The craft the commander was to guide to the beach mustered around our motor launch and after the inevitable confusions that plague any combined operation we turned towards the beach with scores of assault craft plugging along behind us.

Our launch reared and bounced until I thought it would roll over completely. The naval commander, who had served in destroyers for years and who won the Distinguished Service Cross on the North African landing, was sick three times before we got to the calmer waters near the shore. He violently cursed his stomach and the sea. I hung precariously to a stanchion on the tiny bridge and wondered how much a human being could endure at sea. But the infantry, crowded into their landing craft, were even worse off than we were.

We heaved along at six or seven knots. Pachino, four miles from our beach, was blazing now. The air force had hit the town with fire-bombs to give us a beacon. I could dimly see the low black outline of the shore against the glare of the fires. Support craft carrying guns for the beach assault joined us for the final spurt to shore.

A mile from the beach a light flashed to us. We picked it up and, steering for it, came to a canvas kayak with two men who had been taken to this position earlier in the night by a submarine to guide us in. We pulled the two half-frozen men aboard. They had been anchored in their kayak a mile from the beach for hours: now their task was done. We were on the exact course for the beach.

The Canadians were rapidly closing the distance to the beach as the navy opened fire on coastal targets.

A monitor first belched lurid sheets of flame from her two fifteen-inch gun muzzles and we could feel the blast sweep over the ocean, although we were several miles away. To the east, there was steady drumming of naval fire as other big ships of the fleet hit out.

From landward came the roar of exploding shells and our ears dinned with the noise of our own guns. A glimmer of dawn flushed the sky as the first wave of infantry hit the beaches; tracer bullets from enemy pillboxes on the sand spurted at the boats and along the strip of beach.

Our own riflemen and Bren-gunners were in action immediately and some of the tracer stopped abruptly. One cliff-top position on the right flank was more persistent than the others on our sector and out of the darkness came a whoosh and a roar from a rocket craft two hundred yards from us. Flames leaped from rocket-gun barrels on her deck and in a few seconds the cliff-top was blanketed with bursting high explosives. This was the first time rocket craft were used.

Salvo after salvo smashed on the troublesome enemy position as the Canadian infantry and assault engineers waded ashore from landing craft that had hit sand bars and shallow water.

The barbed wire stretching the length of the beach was breached and the Canadians went through into the fields and along the roads. It was nearly daylight. Enemy coast guns were firing on the landing craft. Spouts of water shot into the air as the shells from six-inch Italian guns landed among boats speeding to the beaches, but this shelling was erratic and short-lived.

A couple fell thirty yards or so from our boat as we bumped the sand bar forty feet from the beach and leaped off the deck into waist-deep water to wade ashore.

Enemy machine-guns on the shore which had put up surprisingly weak resistance were overrun by now and the first prisoners were being taken. The attack had come as a complete surprise to the Italian coastal troops on Pachino; the meagre defences folded up with very little fighting on the beaches.

The Royal Canadian Regiment and the Hastings and Prince Edward Regiment carried out the 1st Infantry Brigade assault on the right sector of the beach, with the 48th Highlanders following in reserve, while on the left-hand sector the 2nd Infantry Brigade rapidly overcame all opposition, with the Seaforth Highlanders and the Princess Patricia's Canadian Light Infantry leading the way and the Loyal Edmonton Regiment in reserve. These units won the Canadian bridgehead and the 3rd Infantry Brigade of the Royal 22nd Regiment, the Carleton and York Regiment and the West Nova Scotias came in later with the Three Rivers Tank Regiment. All were under Major-General Simonds, divisional commander. His G.S.O. 1 was Lieutenant-Colonel George Kitching, and his "A and Q" was Lieutenant-Colonel Pres Gilbride.

The sun came up blazing hot and by eight A.M. the roads winding inland from the beach-head were filled with long lines of Canadian troops logging their way forward to new objectives; tanks, guns, Bren-gun carriers and trucks rolling north in clouds of white, choking dust that billowed from their tires and threads like a smoke screen.

Ships crowded to the beach to disgorge their cargo; destroyers and a monitor lay half a mile off shore and pounded at targets miles inland, as the advance gained momentum.

Royal Air Force and American planes patrolled above the beach-head and not a single enemy aircraft showed up to strike at the mass of ships and vehicles and stores along the strip of sand.

The invasion of Sicily was away to a spectacular start in the Canadian areas; it was the same on the beaches where British and American divisions had attacked. It was a success for which no one had dared hope.

*   *   *   *

On the immediate left flank of the Canadians, two Royal Marine Commandos, under Brigadier Laycock, who later succeeded Lord Louis Mountbatten as chief of Combined Operations Headquarters in London, landed and destroyed a coast battery which could have commanded the main Pachino beach.

Men of the 51st Highland Division, veterans of the desert war with the Eighth Army from El Alamein to Tunis, were on the Canadians' right flank and landed on the extreme tip of Pachino peninsula. The 231st Malta Brigade, which had been on the George Cross island throughout the air blitz, landed north of the 51st to get some of its own back. The 50th Division, from the Tees and Tyne, and the 5th Division of the British regular army touched down on beaches near Avola, twelve miles north of Pachino and about the same distance south of Syracuse, the first big port the Eighth Army planned to capture.

In the Gela area, the American Seventh Army sent in the 1st Infantry Division and the 2nd Armoured Division, as well as the 3rd Infantry and the 45th Infantry, the latter coming direct from New York to join the invasion force at sea.

The plan called for a British airborne force and the American 82nd Airborne Division to drop from the skies several hours before H-Hour, when the seaborne forces hit the beaches, but the high wind disrupted their operation. Gliders were blown off their course, paratroops were tossed all over the country and neither group was able to carry out its plan of attack fully.

Some of the British airborne troops, who were supposed to land in the Syracuse area, were blown out to sea and either swam ashore or were drowned. The divisional commander came down in the sea somewhere off Syracuse and floated to the beach.

The Americans were to land in the Gela area and had several specific airfields to capture; but they too were scattered all over the south. Days later we found bands of American paratroopers wandering around in the Canadian sector trying to find their way to the American lines to the west.

This attempt at large-scale use of airborne forces was far less than successful, and as a result steps were taken later, by both the British and American commands, to improve methods of airborne attack.

One of the most successful features of the Sicily invasion was the pre-landing bombing. Through June, day and night bombers flying from North Africa hit at hundreds of targets in Sicily, southern Italy, Corsica and Sardinia. A week before the landing the blitz stepped up and airfields, railway junctions, harbours and communications were plastered with everything the Mediterranean Air Forces could hurl at them.

The damage was staggering. There was scarcely a railway line in Sicily that could be used; major airfields were denied the Germans and the Italians by this bomber onslaught. The great Gerbini airfield group south of Catania was neutralized days before the landing, and when the British troops finally captured it they found scores of abandoned enemy fighters in the dispersal zones, and the buildings and installations smashed as if a tornado had ripped through them.

In our long journey through Sicily, I saw few towns which had not been hit by the bombers. Even remote mountain hamlets, which possibly had the misfortune to have a railway junction, were blasted with high explosives. It was precision bombing with a degree of accuracy and effectiveness never achieved before.

It made you shudder sometimes to view this havoc and the only antidote was to remember the London blitz, the shattered East End and the long lists of casualties posted each day at the town halls of London boroughs.

*　　　*　　　*　　　*

The invasion of Sicily was launched fifty-nine days after the collapse of the German and Italian armies in the Bizerte-Tunis triangle but it had been decided upon by the British and American leaders at the Casablanca conference earlier in the year. Prime Minister Churchill and President Roosevelt, with their army, navy and air force chiefs, left French Morocco with the broad plan in their minds; in the succeeding months, staffs in London and Washington and Algiers and Cairo worked it out in detail as the Eighth and First British Armies, with the Second American Corps and French troops finished off the Axis in North Africa.

I had returned to England from the Tunisian front in anticipation of an operation in which the Canadians would participate with a division or more, and I wasn't in the Canadian camps in southern England long before I was given orders to get my field kit packed again and be ready to move.

Originally, a British division was to go from Britain to join the Eighth Army for the Sicily operation, but it was decided in the spring to give the 1st Canadian Division and the 1st Canadian Armoured Brigade the assignment. The two formations went to Scotland to make their final preparations.

Major-General H. L. N. Salmon was commanding the 1st Division then and he was to take it into action. The plan of the Canadians had to be interlocked with the general Eighth Army plan and a number of Canadian staff officers flew to Algiers and Cairo for conferences.

Called to a meeting of senior commanders in the Middle East, General Salmon got aboard a plane in southwest England that crashed on the take-off, killing him. His loss was a heavy blow to the Canadian Army. He knew the details of the operation so intimately and was such an able leader that it was a difficult problem to find a successor.

General Simonds was Brigadier, General Staff, to General McNaughton at Canadian Army Headquarters at that time. A month before he had been with the Eighth Army for several weeks, studying Montgomery's tactics in the push north from the Mareth Line to Sousse and Sfax. He was the choice. He left Army Headquarters immediately and joined his new division in Scotland.

On June 11, I left London for the Scottish concentration area and the Canadian force went aboard the troopers and landing ships a few days later. Two large-scale manoeuvres followed, with the Division making landings on the broad, sandy beaches on the west coast.

While the staff officers at Divisional Headquarters knew where we were going, the troops had not been briefed and it was not until we were issued with tropical bush-shirts, shorts, slacks and mosquito nets that we realized that we were bound for the Mediterranean.

On June 28, I went to the Headquarters Ship anchored in the Clyde to have a first interview with General Simonds before sailing and only then did he tell us officially that we were going to join the Eighth Army. He refrained from saying anything about the operation and did not name the target. Speculation as we sailed that night ranged over targets everywhere from the Aegean to Sardinia. The Balkans was a popular choice.

The convoy sailed in the evening with a strong escort of destroyers and corvettes, and we settled down to the shipboard routine of eating and sleeping, of limited P.T. on the crowded decks, of lectures and idleness. It was Dominion Day, July 1, when we were briefed and the colonel of the R.C.R.s made the rounds of the ship telling officers and men the background of the operation. The troops listened intently. As the colonel finished there were a few cheers and a smattering of hand-clapping, but no wild enthusiasm.

These troops had waited so long for a campaign that it was almost an anticlimax when they were told that they were going into action with Britain's finest army.

Maps of Sicily were distributed. The plaster model of the Pachino peninsula was taken from its wooden box and placed in a room where everyone could study it, and the men who had taken down all identification marks from their uniforms prior to embarking, as a security measure, now sewed on their "Canada" shoulder flashes again and put up the rectangular red patch of the 1st Canadian Division.

The troops were proud of their red patch, for it marked them as men of the first contingent of Canadians to come to Britain in December, 1939. It was this battle flash which later prompted the Germans, as they fought the Division on the bloody slopes of Nissoria in central Sicily, to dub the Canucks the "Red Patch Devils".

There were few idle moments now aboard the ships; detailed briefing went on day and night over the maps and the plaster model. We were given complete information about the enemy forces in Sicily which included the Sixth Italian Army of four regular divisions—the 4th Livorno, the 26th Assieti, the 28th Aosta and the 54th Napoli—with five third-rate coastal divisions made up mainly of low-category men not fit for first-line formations.

The total Italian force with its army and corps troops and base formations was about two hundred and twenty-nine thousand men. The German force in early July was about two divisions but they were sending more men across Messina straits daily. The Germans were principally in the central sections of Sicily and were also based on Catania on the east coast. Both Italian and German headquarters at the time were at Enna, in the middle of the island.

It was thought the German and Italian air forces had been weakened by the pre-invasion blitz by Allied planes, but Intelligence was not making many predictions about possible air opposition; as far as naval opposition was concerned it was merely indicated that a large portion of the Italian fleet was in Taranto and might come out to fight.

That was the enemy picture as we got it. On our own side, we had General Montgomery leading four full ground divisions of the Eighth Army with two additional brigades and powerful corps and army forces, and General Patton of the Seventh Army with four ground divisions. We had fleets of the Royal Navy and the United States Navy which totalled about three hundred fighting ships of all types. There were battleships operating in Sicilian waters the night of the attack, aircraft carriers, cruisers, destroyers, other escort vessels, such as corvettes and frigates, monitors, river gun-boats, flotillas of motor torpedo boats, flotillas of motor gun-boats, anti-aircraft cruisers and scores of heavily-armed support craft.

Fighter aircraft were lined up on Malta airdromes nose to tail. On the big bomber bases in Tunisia and Algeria, built for the bombing of Sicily and Italy even as the Tunisian campaign was being fought in bitter battles during the depressing months of February and March, there were masses of medium and heavy bombers. By day the Americans flew out, and on the night shift went the Royal Air Force bomber crews, ranging far and wide over the central Mediterranean.

The heavy bombing of Sicily began on July 4, as our convoy passed through the Straits of Gibraltar during the darkness after an abortive submarine attack had been made on our ships just west of the straits. This was one of the half a dozen scares we had on the voyage, with destroyers dashing about and rocking the ocean with depth charges. None of the troopers was hit by subs although many 1st Division vehicles in our other convoy were lost in the Mediterranean, and those losses proved a serious handicap to the Division until replacements caught up with it in central Sicily.

We sailed east in the Mediterranean on a flat sea, with the sun searing hot, and watched the sky for the enemy aircraft that never showed up. Past Oren, past Algiers and Philippeville and Bone on the Algerian coast, the convoy moved unmolested; then we had other giant convoys with us as the assault fleet moved on to its rendezvous south of Malta. None of us had ever seen such a stirring naval spectacle as these hundreds and hundreds of ships with scores of destroyers racing among the ships, signal flags flying and lamps blinking out messages.

It was not until July 6 that we were told the date of D-Day. Saturday, July 10, was to be the day of attack. We listened to the radio news at every broadcast for the story of the Sicily bombing, so important to the success of the landing.

An Intelligence report flashed to our ship that the enemy had ploughed up Pachino airfield and we were of two minds as to the meaning of this. Perhaps the Italians were pulling out or perhaps they knew by now we were going to land there.

Then we went around Cap Bon, down towards Tripoli, swung back on July 9 towards Malta and in the storm the assault went in.

*   *   *   *

As the Canadians and the British thrust inland from the beaches the Italian defences were not much more effective than they had been on the coast. There were some skirmishes around Pachino during the morning and afternoon and by nightfall of that first day in Sicily the invaders had nipped off the whole Pachino peninsula. The attack was running ahead of schedule.

After landing, I slogged up the narrow road leading to Pachino, trying to keep up with the R.C.R.s who had raced ahead. Columns of Italian prisoners, wearing wretched, dirty uniforms, but smiling as if they had won a victory themselves, passed us on the way to the beaches, bound for prison camps in North Africa. Many carried baskets of wine and bread and tried to cadge cigarettes from us.

They were members of a fraud of an army which was defeated before it even fought on its own soil. These men had no heart or will for battle and, except for the odd group, offered little resistance. They were not ready for the attack on Pachino either. since their High Command had believed no Allied landing would occur on the difficult beaches where made. The Italians, and even the Germans, had thought that the shallow water and the sand bars off shore were a natural defence for the southeast tip of the island.

Two miles from the beach we came to an Italian coast battery, knocked out by the R.C.R.s an hour

earlier. Four six-inch guns were there but they were
of 1916 make and had not fired thirty rounds. The
Italian defence system was so poor that they did not
even have these various gun positions linked by telephone to a command post. Runners made the rounds
of the positions on foot with information and targets
for the gunners. It was primitive.

Along the road there were evidences of brief actions
and some dead Italian soldiers lay sprawled in the dust.
As I got nearer to Pachino I could hear the sound of a
fight over the hill ahead. Italian mortar bombs crashed
on the crest but seemed to be firing at nothing in particular. A squadron of British tanks with the 51st
Highland Division crawled up the hill and fired
steadily from a sheltered position. The R.C.R.s and
the Hastings were about a mile ahead and after capturing the important Pachino airfield—which had been
ploughed up very thoroughly—the R.C.R.s attacked
and captured the main Italian coast battery position
for the area, a mile west of Pachino, which was occupied
during the morning by the 51st Division.

The first Canadian casualties in Sicily were suffered
in the attack on the big battery position, which was
also the coast defence headquarters, and three R.C.R.
privates were killed as they stormed dug-in machine-
gun posts in an orchard. They were buried by the
main road.

The airfield had not been captured more than a few
hours before a British construction group was working on it with bulldozers and scrapers, levelling it off
again and preparing it for the Spitfire squadrons that
flew in a day and a half later. They were the first
formations to fly operational missions from a Sicilian
'drome.

By afternoon, the sun was searing hot and beat down

on the troops advancing through the dust over the low undulating hills of the peninsula, with its scrubby farm-house hovels, its barren fields, dejected vineyards and malaria swamps. Thousands of Canadians who had never known heat like this before, had blistering sunburns by evening.

Fighting in the Pachino area where units of the 1st Brigade, commanded by Brigadier Graham, were engaged, was all over by mid-day, and in the meantime the 2nd Brigade moved rapidly inland and swung west over the fields and along one good road towards Ispica, a cliff-top town which was being shelled by a monitor and destroyers that cruised along the coast.

Ispica was occupied after the bombardment and so was Rosolini and a company of Seaforths took over the town of Pozzallo on the coast. The Italians there raised a white flag on the town hall turret as a destroyer nosed alongside the jetty and threatened to throw shells down the main street. This town had been a German headquarters for the coast zone and the Italians said the Germans had gone back to central Sicily a week before.

In the Pozzallo area the commandos got their biggest surprise of the landing when they ran into a squadron of Italian horsed cavalry and wiped it out in a vineyard *mêlée*.

Hoofing back down the road to the beach to write the story of the landing, I passed squadron after squadron of our Sherman tanks rumbling up the line to join the infantry and there were self-propelled guns going up too, as well as heavy mortars and medium machine-guns.

Our strength was building up rapidly and by mid-afternoon the whole Division was ashore. Slumping into a slit-trench by the beach, I wrote my story of the landing and sent it out to Headquarters Ship where it was flashed to London on the air force wireless during the night. Much to my own astonishment it turned out to be the first story out of Sicily. I did not know it myself until days later when some reinforcements joining the Division told me they had heard it quoted as such in a news broadcast they had picked up on their ship coming to Sicily.

It was a world beat by seven and a half hours.

While we had worked out all the communication angles we could to try to get my story out early, there was a lot of sheer luck attached to this scoop.

Our public relations officer on the assault was Major Bill Gilchrist of Saint John, N.B., a former managing editor of *The Telegraph-Journal* there. He was on Headquarters Ship and although we had no contact with each other during the entire voyage from England, I knew he was trying to obtain wireless communication from his ship over which we would be allowed to transmit brief news stories after the landing.

He remained on H.Q. Ship and the copy which I sent from shore by landing craft reached him all right.

By that time, he had an understanding with the staff that some brief news would be transmitted to Malta over the navy, army or air force wireless sets on the ship. That is, if operational traffic were not too heavy.

Actually this was highly irregular, but coming as we did directly from England we had not yet become bound by official red tape on communications and censorship. We knew nothing of the rules laid down for other correspondents who sailed with British and American troops from North Africa.

So we worked out our own scheme. Thanks to Major Gilchrist and our good fortune, it worked perfectly.

The Major had my story approved by the Divisional

Intelligence officer in the absence of a field press censor and raced to the wireless sets. The Intelligence officer really had no authority to pass the copy but from an operational point of view there was nothing objectionable on the grounds of broad security.

The army wireless set was too busy to handle it. So was the naval set. But the air force operators, with a direct link to London, took it. I had typed "Urgent" across the top, which is normal newspaper practice. Without giving it a second thought the operators considered it highest priority. It really had none at all.

They cleared the air force network to London of operational traffic and my five-hundred-word story was beamed through to the Air Ministry direct, where it was received with consternation.

The story was published and broadcast around the world and it blew up a storm at Allied Force Headquarters in Algiers. I had violated all rules, they said in Algiers; I was to be arrested and thrown out of the theatre; the story had got out in error.

The storm, about which I knew nothing for weeks, finally blew over. But Lieutenant-Colonel Cliff Wallace, chief of Canadian public relations in the Mediterranean, had a hectic few days placating half a dozen top-ranking officers in Algiers to keep me out of the hands of the military police. He even had a talk with General Eisenhower about it.

On the beaches, the men who were unloading the ships and craft and establishing the ammunition and supply dumps joked about the "phoney" war, for the only firing they heard, after they landed several hours behind the assault infantry was the booming of the naval guns firing on Ispica. Darkness brought action to the beaches, however, for, running true to form the German bombers came over just as soon as night had fallen. A couple of planes dodged in fast and scattered parachute flares over the beach and the ships lying off the coast. Hundreds of guns from the boats and shore clamoured and the sky was latticed with a thousand streaks of tracer. The bombers flew over it and through it and relay after relay attacked our ships and those of the 51st Division a few miles to the east. They dropped a stick of bombs along the beach and a billow of smoke blacker than night poured starwards in the glare of the flares. A ship down the coast was hit and exploded with a belch of flames. The noise of our own guns tore at our nerves as we lay deep in our slit-trenches, fearing our own shrapnel as much as the bombs. The Germans came back several times during the night and with dawn the bridgehead was quiet again.

The Canadians were in the 30th Corps, under Lieutenant-General Sir Oliver Leese, who later succeeded Montgomery as commander of the Eighth Army, and the Corps Headquarters came ashore on the second day. General Montgomery himself came over from Malta and drove around the bridgehead in his open desert car in which he had ridden from El Alamein, waving that slow informal salute to his troops and stopping frequently to talk to the men on the beaches and on the roads going inland.

I interviewed him as he sat on the steps of his caravan at Corps Headquarters. He was delighted with the performance of the Canadians, saying they had been "terrific" on the beaches. And he was no less pleased with his British troops, the men of the 51st Division in 30th Corps with the Canadians, and the men of the 50th and 5th Divisions in another corps under Lieutenant-General Dempsey, who later commanded the Second Army on the Western Front,

Syracuse had been captured as planned and he gave us the good news that Augusta, farther up the coast towards Catania, had fallen to the British divisions, racing north along the coast road.

General Simonds was driving his Canadians forward hard to take full advantage of the surprise achieved on the landing; the city of Modica fell without a shot being fired. This city in a chasm between grey cliffs, with its fine old buildings, ornate churches and squalid houses, was the headquarters of the 206th Italian Coastal Division. The divisional commander, who won the Military Cross fighting with the Allies in the last war, and his staff, surrendered to an advance party of Canadians.

There had been several short actions on the road to Modica when detachments of Italians had resisted the Canadians at road blocks and bridges but they surrendered as the Canadian artillery went into action. Several thousand Italian prisoners plodded down the roads and created a major problem for the provost who had no plans for handling such a horde. Several enterprising prisoners even organized their own bus service, driving Italian army trucks to and from the front, taking their colleagues to the Pachino beaches where they were embarked. Columns of Italians without any guards were frequently seen and as we passed them going to the front they would grin foolishly and give us the V-sign.

Groups of the more determined ones went off to villages and changing to civilian clothes tried to carry out their own guerilla warfare against the invaders. For several days these snipers were a menace but they soon gave it up. Rumours about the danger of snipers spread through the Canadian lines but there seemed to be more of a threat from trigger-keen Canadian sharpshooters, who were over-conscientious in their job, than from the Italians.

Passing through the towns in the wake of the troops was a regular Roman triumph for us. The towns-people stood on the streets and cheered, threw flowers in our path and shouted for cigarettes, chocolate and biscuits.

It seemed spontaneous enough, and it was a welcome that liberators would get in fiction, but it was always a little embarrassing. The Sicilians were bewildered, poverty-burdened folk who had been ground into the barren earth they tried to farm. It was pathetic to watch them cheer us as we passed—hopefully, humbly, correctly—the way they probably would have cheered even the Germans in an advance like ours. You could not easily forget the sad look in the faces of the old, wrinkled women who had known nothing but the starkest poverty. They would try to smile with the laughing, clapping children and young girls but their smiles were empty and clouded with hopelessness.

We had not been in Sicily many days before we could see the fraud of Italian Fascism; its victims were these crowds of starving, beaten people in every town. Strident, boastful slogans, quoting and extolling Mussolini, his Imperial aims, his army and the future of the Italian people were emblazoned across the face of buildings. How ironical they were to us as we looked around and saw what Fascism meant to Sicily. It was grand villas in the country and towns for the Fascist chiefs and squalor for the people. You had only pity for these folk, duped so completely by the Roman dictator whose regime was toppling even then.

North of Modica the Canadians bivouacked in the fields and groves and rested on July 14 after their four-day blitz from the beaches. General Montgomery came up the line to compliment them on their effort.

It had been four days of long forced marches, of little sleep, of skirmishes and some hot but brief fighting; the outstanding feature was the way in which the Canadians had taken to campaigning and put their training so readily into practice.

*   *   *   *

A strong Canadian patrol of tanks and infantry went westward to the city of Ragusa, the largest community in southeast Sicily, and there linked up with troops of the American 45th Division and paratroopers of the 82nd Airborne. After a fight at Gela against a German force, the Americans speedily exploited their bridgehead and went north and west along a dozen roads. Italian soldiers had surrendered to them by thousands, as they had to the Canadians and the British.

The Canadians rested for less than thirty hours in the Modica area and then moved north through the mountains to Vizzini, twenty miles from Modica, travelling along a narrow road which twisted treacherously along the edges of the dizzy gorges. At every turn the Canadian advance guard expected to run into enemy positions, for everyone was anticipating that soon the Division would be hitting German formations for the first time.

We passed through that jagged belt of mountains, however, without the slightest trouble. The enemy had not had time even to crater the roads. Through the dirty but picturesque mountain-top towns of Giarratana and Monterosso, where there were magnificent opportunities for a stubborn group of defenders to block the advance for days, the Division rolled north. As we came into the long, sweeping valley leading to Vizzini we heard the rumble of the artillery of the 51st Division on our right. The Highlanders were attacking Vizzini, which was held by a determined force of German paratroopers.

British patrols had broken into Vizzini but had been thrown out and the guns now were shelling the town in preparation for another attack. The Canadians pushed ahead fast and occupied hills to the west of Vizzini. Faced with this double threat, the Germans withdrew at night.

For the Canadians, the occupation of Vizzini marked the end of the comparatively easy phase of the invasion. The American Army was making excellent progress in the western and southern parts of the island and the Eighth Army was in possession of the whole of the southeast. The 50th and 5th Divisions, however, which had advanced from Augusta towards Catania, were engaged in bitter fighting between Lentini and Catania and eventually were blocked on the Simeto River line where the bloodiest battles of the campaign were fought for the bridge over the river near the coast.

General Montgomery ordered the Canadians to advance west and north from Vizzini. This was the famous "left hook" tactic of the Eighth Army, an assignment carried out with brilliant success on several occasions in the desert by the New Zealand Division. Now the Canadians were the flying column sent rumbling around on the flank between the British and the Americans to force the Germans to release their hold on the Simeto line.

Still operating on a one-brigade front because of the scarcity of good roads, the Division advanced west from Vizzini without resting. The Hastings and Prince Edward Regiment was in the lead, with tanks of the Three Rivers Regiment.

It was the morning of July 15 and they had gone eight miles and were nearing the hamlet of Grammichele, its grey-stone houses on a slight grade, when the forward troops fell into a German and Italian ambush.

Four German Mark IV tanks on a slope a half mile off the road fired on a column of Canadian Bren-gun carriers and knocked out eight in a few minutes. A German pompom gun mounted on a half-track vehicle sprayed heavy calibre bullets down the road and machine-gunners and riflemen in the buildings on the edge of the town opened up on the Hastings.

The Canadians leaped from their blazing carriers and took shelter from the fire from the town and the tanks on the slope. Officers and non-commissioned officers rallied the platoons and they edged forward gradually, returning the fire. The rest of the regiment had been ordered to stop and a squadron of Canadian tanks roared over the fields to engage the German tanks.

The tanks surprised the Germans as much as the ambush did the Canadians. There was a sharp exchange of shelling, with the Canadian crews gradually closing the range until they hit one of the German tanks and its crew piled out and fled. Another was smashed as it tried to move off and the pompom vehicle was smashed, while several Canadian tanks were hit in the action.

The infantrymen rushed the buildings during the tank fight and threw the Germans out of the town, taking a few Nazi prisoners, the first they had captured in Sicily. The Germans retreated to the next town and left three hundred Italian soldiers to fend for themselves. They surrendered as soon as the Canadians got to them.

That little initial scrap with the Germans was a

good tonic for the Canadians, even though only a few hundred of them were actually engaged in the fighting. They went through Grammichele without pausing and followed hot on the heels of the enemy towards Caltagirone, a city eight miles farther along this line of the Canadian advance.

The 48th Highlanders passed through the Hastings and under a full moon moved stealthily through the shadowy streets of Caltagirone.

By dawn the 48th had combed the city with its patrols and there wasn't a German or even an Italian soldier in the place. The Hermann Goering troops had pulled out again and moved back towards Enna, the Canadians' next goal.

In five days the Division had advanced sixty miles and the infantry had marched most of that distance on foot. The Canadians had had a good taste of campaigning in the heat and the dust and were holding their own with the experienced divisions in the Eighth Army. General Montgomery was pleased as Punch and General Leese sent Simonds a message saying: "Congratulations; keep it up."

It was a breath-taking business keeping up with the speeding Division and trying to write its day-to-day story as it happened. We could never bivouac in the same place for two nights and we bounced around in a jeep throughout the daylight hours, going to the forward units to check on some incident and then rushing back to headquarters to get more information. Like the troops, the correspondents looked like labourers who had slaved a month in a flour mill. We were covered with fine white dust after we had been on the road for half an hour and even when we washed it off we still had a ghostly pallor.

Our bush-shirts and shorts and socks were impregnated with dust; we wore goggles and tied handkerchiefs over our mouths as we rolled along in truck, artillery and tank convoys which clogged the highway from dawn to dusk and into the night.

From the start the food was not bad. Within two days of landing we were receiving the British "compo" ration in the wooden boxes. There were tinned meat and stews, hardtack that was edible, puddings and steak-and-kidney pies, bully-beef, sardines, cheese, jams and a powdered sugar-milk-and-tea compound which made a satisfying brew. There were six varieties of these "compo" packs and in some we would get tinned fruit, which was a real delicacy. For breakfast we always had tinned sausage or slabs of bacon and although the food became monotonous there were few complaints about "compo" during the campaign.

It was a treat, though, to run over to the American lines on our left occasionally, especially when the hospitable 1st Infantry Division under Major-General Terry Allen was our running mate, and pick up a box or two of the American "C" ration with coffee, which we never had in our own issue. We liked the Spam in those days as a change and curiously the Americans would devour our bully-beef with relish. The Americans were fed up with Spam and we had bully on our Indian list.

Water was a continual problem from the beginning to the end of the campaign. We seldom ran short of water to drink if we were careful with our water bottles, but getting water for washing was a great difficulty. We went for weeks without baths and the only opportunity we'd get to clean up would be in some horse-trough in a town or in infrequent streams where the water was soapy from a hundred men bathing there before you.

Fleas and bugs, scorpions and the ubiquitous mosquito were campaign menaces and we religiously followed our anti-malaria rules, drilled into us verbally by medical officers and by army signs on the roads which cautioned us again and again to use our mosquito nets every night when we slept and to take our yellow mepacrin pills regularly.

In this early stage of the campaign casualties from the sun and from malaria were far higher than from actual battle wounds. The medical services moved right along with the Division and three field ambulances followed up the front-line troops, setting up their field hospitals and operating rooms in former Italian municipal hospitals, in schools or in the fields. A large amount of their medical equipment had been sunk on the way out and captured Italian Army medical stores were readily put to Canadian use.

The Division took on the dusty, battered appearance of the Eighth Army "desert rats". Their vehicles and guns and tanks became as white and grimy as the troops who handled them. You could not distinguish the Canadian formation from the 51st except that many of our vehicles were newer and we did not have Arabic markings on our trucks, reminiscent of the perilous days of El Alamein when the Germans were crowding on the rim of the valley of the Nile—less than a year before.

In the Canadians' wide flanking movement towards Enna they operated pretty much alone. One medium regiment of British artillery and a British regiment of twenty-five-pounders on Valentine tank chassis were with us, but it was an essentially Canadian advance and there was little direct contact with British formations, or even with American, until near the end of the campaign.

General Simonds ran his own show on the orders that came down from Army and 30th Corps Headquarters but the higher formations showed unusual interest in the progress and tactics of the Division, and every few days either General Montgomery or General Leese would drive to the Canadian sector for long talks with General Simonds.

They took pains to guide the keen and able Canadian general, fighting his first campaign. At the start they almost took him by the hand and showed him the way but later on, as the actual battles were fought, General Simonds was left alone to carry out his own ideas. The British were confident by then he would do well, and he did. Protégé first of General McNaughton, then of General Montgomery, he was one of the finds of the Mediterranean theatre. He was rewarded later with command of the 2nd Canadian Corps for the Western Front campaign.

*   *   *   *

From Caltagirone, the largest city the Canadians had occupied, the 2nd Brigade went forward through more mountains towards Piazza Armerina. Meanwhile, I lingered a few hours in the heavily bombed city, talking with the 48th in the streets and watching the Italian citizens making a languid effort to sweep up the debris from the fronts of stores. The barber shops, which are the communal centre of Italian towns and the gathering places on the main streets where all the local gossip is exchanged, were opening up. They are to Italian towns what pubs are to British towns.

Grimy Canadian soldiers went in for haircuts and shaves and the barbers did a thriving business, spraying the warriors with scent with a finishing flourish and sending them out to the bawdy comments of pals in their platoons.

The 48th relaxed in town and some soldiers, finding a couple of buggies and spirited horses in the stable of a Fascist chief, who had fled days before, harnessed them up and trotted through the town in elegant style. One Torontonian wore a huge straw hat and he waved it elaborately as he swept by his company, bivouacked in a bomb-cratered park. Several large bottles of Italian *vino*—raw and red—clinked suspiciously in the back seat of the buggy.

It was dark before we left Caltagirone to catch up with the advance formation of the Division and we soon found that it had been a mistake to dally in the city. We went ten miles in our jeep along a highway in the bright moonlight and did not see a soul, except a lone dispatch rider heading back to Caltagirone at top speed. We didn't know where the Germans were and were not at all certain where our own troops were. The little towns through which we passed were deserted.

My imagination began to run wild and I thought every sinister, evil-smelling alleyway held a German patrol or a machine-gun. We were becoming very uneasy about continuing this strange night ride when we met a Canadian provost corporal at a cross-roads. The Division, he said, was five miles farther on and still moving. On we went and joined speeding convoys of trucks and tanks making use of the moonlight to catch up with the Germans, withdrawing rapidly on Enna.

Headquarters had moved off the main road to halt until dawn and we raced up and down sideroads for an hour and a half until we located them by an old Italian Army barracks near the hamlet of San Michele. The night before the Germans had bivouacked in that very spot and we unrolled our blankets under the

orange trees where the ground was littered with empty
German ration boxes and copies of recent Berlin newspapers. Some of us should have become casualties
that night, for the Germans had scattered glass vials
of sulphuric acid through the orchard. We did not
discover these villainous booby traps until daylight
and picked them up carefully before any had been
broken. They would have exploded and given bad
burns.

The chapel bells at the monastery of San Michele
tinkled at daybreak and from the distant hills around
Piazza Armerina rolled the crash of artillery. The
German rear-guard of the Hermann Goering Division
had taken up position on the slopes south of Piazza
Armerina and the Edmonton Regiment was first to
meet them on this hot July 16.

From this point to Aderno, the Germans used the
same tactics they had previously employed, digging in
quickly and setting up machine-guns and heavy mortars, with the infantrymen supported by a few tanks
and a few guns. It was their system for covering their
inevitable withdrawal, and every time they made a
stand the Canadians had to mount artillery-infantry-
tank attacks and blast them back.

The Edmontons advanced up the plain towards the
German positions and were mortared. The companies
scattered into gulleys and worked their way forward
field by field. General Simonds himself and several of
his staff officers went forward to reconnoitre and prepare the final attack, and the party was trapped by
mortar concentrations and shelling. A handy ditch
was the only refuge and for an hour the staff officers
were pinned down while the mortars and shells landed
around the ditch, some coming within a few feet.

Canadian tanks came up to help the Edmontons,

and with artillery, mortars and machine-guns the Canadian attack pushed the enemy off the slope. The Germans jumped into their trucks and roared through Piazza Armerina into the hills north of the city with the whole 2nd Brigade, led by the then Brigadier Chris Vokes, and the tanks pursuing them.

The enemy left a score of dead in their trenches; a few prisoners were taken by the Edmontons.

This brisk fight revealed that the Germans were using a highly mobile battle group to delay the 1st Division and General Simonds was determined to trap it and knock it out. He gave the Division no rest, and the infantrymen were nearly exhausted by this long advance. The Germans were cratering the roads now too, and north of Piazza Armerina several huge blow-ups occurred at bridges and at turns in the road.

At these craters the Canadian advance guard skirmished with small German parties which tried to cover the craters with machine-gun fire to prevent the engineers repairing them rapidly. There would be scraps in the groves and on the knolls by the side of the road where the demolition had been made; then the Germans would be overwhelmed and driven back or taken prisoners.

More and more prisoners kept coming down the line from this one-road front, sometimes fifty and sixty at a time. They seemed so young, these Nazis. They were seventeen and eighteen and sometimes over twenty, but it was seldom you found these Hermann Goering troops south of Enna much past their 'teens. For every real German there were at least two conscripts from Poland, or the states of central or southeastern Europe. The conscripts made no boasts and indicated clearly they were glad to be finished with the war.

They would pass us on the road, in their grey-green tunics and trousers, wearing short jack-boots, or in their dark khaki summer drill of shirts and slacks much like our own. Practically all of them wore the cloth peak-caps of the German Army; few had helmets. They were short, healthy-looking young men, and good soldiers. They did not smile and laugh and wave to us as the abject Italian prisoners had the week before when they flooded down the roads without escorts. These Germans and satellite soldiers had to be guarded.

Despite the road demolitions and the harassing opposition along the road to Enna, the Canadians moved due north for nearly twenty miles to a point where the road forked east and west, the west fork going to Enna and the east fork meandering to Valguarnera, southeast of the central city of Sicily.

We had time to catch our breath on this move north and the 3rd Infantry Brigade, which was dogged with hard luck as far as many dramatic actions were concerned throughout the campaign, took the lead as the Division neared this fork in the road. The 3rd Brigade was led by Brigadier Penhale.

The dirt road wound through folds in the hills at this point and the Germans, taking advantage of the manner in which the hills dominated the road and the approaches from the south, turned it into another defensive point. As they had done at Piazza Armerina, they dug in machine-guns and placed their mortars in good positions. They had some guns sited on the road up which the Royal 22nd Regiment, commanded by Lieutenant-Colonel Bernatchez, came on the night of July 17-18. The French-speaking regiment reached the base of the hills, where the German positions were located, during the night and were fired on. The

Canadians dispersed and fought back but they were in a bad position and it was impossible to dislodge the Germans from those hill positions without support. Reports were sent back to Divisional Headquarters down the road and the 22nd hung on in the face of the German fire until a full-scale 3rd Brigade attack, with support of four regiments of artillery, was mounted and launched early on the afternoon of the 18th.

I had gone forward to a slope just behind the 22nd's positions when the Divisional Artillery barrage opened shortly after noon. They had been ranging on the fork of the roads and on the enemy trenches on the slopes for an hour before and now they hit out furiously. There were only 120 guns in that shoot and it was small compared to ones which followed it, but it was a milestone for the Canadian Army—the first divisional shoot for the Royal Canadian Artillery in this war.

The sugar-loaf hill to the west of the fork was plastered with shell bursts. Every time I watch a barrage like that I imagine I see a grey forest of trees growing suddenly and magically before my eyes. As a shell hits the brown earth, the grey smoke billows up like a full-blown tree sprouting from the soil. There were half a dozen at first, well scattered, and then twenty, fifty, a hundred or more, crowding each other for space. The hill-side was covered with the grey forest and then the smoke drifted and merged into a dirty, grey curtain over the brown hill-side.

You heard the grumble of the guns miles behind, and the swish and whine of the shells overhead like a long train going through a tunnel. There wasn't much commotion on the hill-side target. Twenty-five-pounder shells dig only a shallow crater, usually just a scoop in the ground about five inches deep, with the blast spreading for fifty yards or more around.

The smoky hill flickered with bursts of shells, but the bursts did not seem large. They just sparked and were followed by more sparks.

The concentration lasted for more than half an hour, creeping slowly down the side of the hill, across the fork in the road and up the slope on the eastern side. There was not a shot fired in response by German guns lying on the opposite slopes.

The Royal 22nd and the Carleton and Yorks, commanded by Lieutenant-Colonel Tweedie, advanced straight at the German hill positions close behind the barrage. They were so close that at one time some of our own shells fell in the Canadian lines. The West Nova Scotia Regiment, under Lieutenant-Colonel Pat Bogert, wheeled around on the flank to the west to jolt the enemy unexpectedly.

The Canadian tanks and the British self-propelled guns climbed a hill overlooking the battle-ground and fired across the valley at German machine-gun nests. The infantry stormed the hills with bayonets fixed and Bren and Tommy-guns firing.

The German battle group on the hills stood to fight for several hours and the clatter of machine-guns and the sharp crack of rifle fire echoed along the road where we lay watching this battle spectacle. We could see the Canadians closing in on the German positions, little clusters of men in dusty khaki moving cautiously forward and then running and falling flat as they took cover. Some men were hit and fell and didn't move.

The others couldn't stop, and kept going, firing, dodging, creeping, sweating forward. Stretcher-bearers, with their Red Cross arm-bands standing out clearly, reached the fallen men and bound them up or left them dead on the brown, scorched earth.

By the end of the afternoon the fight was over and

the line of hills and the fork in the road had been captured by the Canadians. The German force, badly mauled and suffering heavy casualties, withdrew towards Valguarnera, eight miles to the east.

The Canadians made their first haul of the campaign and although they had not "bagged" the whole German battle group they had hit it hard. More than thirty German machine-guns were captured, with thousands of rounds of ammunition. A German 88mm. gun on a half-track was knocked out and some armoured cars were burning along the roadside. It was a small victory, seen against the back-drop of the whole campaign, but for the Canadians it was an important action; for it was a vital step forward in the gradual inoculation to battle which helped make the Division one of the finest fighting outfits in the Mediterranean theatre.

I walked over the German positions and saw they had dug their defence positions so deeply that only direct hits by shells and mortars would have destroyed them. It had been our infantry, with bayonets and machine-guns, closing right in that had driven them out. Captured equipment was stacked by the roadside and you could have your pick of fifty German helmets. They made good wash buckets.

From the fork we could see Enna, clustered on the top of a sheer cliff twelve miles away and looking for all the world like a fairy city in Grimm's Tales.

The Canadians had planned to strike at Enna but the whole Division was switched along the road to Valguarnera, by-passing to the south and east of Enna. General Simonds, however, sent a fighting patrol to Enna. It was held up every few miles by gaping craters in the roads. When it did reach the city the Canadians found the Americans had occupied it a few hours before, coming in from the southwest and the west after taking the city of Caltanissetta and the town of Villarosa. There had been no fight for Enna. The Americans had plans to besiege the city and their artillery was deployed in the fields below the cliffs to hammer Enna into submission, but before the bombardment began the German force fled northwest to Leonforte and Assoro where they prepared to make a firm stand in the towns and along the hills and cliffs.

*   *   *   *

More than half of Sicily had been occupied by July 19 after only nine days' campaigning. On the eastern side of the island the right flank of the Eighth Army was still held up at the Simeto River and a grim and costly battle was in progress there. From our camps south of Enna we could see the sky flaming with gun flashes at night over the battle area. The Germans had strong positions on a line of hills on the outskirts of the city of Catania, and with concentrations of guns raked the Gerbini and Lentini plains which the British were trying to cross. General Montgomery maintained pressure on the Simeto River sector with the 5th and 50th Divisions. He ordered the 51st to sweep around to the left of the line inside the Canadians, who were to continue their wide flanking movement and complete the "left hook" by striking east to Mount Etna from the Enna area. The Malta Brigade was sent across the front to work between the 51st and the Canadians and eventually to come under Canadian command.

While this deployment was under way, the crack 78th Division, which had fought with such distinction in Tunisia the winter before, landed secretly in Sicily and moved forward, without the Germans having an inkling that it had left North Africa.

The Americans had overrun the western part of Sicily and their 1st Infantry Division came up on the Canadians' left flank.

While the battle for the road fork was going on, the Canadian 1st Brigade went over the hills to the east and descended on Valguarnera, a wretched, dirty town crowded in a confusion of ancient stone houses, tiled roofs and open drains on a hill-top, where the Germans, as usual, had set up their guns. Valguarnera was a tongue-twister for the Canadians; it became "Valcartier". The R.C.R.s and the Hastings attacked these hill positions and stubbornly pushed the enemy back on the town. The 48th, led by Lieutenant-Colonel Ian Johnston, engaging in their first action, joined in the fight and some of the most gallant exploits of the Valguarnera action were achieved by the Highlanders as they cleaned out a line of machine-gun posts anchoring the defence system around the town. They were the first into Valguarnera in strength.

The Germans had some heavy tanks in Valguarnera and the infantry had to deal with them too. In addition to the 1st Brigade, the Royal 22nd, following the fight at the forks, rolled right along the road to Valguarnera and also were in action in the fight for the hills dominating the town. It was here, too, that the gunners of an anti-aircraft Bofors battery, bored stiff in a campaign with no enemy planes to engage, gave the infantry support by firing on pillboxes and haystacks with their 40mm. shells. It was unorthodox but effective.

The German battle group, forced to fight two actions in one day, was badly mauled by now and fell back on Leonforte, a sizeable town twenty miles north of Valguarnera, pursued by the 1st and 2nd Brigades, which had come up for the advance over the rolling plain stretching north from Valguarnera.

This advance was comparatively slow, for mine fields had been laid on the plain and the enemy was also able to shell and mortar the Canadians.

I made a diversion and broke away from the advance to take a side road to Enna, climbing over road demolitions and a blown railway bridge and trudging up a heart-breaking cliff road until a villainous-looking Sicilian gave me a lift on a mule; the American outposts finally picked me up and drove me into the city in a command car.

Enna was the only Sicilian city I saw, with the exception of Catania and Syracuse, that seemed to belong to this century. There were several fine streets in the city, perched like an eagle's nest high on a crest dominating the farmlands and vineyards for miles around. There was a modern luxury hotel and the Fascist Headquarters was a magnificent structure of stone and marble which the British and American civil affairs officers of A.M.G.O.T.—Allied Military Government of Occupied Territories—were now occupying.

The Amgot officers were a harassed group in Enna, as they were in practically every community, trying to keep the local administration going, trying to feed the starving people and bring some order from the confusion into which Sicily was thrown by the collapse of the Italian administration.

Amgot had many problems and there were many muddles and misunderstandings as this new, and in many respects experimental, organization sought to do its job. The organization was very short-handed and many of the officers seemed quite unsuited for the task. There were some who could not even speak Italian or Sicilian.

Amgot was no great success in those early days.

I went to the Italian Sixth Army headquarters building, wrecked by the Italians before they fled. The offices and hallways were littered with smashed typewriters, old army orders, broken furniture and piles of documents and paper. Italian flags lay crumpled on the dusty floor and an impassive American sentry stood guard over the shambles.

There was scarcely any food in Enna for civilians, and children and women and even men screamed at the soldiers for biscuits and chocolate and cigarettes. But it was the same in any town. Everyone was short of everything. Cigarettes, especially, were like gold for barter.

Enna citizens lined up at food stores for small loaves of bread—that was about all they could get. The Germans had wrecked the city water supply before withdrawing and there were only one or two dirty wells from which the thirty thousand civilians could draw water. They drank it, somehow, without any apparent ill effects.

Yet on the main streets the barber shops were open and some gift shops were selling souvenirs to American doughboys; and pretty women in clean print frocks walked along the boulevard with its palms and orange trees.

Enna, with its squalor and its startling contrasts, was worth seeing; but the battle for Leonforte had started. From the promenade in front of the Grand Albergo hotel we could see Leonforte on the next high ridge fifteen miles to the northeast, clouded in grey smoke from the Canadian barrage laid on the town.

Citizens of Enna stood by the ornate stone balustrade at the cliff's edge and watched the bombardment with the casual interest of spectators at a dull sports meet. The war had come and gone for them and Enna had not been devastated. It had been bombed a few times, but not heavily, and now the people were thankfully settling back into the rut of their old life and didn't care what happened fifteen miles away.

I had hitch-hiked from our own lines to Enna and it would have been a long march back, but the men of the 1st American Division figured anyone from the Canadian Division was a friend of theirs and an artillery captain took me off in his jeep to their camp on the city's outskirts. In the evening we yarned and ate American rations with coffee to wash down the stew. The captain delivered me back to Canadian Headquarters by dark. That was the kind of hospitality Canadians got from the Americans in that campaign and it was reciprocated every time opportunity offered.

*   *   *   *

The three-day battle for the neighbouring towns of Leonforte and Assoro, on the cliffs at the entrance to the Agira valley running due east to Mount Etna, was the most important engagement the Canadians fought in Sicily.

The 1st and 2nd Brigades completed their advance over the plain leading to the cliffs, making steady progress against the shelling which fired the grain fields and charred them black, as if a prairie fire had swept the farm lands. The Canadian infantry went over these smoking fields with their tanks and guns, and on the night of July 20 a two-pronged attack went in, with troops of the 2nd Brigade assaulting Leonforte and the 1st Brigade attacking the ridges and cliffs with Assoro, which was on the highest point by the ruins of a Norman castle, as their goal.

German *Panzer* Grenadiers were holding the towns, with infantry, tanks and guns, and they had machine-guns in caves honeycombing the cliffs. The roads of approach curled around steep hills; it was suicide to advance directly along these roads to the objectives.

Canadian artillery hammered cliff, hill and town as the evening dragged into the twilight and in the darkness the infantry began their advance, carefully picking their way forward and infiltrating the enemy positions with the skill of long practice in training, now tested and found successful in battle.

Of all the actions in Sicily, I look back on this exploit of the Hastings at Assoro as the most daring and spectacular. A reconnaissance of the area to be attacked had been attempted by the Hastings C.O., Lieutenant-Colonel Sutcliffe, with some of his battalion officers, that afternoon; they were in an orchard a mile from the base of the Assoro cliffs when they were fired upon by German 88mm. guns.

They raced for cover and the colonel was killed as he fell into a slit-trench. Only a few hours before, I had seen him and had been given a captured German infantry assault car by one of the members of the regiment, for the Hastings had so many captured vehicles they did not know what to do with them all.

This car was a superb vehicle. Built on the lines of a big and powerful truck it could carry eight infantrymen in the back, facing each other, and three persons in the front seat. It reminded me of photographs of cars used by German soldiers occupying Prague or Vienna, with the Huns sitting bolt upright in the back seats, holding their rifles tightly. This car was a windfall to us, for the Division was still short of transport and could not spare many vehicles for correspondents. We labelled it "Press" on both sides in big letters, drove it for weeks, took it to Italy with us and it wound up on a rubbish heap outside Ortona, a good car.

The plan the colonel had prepared for the Hastings was executed as he would have wished. Major the Lord Tweedsmuir, son of the late Governor-General of Canada, was second-in-command of the unit and led the Hastings to carry it out. The Germans were defending the forward slopes and the cliffs on the four-mile ridge between Leonforte and Assoro while on the eastern flank was a precipice, well over two thousand feet high, with narrow vineyard terraces indenting it from bottom to top. It appeared to the enemy to be a natural defence, impossible to scale, but up this precipice the Hastings went to catch the Germans unaware.

These troops from eastern Ontario farms and towns filed through a narrow valley in the moonlight unseen by the enemy, who were anticipating a frontal attack on the Leonforte-Assoro ridge and were ready with machine-guns and mortars. Out of the shadows loomed a black shape coming along the path the Canadians were taking and the forward troops thought for sure they had been discovered. The shape turned out to be a bullock being driven along by a nocturnal Italian who had no interest in the war.

One company, stripped of heavy kit and loaded with Bren guns and clips, led the way as the regiment began to claw its way up the precipice. There was a military precedent in Canadian history for this sort of a scheme, for Wolfe's troops scaled the cliffs at Quebec back in the middle of the eighteenth century to win Canada from the French. But nobody was thinking of history this tense night. Men sweated with their burden of arms and ammunition, cursed softly but vehemently as they slipped on a root or a vine and crawled from one terrace to another up this almost perpendicular cliff.

Just before dawn the Hastings reached the top and the forward troops sheltered at the base of the Norman castle. Their objective had been achieved without opposition; now they had to fight it out and cling to their precarious pinnacle which they had won with such physical labour.

Three Germans in an observation post near the castle were surprised and disposed of quietly. As daylight came the Hastings opened fire, shooting from the rear and throwing into confusion the Germans who were manning the forward slopes looking to the south and west.

The Germans realized then that they had been fooled by the cliff-scaling Canadians and concentrated on efforts to drive the invaders from the cliff-top. They sniped them and counter-attacked them during the day, and every hour brought new shelling of the positions where the Canadians were now dug in deeply, firing back at the enemy with everything they had.

By afternoon the Hastings were running short of ammunition and were practically out of rations, for they had not been able to carry much up the cliff with them. The 1st Brigade tried to get trucks through to them on the road which twisted up the cliff-side, but the Germans shelled the convoy of Bren-gun carriers and trucks before it got half-way up and knocked out half a dozen of them. Nothing got through. At nightfall the Hastings sent a party through the German lines to reach Brigade headquarters, get rations and ammunition and bring them back. The R.C.R.s, in reserve for this attack, went to work and the men packed forward the urgently needed ammunition and food. Somehow they got enough through to the Hastings to enable them to hold on, although they had suffered more than one hundred and twenty-five casualties.

At daylight the Hastings took the offensive and engaged the Germans who were in the ancient town of Assoro, just two hundred yards from the cliff-top trenches where the Ontario troops were dispersed in a couple of hundred fox-holes. German trucks and other vehicles, full of troops, were shot up and it was not long before groups of Hastings were skirmishing in the outskirts of the little tumbledown town, in the shadow of a large, centuries-old church which had been shattered by shells.

During the night the 48th Highlanders assaulted the ridge from the front and with some Canadian tanks working alongside them, drove the Germans back over the crest. The pressure from the Canadians cleared the Germans from the whole ridge. The town of Assoro fell to the Canadians after more hand-to-hand fighting in the streets. The 48th pushed on for two miles along the Agira road, while the Hastings rested on the cliff-top by the castle.

I reached them on this peak, the highest in those rugged hills and cliffs from there to Mount Etna, after their battle, and looked down the cliff-face they had climbed. It made you dizzy just to glance into the gulch. The Hastings were still being shelled spasmodically and an hour before I got to the battalion, heavy shells hit the church in Assoro again. Four Canadian soldiers lay dead by a well in the cloisters as we walked through to the castle. The padre was having graves dug by the church wall and up on the cliff-top the Hastings were striking back at the Germans.

I found several officers, including Major Tweedsmuir, crouched in an observation post, looking through a captured German artillery observation periscope at German machine-gun positions in an olive grove a mile away towards Nissoria, next town on the

Agira road. They relayed the locations of the German positions back to the Canadian artillery miles behind them and within ten minutes shells were bursting among the enemy.

We could see Germans running through the grove for shelter in a valley behind. The Hastings grinned. They had taken a pounding like that the day before and stuck it out.

This Assoro cliff-top was the lookout for the whole Canadian battle-front. From it you had a panorama of thirty miles of Sicilian mountains, sloping valleys, deep chasms, dusty roads, brown farm land, vineyards and green groves. Far to the east, volcanic Mount Etna reared into the sky like a grey-blue cloud and a wisp of smoke curled from its crater as it would on a tourist poster.

While this grim drama of Assoro was being enacted, an even more bitter and a larger action was being fought by the 2nd Brigade attacking Leonforte.

The Seaforths, led by Lieutenant-Colonel Hoffmeister, and the Edmontons, commanded by Lieutenant-Colonel Jefferson, struck at the town after the Canadian gunners had shelled the approaches and the place itself for hours. The Canadian infantry went in at night, working along the cliffs and the hills on either side until they dropped down into the narrow, cobblestone streets and alleys where the Germans lurked.

Throughout the night, fighting raged in the streets and on the slopes. It was rough and bloody fighting, with neither side giving or asking quarter. The Germans had several tanks in the town and plenty of machine-guns. Tracer shells cannoned down the streets, blasting into walls and exploding with deafening roars. The machine-gunners laced the main street with tracer.

The Canadians fought their way into the centre of the town, moving in small groups, usually less than a platoon of thirty men. They fought hand-to-hand actions in houses and skirmishes at nearly every corner. German snipers were on the roof-tops, lying behind tottering chimney-pots or were in top-storey rooms. The Highlanders and the Edmontons carried the fight to the enemy wherever they found them, in the wildest fighting they had known in Sicily; the intensity of this action was not equalled until the Christmas week fight for Ortona five months later in Italy, when the same regiments fought together in the rubble.

All night long, Leonforte was a town of sudden death in the darkness; killed and wounded lay in the streets. Colonel Jefferson of the Edmontons with several officers and more than one hundred men were cut off by the Germans in the centre of Leonforte. They were hemmed into three or four houses and fought back at the Germans, firing machine-guns from the windows, tossing grenades into the streets and sniping hour after hour with rifles and Tommy-guns. The Germans came at them with their heavy machine-guns and their "potato masher" stick grenades but could not budge the besieged Edmontons.

The *mêlée* in the streets overflowed into the hills around and on the slopes Seaforth and Edmonton companies attacked dug-in German machine-gun posts.

The battle swayed back and forth in wild confusion. The Canadians would capture a couple of streets, they would be counter-attacked by tanks and infantry and would have to yield. Then they would form up and drive the Germans back towards the north end of the town, which rocked to the crash of the guns.

Just after dark, when the infantry had begun their

advance on the town, a detachment of Royal Canadian Engineers crept down a steep hill and along the winding road that crossed a gulch in the valley and then curved sharply to edge along a cliff for four hundred yards until it disappeared into the tangle of Leonforte streets.

The narrow bridge over the gulch had been blown by the Germans and it had to be repaired before the Canadian tanks, guns and vehicles could move into the town. The sappers worked for three hours without interruption by the enemy, although they could hear the battle raging just up the road. Then groups of infantry came slogging back down the road. A few minutes later three German tanks rumbled down the road, halted, fired a couple of rounds over the bridge, and withdrew to the shelter of the buildings on the edge of Leonforte.

The sappers came out of the ditches and continued their work. They had hammered down only a few more planks when German machine-gunners fired on them and some more shells hit the hill just behind them. The engineers worked on under this attack and by two A.M. had the bridge finished. They then settled down in the ditches and slit-trenches by their bridge and stuck there, yielding not an inch, until dawn when a second Canadian attack went in to clear Leonforte of Germany infantry and tanks.

If these sappers had not completed the bridge and then defended it stubbornly under intense fire all the rest of the night, the successful attack could never have been made.

It started at dawn when Canadian anti-tank guns sped along the road and smashed up machine-gun posts which had harried the engineers from the bank on the Leonforte side of the gulch. The Princess

Patricias then came rolling along, with the leading company, led by Major Rowan Coleman of Montreal, riding on tanks and Bren carriers and guns. The rest rushed forward in trucks behind them. Over the bridge the Patricias went as German guns slammed shells at them from the town. The anti-tank gunners and the engineers joined in the attack up the road from the bridge to the outskirts and this unorthodox collection of assault troops stormed into the street.

I was with Brigadier Vokes of the 2nd Brigade in an orchard about half a mile from the town as the assault was going on, and between salvos of mortar bombs, which lit in the valley below us, he told the story and grimly said he thought he had lost the Seaforths and Edmontons during the night. He was on the point of exhaustion and in the turmoil of the wild fight in the streets nobody could say what the exact situation was.

But it wasn't as bad as we thought. In fact, the Germans were being pushed out of the town at that moment.

The Seaforths and the Edmontons had scattered all over the town and the surrounding hills, but in small groups they had fought so well that the enemy was shaken. It was too much for them when the Patricias, commanded by Lieutenant-Colonel Lindsay, hit them with tanks and guns on this morning of July 22. They were edged out of the houses and streets by late afternoon.

The group of Edmontons marooned in the centre of the town were relieved just as their ammunition was practically gone and as the Germans were preparing a systematic extermination of every Canadian in that section. Taking one house at a time and cleaning it out thoroughly, they were about five houses away from the Edmontons when the Patricias stormed up the streets. There were wild shouts of welcome and an Edmonton officer rushed from one house to present a Patricia company commander with a bottle of wine.

Several tanks edged into side alleys and as two German tanks came down the main street to attack the Patricias, the Canadian tank gunners let them have it at point-blank range. One German tank had its turret blown completely off by a 75mm. shell at thirty yards and the other tank was also stopped abruptly with two holes through its turret.

The guns and tanks followed the infantry through the place as the Patricias were joined by the Edmontons and Seaforths still in the town and on the hills in a complete clean-up of the area. The enemy did not give up easily and fought stubbornly for hours. It wasn't any use. They were overwhelmed by the ferocity and concentration of this street-by-street advance of the 2nd Brigade and withdrew northwest along the Agira valley road.

When I got into the town they had finished collecting the German dead from the streets and were burying them on the outskirts. Dead were still lying in the hills, though, by the stone fences and through the tangled vineyards. The sickening sweet, earthy smell of the dead hung over the town as it baked in the shimmering sun.

The weary 2nd Brigade bivouacked on the northeast outskirts to rest as the 1st Brigade passed on to continue the attack towards Nissoria, next town in the valley, eight miles away.

*   *   *   *

The Americans on the left were advancing now on Nicosia, twelve miles to the north and also making good progress along the north coast road. The Germans were being hemmed into northeastern Sicily but they still were strongly resisting the British Division along the Simeto River line.

The objective of the Canadians now was to strike east to Mount Etna and bring pressure to bear as fast as possible on the defence line around Mount Etna. This would aid the new attack being planned at the Simeto.

General Simonds massed his artillery along the road to Nissoria and began the long barrages that went on day and night during the march to Mount Etna. Few hours passed now when the twenty-five-pounders or the mediums were not shelling the hills ahead of the Canadian infantry and tanks. We lived with the gun-fire and at night we could not sleep unless we picked a bivouac a mile or so away from the artillery positions. The darkness flared with our gun-fire and on the left we could see the American artillery flashing in the darkness; on the right there were the British guns, pounding, pounding away without let-up.

The 1st Brigade marched eastward and the 48th Highlanders fought a brisk action at the cross-roads three miles from Leonforte where the road forks north to Nicosia, at which town the Americans were engaged.

The Highlanders had come down from the Assoro heights and went through the pine groves to battle this German rear-guard, which fell back to join up with the main German force digging in now at Nissoria, a small, dejected, lonely town lying at the foot of a slope which the enemy had chosen for their next stand.

On a hot Saturday afternoon, July 24, the 1st Brigade opened the attack on Nissoria.

From a trench on the crest of Assoro, I had a bird's-eye view of the narrow front and watched the R.C.R.s go along the road and through the fields in the valley below. Our tanks were with them and the Divisional Artillery was ploughing the area ahead of the troops with high explosives. The tanks were from the Three Rivers Regiment, which, under Lieutenant-Colonel Booth, fought with the 1st Division through Sicily. He was later killed as a brigadier in the battle of Falaise in Normandy.

Shells whooshed over our heads there on the Assoro cliff and the barrage grumbled eastward with shells exploding in a mile-wide belt as the range was lengthened up the road.

A trail of smoke was laid by the artillery beyond Nissoria and the grey smoke from the gun-fire veiled the battle-field. The sound of the artillery was like an autumn gale.

A red flare was lit on Assoro like some medieval beacon to guide the American and British planes which were to bomb the town of Agira, majestically poised and shimmering in the sun eight miles away on the next great crest.

The planes darted over Agira and the town was wreathed in black and grey smoke.

Here was war with its principal weapons in action spread out before my eyes. It was like watching a sand-table miniature from far up there on Assoro, but for our infantry slogging up the road to Nissoria it was grim and real. They scrambled over the stony fields and through the inevitable vineyards and olive groves, tiny figures in khaki bush-shirts and shorts, with the red patches on their sleeves.

The Germans mortared the infantry and bombs burst along the road and in the groves, kicking up ugly clouds of dirty brown dust and black smoke. You heard the shrill whine of shrapnel. Through the mortar fire the regiment kept going, to close in on Nissoria, with its one main street and a maze of alleyways branching off it. The German gunners shelled the approaches and machine-guns clattered on the outskirts. This was a difficult attack for the R.C.R.s in broad daylight but they reached the town and the tanks roared straight down the main street.

The German outposts in the town had withdrawn rapidly as the Canadians advanced the last few hundred yards and they raced for cover just eastward as the tanks and infantry entered, leaving Nissoria to be occupied.

The R.C.R.s went through the streets and continued their attack towards the knoll and other slightly rolling hills on the far side. The Germans were in strong positions on that knoll and along the hills.

As the tanks thundered along the road German anti-tank guns, carefully camouflaged at a corner, fired on them at less than two hundred yards. They could not miss. Five Canadian tanks were knocked out, while the others, coming behind them, deployed and fought back with guns blazing.

The infantry worked into the hills and there was a mad fight around a red-plaster building by the roadside. The fighting spread from hill to hill and the forward companies of the regiment got more than a mile and a half past Nissoria in heavy going.

It was obvious, though, that it would take a stronger force than this to drive the Germans from the hills and the R.C.R.s were ordered to fall back in the evening.

They came back, grimy from the battle and sad in their hearts, for they had lost their commanding officer, Ralph Crowe, on the slope beyond Nissoria.

In the confusion of the Nissoria battle some Cana-

dians went right through the German lines until
they were practically into Agira. Two privates thought
the town had been captured and coming upon a
German staff car, with nobody in it but the driver,
captured the driver and the car and then realized they
were miles ahead of the Canadian attack. They abandoned the car but stealthily made their way back to
Nissoria with the prisoner. He turned out to be the
driver for the German district commander and was
one of the most valuable prisoners captured in the
fighting in the Agira valley.

The Hastings continued pressure on the Nissoria
slopes after dark and there was more fighting on the
terraced hills before they too were ordered to withdraw while a new attack was mounted. The Canadian
artillery struck at the hills again with deadly shell-fire
and on the Nissoria road the 48th Highlanders prepared a third attack which went in the next night,
Sunday.

The Germans had re-formed on the slopes and
moved in more machine-guns, artillery and tanks in
stubborn determination to delay the Canadians, who
were the only division of the Eighth Army attacking
at that time.

After dark the Highlanders crept through the small
valley between the slope and the town and made good
progress up the slope, crawling over the stone walls
which criss-crossed it and creeping through the
orchards until they were practically into the German
positions. The enemy machine-gunners blasted at
them in a stormy burst of firing as the Highlanders
opened up themselves and German mortars hit the
hill-side.

Platoons fought up and down the hill-side and
several times the Highlanders went in with the

bayonet. One group advanced straight into the German line for 150 yards, cleaning out everything before them and winding up this sortie by capturing an 88mm. gun, killing the fifteen Germans in the gunpit.

The slope was covered with trenches, hastily dug by the Germans, and they had good machine-gun positions at corners of the stone walls. They had been shaken by the artillery barrage, which had covered the area so thoroughly that a shell had exploded about every ten feet. Still they hung on. Hour after hour the night battle raged and with another formation now ready to make the final assault the following night the 48th came out of the line at dawn. Their gallant and bloody struggle had softened up the German defenders for the successful thrust to follow.

As we ate our breakfast the morning of July 26, we heard the BBC eight o'clock broadcast give the news of Mussolini's resignation. Giovanni, our Italian mess orderly, nearly dropped the tea in his excitement and gleefully drew his finger across his throat in a significant gesture. Giovanni was a peasant boy from the hills around Rome and had been captured by—or rather gave himself up to—the Canadians early in the campaign. Instead of going to a prison camp he was made our mess orderly and a good one he was. He now wore a Canadian cap and badge with his Italian uniform.

Simple little Giovanni was delighted and he babbled away about the iniquities of Mussolini. He had suppressed his feelings for a long time about the Fascists and now he burst out with: "Look at our people. Look at their boots and their clothes. He has starved them and ruined our fine country."

Then he looked a little sheepish and went back for more tea.

If Giovanni reacted like that, what would the people in the towns be like? we asked ourselves; so off we drove to Leonforte before the big night attack. I got a Canadian signalman whose parents had gone from Italy to settle in Cochrane, Ont., and who spoke excellent Sicilian, to come with us, and on the main street he told a group of old men, boys in their 'teens and wrinkled old women the news of Mussolini's downfall.

I had never seen such a spontaneous outburst of emotion. *"Bravo, bravo,"* they shouted, and clapped their hands and grabbed our arms and embraced us. The news flashed from group to group until the main street of Leonforte, with the two hulks of German tanks still lying at the corner, was filled with their cheers and the clamour of these excited, joyous folk.

They shrieked in shrill Italian, "Death to Mussolini!", and tore posters from the walls of the stores and defaced pictures of the grimacing dictator. A *carabiniere* ran off to get a bottle of wine and we had a dozen invitations to imbibe as Leonforte celebrated.

Canadian patrols in the streets thought a riot was brewing and a corporal rushed up to ask me in a rather belligerent manner what it was all about. I suppose he thought I was inciting the locals. As I told him the news, he too was engulfed in the celebration and I later saw him sharing a jug of wine with an old man who had been the socialist mayor of Leonforte more than twenty years before and who was going to make his come-back now.

The shadows of two-score years of Fascism slipped away from those people's lives that morning and I felt I was seeing happy Italians for the first time since we had landed. Even the smiles of the old women sparkled.

They believed this would now bring peace to Sicily

and Italy and prophetically the men told me that Marshal Badoglio would aid the Allies now that he was in charge in Rome. The Marshal would bring peace to this country and there would be no more fighting.

And as they spoke these hopeful words, our guns were rolling through the streets, and along the road the western infantry regiments were moving to the starting-line for another crack at the Nissoria slopes.

It was another night attack and the Patricias lay low in the groves on the northern edge of Nissoria until dusk, then edged down into the valley and slowly went up the slope where three other battalions had faced the German fire.

For several hours before the Patricias attacked, the Divisional Artillery raked the slopes in the heaviest concentration it had laid down on that area. German prisoners who came down the line later in dazed conditions mumbled that the gun-fire had been terrifying. It was followed by the crack Patricias going in with bayonets fixed.

They got onto the ridge after battling their way through a maze of dug-outs and narrow trenches and stormed the high point on the hill where the strongest positions were located. In the darkness Canadian tanks also chewed their way along the slope and several tanks got right among the German infantry. It was a nightmare for the tank crews as they clanked around on the slope, fired at frequently by marauding German tanks and plagued by the German infantry, who had to be beaten off with machine-guns and even hand grenades when they threatened to rush the tanks.

In the early hours of the morning, July 27, the Patricias broke through the enemy positions and the Germans retreated, falling back as quickly as they could along the Agira road. The Seaforth High-landers followed up the Patricias' success and passing through them tore along the road in pursuit. The Edmontons joined in the attack at this point and on two hills flanking the main road on the outskirts of Agira the Germans made another stand.

One German force was in a cemetery on the north side of the road and set up its machine-guns among the vaults and tombstones, while another was among the trees and in the sandpits and scrub on the south of the road.

Accurate mortar fire prevented the Canadians from going down the road and the Edmontons cut well off to the north to attack the hill which went by the name "Cemetery Hill". The Seaforths curved to the south and went for the other hill.

The hill battles were stiff; troops of the Hermann Goering Division and the 15th *Panzer* Grenadiers opposed the Canadians as the action rumbled on through the day. The westerners worked their way up the steep slopes, and the Edmontons had to storm a cliff finally to break into the cemetery and drive the Germans out.

By the morning of July 28 the Canadians held the hills with their German dead. The remnant of the enemy force which had made the stand fled in disorder over the hills and down the roads past Agira. Canadian machine-gunners and tank-gunners on high ground northwest of Agira scattered them still more as they retreated and the artillery shot them up every time they stopped.

That afternoon the Patricias occupied Agira and the long toil down the Agira valley was over.

The Canadian Division had been aided in the capture of Agira by the Malta Brigade, which was placed temporarily under command of General Simonds and advanced from the south. After the fall of the town, it went east towards Regalbuto though some units got some well-earned rest around Agira.

In the attack from Leonforte to Agira, General Simonds had gambled, for his left flank was uncovered practically all the way. Opposition at Nicosia had held up the Americans. They were not able to pivot as rapidly as had been expected and thus keep up with the Canadian drive east.

Despite the threat of an attack on the flank, the Canadians went right ahead and the gamble succeeded magnificently. If the Germans had attacked in strength from the north during the advance from Leonforte to Agira the 1st Division would have been in a difficult position for a while. But the attack never came. There was only one incident when it was thought that a counter-attack would materialize and this was during the battle of Leonforte. One evening a report came down the line that the Germans were massing to hit the Canadians a knock-out blow. Our anti-tank guns were rushed forward. It was an empty rumour, for the Germans remained lurking in their positions and never took the offensive.

The 1st Division now looked to Regalbuto as the next town to attack and on the blue slopes of Mount Etna, towering against the sky, there was Aderno, a town which was the keystone of the Germans' Mount Etna line.

The Eighth Army, held up still on the Simeto but edging troops around on the German flank, was closing the pincers on the enemy, holding around the south and southwest of Mount Etna, and the Americans were advancing steadily now on the Canadians' left. The climax of the campaign was slowly approaching. The **enemy was being cooped up in northeast Sicily.**

While the 1st Brigade and the Malta Brigade methodically advanced on Regalbuto, the 3rd Infantry Brigade was fighting its own war south of Regalbuto in rolling hills which climbed eastward until they merged with the lava folds of Etna.

Shortly after the fall of Valguarnera and when the 1st and 2nd Brigades attacked Assoro and Leonforte, the 3rd Brigade branched off and, taking a good road which parallels the Leonforte-Agira-Regalbuto road between six and ten miles south, the Brigade struck east as fast as it could move.

It had been put under command of the 78th Division, which was now moving into position on the right of the 1st Division to lend a hand in breaking the Etna line. This was the Division which came secretly from North Africa and even as it went into the battle-line the Germans still did not seem to have any idea that it was in Sicily, much less about to attack.

The town of Catenanuova, seven miles south of Regalbuto, was the Canadian Brigade's objective and after skirmishing with German rear-guards along the highway, which streaks down a broad plain, and being slowed down many times by mine fields which the Canadians had to negotiate with skill and care, the fight for the town began.

A "Jock Column" of the Royal 22nd Regiment, with anti-tank guns, spearheaded this thrust and several times on the advance along the plain road the column was mortared and sniped by patrols. A few miles west of Catenanuova, the Germans, following their usual game, dug in on two hills—Santa Maria, north of the road, and Mount Scapello, south of the highway.

The Royal 22nd experienced their hardest fighting of the Sicilian campaign on those two hills and the French-speaking soldiers of that famous regiment displayed superb gallantry against troops which had been ordered to resist at all cost.

One company occupied Santa Maria. Before withdrawing, the Germans had taken ranges for their own artillery to fire on this hill and as soon as the Canadians got into position on the top they were shelled. It went on for hours. Mount Scapello was taken by another company and it too was shelled during the day—July 27.

After an hour or so of shell-fire the German infantry would attack Santa Maria and the Canadian losses piled up. The company refused to budge, despite alternative shelling and infantry attacks. In the evening the colonel told them to come out but just at darkness they had to beat off a last counter-attack with bayonets and grenades.

Only forty-one men in the company came off Santa Maria and they brought their wounded with them as they joined the other company holding on Mount Scapello.

The rest of the Brigade had come up by this time and the West Novas on the night of July 29-30 moved down the slope of Mount Scapello, behind a fierce barrage laid down by the British gunners of the 78th Division. The West Novas crossed the dried-out bed of the Dittaino River, which is in front of the town, and entered Catenanuova. The only sign of the enemy was some random sniping with Very lights which shot into the sky and illuminated the streets.

As they worked into the town, various platoons had some street-fighting. Several German tanks attacked but were driven off. The town was cleared well before dawn, though, with the Carleton and Yorks aiding a Maritime unit, particularly in destroying German mortars in an orchard on the fringe of the town.

On July 30, the Canadians over the Dittaino were shelled persistently and the river-bed was so well covered with mortars and guns that they could not get transport across with rations or water. The Maritimers were running short of ammunition too.

A field company of the Royal Canadian Engineers was sent forward and under this shelling and mortaring the sappers worked all afternoon putting a road across the river-bed. Canadian tanks prowled along the banks trying to cover the sappers, as they laboured in the steaming heat and the dust, by laying smoke-screens and shooting up any targets they could spot.

By nightfall the roadway had been completed and guns and vehicles were going over into the new bridge-head. British infantry also went over the river-bed and relieved the Canadians. The Royal 22nd retook Santa Maria and the 3rd Brigade then swung northeast through big hills to link up again with the 1st Division.

Regalbuto to the north was hemmed in by the 1st Brigade and the Malta Brigade and the Germans made several strong counter-attacks on the Malta Brigade without being able to break the hold the two formations had on the town, which had been bombed into a ruin by American medium bombers.

The Allies owned the air in those days and you were awakened at the first glimmer of dawn by squadrons of bombers and fighters—our squadrons—droning over our lines to strike at enemy-held towns and German concentrations. I saw only three attacks by German aircraft during that trip through central Sicily.

One evening fighter bombers struck at our gun positions and the next morning a dozen fighters zoomed down the valley, with cannons crackling, and shot up transport on the road which ran past our camp. Those forays cost them heavily and four planes were knocked down by Canadian anti-aircraft gunners, who had scarcely fired a shot at aircraft since they had left the Pachino beaches.

Another day when I was at 78th Division Headquarters nine enemy fighter bombers zoomed over, dropped a few bombs and scurried back to their base.

After visiting the Catenanuova sector and seeing the fight for the bridgehead over the river-bed, I drove back to Divisional Headquarters which was still south of Agira, among the trees where the Germans had had an ammunition dump. Stacks of 88mm. shells, mines and mortar bombs were still there, evidence of the haste with which they had moved back from their Agira positions.

We had a quiet two days and in my diary I wrote: "The advance has slowed down, while we get ready. Perhaps in a day or so the finale will start. We're taking it easy for the first time in three days."

On August 2 there were sudden developments. Regalbuto fell at 12.15 P.M. and the Malta Brigade occupied the town, painting huge red Maltese crosses on the heavy wooden door of the town hall and on the ornate façade of the Fascist headquarters. The 1st Brigade had moved around to the north and east and held firm positions looking east down the Salso River valley to Aderno, set on a plateau on the lower slope of Mount Etna.

At three P.M. the same day the amazing news came through that the cliff-top town of Centuripe, between Catenanuova and Aderno and six miles southeast of Regalbuto, had been stormed and captured by the British 78th Division, with the 3rd Canadian Brigade covering the left flank of the attack as the Brigade moved up to rejoin the 1st Division.

The British troops called this craggy town "Cherry-

ripe" and from Catenanuova it looked as tough a
position to take as Longstop Hill in Tunisia, down the
road from Medjez el Bab, where the same 78th Division had added to its great name by storming it in the
final break-through to Tunis.

German fortress troops held Centuripe and the 78th
prepared for the infantry assault by shelling the town
for hours with its twenty-five-pounders, a technique to
which we had become accustomed since the first divisional barrage at the battle for the road-fork south of
Enna, and had seen applied in every attack since then.

From the Canadian lines we heard the guns of the
78th rumbling all night before Centuripe was taken,
and some Canadian batteries, in position around
Regalbuto, switched to targets in the 78th Division's
sector. Some forward elements of the 78th got into
Centuripe during the night but were driven out again
and in a masterly early-afternoon assault this Division,
as keen and skilled as any in the British Army, took
Centuripe and looked six miles over the Simeto River
valley to Aderno.

As Regalbuto fell, the Canadian Division leaped
forward and concentrated in the hills north of the
town for the attack down the valley of the Salso, which
links with the Simeto River valley in front of Aderno.

Canadian patrols were already pushing east, going
through the German lines to shoot up transport on
the roads and to lay mines. And through the high hills
on the northern side of the Salso valley the Edmonton
Regiment was fighting guerilla actions by platoons
and companies with spartan endurance under terrible
conditions.

German detachments held half a dozen of these
hills, heavily armed with mortars and automatic
weapons, and every hill they came to meant some kind

of a fight for these rugged troops from the farms, foot-hill ranches and northern communities of Alberta.

The Royal Canadian Army Service Corps organized a mule-transport company for this push through the mountains and located a dozen or so former western cowboys as the *cadre* for the company. Farmers and ranchers were taken from infantry and artillery units and put in this new company. Donkeys, horses and mules were rounded up on Sicilian farms from Enna to Regalbuto. They were a scruffy collection of animals when they reached the divisional area but the Canadians-turned-muleteers, delighted at working with horses and mules again, groomed them until they looked like horse-show entries.

Pack saddles were sent to the Division by Corps and the mule trains began to operate to the Edmontons in the mountains on the Division's left flank. The mule trains were mortared and machine-gunned and sniped as they trekked along the valleys and over the rugged, craggy hills but they got through to keep the Edmontons supplied with ammunition, water and rations.

While the Edmontons sweated their way through the mountains, Royal Canadian Engineers went forward from the Canadian area north of Regalbuto and, under continual fire from German mortars on the hills around them, built a road over the Salso river-bed and along the valley for the attack about to be made straight down the valley. This was a fine achievement for the Canadian sappers who already had done so well in the campaign.

The Edmontons skirmished and battered their way along the line of mountains and hills and came to Hill 736 and Mount Revisotto, about five miles northwest of Aderno. Major Archie Donald of Edmonton got a couple of platoons together and with the support of a couple of guns and a few mortars, the infantrymen stormed up the face of a cliff to knock the Germans off the top and capture Hill 736.

The strangest scene in the fight was a Canadian machine-gunner, crouched over his Vickers on another crest near Hill 736 with a battered Italian fedora he had picked up in a captured town, sweeping the top of the objective and pegging at every German who showed his head. After each long burst he jerked his fedora down over his eyes a little more as if chalking up another score.

While this little attack—but one which was completely successful and which was an integral part of the advance—was winding up, two companies of Edmontons went up the rocky slope of Mount Revisotto. It was a climb of at least two miles against German opposition all the way. With the determination that was a hall-mark of that great regiment, which I personally thought the finest in the 1st Division during the Sicilian campaign, the infantrymen reached their objectives on the crest and drove what were left of the German defenders down into the valley beyond.

The Edmontons' job was finished and they held firm on their hard-won crests, while the Seaforths and the Three Rivers tanks, with a squadron of the Princess Louise Dragoon Guards, reconnaissance unit of the Division, struck down the Salso River valley. With these troops went anti-tank guns and British self-propelled artillery.

The force fought its way for eight miles along the Salso valley, taking hills on its flanks and linking in with the Edmontons' advance directly to the north. The Seaforths and the tanks used the road the Canadian sappers had built, and their vehicles and transport whirled along the valley without danger of bogging in the loose sand or shale or running into mine fields.

On August 5 the main attack was launched to capture the high ground overlooking the Simeto River valley right in front of Aderno. It was a set-piece action and General Montgomery and General Simonds watched it from a hill-top.

First the "recce" squadron went forward. This squadron had landed with the Division at Pachino but had had tough luck most of the way, for there were few opportunities for it to carry out its proper role on the narrow, winding roads on which the Division had advanced.

But here in the last big fight, they had their chance and got to within three hundred yards of the ridge, when they were fired upon. As the fight began, the Seaforths were rushed forward, many of them riding on the turrets and hulls of the tanks and jumping off short of the objective. They assaulted the ridge on foot as the tanks shelled the Germans and the armoured cars of the P.L.D.G.s shot up the enemy with machine-guns.

Company after company of infantry joined in the battle. Lieutenant-Colonel Hoffmeister of the Seaforths rode with Lieutenant-Colonel Booth of the tank regiment in a tank from which they controlled the action as the fight roared on from hour to hour.

The infantry, with the tanks working near them, closed in on the Germans. In a final burst of fighting at from thirty to forty yards range, with the Seaforths tossing grenades like baseballs, the German force was routed after suffering extremely high casualties. The Seaforths and tanks stopped here and, under desultory mortar fire from Germans around Aderno, rested after carrying out what was almost a perfect manoeuvre in the eyes of the two generals on the hill-top.

Meanwhile, the Patricias were also moving east to the Simeto and they occupied Mount Seggio on the edge of the Simeto valley, after fighting their way over the slopes of the mountain crest.

Along the whole Eighth Army front from Aderno to Catania the German defence was breaking up. On August 6 we got word that Catania had fallen. British troops had entered it and the Germans who had held so long on the Catania front were retreating rapidly northward on the one road which goes through the bottleneck between Etna and the sea.

Misterbianco and Paterno, the two main towns between Catania and Aderno on the highway linking the two places, were also taken by the British.

The pressure of the 50th, 5th and 51st Divisions on the Catania front had forced the Germans to withdraw from the Simeto River line, retreat over the Gerbini plains and the great airfields and even leave Catania to the victorious Tommies.

The Canadian left-hook and the pressure of the 78th Division on Aderno had the effect General Montgomery wanted. The attack of these two divisions pinched the whole German flank and broke the Mount Etna line dead in its centre at Aderno.

The Germans had tried to save their fine defence line hinged on Catania and Etna but were forced by the growing threat on the western flank to send troops from Catania to Paterno and Aderno. It weakened them. It was useless for them to try to hold off the Eighth Army any longer and away they went north.

On the left of the Canadians, the Americans captured Troina and swept along the corkscrew road towards Randazzo, while farther north on the coast

road they were fighting their way past scores of road
demolitions. The work of the American engineers
was lauded by everyone who saw them at their job.

On that August 6 I drove through the Canadian
lines to within a few miles of Aderno and as we sat
in our jeep by the roadside American medium
bombers attacked the city, and several squadrons
circled over its southern side and let their bombs go.
A giant billow of grey-yellow smoke rose and drifted
up the side of Mount Etna.

Other squadrons followed up the attack by bombing
the north side and centre, and Aderno was blotted
out completely by the smoke.

There was no ack-ack fire. It was a strange, eerie
kind of bombing, and sitting there in the hot sun on
the dusty road something told us that the Mount Etna
line was broken and that the campaign was practically
over.

It was the same feeling you get on a Dominion
election night in a Canadian newspaper office with
results pouring in from all over the country. There
comes a time when the election tide turns one way or
the other and you realize that a certain party has won,
even though the official concession can not be made
until later.

That was the way I felt as I watched the bombers
wing back to base and saw Aderno smoulder and
smoke. I felt like shouting that the campaign was over,
that Sicily was ours. I had a queer elation and relief.
The long journey was nearly finished and soon we
could rest and sleep long hours, eat food at our leisure
and enjoy life after this grind from Pachino to Etna.

The Canadians had one more job to do and they
did it with a flourish. They occupied the west bank
of the Simeto, which bubbled cool and entrancingly

down from the springs on Etna. It was the first flowing
river we had seen in Sicily and it fascinated us just to
look at it and admire it gurgling past. We forgot the
dust and the heat that had become such a part of our
daily lives.

The Royal 22nd went over the Simeto in a night
foray and gained a firm bridgehead against minor
opposition. On the night of August 6-7, the 78th
Division went for Aderno with infantry going up the
road after a thundering artillery barrage had demolished what buildings were left following the bombing.

There was little fighting for Aderno. It was really
an occupation. After daylight I went into the city
with the East Surreys, a regiment I'd known well in
Tunisia, and saw the appalling devastation wrought
by our bombs and shells. For blocks and blocks, rubble
lay heaped in the streets and there was scarcely a house
or building which had not been blown apart. Dead
soldiers and some civilians were lying on the main
street and there were many bodies in the ruins. The
city smelled of death and gaping bomb-craters fur-
rowed its parks, their palm trees shredded by shrapnel.

The Surreys with the rest of the 78th Division
pushed north from Aderno along the road to Bronte
and Randazzo, and the 3rd Brigade merely held the
flank on the Simeto River. The campaign was over
for the Canadians. The 78th was taking up the chase
and would join the Americans for the final phase in
the northeast tip of Sicily.

Since July 10 the Canadians had been on the move.
Now they were out of the line for a rest and they
settled down right where they had stopped in the
verdant Simeto valley, beside the ice-cool river and
amid the orange groves and the vegetable gardens.
This was paradise.

They bathed in the river and there were swimming holes all along the banks where the Canadians were encamped. For most of us it was our first real bath since we had left Britain away back in June. So we luxuriated in the abundant fresh water and gorged on fresh tomatoes, oranges, peaches and grapes that grew there.

This was a happy camp for the weary Canadian warriors; and they remained there for three days as fighting went on and Bronte and Randazzo fell in quick succession.

*   *   *   *

In addition to the Canadian Division and the Three Rivers Tank Regiment, which were always on the extreme left of the Eighth Army, two other tank regiments, the Ontario and the Calgary, and headquarters of the 1st Canadian Armoured Brigade, which had come from Britain with the same convoy as the Infantry Division, were on the Catania front during the battle there.

It had been anticipated that a tank battle might be fought on the Gerbini plain south of Catania but it did not develop and the Canadian tankmen, anxious to get into action, stewed around for weeks without firing a shot. The big, burly, competent commander, Brigadier Bob Wyman of Edmonton, was fit to be tied.

His headquarters and the two regiments had landed at Syracuse after its capture, burning for action. They envied the Three Rivers tanks with the 1st Division, fighting almost daily as the Division bumped the Germans.

The Ontarios and Calgarys moved up to the Simeto River line south of Catania and as the bitter battle was fought out there, they were held in reserve behind the 50th and 5th Divisions.

Finally, as the Eighth Army advanced and occupied Catania, the Ontarios were given the assignment of supporting a British infantry brigade in an attack which swung around the west of the city and ended on lava slopes between Etna and the sea. It was not a large show and was comparatively easy, but the Ontarios were pleased they had seen at least some action. The Calgarys didn't draw any tasks and Brigade Headquarters did not have any battles of its own to fight but their turns came later in Italy.

*   *   *   *

All the Canadians were grouped together around August 12 in rest camps near Lentini, twelve miles south of Catania. And what a miserable place it was! We had our camp at Headquarters and there were bugs and mosquitos galore. One by one we took sick with dysentery or sand-fly fever or malaria. The sun seared the baked clay soil; as a rest camp it was a terrible failure. Some of the regiments were better off, for they were up in some hills, where it was cool at night and where the mosquito menace was not so serious.

In desperation we looked around for a building to live in, away from this depressing bivouac, and one of the officers found us the Villa at Acireale, a dozen miles north of Catania. It was a huge house, set among the vineyards on the slope of Etna, and from our balconies we had a magnificent view of the sea and the sweep of the coast and the toe of Italy in the mist to the north. We lived splendidly there.

By the 13th of August the German evacuation of their Sicilian force was in full swing across the Messina Straits and the British troops were having a slow time of it moving along the coast road through the luxury resort of Taormina towards Messina. Demolitions blocked their way at every turn and the cliff road was blown clear into the sea at some points. Sappers of a Canadian tunnelling company worked on some of the worst repair jobs.

The Americans were closing in on Messina on the north coast road, but they too faced frequent demolitions.

Day and night the Allied planes bombed Messina and the beaches on the Straits where the Germans were embarking for Italy. The flak concentrations around the Straits were tremendous and the Germans got most of their force out as the rear-guards and the demolitions held up the men of the Eighth and Seventh Armies.

To speed their advance a British brigade landed from the sea eight miles south of Messina, with infantry and tanks, and were promptly shelled from the Italian mainland. They found the roads badly cratered and their advance was tedious.

The fall of Messina was the only story left in the Sicilian campaign. On the morning of August 17 I went to Army Headquarters with two other correspondents for the usual morning conference with the Intelligence officer.

There was no one else there. All the other correspondents had gone off to witness the capture of the city and were stuck somewhere along the terrible roads.

An officer came out of his tent and casually said: "I've got a little news for you this morning. The city of Messina has fallen. The Americans entered it and British troops from the force that landed south of the city have also been in. That is about all. Oh, yes, our artillery is shelling the mainland now."

The Sicilian campaign was officially over. We

hammered out the story, got it away on the noon plane to Malta where the cable head was located. It was the first news to get out on Messina's fall. It was a hunch that took us to Army Headquarters that morning. Scoops in Sicily were made of flimsy stuff like that.

General Montgomery issued an order of the day on August 18, written in his usual trenchant style. This was it:

"The campaign in Sicily is over. We landed on this island on July 10. By July 20, together with our American Allies, we had driven the enemy into the northeast corner of the island. On July 30 I told you we would now drive the Germans out of Sicily. And by August 17 the Germans had been driven out and the Allied Armies, American and British, were in possession of the whole island. In February last the Italian overseas Empire had ceased to exist. Today, August 17, 1943, we have captured our first slice of the Italian home country. In these tremendous events you, the soldiers of the Eighth Army, have played a very notable part. By your splendid fighting qualities and devotion to duty you have helped change the whole course of the war. It is difficult to find words to tell you my true feelings. Since I assumed command of the Eighth Army in August, 1942, exactly one year ago, you have given me your confidence and you have never failed to respond to all calls I have made on you. I thank you all and I say to you: Well done. Well done, indeed. Together, you and I, we will see this thing through to the end. Good luck to you all."

It was signed B. L. Montgomery, General, Eighth Army.

There wasn't much to do now until the next job and we loafed at the Villa, ate well off a white tablecloth in a regular mess we had set up, wandered around

Catania and the little towns on Etna and went up to Taormina, the former luxury resort north of us on the coast where the wealthy came in peacetime to holiday from all over the world.

We bought coral jewellery and Sicilian trinkets and sent them home, tried to learn a little more Italian from the folks in the nearby town, and had friends to the villa for dinners and to share our wines.

It was a pleasant ten days and the troops were enjoying themselves as well. They swam in the sea, held sport meets in their camps and rested until they were back in top form again. They refitted and prepared for the next job which we knew was not far off. At Divisional Headquarters, the staff worked hard, with little time for relaxation, on the plan for the invasion of Italy.

General McNaughton came from England to see the Canadian troops and to look over the battle-fields where his men had fought. General Montgomery inspected the Canadians, too, and said, "I regard you now as one of the veteran divisions of the Eighth Army."

One day we went to Army Group Headquarters south of Syracuse and met General Sir Harold Alexander, the Commander. Urbane, grave and looking very much the Guards officer, he stood in his map-room tent and reviewed the campaign. He said the Germans had been in the wrong parts of the island to defend Sicily properly when the landings were made. Then they had been split up into battle groups and shuttled about. The German soldier was a magnificent fighter, though, even without air cover, but towards the end the enemy got very tired and the continuous attacks by the Allied forces had finally broken the defenders.

I asked him about the Canadians and he said with a smile that he had had excellent reports on them.

Back at the Villa, we continued to live in the grand style—a dozen correspondents with the conducting officers of the Public Relations unit and our drivers. I wanted it to go on for weeks, for most of us had recovered from bouts with fever and dysentery and life was very enjoyable there at Acireale.

But tanks, guns and vehicles, and hundreds of amphibious "ducks" were moving north on the coast road, choking it for ten miles at a stretch. On the last day of August we woke to see a British naval force of battleships and destroyers sailing north for the tip of Italy. Two hours later we heard the grumble of their guns. They were shelling Fort Hill at Reggio.

Allied guns on the Sicily side of the Straits had been engaging German and Italian guns on the opposite shore for days.

Our holiday was soon to be over.

XVI

FROM REGGIO TO THE PO

In THE Sicilian ports of Catania, Augusta and Syracuse as August ended, ships were loading with tanks, vehicles and stores, and on the sandy beaches between Taormina and Messina the landing craft were massing for the assault on the toe of Italy's boot.

From the mainland, the Italians and Germans saw the beaches become more crowded each day and watched great convoys of vehicles moving to the concentration areas along the one road skirting the sea at the foot of the mountains.

The 5th British Division moved to camps just south of Messina. Below them were the 1st Canadian Division and the tanks of the 1st Armoured Brigade. To these two assault divisions of the Eighth Army had been given the task of gaining the first foothold on the mainland of Europe.

In the early afternoon of September 2 we left our villa reluctantly, said goodbye to the comparative luxury and comfort we had enjoyed in the fortnight since Sicily was won, and drove north in our jeeps along the vehicle-jammed road to Saint Teresa de Riva, a hamlet by the coast eight miles north of Taormina. There Canadian Headquarters was located among the trees just off the dusty, noisy highway.

It took us most of the afternoon to make our way through the invasion traffic and reach Headquarters for a briefing by General Simonds.

Finally all the Canadian correspondents assembled

in the Commander's tent. Pointing to his battle map, he told us the plan. Tomorrow, the fourth anniversary of the start of the war, was D-Day for the invasion of Italy. We would land at dawn or shortly before. The Canadian Division would attack on a good beach north of Reggio, and between Reggio and San Giovanni, opposite Messina, the 5th British Division would land.

The 3rd Infantry Brigade was to lead the Canadian attack, followed in by the other two infantry brigades. Brigadier Penhale led the Brigade. The object was to gain a foothold on the mainland, free the Messina Straits for Allied shipping, capture Reggio and the airfield south of the city, and then move northeast into the Calabrian mountains to cut the lateral roads.

Four hundred guns would cover the landing from the Sicily shore, with warships operating in the Straits to lend more fire support with their big guns. The Eighth Army artillery already had complete domination over the landing area and every enemy gun which opened up now received a counter-battery blast from at least eighty guns from Sicily.

Nobody around Headquarters seemed certain whether it would be a tough landing or not. Some officers said it would be easy. Others shook their heads doubtfully and said, "Nice to have known you," when you told them you were with the assault brigade.

Commandos had gone ashore on the mainland a couple of nights before, landing at Melito on the bulge of the toe south of Reggio, but had not yet been able to send back much detailed information. Some of the landing parties had been shot up and the main force was scattered through the hills.

We left Headquarters with mixed feelings and I personally wasn't optimistic. This was my fourth landing of the war and I was beginning to wonder just how far my luck would stretch in these uncertain adventures in combined operations.

The 3rd Brigade was encamped at Mili Marina, seven miles across the Straits from Reggio.

So we hustled along the road, going north in the evening twilight, dodging through the traffic with our jeeps piled with kit and typewriters. The Sicilians sat outside the shops and their houses in the coast towns through which the convoys sped, waving and cheering the soldiers on their way. They seemed to know as well as we did that something was up. Your imagination began to play tricks and you saw sinister spies in those groups of grinning Sicilians.

Every few miles along the coast we passed transport and guns lined up on the beaches, traffic lanes marked with white tape, waiting to move onto landing craft. Everything was in readiness for the take-off and in the camps by the highway the troops were having their last meal in Sicily.

Just before dark we reached 3rd Brigade Headquarters in a small villa set off the road in a garden and hidden by trees.

Reggio seemed very close across the water and its white buildings stood out against the darkening hills and mountains rearing behind the largest city on the Italian toe.

From the beach the ground rose sharply and behind a few lines of hills and cliffs, the terrain rolled back to plateaus and a tangle of pine-clad mountains. Calabria looked forbidding and dangerous as darkness fell and the stars came out.

We talked with the 3rd Brigade staff, learned where we were placed in the assault craft, munched hardtack and bully-beef and lay down on the grass under the trees to wait for orders to move to the boats. Around Headquarters the troops were dispersed and groups of assault infantry sat around yarning and joking. Some of them sang "Mexicali Rose", following it up with a medley of tunes that drifted off into "Sweet Adeline" and rowdy army songs. They were light-hearted and eager.

The crossing of Messina narrows wasn't worrying these old campaigners. Now they knew how to relax.

Towards midnight red flares shot up from the Italian shore and the narrows was illuminated for miles. The flares drifted slowly down and then snuffed out in the water. Ten minutes later there were more and then it was dark again. We didn't know what to make of them but they did not contribute to peace of mind at this stage.

At one A.M. an officer walked from group to group and told us to prepare to go to the beach and to follow the guide along the white tapes marking out our path.

So we pulled on our webbing, adjusted our packs and formed up. There was no talking now. Everything was very still. We moved off to the crunch of boots on the gravel path and occasionally a heel-plate kicked a spark from a flint stone. Our route took us down the road and then through a lane to the beach, marked with dim coloured lamps. The landing craft were nosed up against the sand with ramps down.

Members of the beach organization guided us to the right craft and an officer with an Oxford accent gave orders in a very slow and steady voice through a megaphone. His voice sounded loud; you wondered if it would carry to Italy. The engines in the craft started up and they sounded much too noisy.

There was the crunch, crunch, crunch of a thousand boots on the sand and hobnails on the metal ramps as the infantry went aboard.

The Italian shore was quiet and dark. There were no more flares. The night was perfect for the attack, with sea calm and sky clear. A slight haze crept over the water now, and it was helpful.

I had expected German night bombers would attack the take-off beaches some time during the night and bomb in the light of flares, for the craft were close together on the shore and made a wonderful target. But there was no interference. The embarkation was carried out without a hitch; I had never seen a combined operation start so efficiently. There was none of the usual last-minute confusion.

I was in a craft with Brigadier Penhale, commanding the 3rd Brigade, as well as several Brigade staff officers and about a platoon of infantry. It was a flotilla leader and as we pulled off the beach I heard a Canadian voice giving orders to the naval crew. I wasn't much surprised for I'd found Canadian naval officers on many ships and craft in the Mediterranean, but after talking to this officer I discovered that it was a flotilla of the Royal Canadian Navy that was helping to take the Brigade to Italy that night. This was indeed a Canadian attack on the Reggio sector.

Our craft swung well clear of the beach and circled, while a dozen others joined us as we sailed into the Straits in the direction of San Giovanni. A strong current runs through the narrows and we had to cope with it by cutting across at an angle, heading into the current.

Flotillas of other landing craft were on our beam and the water along the Sicily shore was crowded with the invasion fleet as it crept into the stream. Those who saw this spectacle from the heights overlooking the Straits described it as the most dramatic sight they had ever seen.

In the assault craft it was just like any other landing
job. You were crowded into a corner between a couple
of riflemen and a jeep carrying the brigadier's wireless
set, and you stood on your kit to look over the bul-
warks. You didn't see much; just shadows of the
nearby craft, the white plume of their wash, the stars
and the clear sky. The air was cool and you buttoned
up your bush-shirt and wished you had put on an extra
one. Your tin hat pinched your head as usual and
felt heavy. Then you got very, very sleepy. Here you
were, getting into the middle of the Straits of Messina
on one of the great nights in history—and you felt
like dozing off. A sailor behind you was sound asleep
on a pile of kit and you stepped on him and he cursed
quietly as you apologized. An officer went to sleep
beside you and the two riflemen slumped down also,
and you lost your effective support in the packed little
craft.

The Canadian naval lieutenant gave orders to the
wheelsman. Except for the throb of the motors, that
was the only sound. You didn't fall asleep because
you knew that the artillery would open up at 3.30
A.M. Right on the dot the guns began to fire. First
the batteries near Messina flashed in the darkness; just
a dozen or so guns. Down the coast the flicker of gun-
flashes passed like a breeze whipping through wheat.
The sound reached us there in the stream and as we
watched and listened, the entire Sicily shore from
above Messina to Mili Marina, covering a distance of
about ten miles, flamed and flashed as if it were exploding in one destructive and supernatural eruption.

Hundreds of shells shrieked and whined over our
heads and the coast of Sicily was a long belt of dazzling
fire from the massed guns. The cannonading drowned
out every other sound.

As we reached mid-stream, tracer shells streaked from Sicily right across the Straits towards the beach north of Reggio where we were to land. These were from a heavy anti-aircraft gun, firing its red tracer as a navigational guide for our craft. The difficulty was, however, that the tracer seemed to curve as wildly as a hooked niblick shot and you couldn't get much direction from it.

As the barrage got under way, glaring blue beams from six searchlights reached straight into the sky. The searchlights were located at intervals along the coast south of Messina and they, too, were to aid the navy in its navigation.

Now we had the roaring, flame-spurting guns, the searchlights, the tracers, we smelled the cordite and gunpowder, and smoke mixed with the sea haze. Tense excitement now gripped the troops in those large flotillas of landing craft carrying the assault forces of two divisions across Messina Straits. Warships of the Royal Navy sailed slowly into the Straits and joined in the artillery assault on the coast, their big guns spouting flame and steel. The blast swept past us like a sudden, fierce gust of wind.

We were more than half-way across and mountains of Italy loomed black ahead. There had been scarcely a response from the enemy coast to our mighty bombardment. Now and then I saw flashes from the hills and from the beaches; they looked as if they might be guns firing. Some of them probably were, but such guns were quickly engaged by overwhelming force in a counter-battery shoot by the Eighth Army artillery.

It was less than three-quarters of a mile to the shore now and signalmen manning the wireless set in the brigadier's jeep put on their earphones and kept a listening watch. Wireless silence had to be observed until the first troops touched down, but then they would flash a report to the brigadier. These were the anxious moments.

The wireless came to life with a sputter. The Carleton and York Regiment, led by Lieutenant-Colonel John Pangman of Toronto, was reporting. The first companies had touched down at 5.15 A.M. on the correct beach north of Reggio. There had been no opposition. Ten minutes later Lieutenant-Colonel Pat Bogert reported that his West Nova Scotia Regiment had landed on the left flank of the Carleton and Yorks with no opposition. They had not been put down in exactly the right place, however, and were making their way south towards Reggio to advance on their objectives. The current in the Straits had played tricks with navigation despite all the precautions.

The artillery barrage, which had fired steadily for two hours, began to ease off, but several hundred guns were still shelling inland targets. Smoke and dust drifted over the Straits. We closed in on the shore through this choking pall as dawn broke.

The Royal 22nd Regiment was in craft around us and Lieutenant-Colonel Bernatchez came alongside in his landing craft to confer with Brigadier Penhale. The French-speaking unit was to land behind the Carleton and Yorks and we sailed along the coast to that beach with them, about one hundred and fifty yards off shore. Through patches of smoke we saw several big fires blazing in buildings on the northern outskirts of Reggio. Houses along the coast had been shattered by the barrage and the beaches were scenes of destruction. Reggio was smoking and troops were running over the beaches and marching along the beach roads. A British battalion, landed by mistake in the Canadian sector, was moving north in a long file towards San Giovanni.

More wireless reports came through from the Carleton and Yorks. They had entered the outskirts of Reggio and occupied the important bridge over which the main approach to the centre of the city had to be made.

So far there had not been any opposition, and then there were puffs of black smoke in the sky and the sound of exploding shells. German 88mm. guns were ranging on the landing craft. Some bits of shrapnel whined past. British guns lashed out from Sicily in a new outburst of firing.

Our craft swung into the beach. The ramp came down and we ran off to make a dry landing. It was even easier than at Pachino two months before. The beach organization was beginning to function and traffic lanes from the beach were being opened. The engineers prepared demolitions to blow away obstacles and clear the beach exits for the tanks and guns and transport that were following us in tank landing ships, now waiting in the narrows for the signal to beach.

We stacked our kit on the beach and went up the slope to the coast highway, swung right and caught up with the Carleton and Yorks as they occupied Reggio. The city was practically empty of civilians. One old lady who had endured the bombardment, stood by her ruined home and waved pathetically to us. She was nearly out of her head. A *carabiniere* came along on his bicycle, looking neat and friendly, and told us that the Germans had gone away in a great hurry.

The city was a shambles, with telephone lines hanging limply across streets littered with blocks of concrete, bricks and debris. For blocks and blocks there was not a house which had not been hit by shells, or by the bombs showered on Reggio in the days before the landing. Civilians had looted the wrecked shops. There had been no civil administration in the city for days and the civilians had run riot.

Italian coastal defence troops surrendered everywhere. They first came in by hundreds and then by battalions. Without guards they passed back to the beaches to be taken away.

On the main square in the centre of Reggio a few officers who remained formally turned over the city to the Canadians. The Carleton and Yorks went right through it and took over the airport two miles to the south.

The West Novas marched to the top of Fort Hill, a formidable fortress dominating the city and the beaches, and occupied it without the slightest trouble. The garrison had been hiding in the caves and among the rocks and gave itself up. The Royal 22nd advanced immediately into the mountains and, although they were fired on briefly by German guns, they passed target information back to British artillery and the guns were soon silenced.

This had been a ludicrously easy invasion of the European mainland—far easier than even the most optimistic commanders had expected.

Even the two-hour barrage by the four hundred guns and the warships scarcely seemed to have been necessary.

While this operation was being carried out with such success, and with very few casualties, the Italian armistice was signed in Sicily; this was something about which we were completely in the dark. It had been rumoured that negotiations were going on; that certain Italian aircraft had been given safe passage to Sicilian airfields on several occasions during the last two weeks. But we didn't know that Italy had capitulated. We went about Reggio, astounded at the lack of resistance. The Germans weren't going to let the Eighth Army have its bridgehead, though, without some interference and as we sat in a cave a few hundred yards from the main Reggio beach writing our landing stories, the tank-landing ships coming in were shelled by enemy batteries firing their parting shots from the mountains behind us. Shells splashed around the ships but none was hit and in ten minutes the shelling stopped. British self-propelled guns were ashore by now and they went into action, engaging targets along the mountain roads.

As we typed away, I heard the drone of planes and out of the sun darted a small flight of German fighter bombers. We fell flat in the cave mouth as they went into a long dive, and watched the red-painted bombs flash past the face of the cliff and explode on the beach near unloading landing ships. Flak guns fired from the ships and then the aircraft were gone. It was little more than a token raid. There were more of these small, nuisance attacks during the morning and afternoon of that first day, but our Bofors anti-aircraft guns were soon ashore and they made it highly dangerous for the hit-and-run planes, downing several of them.

The Ontario Tank Regiment landed with the 5th Division to the north of us and the 1st and 2nd Brigades followed the 3rd Brigade in on the Reggio beaches. They sailed from Saint Teresa.

Trucks and guns for the Division poured ashore and, after re-forming, the Canadians struck into the mountains towards Saint Stefano and Gambarie, and Delianuova on the first lateral road across Calabria. The long trek into southern Italy had begun and for the next two weeks the advance continued, with the Canadians travelling four hundred miles, overcoming scores and scores of big demolitions in roads and at bridges until they finally caught up with the German rear-guard at Potenza, east of Salerno Bay.

* * * *

In the hills behind Reggio we found fourteen Allied prisoners of war in a hospital. They had been released by the Canadians and now, overwhelmed with relief and joy, they waited in the ward to leave Italy. They were all badly wounded cases, some without legs or arms. They told us the story of the weeks preceding the invasion and of the terrifying experience of being on the receiving end of the Eighth Army barrage. They called it "colossal".

There were nine Britons, one Frenchman and an Arab who had been wounded and captured by the Germans in Tunisia and had been brought to this Reggio hospital, run by an Italian religious order. Three Americans were there too, survivors from a Flying Fortress which had crashed after bombing the city.

A company of German infantry, camped across the road until two days before, had suddenly packed up and rushed back into the mountains in trucks. Other German units had also been in Reggio and San Giovanni. They seemed to have been preparing to defend the beaches but at the last minute had withdrawn hastily.

The Allied prisoners could see the invasion preparations on the Sicily beaches from the roof of the hospital where they were allowed to exercise, and for days they had been puzzled why the attack had not come. They made bets among themselves on the time of the attack and planned to escape and cross the Straits to report to the British, but they could not get any guarantee from Italian friends that they could get a boat.

They realized the attack was on when the barrage opened up and shells fell close to the hospital. This building was a mile or so inland and it was not hit, being on the fringe of the heavy concentration zone.

At dawn they went to the roof to watch the invasion fleets stream over the narrows, and their Italian guards then stacked their guns in the corner and shrugged their shoulders. The war was over for them, they said, and they were nearly as delighted as the prisoners who watched their liberators come up the hill.

I have never seen such thankful men as these Allied soldiers now freed from their months of confinement. They had been treated well by the nuns in the hospital and by most of the Italian guards, but there was always the threat hanging over them that the Germans would move them farther into Italy. Talking to those happy released prisoners, choked up with emotion swelling from their relief and gratitude, was the brightest hour in that first day in Italy.

*   *   *   *

The Germans had about seven divisions in Italy at the beginning of September. One of them was in Calabria. The German Commander, Kesselring, saw the impossibility of defending the toe, and even the foot, with the Allies owning the sea, and decided to make his stand on the Naples line.

He even decided against suicide stands in the Reggio area, although it appears he played with this idea until a few days before the landing. Then he pulled out the defence force and ordered them to withdraw along the coast roads and through the mountains, the engineers blowing the roads and bridges as they went.

So as the enemy faded back, the 5th Division went up the west coast road and the Canadians made their way through the heart of the mountains, opposed by demolitions but little else. The elusive German rear-guards kept one day or two ahead of them.

By September 8 the 1st Division was working its way past Delianuova and in the late afternoon over the field wireless sets heard the news of the Italian capitulation. The little mountain hamlet of Delia-nuova went mad with excitement. Far into the night the celebration continued, with everyone in town treating the Canadians to bottles of *vino* and finally opening up the big demijohns.

The capitulation was the best news since we landed in Sicily and the elation of the troops was tremendous. One Canadian Commander, enthused at the prospects, told me he thought the war might be over by Christmas. And that wasn't his view only. He said it was a reflection of opinion held by some of those higher up.

The Allied armada was sailing to Salerno Bay that night and at dawn the Americans and British of the Fifth Army hit the beaches and the bitter battle for the beach-head began. The fight was touch-and-go for days and it was imperative that the Eighth Army push through southern Italy rapidly to relieve the pressure on the Fifth.

General Simonds drove the Division day and night. Through the mountains the Canadians pushed; the engineers worked wonders repairing roads and getting transport over the rough spots. The country was magnificent in its beauty and we had time to admire the great valleys and gorges, the pine forests and mountain hamlets, with their ski chalets, as we drove along. The air was clear and crisp and the mountains made you homesick, they looked so much like the Laurentians or parts of the Rockies.

The Canadians reached Cittanova and then swung

east to the east-coast road, going through Locri, on the coast and north to Catanzaro, the largest city after Reggio to be occupied.

Once the troops got out of the mountains the advance gained speed and the race through southern Italy became easier.

Ahead of the main body of the Division went the Locri Force, a battle group formed to spearhead the advance. It included a squadron of Princess Louise Dragoon Guards, a squadron of tanks from the Calgary Regiment, and a company of Carleton and York infantry. It made the reconnaissance and was ready to fight any rear-guard it caught up with. Over demolitions and around blown bridges it sped along to Catanzaro.

Supplies were moving up to the Canadians by sea now as well as by land. Royal Canadian Army Service Corps drivers were performing the virtually impossible, keeping their trucks rolling day and night over mountain roads where the slightest misjudgment in driving could mean death in a gorge hundreds of feet below. They equalled and even surpassed their fine job in Sicily as they maintained the Division over the lines of communications lengthening through rugged Calabria.

The Battle of Salerno still raged indecisively and the Germans were fighting fiercely to shove the Fifth Army into the sea. A British landing ahead of the 5th Division on the west coast had helped the advance, but it became more urgent than ever for the Canadians to reach Potenza. The columns sped to Cotrone on the bulging part of the Italian foot; led by a battle group of the West Novas and a squadron of Calgary tanks, the Division kept up the fast pace, raced along the road skirting the Gulf of Taranto, reached Rotondella, and then struck inland towards the goal of Potenza.

The four-hundred-mile move from Reggio was achieved in two weeks and it must have been a surprise to the Germans. It was made possible by masterly work on the part of the Canadian sappers, by determination on the part of the Locri Force and by the physical stamina of the troops themselves.

Not a formation rested for more than half a day at a time on that long and difficult journey into the first action at Potenza. Away back at Delianuova I went down with fever and after driving in a truck to Locri, trying to beat it off and keep up with the Division, found it had me beaten and at Locri I gave myself up to the Medical Corps.

It meant a long journey back to a field ambulance in Reggio, where I'd started this campaign, and I'd not been admitted to the field ambulance more than a couple of hours before it packed up and was off in pursuit of the Division far off in the mountains. I was transferred to a British casualty clearing station in a former Italian school and they drugged me for days with quinine until the malaria was under control.

In a week I was able to get out of the C.C.S. The Canadians were far up the coast, swinging along the Gulf of Taranto.

Propped up in a jeep and feeling mighty groggy from the effects of the quinine, I drove hard for three days to catch even the rear echelons of the Division and it wasn't until I got on the Potenza road that I finally reached Divisional Headquarters again.

Once it got going on clear roads, the Division rolled like mercury.

*   *   *   *

Potenza was the most modern city we had seen in Italy to that time. It was built on the northern slope of a broad valley and a line of fine new apartment blocks stretched along the south side, a few hundred yards up the slope from the railway yards and the junction of several main roads.

This city was important to the Germans for the railway and for the roads. Detachments of German parachutists had been rushed from Salerno Bay to oppose the Canadians speeding north through the mountains. The West Novas and the tanks leading the Division came within sight of the city at nightfall on September 18 and apparently surprised the enemy by arriving so soon.

The German force was not large. They had probably intended to pack in more troops and make a firm defence at Potenza but the Canadians moved right in on them, with the sappers clearing the approaches to the city of mines and obstacles. The bridges over the dried-out river-bed, which made a deep gouge in the valley, had been blown shortly before the Canadians entered the valley.

The infantry and tanks advanced through the valley in the darkness and just before midnight the leading patrols bumped the first enemy machine-gun posts. Tracer bullets flashed and there were skirmishes near the apartment houses and in the railway yard where the parachutists had dug in or set up machine-guns behind strong brick and stone walls.

In the morning Canadian artillery shelled the city and it was enveloped in billows of smoke as high explosives crashed down. The parachutists hung on until shortly after noon, when the Canadian tanks surged through the valley, clanked across the river-bed and roared across the devastated railway yard into the city. Their guns fired 75mm. shells and machine-gun bullets into the apartment houses and the infantry stormed into the city close behind them.

The brief siege was over. A few German prisoners were taken, the first of the Italian campaign for the Canadians, and others who had not been killed in the fight scurried north into the hills. The Division rolled up to Potenza on the heels of the advanced guard and in the hills around, the units rested for ten days, the first real respite for the troops in the long advance from Reggio.

Patrols went north on the Melfi road and also prodded westward to establish contact with the 5th British Division and elements of the Fifth Army which had won its battle at Salerno and was now pressing the Germans back on Naples.

While the Canadians pushed north towards Potenza from the Calabrian mountains, Taranto had been occupied by British infantry and British airborne troops had been brought in by sea to occupy the heel of Italy and fan out towards Bari on the Adriatic coast. Other British formations followed this force in and the Eighth Army grew steadily in strength for the big push north along the Apennines and the east coast. The Allied line across Italy was taking shape.

Allied fighters had been flying from Italian bases for ten days and now the medium bombers were beginning to operate from airfields on the mainland. German air opposition was negligible and the havoc of our bombing was seen in every town through which we passed.

At Potenza, for example, the railway yard and the junctions had been devastated. Railway engines, trucks and trains had been blown to pieces and the wreckage lay heaped by the siding. The city itself had been hit in several spots and road junctions had been cratered.

As in Sicily, it was the same story all along our route. The railway yards had been hit heavily at places like Catanzaro, Controne and Locri. In many towns, the bombing had filled whole streets with rubble; this delayed our advance until the bulldozers came up and cleared away the debris.

Not much had been missed by the medium bombers. Even in the mountains, you would see bomb craters and wrecked houses, and at one lonely town where there was a small railway junction I counted fifty bomb craters on and around the junction.

The German rail communications had been completely crippled by this air assault, methodical and relentless for weeks.

You felt sorry for the poor Italian civilians. When the trains stopped, their supplies stopped, and frequently you'd hear the townfolk say they were starving because the "train from Naples hasn't come".

*   *   *   *

At Potenza I left the 1st Division and the Italian war to return to England for a rest and to get fit again for the Second Front attack which we felt then would come by the following March. It was a premature forecast as it turned out, but at the time it seemed to be a strong possibility.

It had been the finest assignment any Canadian correspondent could have wished for—covering the "Red Patch" Division from Pachino to Potenza—and I tossed my kit in the truck that sparkling autumn morning in front of Potenza with sincere regret at leaving so many good friends in such a fighting outfit.

I'd lived with them at the front and written a hundred thousand words or more about their campaign. Now I was going—after three months of watching their battles and sharing their grub and their bivouacs.

It was almost like saying goodbye to your family.

You were saying goodbye to men whom you hoped you'd know as friends for the rest of your life.

From General Simonds and his Headquarters staff, down through the brigades and battalions, and throughout the 1st Armoured Brigade, everyone had helped me, as they helped the other correspondents, to gather the campaign news.

But I was glad to be going away from the heat and the dust of the roads and the camps, to be leaving the mosquitos and the flies, for London and the other Canadian camps by the quiet towns of southern England.

For the better part of a year I'd been covering the Mediterranean war and had seen Allied fortunes rise from the muddy stalemate in the Tunisian mountains to the flaming victories that carried the British, American and Canadian troops down the bloody road to Rome. I was getting very weary.

Still, as I drove out of our camp that morning for the airfield down on Taranto Bay where I got the plane for Catania and Algiers, I found that deep down I hated to go.

Comradeship of war is a gripping thing; and it is hard to break away from it. As we drove south through the mountains, I thought of the stormy night off the Pachino beaches and the dramatic landing; the stirring climb of the Hastings and Prince Edward Regiment at Assoro and the battle of the 2nd Brigade at Leonforte; I remembered the stories of the struggle of the Royal 22nd Regiment at Catenanuova—the hill of Santa Maria; the rugged Edmontons in the mountain push to the Simeto; the crossing of Messina Straits.

I thought of good friends lying now in the graves by the roadsides of Sicily under white crosses, with their helmets on the mound of earth.

I remembered the flaming night barrages and the long log of towns which had fallen to the Canadians. I remembered the cheerful greetings you'd always get from these fighting men as you visited the front, no matter how tough the going.

A hundred more memories of the magnificent 1st Division crowded on my mind as I flew back to England. It is a gallant outfit.

*   *   *   *

At Potenza, General Simonds contracted jaundice and Brigadier Chris Vokes became temporary Commander of the Division. General Simonds had shown brilliant leadership and had won a fine name for himself and his troops in the Mediterranean. He was marked for promotion; it was inevitable. Later in the year he took command of the 5th Division which came to Italy in November with the 1st Canadian Corps, but he did not rest long there. He returned to England for the Normandy invasion.

It was at Campobasso in late October that Brigadier Vokes was promoted to major-general and given full command of the 1st Division. Here was a completely different type of soldier from dapper, polished General Simonds. General Vokes was bluff and rough, and had done a fine job with the 2nd Brigade right from Pachino. It was difficult for anyone to succeed Simonds, who had had such achievements, but Vokes filled his shoes capably and the Division went on to fight some of its greatest battles and win some of its most shining victories under his command.

In late September, the Division moved from Potenza east to Gravina and then north through Spinazzola and Canosa and along the hard black macadam road sweeping across the Foggia plains, where clusters of fine airfields were located.

A "Jock Column" headed the Division and the town of Foggia was occupied without opposition. From Foggia the Division turned west again, going into the rugged Abruzze hills as the fall rain started. It was the herald of terrible weather that was to plague it through the winter with cold and mud.

Twenty miles west of Foggia the 1st Brigade caught up with the Germans at Motta, a hamlet in the hills where the highway becomes a corkscrew.

The Royal Canadian Regiment attacked behind artillery concentrations of medium and field artillery and with the support of the Calgary Tank Regiment. On October 2, the regiment took Motta, while the Hastings and Prince Edward Regiment went through the hills on the north on a back-breaking cross-country march to take Monte Miano, which dominates the San Marco ridge.

The 48th went through the R.C.R.s and took Volturara, six miles down the road from Motta, and then the Royal 22nd Regiment of the 3rd Brigade went on towards Gambatesa, another eight miles along the road, in the face of fierce shelling.

The 2nd Brigade worked through the hills on the south of the 3rd and 1st Brigade axis, and the Seaforth Highlanders and the Loyal Edmonton Regiment cleaned out Baselice and Castelvetere.

The rain kept falling and the troops made their way laboriously up greasy slopes and muddy trails and roads. Transport bogged in quagmires. Mule trains, driven by North African Arabs, were used as the Canadians slogged forward through this sodden country.

Gambatesa fell to the Carleton and Yorks after the West Novas captured the heights around the town, and eight miles to the south the Seaforths fought a brisk action against German tanks and self-propelled guns.

On the main road the Royal 22nd captured Jelsi, and now the Division began to close in on Campobasso.

The Germans kept withdrawing behind heavy artillery and mortar fire that hounded the Canadians as they moved from hill to hill and town to town.

Finally on October 13, the R.C.R.s occupied Campobasso in a strong attack with the Hastings and the 48th. The opposition they had expected did not develop.

Six miles southwest of Campobasso, at Vinchiaturo, the enemy offered strongest resistance and fought the 2nd Brigade with tanks and guns, even employing railway artillery before pulling out to fall back on the Biferno River. This stream flows through the hills north of Vinchiaturo and Campobasso.

The Canadians followed up the capture of these two important towns by marching on the German positions along the Biferno on a twenty-mile front.

Strong artillery concentrations aided the advance, and air support was provided for the infantry as they swept over the brown and green mottled hills and shook the enemy loose from the dozen towns they held on the Biferno.

For days the great artillery barrages raged and there were violent duels with enemy guns hidden in the muddy hills.

The Division attacked with the 2nd Brigade in the centre, the 1st on the right and the 3rd on the left, and after a twelve-mile march the Seaforths stormed a ridge to capture Baranello, and cleared the town house by house in close combat.

This was the first chief objective to be taken on the south side of the Biferno and it was followed by an

attack by the Hastings which bagged the towns of
Montagano, on a 2,500-foot hill, and San Stefano.
The Germans resisted these thrusts particularly with
their mortars and artillery, and even when the towns
fell and they had withdrawn they hit the Canadians
hard with shells and bombs.

On the left flank the Carleton and Yorks went across
country and took Guardiaregia, six miles south of
Vinchiaturo, and the Canadian artillery moved up
swiftly into new gun positions to plaster Campochiara
with twenty-five-pounder shells.

The attack over the Biferno River itself now was
ready and it was the Edmontons, who fought so well
in Sicily, who won the first bridgehead. At night they
waded the icy river and by dawn had advanced two
thousand feet up the opposite slope to the outskirts of
Colle d'Anchise. The Alberta infantry had been protected by a thick fog and when it lifted with the dawn
they were heavily engaged and fought all day against
the enemy on the slope and around the town. They
were shelled and mortared and enemy tanks prowled
the slope but they fought back and by nightfall the
Germans had had enough. They retreated and the
Canadians had their first grip on the north side of the
Biferno.

The Princess Patricia's Canadian Light Infantry
followed up the Edmontons' success, crossed the river
and took the battered town of Spinete, four miles
farther into the German territory.

Meanwhile the 1st Brigade on the right crossed the
river too, with the R.C.R.s first fording it under shell-
fire, followed by the 48th. The Highlanders battled
their way right to Torella and the Hastings came up
fast to capture the neighbouring town of Molise.

The 3rd Brigade worked its way north over the

head-waters of the Biferno, and by November 7 the German line on the Biferno had been shattered by this three-brigade attack.

The Division held firm on the hard-won Biferno River line and back in the mountains at Campobasso the Canadians found a haven from battle. It was re-named Canada Town and the big square in the heart of the town was called Piccadilly Circus. The Auxiliary Services opened an officers' club and called it Aldershot Officers' Club, and the other ranks had their Beaver Club, named after the famous rendezvous for Canadian servicemen in London. There were movies and recreation rooms. Thousands of Canadian soldiers remember Campobasso as Canada Town where they enjoyed some of their best times in Italy.

The crossing of the Biferno marked the end of the second phase of the Canadians' campaign in Italy, but as the 1st Division consolidated on the northern slopes of the river, Canadian tanks of the Three Rivers Regiment were in action on October 6 in a battle at Termoli, forty miles from the Canadian area and at the mouth of the Biferno River.

To complete the Eighth Army line on the Biferno, the 78th British Division was coming north along the coast road and British commandos had made a small landing at Termoli on October 2. A strong German force was moving on the seaside town, however, and on the morning of October 6 the Irish Brigade landed from the sea, ahead of the main force of the Division still miles down the coast.

The Three Rivers Regiment had been ordered, on October 5, to rush across country forty miles to Termoli to support the Irish Brigade and the beleaguered defenders of the town. The Canadian tanks roared through the night and went into action without even time to refuel, although they had scarcely enough gasoline in their fuel tanks to last the day.

On the outskirts of the town the battle was joined with the Canadian tanks and some from the City of London Yeomanry fighting about thirty German Mark IV specials, with added armoured plating around the turrets and long 75mm. guns.

At ranges often less than one hundred yards the tanks locked in a slithery struggle that raged over the greasy fields and through the olive grove just outside Termoli. It was as bitter fighting as any of the men of the Eighth Army had known in Italy. The Germans pressed their attacks so far that once they got right into the streets of Termoli before they were driven back.

The fighting stormed back and forth all day and by late afternoon the Canadians had knocked out ten German tanks and the City of London Yeomanry had accounted for four. The Canadians lost only two.

The Germans were driven from a cemetery they were holding on the flat farmland and also off a commanding ridge. The battle was won and the British infantry moved up and held the ground.

That wild cross-country dash and action fought by the Three Rivers tanks had saved Termoli. The 78th Division was given a firm base for the advance on the Sangro River, thirty-five miles to the north.

*   *   *   *

On the north bank of the Sangro River, the Germans had constructed what they intended to be their winter line on the Adriatic. Here they hoped to hold off the Eighth Army, possibly until spring. It was an extremely strong position, and a great deal of labour had gone into the construction of dug-outs, gun positions and trench systems. The Sangro is about forty

yards wide and was flowing swiftly in flood in late
November through a three-mile-wide, sweeping valley.

This was the obstacle that the 78th Division, with
the Indians and the New Zealanders, tackled while the
Canadians made ready to pass through them and
strike north.

In weather that even General Montgomery described
as "appalling", with rain lashing the muddy battle-
ground, the Eighth Army slashed at the German
positions.

It took a week of wet and bloody fighting, but by
November 24 the 78th Division had won a bridgehead
over the swollen river near its mouth and the German
defence crumbled. The Germans, staggered by the
loss of the Sangro line, fell back on the Moro, ten miles
farther north, and rushed up new defensive positions.

The 78th Division advanced along the coast road as
far as the Moro valley and the Canadians followed
them up and took over.

The three-week battle for the Moro valley and
Ortona opened on December 6, when the Princess
Patricias and the Seaforth Highlanders swung off the
San Vito-San Leonardo road, jumped over the narrow
Moro River and took up positions around the hamlet
of Roatti, four miles from the Adriatic.

The Germans of the 90th *Panzer* Grenadier
Division, holding the Moro line, counter-attacked
immediately and the Seaforths were forced back. The
Patricias hung on and then were withdrawn too, south
of the Moro. The Indian Division, which had fought
on the Sangro, moved up into this area and the Canadians now concentrated on crossing the river and
valley south of San Leonardo, a mile and a half from
the mouth of the river.

While the abortive Roatti attack was being made on

December 6, a diversionary thrust was carried out by the Hastings and Prince Edward Regiment over the river at the coast and this thrust was a success which had not been anticipated. One company got over the river and was able to hold its gain, and the rest of this battalion went forward and joined it.

The Germans were extremely strong on the coast sector, however, and seemed to be concentrated astride the coast road in greater strength than on the other road which winds inland through San Leonardo.

It was logical for the Germans to expect the Canadians to make the main attack along the coast road, and perhaps it was a fluke that the Canadians didn't. But on the maps the Canadians were using, and from which the preliminary battle plans were made before a reconnaissance could be carried out on the terrain itself, the coast road, which actually was the main road, was erroneously shown as a very poor secondary track. The road through San Leonardo was shown to be the main road, while it actually was the secondary road.

The Canadians launched the main attack up the San Leonardo road. I'm not certain whether the faulty maps explained the direction taken but at any rate the enemy had to do some rapid switching of dispositions from the main highway on the coast to meet the strong Canadian attack on the inland road.

The Hastings on the coast were being hammered day and night by German guns and mortars but they held their positions north of the river and stubbornly refused to budge, beating off one counter-attack after another.

On December 8, the Royal Canadian Regiment and the 48th Highlanders opened the main attack for the San Leonardo bridgehead and after a stormy barrage by Canadian and British guns, in which the three field regiments of Canadian artillery alone fired more than 23,000 twenty-five-pounder shells, the infantry stormed up the slope on the north side of the Moro.

The R.C.R.s went around on the right of San Leonardo and the 48th occupied ground on the left and were able to hold there.

The enemy attacked the R.C.R.s with tanks, self-propelled guns and heavy artillery fire and for twenty-four hours the combat raged. At one point a company was in the streets of San Leonardo for a while.

The R.C.R.s performed wonders in that *mêlée* and inflicted far more casualties on the enemy than they suffered, but the persistence of the German counter-attacks forced a change in plans and the regiment was withdrawn, in good order, back across the Moro.

The 2nd Brigade was put into the battle the next day, and the Seaforths and Patricias swept forward to capture San Leonardo and moved up the winding road which joins the Ortona-Orsogna highway at a cross-roads about two miles north of that town.

The Loyal Edmonton Regiment went into action on December 10 and drove north and east of San Leonardo, meeting stiff resistance. The Germans contested every yard of ground.

The Carleton and York Regiment leap-frogged the Patricias north of San Leonardo and went for the cross-roads, but the enemy was entrenched in a gully just south of the cross-roads and would not yield.

The grimmest and hardest action that the Division had fought until then was waged over rich, rolling farmland, with the pale blue Adriatic on the east and the snow-capped Apennines on the west. From the Moro the land rolled back in verdant shoulders separated by sloping valleys with their olive groves, farm-houses and green-brown fields. The black earth was damp and soggy from the rains and the fields were criss-crossed with ruts of tanks and vehicles and guns.

Day after day, and every night, the Moro valley echoed to the thunder of barrages fired by nine artillery regiments supporting the Canadian attack, with guns of the Indian Division on the left joining in when convenient targets offered.

The German guns answered with more earthshaking salvos and even Canadian Headquarters back on the road near San Vito, which seemed a "safe" distance behind the line, was shelled. Rear Divisional Headquarters itself was bombed and strafed, and there were few spots in the valley where you could feel immune from German fire.

The Saskatoon Light Infantry, the support battalion of the Division, had a real opportunity here to fire its new 4.2 mortars and to employ its Vickers machineguns. Previously the regiment had been able to get into action only in comparatively small groups, but here on the Moro it did everything it wanted.

*   *   *   *

Allied bombers shuttled back and forth over the German lines, hitting them with high explosives, and Allied fighters provided continual cover.

For the first time in the Canadians' experience the German Air Force really joined in the battle and fighter bombers and fighters made daring raids, dropping bombs and shooting up camps and positions.

On both sides of the Moro there were strong concentrations of anti-aircraft guns. The river was the dividing line. The black puffs of bursting flak north of the river would indicate the German ack-ack and in a clean-cut line south of the river you could see the white puffs of the Canadian flak.

Tanks of the 1st Canadian Armoured Brigade worked right with the infantry from the start of the battle to the end, churning up the sodden soil of the valley and engaging every enemy target with their 75mm. guns and machine-guns.

To break the deadlock at the cross-roads, troops of the West Nova Scotia Regiment and some tanks went west from San Leonardo to try and cut the Ortona-Orsogna lateral road. This combat group was joined by a depleted company of Seaforths and the Highlanders with some tanks worked their way on to the lateral road.

This small detachment of infantry and tanks then swung east on the road, proceeding towards the cross-roads, and the coast and the Canadians knocked out three tanks and took a number of prisoners. This little sortie revealed that the Germans were weak on that particular sector and that an attack over the lateral highway would likely succeed.

But before the attack that put the Canadians across the road, the Royal 22nd Regiment exploited the success of the combat group on the left flank, and stormed and captured the tiny settlement of Berardi. The French-speaking infantrymen were supported by tanks, and it was here that the then Captain Paul Triquet won the Victoria Cross—the first awarded in Italy—when he led his company, with the tanks alongside his men, across a heavily-defended gully and into the enemy-held hamlet.

His company was the spearhead and when the rest of the battalion came into Berardi the next day, only Captain Triquet and nine men from his company were still in action.

The 90th German Division had been badly mauled by these continual Canadian attacks along the Moro front and on December 15 it was withdrawn from the line and replaced by the 1st German Parachute Division, the best defensive formation of the German Army then in Italy.

It was inevitable that the Canadian Division had to stop for a breathing spell after ten days' constant fighting but on December 18 the R.C.R.s and the 48th attacked on the left flank where the combat group of Seaforths and tanks had found the German line thin.

A four-hour barrage, in which field guns alone fired one hundred thousand rounds, preceded the attack and a force of infantry and tanks smashed over the highway. They gained positions northwest of the cross-road and the gully which had been contested so long.

The second wave in the attack ran into heavy opposition and found difficulty in reaching objectives north of the highway. The Germans continued to resist at the cross-roads and particularly in the gully.

But the German defence along the highway had been pierced by this attack of the 1st Brigade infantry battalions and the tanks, and the battle for cross-roads and gully was also about won. The Carleton and Yorks cleaned out the gully. December 19 was "mopping up" day along the highway as the Edmontons moved on Ortona itself.

On December 20, the Edmontons fought their way into the outskirts of the town and for the next eight days this regiment and the Seaforths, who followed the Edmontons in, battled from house to house and finally cleared the town of the German paratroops, who resisted with fanatical zeal.

The Edmontons went into Ortona from the southwest along the lateral road from the cross-roads, while the Seaforths went up the coast road from the south from positions which the Hastings had been holding.

Both Canadian and German artillery shelled the approaches to Ortona, with its normal population of eleven thousand, as the attack was launched and the town, on a cliff two hundred feet above the sea, was shrouded in smoke and dust.

Canadian tanks moved in with infantry, firing as they descended on Ortona. The roads were heavily mined and sappers had to go ahead to clear the route and check for booby-traps.

Street fighting developed as soon as the two Canadian units got among the houses. The town was about a mile long and the Edmontons began to work through the eastern two-thirds by the sea, with the Seaforths handling the western section.

The tanks rumbled about the streets, firing into houses and laying smoke screens, and anti-tank guns were brought into Ortona to blast away walls and drive out the paratroops who made each solid stone house a fortress.

Germans were all over the town and from room to room, house to house, and street to street, the battle raged. This surpassed anything the Canadians had seen in battle for close-quarters ferocity. One German tank was in Ortona and its crew finally ran it into a cellar, collapsed the building on top of it and used it as a stationary gun-post.

The streets were piled with the wreckage of buildings and as the fight roared to its climax, Ortona took on the appearance of a Roman ruin.

From the hills north of the town the Germans fired their *Nebelwerfers*—six-barrelled rocket mortars firing a huge bomb about two feet long and eight inches thick, loaded with one hundred pounds of high explosive. They crashed into the Canadian lines with a sound like the end of the world.

The weather was cold and miserable and the sky overcast, and in this turmoil of battle the Edmontons and the Seaforths spent their first Christmas in action.

It was far from being a merry Christmas, but the Seaforths held a party in a church a few score yards away from a German position and every platoon on every ruined street had some kind of Yuletide celebration, with extra rations and even some fowl.

The Germans barricaded themselves in houses and strong buildings, and the Canadian engineers and infantry had to dynamite their way through floors and walls to get them out. Very few of the enemy surrendered in this Little Stalingrad of the Adriatic. Several who tried to surrender were shot by their comrades. One German machine-gunner was blinded by shrapnel but kept firing his gun by sound, with blood pouring from his head wounds, until he was captured. He spoke defiantly to his captors even then and said: "I'm a good German soldier. I hope my son grows up to be a good German soldier." He wouldn't give in.

It was on Christmas Day that the Germans used flame-throwers against the Canadians and they went into action with a blistering roar, shooting streaks of flame seventy-five yards. Canadian anti-tank guns shot them up and prevented them from being effective.

As the street fighting continued without let-up, troops of the 1st Brigade attacked enemy positions covering Ortona's western flank and fought all Christmas Day in the wet gullies under fire.

Along the whole flaming front the men of the Medical Corps performed valiant deeds, bringing out the casualties and tending the wounded as they fell. And the padres worked with them, comforting the dying and helping with the injured.

By December 27, the German defenders had been

driven to the northern end of the town and the pressure from the west was becoming more menacing to the enemy. Their escape route from Ortona was threatened.

The next day, the Germans gave up the struggle. They retired from Ortona and withdrew three miles up the coast to a hill called "Point 59", from which they were driven by the Carleton and Yorks. They later fell back on the Arielli River line.

Unshaven, their uniforms in tatters, nearly exhausted, but triumphant, the Seaforths and Edmontons relaxed.

It rained and it was cold and the front became quiet, with little activity other than patrols. The Canadians had won their greatest victory since the landing at Pachino.

*   *   *   *

The victory at Ortona was not achieved cheaply. The Division's losses were heavier in that action than at any time since they landed in Sicily. From September 3 to January 8, the official figures covering the Moro and Ortona battles and the few actions before them showed casualties were 3,869—with 879 killed, 2,841 wounded and 149 missing. In the whole period from July 10 to November 23, which included the entire Sicilian campaign, they were only 3,453.

But the Canadians had driven the 90th German Division out of the Moro line and had mauled the 1st Parachute Division badly, particularly in the battle through the streets of Ortona.

*   *   *   *

General Crerar, then the 1st Corps Commander, came out with his staff and established Headquarters temporarily at beautiful Taormina in Sicily.

In late January, 1944, however, the entire Corps was concentrated on the Adriatic sector of the Eighth Army line and here the two Canadian divisions—the 1st and the 5th—maintained pressure on the German forces fending the Eighth Army off from the vital Pescara-Chieti-Rome highway.

The Canadians made several sallies against the Arielli River line, where the enemy held during those winter months. But these efforts were more in the way of giving the new formations battle training than anything else. The weather was too inclement to attempt a full-scale offensive on the Adriatic sector but the Corps proved in those days that it could rapidly pick up the angles of campaigning. Constant patrolling was done and General Crerar handled his command extremely well in this period of comparative lull.

In the late winter he returned to England and was given command of the First Canadian Army. Lieutenant-General E. L. M. Burns took over command of the Corps in Italy and Brigadier Hoffmeister, who was commanding the 2nd Brigade and had previously led the Seaforths, was promoted major-general and given command of the 5th Division.

In April the Canadian Corps moved from the Adriatic sector in deepest secrecy and concentrated on the Cassino front for the great attack down the Liri River valley towards Rome.

In mid-May the attack developed and the Corps, fighting a full-scale action for the first time, rolled up the Germans in its path and struck a mighty blow for the Eighth Army as it flooded down the Liri valley, while the Fifth Army cracked at the enemy along the west coast and linked up with the Anzio-Nettuno bridgehead.

The Canadian Corps was the formation which pierced the vaunted Hitler Line behind Cassino and paved the way for the push down Highway 6—the home stretch to Rome.

*   *   *   *

First Canadians in the new battle were veteran tank crews of 1st Armoured Brigade who supported the 8th Indian Division in crossing the deep, fast-flowing Rapido River in the early hours of May 12. A few hours earlier a barrage of 2,000 guns, many of them Canadian, signalled the start of the two-army offensive.

The Canadian Corps was the ace in the hole in this spring drive and was held in reserve for nearly a week until British troops of the 4th Division and the Indians, with their Canadian tanks, had smashed through the stubborn, prepared defences of the Gustav Line. General Vokes' experienced 1st Division infantry were chosen to lead the Canadian assault.

They took over from the Indians after the fall of Pignataro and pushed rapidly to the Hitler Line. Two feints, by the 48th Highlanders on the left and the Royal 22nd on the right, proved the line as strong as was feared and a two-brigade assault was teed up for May 23.

The Carleton and Yorks, the Seaforths and Patricias led the way. Eight hundred guns fired an opening barrage, then the Canadians, with support from British-manned Churchill and Sherman tanks, went in.

The fighting that day was as bloody as anything at the Moro, for the Germans had prepared their defences for months and had the support of a large number of tanks, self-propelled 75mm. and 88mm. guns and innumerable mortars and machine-guns. Casualties were heavy, but by evening a hole was carved through the line and the Royal 22nd, West Novas and Edmontons mopped up.

That same night General Hoffmeister's Division began to pass through the 1st Division and when morning came, the Germans were on the run. The pace set May 24 by this Division, getting its first real battle test, was terrific. At three o'clock in the afternoon reconnaissance tanks of the Lord Strathcona's Horse and a company of infantry crossed the Melfa River, five miles beyond the Hitler Line. This was three days ahead of schedule.

Once at the Melfa, the Germans tried to make a stand, throwing in Panther tanks, but the Canadians forced the enemy beyond the wide-bedded stream after the fiercest tank battles since Termoli. Sixteen German tanks or self-propelled guns were knocked out for a similar Canadian loss.

The Melfa battle brought Canada her second Victoria Cross of the Italian campaign. It went to Major J. K. Mahony, New Westminster, B. C., who took his company of the Westminster Motor Battalion across the river with the "recce" tanks and held on, though wounded, against repeated counter-attacks until reinforcements arrived.

From the Melfa the Canadians moved swiftly as the Germans withdrew their beaten troops. Mines, mortars, shells and occasional machine-guns were the chief opposition, and General Hoffmeister's infantry and armour pushed forward out of the Liri valley into the Sacco, through the towns of Ceprano, Pofi and Arnara.

Then the 1st Division continued the pursuit through Frosinone, Ferentino and Anagni, near where the link-up between Canadians of the Eighth Army and Americans of the Fifth ended that phase of the Corps' Italian campaigning. Both divisions began a long rest period a few days before Rome fell.

It had been a brilliant and successful inauguration for the Corps. Casualties were heavy, 2,000 including 412 killed and 271 missing, but it paved the way for the capture of Rome and went a long way towards achieving one of the main objectives of the campaign —to kill and capture Germans. The enemy lost 1,711 prisoners to the Canadians and their losses in dead and wounded must have been equally great.

* * * *

Canadian troops—a small group of them—fought too with the Fifth Army during the winter in the gruelling mountain warfare on the Cassino front.

They were members of the American-Canadian Special Service Force and they did themselves proud in that rugged fighting. These men originally were members of a Canadian parachute battalion but were merged with the American Special Service troops to form this unique super-commando outfit. They trained for months in Montana and were skilled airborne troops as well as men versed in commando and guerrilla tasks.

This same force later fought in the Anzio-Nettuno bridgehead, and the Canadians in it were the only troops from the Dominion to share in that struggle, which had its magnificent climax in late May when the bridgehead force broke out to link with the advance of the Fifth and Eighth Armies from down the line.

* * * *

In the rapid pursuit into the north that followed on the defeat of the German armies before Rome, Canadian participation was limited to the independent 1st Armoured Brigade, fighting with the British 13th Corps with which it had assaulted the Gustav and Hitler lines and marched on Rome.

To its already distinguished record, the Brigade began to add in late June the actions it joined on the flanks of Lake Trasimeno, through the Chiana valley, and over the rustic acres that had to be won, against ever-stiffening resistance, in the preliminaries to the fall of Florence. It was their tanks, swinging in from the left flank of the major thrust powered by New Zealanders and South Africans, that were first into Florence.

Behind Florence, a sneering barrier to industrial northern Italy, to the Po valley, and to Germany itself, loomed the Apennines, here at last running themselves out in one final alliance with the enemy that presented the Germans with a natural rampart virtually crossing Italy from the one sea to the other, from east to west. Into that massive barrier pressed the Fifth Army in late summer and with them, still as part of the 13th Corps, went the 1st Armoured Brigade.

It was there, among the most forbidding terrain, that the Fifth Army was to be locked for months in harsh fighting that was directed towards the capture of Bologna.

The Apennines virtually flung themselves across the thin body of Italy. Virtually, but not entirely. On the Adriatic coast, the mountains lost their temper and for roughly fifteen miles inland there beckoned a lazily rolling avenue into the Po valley. It was into that slender bottle-neck that the Eighth Army was poured in a swift, secretive stroke aimed, the Army Commander, Sir Oliver Leese, said, at a "ruthless advance to the Po".

It was here, too, that the Canadian Corps moved back into battle, refreshed after nearly three months of rest in the south. And it was in these somnolent farmlands before Rimini that its battalions fought actions of a bitterness that had no parallel in Italy, save the violence of Ortona and the Moro valley.

Seldom has a campaign bred more initial optimism and more subsequent gloom. There was every indication at first that the Germans had been out-foxed by the gigantic secret preparations, every indication that the thrust to the Po valley would be swift, brilliant, confounding.

Poles on the coastal right, Canadians of both the 1st and 5th Divisions as the central spearhead, Britons and Indians of the 5th Corps on the left moved in the final week of August with only moderate difficulties to the hills overlooking the Foglia River. Behind it, across the bare, rural slopes were interlaced the earth-works, the dug-outs, the mines the Germans had strung over these few miles to complete the work nature had done so thoroughly the rest of the way.

But it was not here that the Canadians or the British or the Indians were put to their severest test. The breaching of this Gothic Line proper was a rapid, courageous execution of a clever plan that had the Allied troops in control of the slopes dominating the surrounding countryside within a matter of relatively few hours. But the Germans, under-manned, unprepared here, fell back, rallied, reinforced with classic precision. And they stopped the Canadians and their Allies short of the valley and made them fight for every inch and every acre and, it developed, accomplished their purpose—that of stemming the Allied tide until the mud of autumn would make the Lombardy plains not an enemy but an ally.

The Canadians struggled across the Marecchia River and into the plains as September entered her final week. It rained that day. It rained intermittently, bitterly, for days and weeks after. And the troops who had breached the Gothic Line, erased the paratroops from the San Fortunato feature, thrown the Germans from Rimini airfield, reduced the key obstacle of Coriano ridge, against the heaviest concentrations of artillery they had yet encountered, against German divisions which multiplied with a swiftness that could only be explained by the main roads stemming from Rimini, found themselves now not racing for the Po River but forcing the enemy back across one alternately tiny and rampant stream after another. For days and weeks the Eighth cursed its destinies in the mud of the Lombardy plains.

The weight shifted south, along the Rimini-Bologna highway. The 1st Division speared the attack briefly and Private "Smokey" Smith of New Westminster, B. C., a member of the Seaforth Highlanders of Canada, won the Victoria Cross for his part in holding a river bridgehead in the fighting around Cesena. His was the first V.C. won by a Canadian other rank in this war.

The Canadians came out, rested, went in again in December as the extreme right flank of the Eighth's right hook, designed to help the Fifth Army emerge from the Apennines, win Bologna and confront the Germans with abundant arguments for withdrawal to the Po. Through December, through Christmas, they fought the actions that grabbed Ravenna, cleared the elongated stretch of land between Lake Comacchio and the Adriatic and threw back enemy forces from many acres of dank Italian soil.

It was a re-organized Corps that returned to action in late August. The 1st Division, under General Vokes, consisted of the infantry and support units which had originally landed at Reggio, plus the Royal Canadian Dragoons as reconnaissance battalion, the latter transferred from Corps Headquarters.

The 5th Division, under General Hoffmeister, now consisted of three armoured units, the 8th Princess Louise New Brunswick Hussars, Lord Strathcona Horse and British Columbia Dragoons, a veteran infantry brigade composed of the Perth, Irish and Cape Breton Highlander Regiments, and other units including the Westminster Regiment, formerly motorized infantry, and the Lanark and Renfrew Scottish, a new unit reared around the framework of a former Corps light anti-aircraft unit. Also with the Canadian Corps were the 4th Princess Louise Dragoons Guards, formerly 1st Division "recce" battalion.

The 5th Division's support battalion was the Princess Louise Fusiliers and its "recce" battalion the Governor-General's Horse Guards.

Canadian troops had shared in practically every phase of the Eighth Army's hard, slugging advance up the length of Italy and as the great Russian offensive burst into Germany and the Allies' armies on the Western Front smashed forward into the Reich, the Canadian Corps was looking down the Po valley. Ahead was the ancient city of Venice—beyond were the frontiers of southern Germany.

The Canadians' last role in Italy was one of static warfare along the diked banks of the Senio River. They had flung the Germans back to that line late in December.

Their Eighth Army comrades struck out from there in a new offensive—the "final" offensive in Italy, Allied Commander Mark Clark called it—in April but the Canadians were not with them. They were massing in western Europe with the other Canadian divisions under the wing of an army that now more than ever before was truly a First Canadian Army.